# HISTORIC PHOTOS OF SONOMA COUNTY

TEXT AND CAPTIONS BY LEE TORLIATT

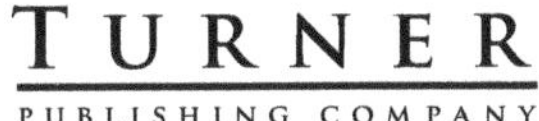

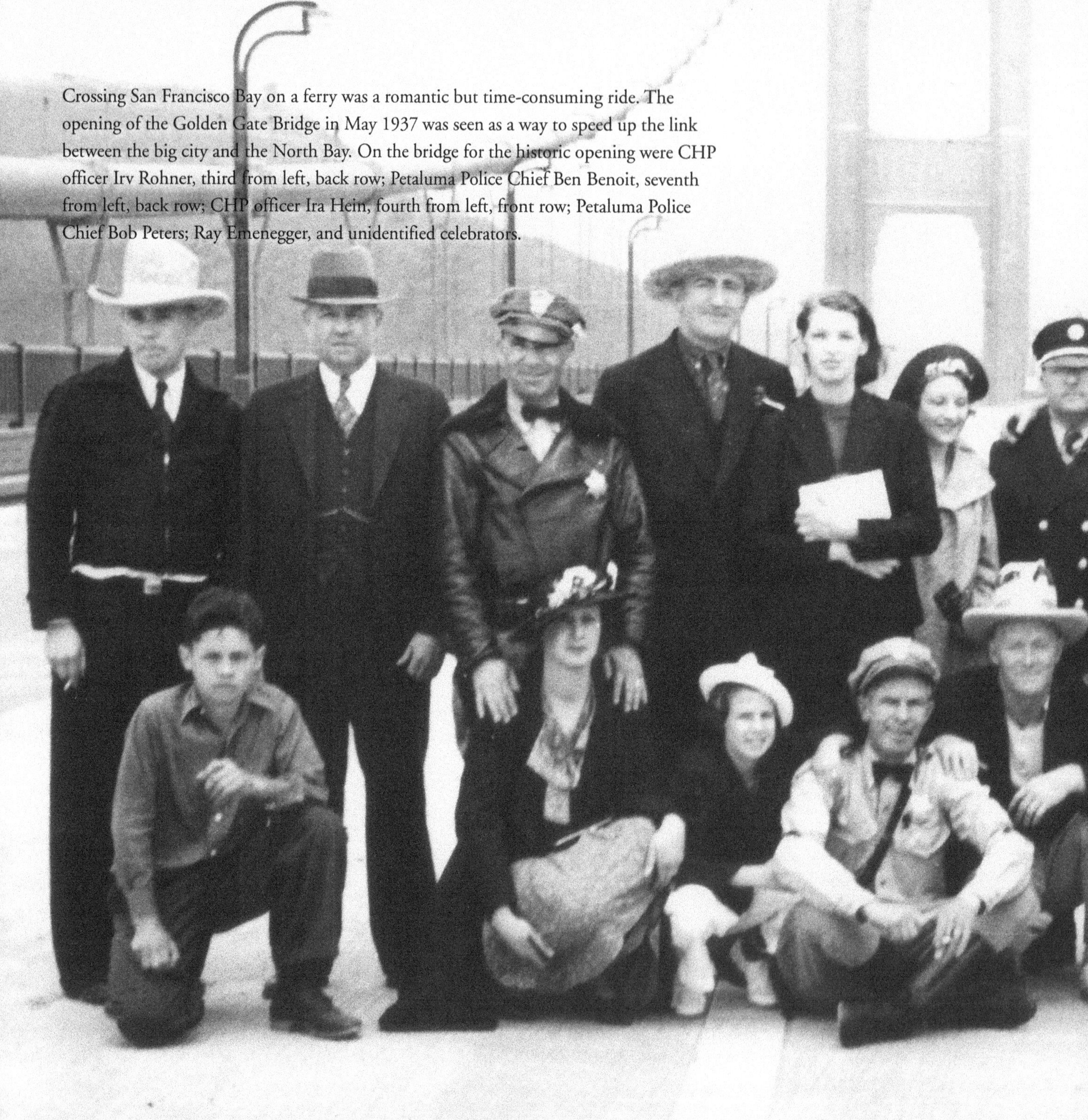

Crossing San Francisco Bay on a ferry was a romantic but time-consuming ride. The opening of the Golden Gate Bridge in May 1937 was seen as a way to speed up the link between the big city and the North Bay. On the bridge for the historic opening were CHP officer Irv Rohner, third from left, back row; Petaluma Police Chief Ben Benoit, seventh from left, back row; CHP officer Ira Hein, fourth from left, front row; Petaluma Police Chief Bob Peters; Ray Emenegger, and unidentified celebrators.

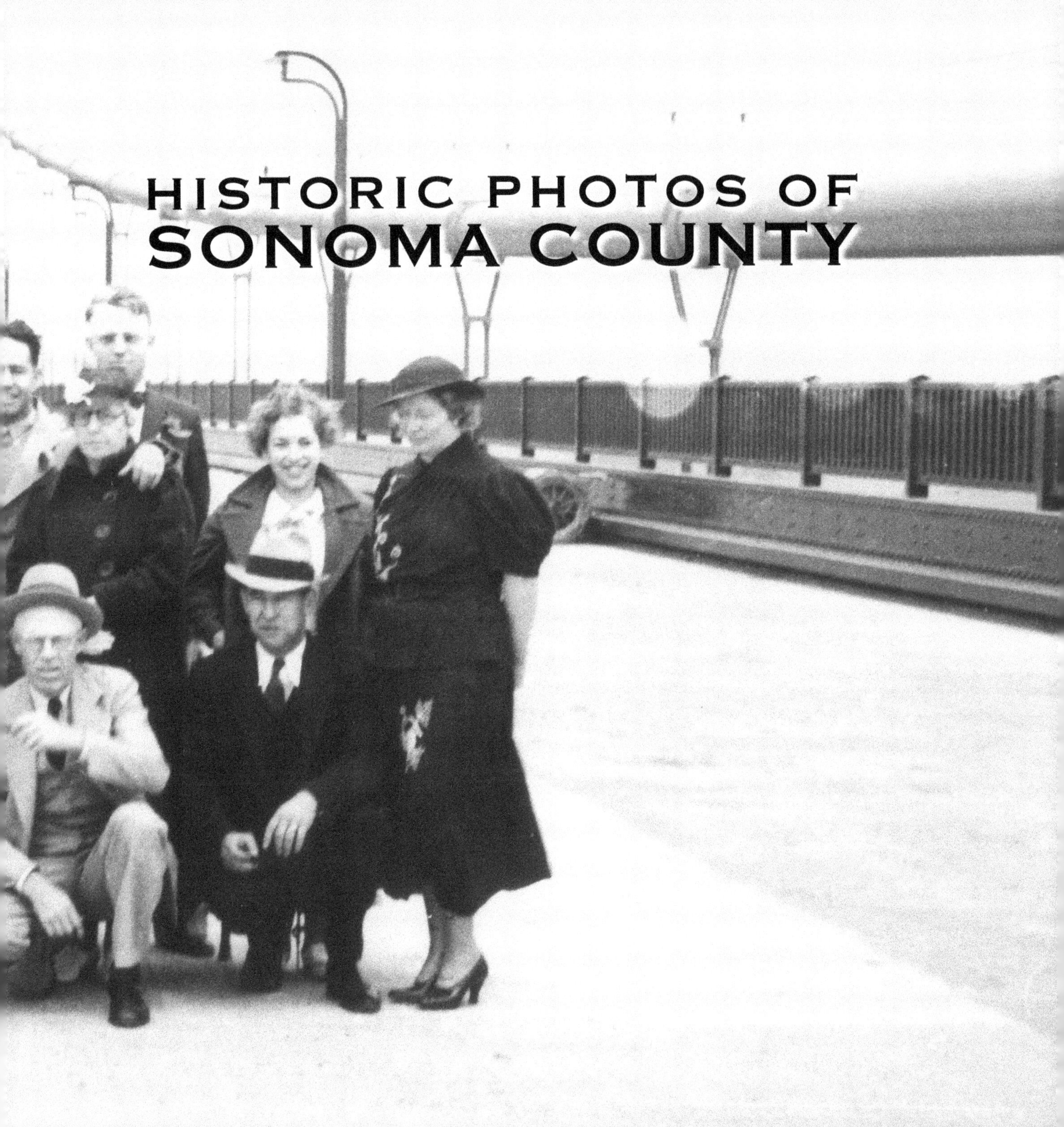
HISTORIC PHOTOS OF
SONOMA COUNTY

Turner Publishing Company
4507 Charlotte Avenue • Suite 100
Nashville, Tennessee 37209
(615) 255-2665

www.turnerpublishing.com

*Historic Photos of Sonoma County*



Library of Congress Control Number: 2007933774

ISBN-13: 978-1-59652-409-5

ISBN: 978-1-68336-989-9 (hc)

Printed in the United States of America

08 09 10 11 12 13 14 15—0 9 8 7 6 5 4 3 2 1

# Contents

Petaluma had its Leghorns and Santa Rosa had its Rosebuds, but the most unusual semipro baseball team in the post–World War II era was The Fighting Irish of Occidental. The team, manned mostly by people of Italian background with Irish nicknames, finished fourth in the Sonoma County League in 1947. Players included Dan "Mahoney" Gonnella and Dan "McGee" Gonnella. One player of actual Irish descent, Charles Kelly, managed to slip onto the team.

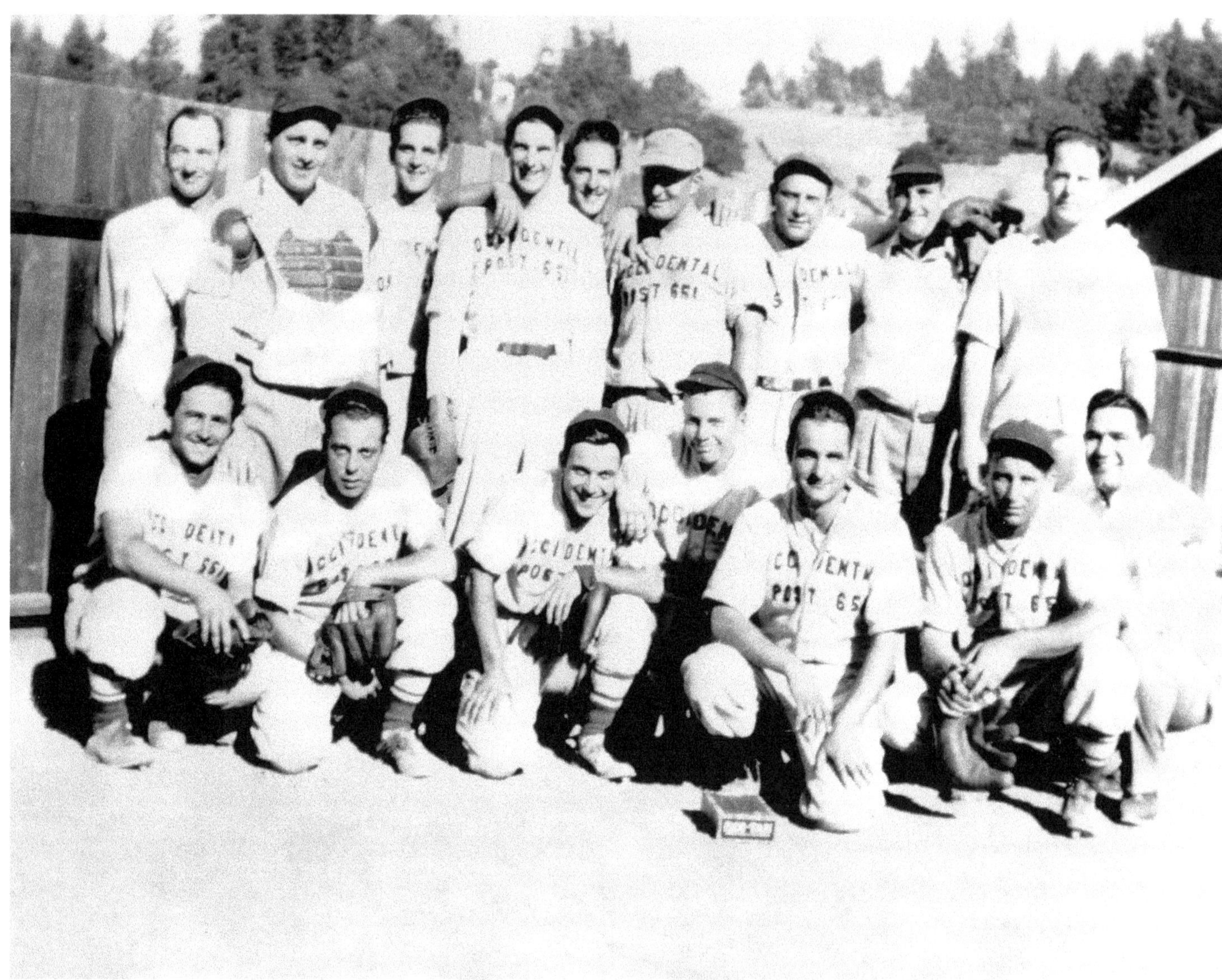

ACKNOWLEDGMENTS

This volume, *Historic Photos of Sonoma County,* is the result of the cooperation and efforts of many individuals, organizations, and corporations. It is with great thanks that we acknowledge the valuable contribution of the following for their generous support:

Harold Lapham Collection
Lee Torliatt Collection
Library of Congress
Sonoma County Library
Sonoma County Museum

# PREFACE

Sonoma County has thousands of historic photographs that reside in archives, both locally and nationally. This book began with the observation that, while those photographs are of great interest to many, they are not easily accessible. During a time when Sonoma County is looking ahead and evaluating its future course, many people are asking, "How do we treat the past?" These decisions affect every aspect of the county—architecture, public spaces, commerce, infrastructure—and these, in turn, affect the way that people live their lives. This book seeks to provide easy access to a valuable, objective look into the history of Sonoma County.

The power of photographs is that they are less subjective than words in their treatment of history. Although the photographer can make decisions regarding subject matter and how to capture and present it, photographs do not provide the breadth of interpretation that text does. For this reason, they offer an original, untainted perspective that allows the viewer to interpret and observe.

This project represents countless hours of review and research. The researchers and writer have reviewed thousands of photographs in numerous archives. We greatly appreciate the generous assistance of the individuals and organizations listed in the acknowledgments of this work, without whom this project could not have been completed.

The goal in publishing this work is to provide broader access to this set of extraordinary photographs that seek to inspire, provide perspective, and evoke insight that might assist people who are responsible for determining Sonoma County's future. In addition, the book seeks to preserve the past with adequate respect and reverence.

With the exception of touching up imperfections caused by the damage of time and cropping where necessary, no other changes have been made. The focus and clarity of many images is limited to the technology and the ability of the photographer at the time they were taken.

The work is divided into eras. Beginning with some of the earliest known photographs of Sonoma County, the first section records images from the 1850s through the 1906 earthquake. The second section spans the period of recovery and rebuilding and depicts the ever-increasing role of winemaking in the region's economy. Section Three moves from the Prohibition era through the Great Depression to the opening of the Golden Gate Bridge. The last section shows the growth of industry, education, and planned communities in the post–World War II era through the end of the 1970s.

In each of these sections we have made an effort to capture various aspects of life through our selection of photographs. People, commerce, transportation, infrastructure, religious institutions, and educational institutions have been included to provide a broad perspective.

We encourage readers to reflect as they travel in Sonoma County. It is the publisher's hope that in utilizing this work, longtime residents will learn something new and that new residents will gain a perspective on where Sonoma County has been, so that each can contribute to its future.

*Todd Bottorff, Publisher*

The Mexican government sent a young general, twenty-five-year-old Mariano Vallejo, to set up a pueblo in Sonoma in 1833. Despite major political changes, Vallejo survived to be one of the influential leaders of Sonoma County until his death in 1892. He was an impressive sight riding in his elegant coach on the streets of Sonoma.

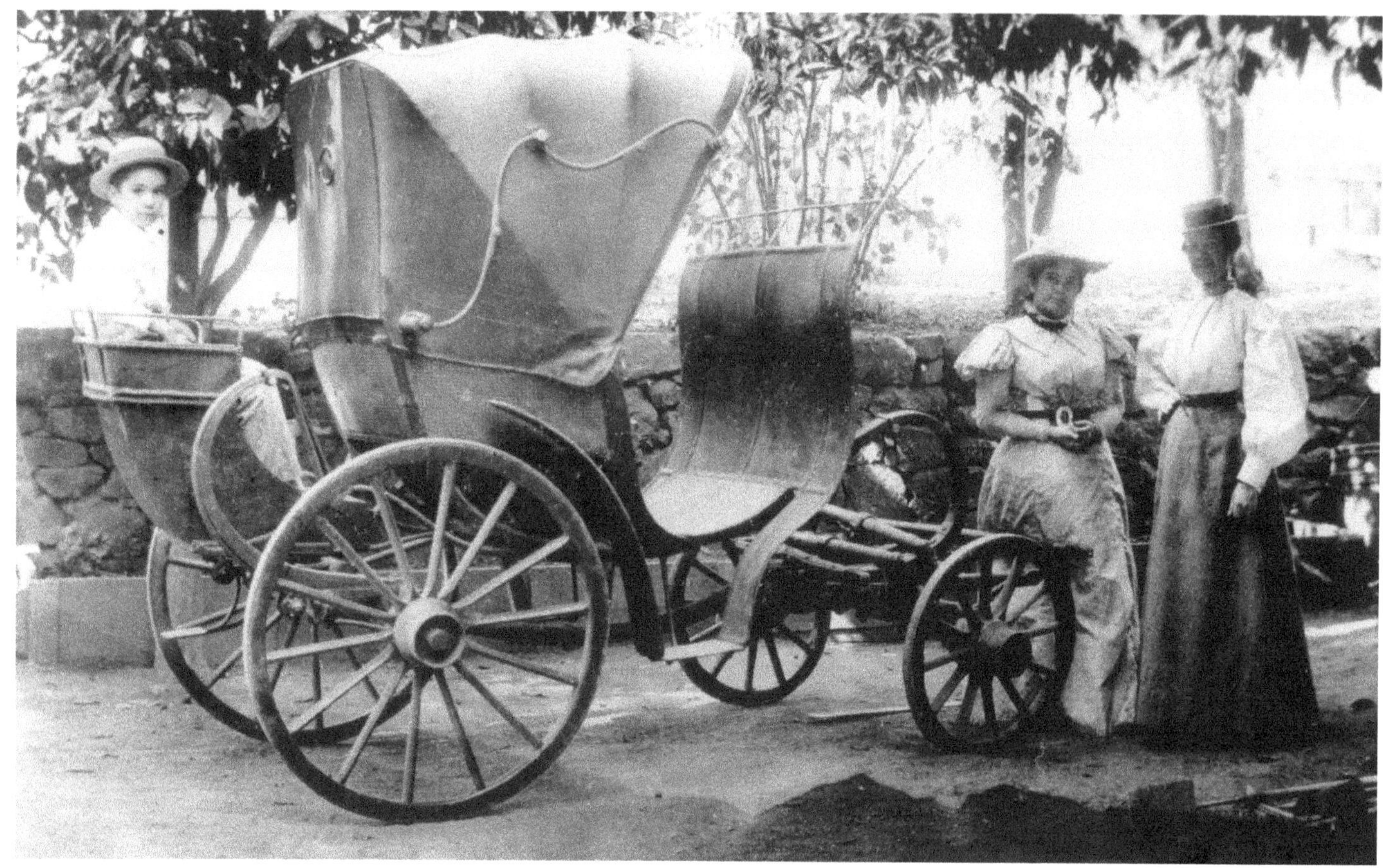

# FROM EARLY DAYS TO THE 1906 EARTHQUAKE

## (1850s–1906)

Famed botanist Luther Burbank, a man who loved nature, called Sonoma County "the chosen spot" on earth. It was a land that had fertile soil, rich waterways, a mild climate, and many other amenities that attracted outsiders. First came the Miwok, Pomo, and Wappo Indians, who were on the scene when the European powers stepped up their exploration of the New World in the sixteenth century.

The Spanish, the English, and later the Russians emerged as competitors for domination on the north coast. Even though the site of Sir Francis Drake's landing remains shrouded in controversy, it is clear that the British explorer made a stop somewhere around Bodega Bay for five weeks in his ship the *Golden Hinde* in 1579. The Spanish, operating out of Mexico, moved into the Bodega area with ill-founded hopes of creating a garrison in the late 18th century. The Russians landed and set up a colony on the coast at Fort Ross in 1812. Irritated by this intrusion, the Spanish (and later the new Mexican government) moved north to set up the last mission in Sonoma. By the 1820s, the Spanish had been pushed out by the new Mexican government, and by the 1840s the Russians were closing down Fort Ross and heading for home.

California was divided into a series of ranchos, one of which went to Mariano Guadalupe Vallejo, a dominant figure in Sonoma County for many decades. Conflict arose between the Mexican government and the American explorers coming from the east. The Mexican-American War (1846–48) led to the annexation of California by the United States in 1848. When gold was discovered in California the following year, prospectors called Forty-Niners swarmed in to seek their fortunes.

The miners rushed off to the gold fields, but when the boom ran its course, they turned into settlers, and what better place than Sonoma County? David Wharff told of how he came up the Petaluma River to set up his farm in tiny Penngrove, a few miles from Petaluma. Crops grew well, and roaming game provided food for the table, but there was not enough land to satisfy the demands of all the settlers, which led to intense struggles between property owners and large numbers of squatters. Nevertheless, it was a land of opportunity, and new residents arrived on a regular basis.

Sonoma County became the supplier for the burgeoning urban population around San Francisco. Lumber, eggs, apples, prunes, milk, butter, grapes for wine, and hops for beer were readily available. People got around by stagecoach, steamboats, and railroads. The first big shock came in 1906, with the giant earthquake that shook San Francisco and Sonoma County.

A photograph taken in 1867 shows the old Barracks in Sonoma with the Mission San Francisco Solano in the background. The Mexican government moved to establish itself in Sonoma County to discourage expansion by the Russian coastal colony at Fort Ross.

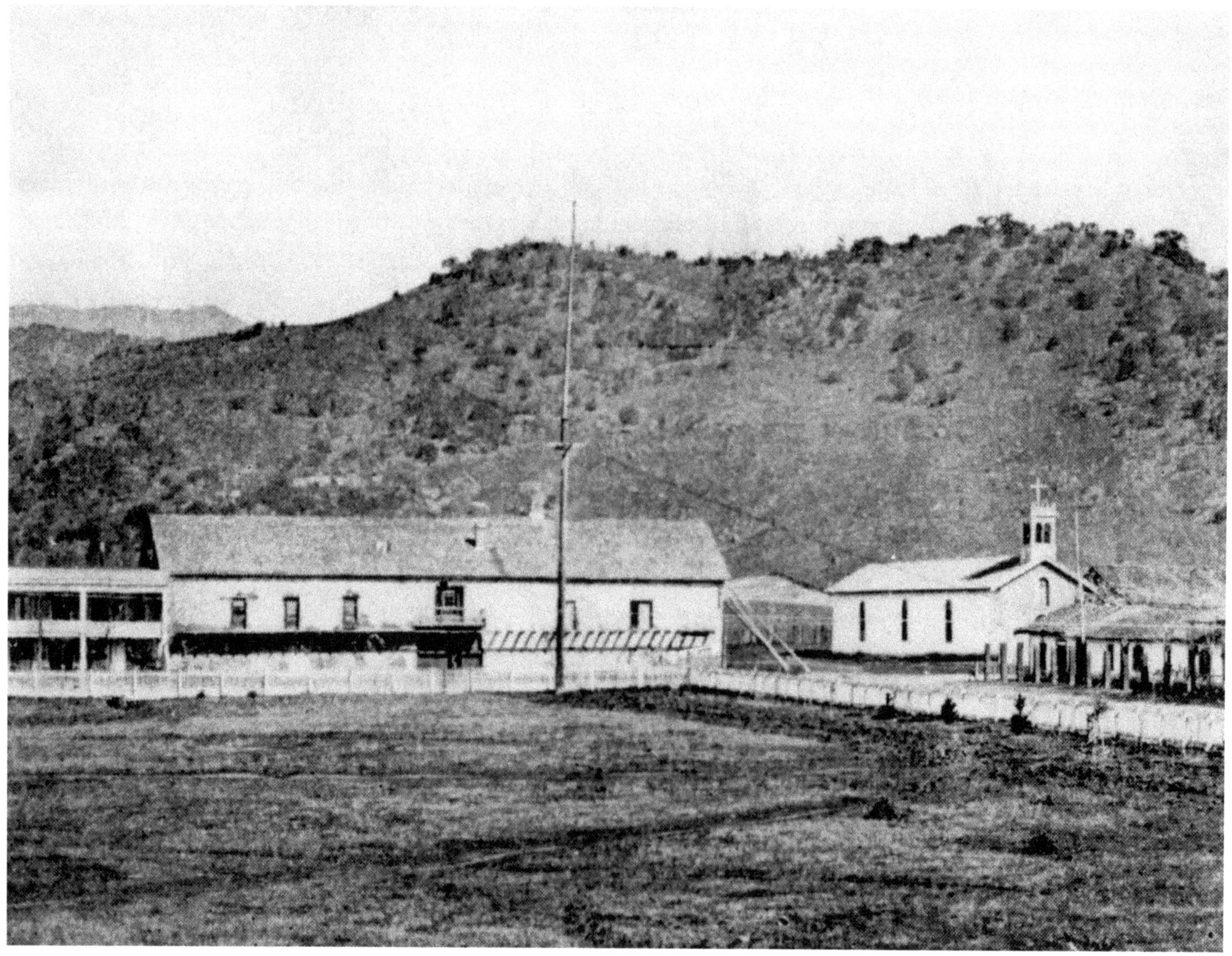

The Gowen building next door collapsed during construction, but the three-story Phoenix Block, a dream of Dr. William R. Wells, got built in Petaluma in 1855–56. Located on Main Street, it was considered Petaluma's first "skyscraper." The building included stores that sold drugs, hardware, dry goods, and stationary and books. This tintype photo was taken in the late 1850s.

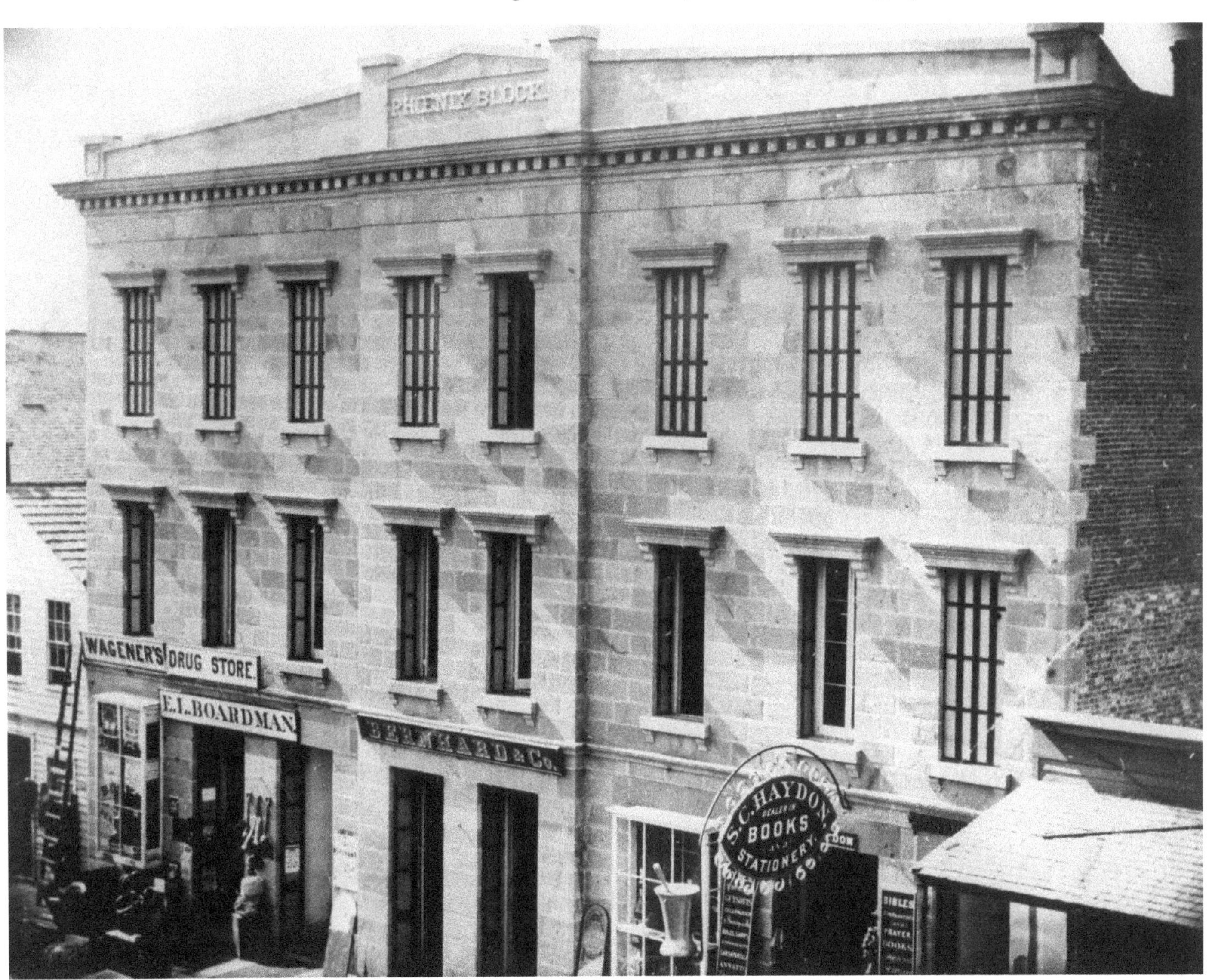

The Sonoma Plaza in 1870 was a major gathering place for residents of the city. While the community lost its place as the county seat to Santa Rosa in a heated election in the 1850s, it gained from the arrival of Agostin Haraszthy, a Hungarian noble who brought wine grapes to the area. Other growers have carried the Haraszthy tradition into the twenty-first century.

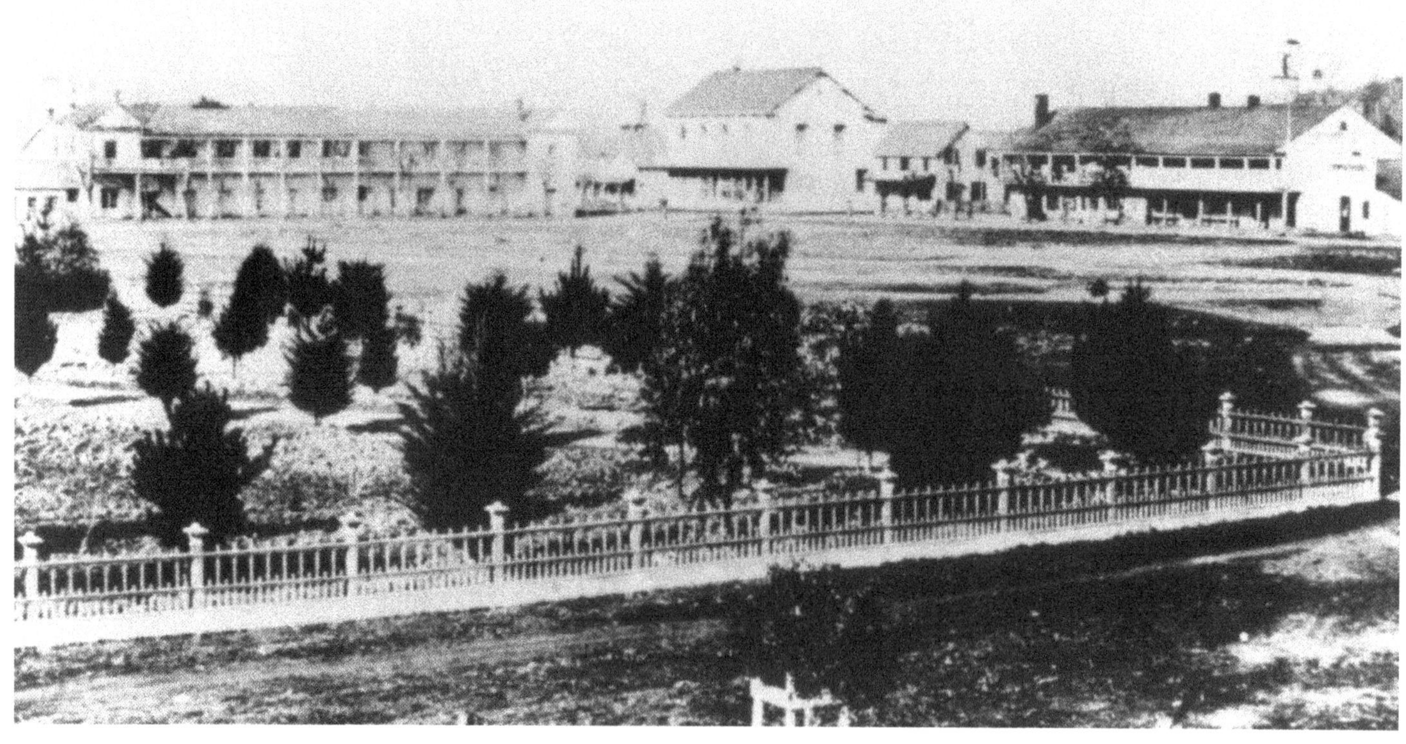

From the early 1850s, Santa Rosa jockeyed with Healdsburg, Petaluma, and Sonoma to determine location of the county seat. Over loud protests, Santa Rosa built a courthouse that opened for business in 1856. Construction of a new courthouse (below), begun in the 1870s, was completed in 1884.

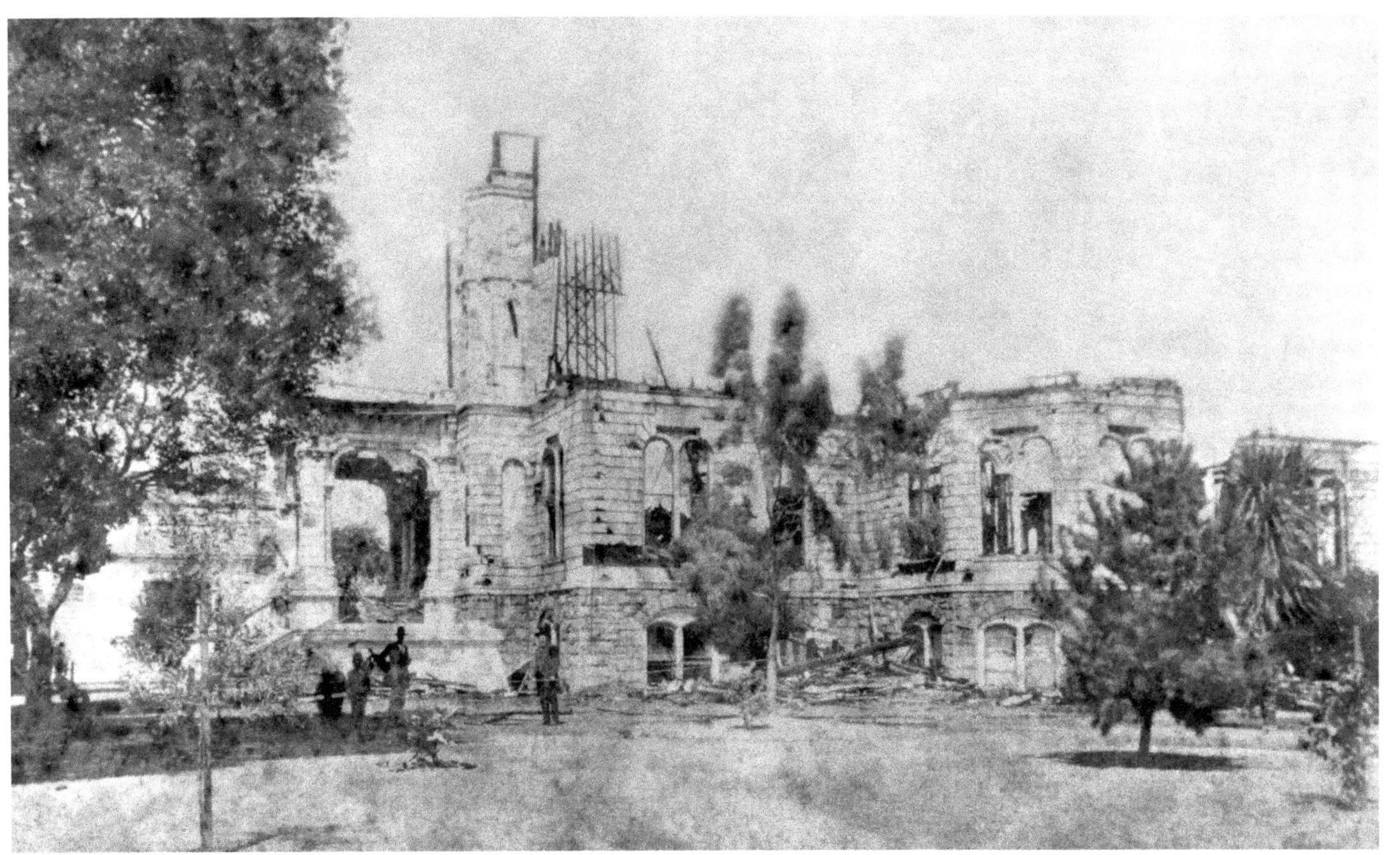

As stagecoaches, trains, and wagons carried travelers through the far reaches of the north coast, hotels and resorts sprang up to serve their needs. One of the most prominent of the 1870s was the three-story Grand Hotel at 3rd and Main streets in the heart of downtown Santa Rosa. Stanley, Jeblett & Julliard sold stoves, hardware, and agricultural implements from the same building.

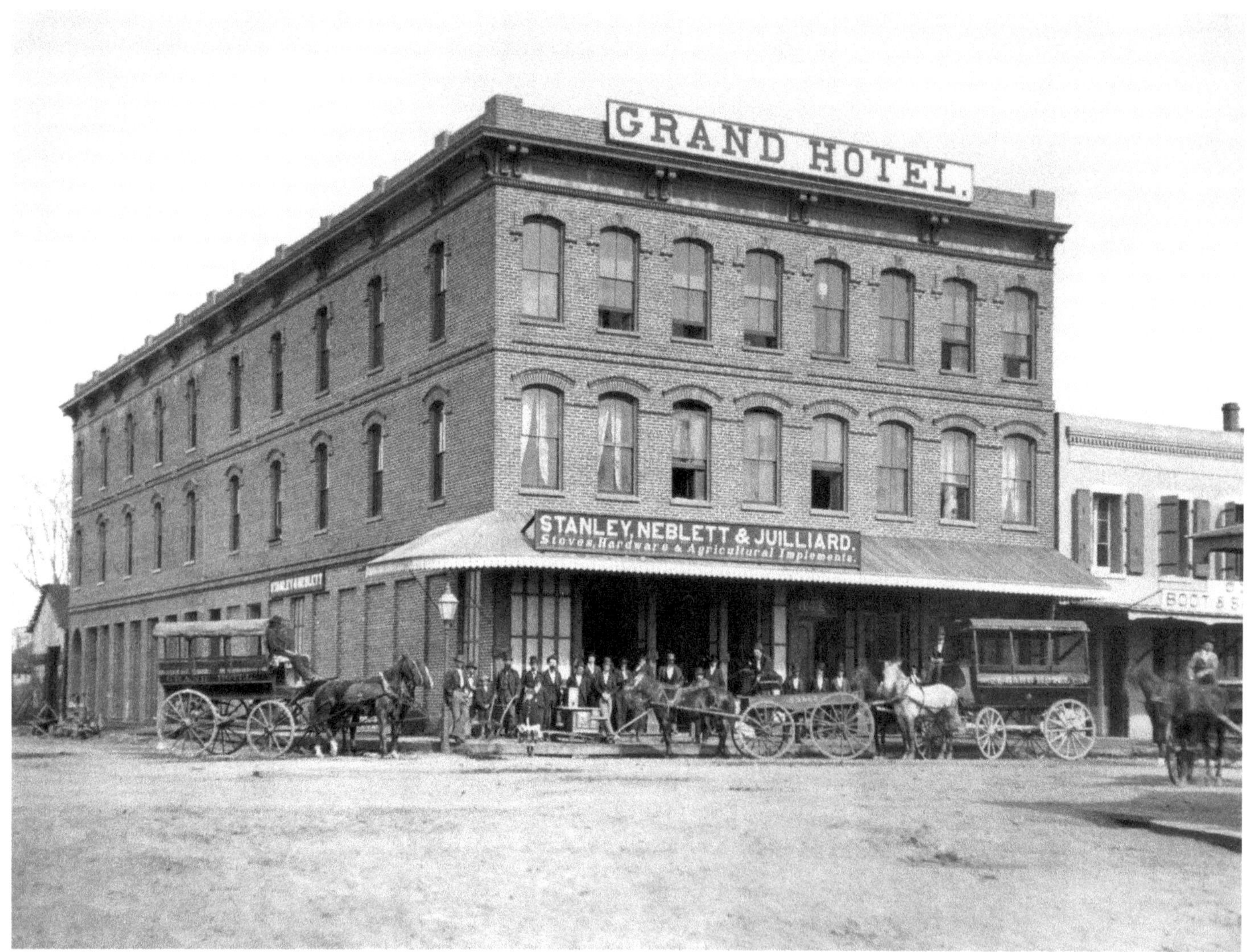

View of 4th Street in Santa Rosa taken from Exchange Avenue around 1875, showing (from right) the courthouse, fire station, a restaurant, and a stationary and variety store. The growing community welcomed completion of the Donahue rail line from Petaluma to Santa Rosa in 1870, which opened the door to expanded contact with the San Francisco market. Population in the county seat jumped from less than 1,000 in 1870 to 6,500 by 1900.

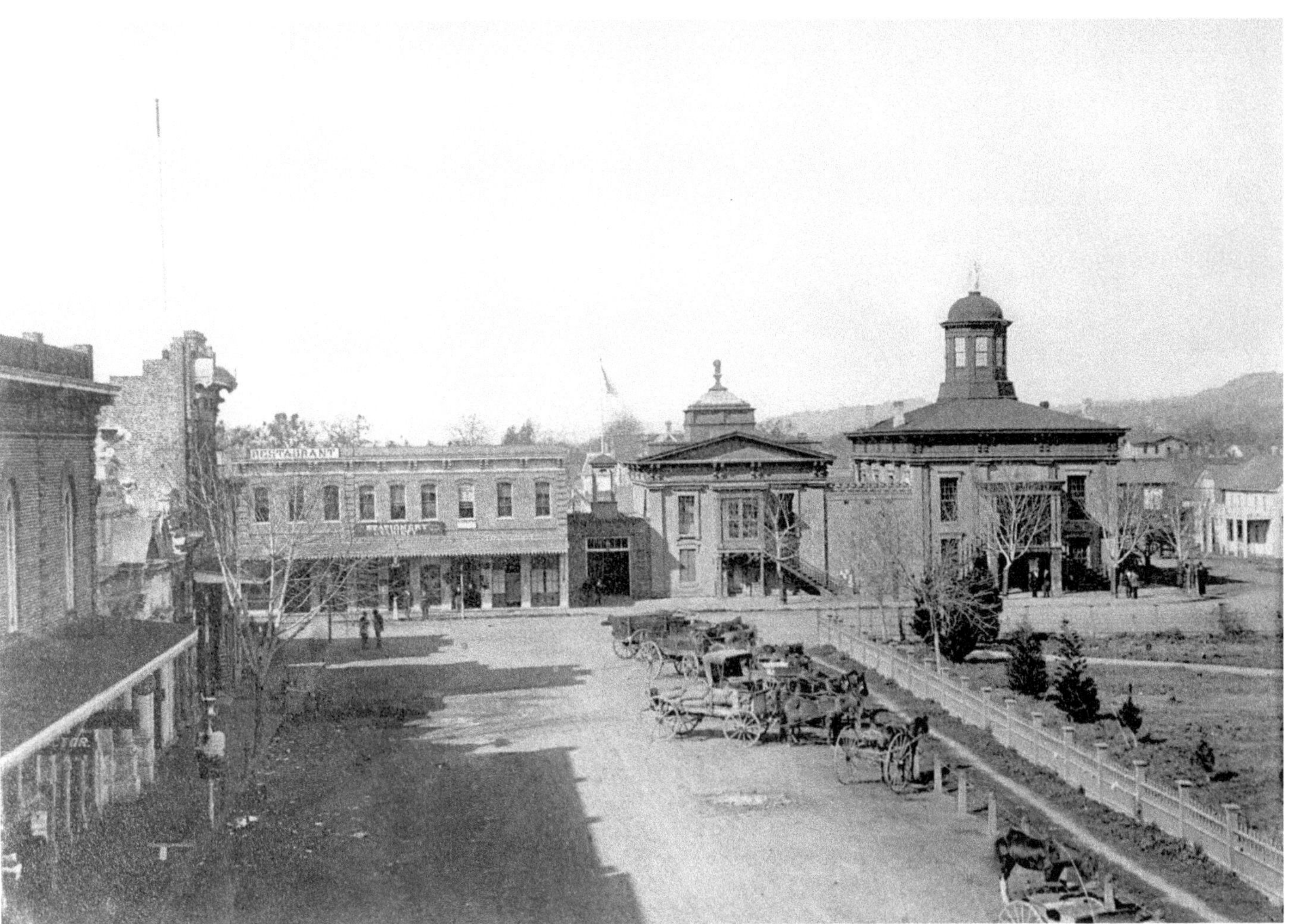

A view of Santa Rosa's "main drag" at 4th and Hinton streets in 1876. The smell of prosperity was in the air with the completion of the Donahue rail line, a new bridge was being built over Santa Rosa Creek, several hotels were providing comfortable stays for visitors, and the city was enjoying the fact that it had recently become a two-newspaper town.

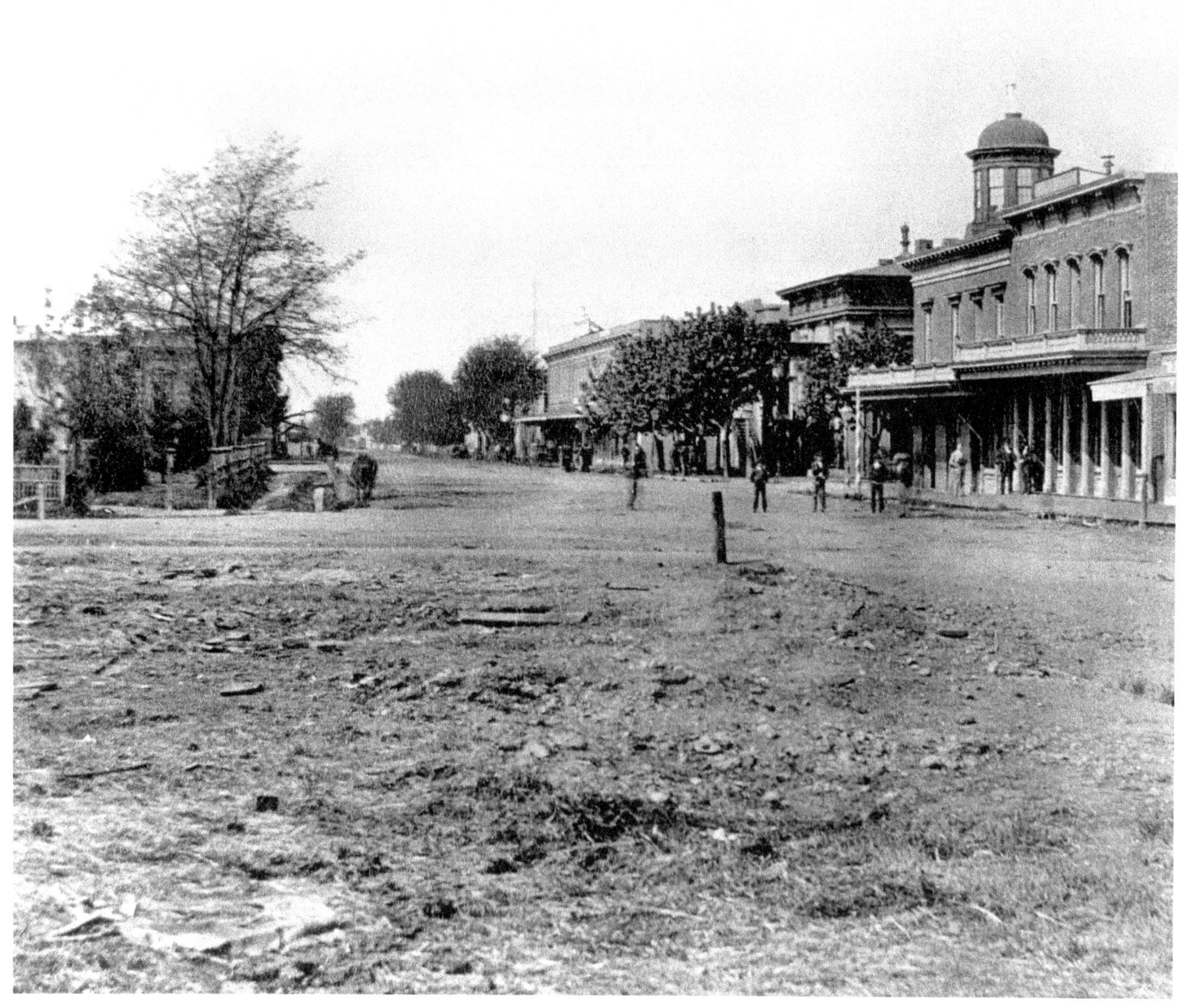

Youngsters gathered in front of the Windsor School for a group photo. In the late 1870s, there was just one school, one church, thirty residences, and a population of about 250. More grammar schools were built, especially after Windsor divided into two communities, East and West, in the 1870s. Teachers often taught several grades and the emphasis was on the basics—reading, writing, and arithmetic.

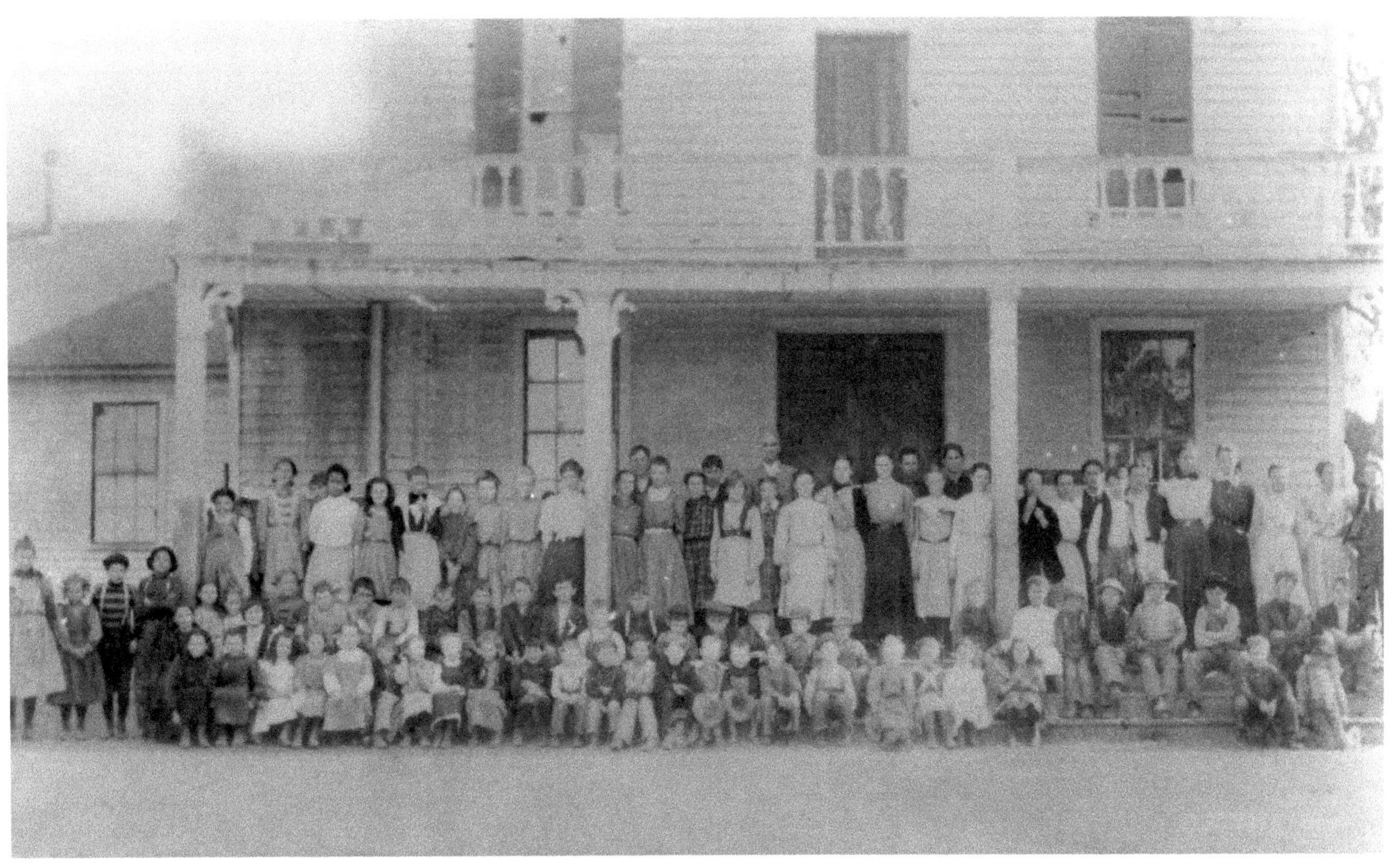

A bridge over Santa Rosa Creek in Santa Rosa helped traffic to flow smoothly in the 1870s, especially when major storms caused periodic flooding. Such road improvements and the arrival of the railroad helped Santa Rosa expand its economy.

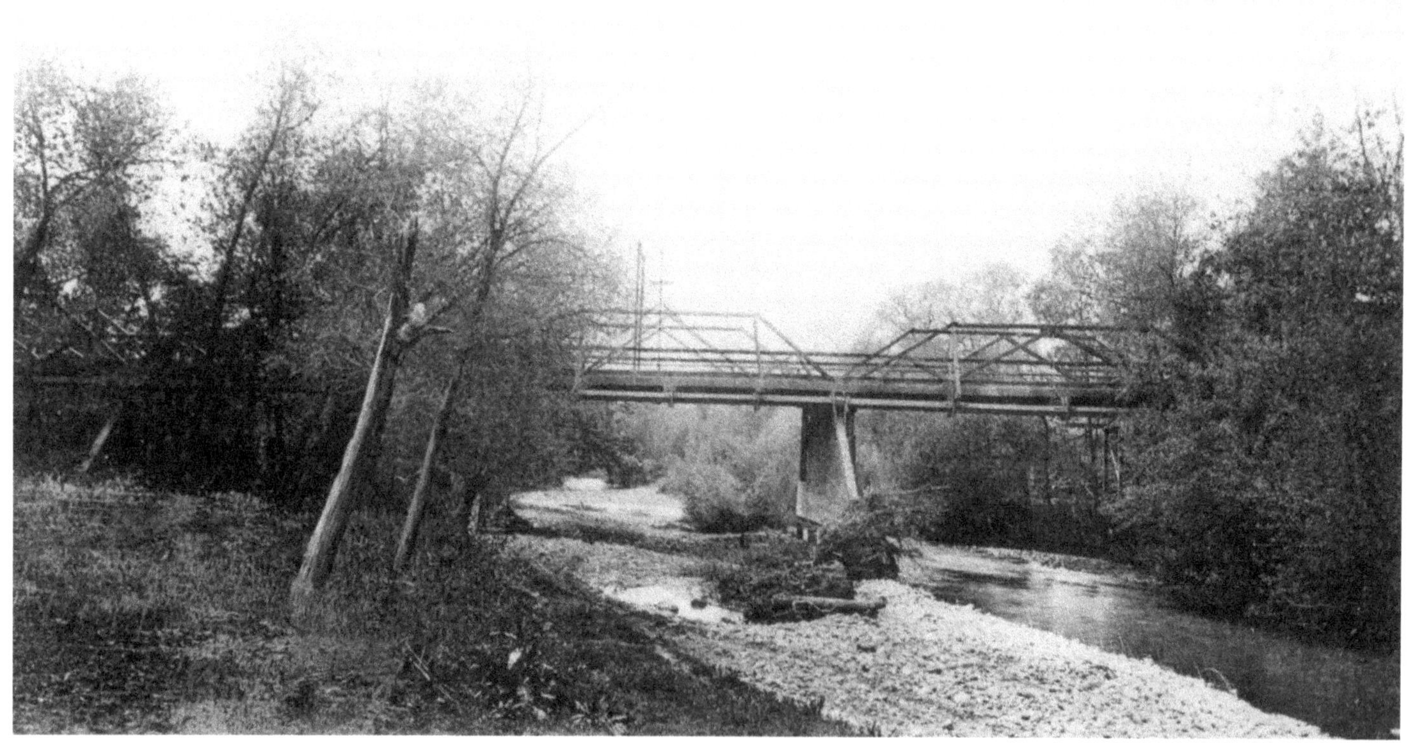

If they were to be of help on the farms or in providing transportation, horses needed tender, loving care. M. V. Hall opened the first livery stable in Cloverdale around 1870. It was located at the northeast corner of West Street at Second. Horses were used heavily around Cloverdale, since stagecoach roads branched out from the city in many directions.

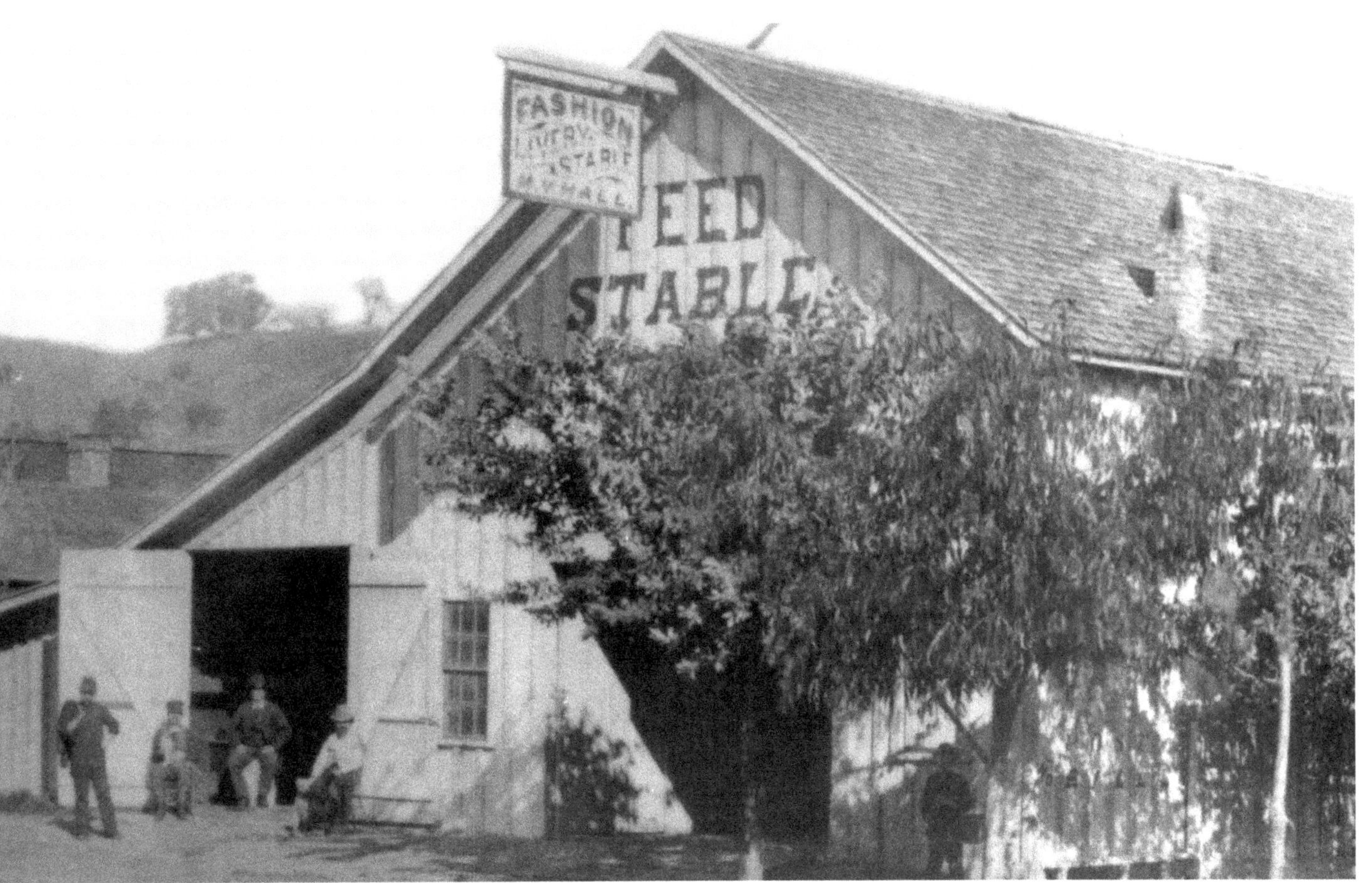

A typical scene in the 1870s showed loggers cutting redwoods in the Guerneville area. It was recognized early on that Sonoma County had great wealth in its timber. The wood was used as railroad ties in the Sierras and other parts of the United States, and as far away as Lima, Peru. A young Irish pioneer, James Dawson, working by hand, whipsawed a large load of lumber he delivered by ox team to General Mariano Vallejo in Sonoma.

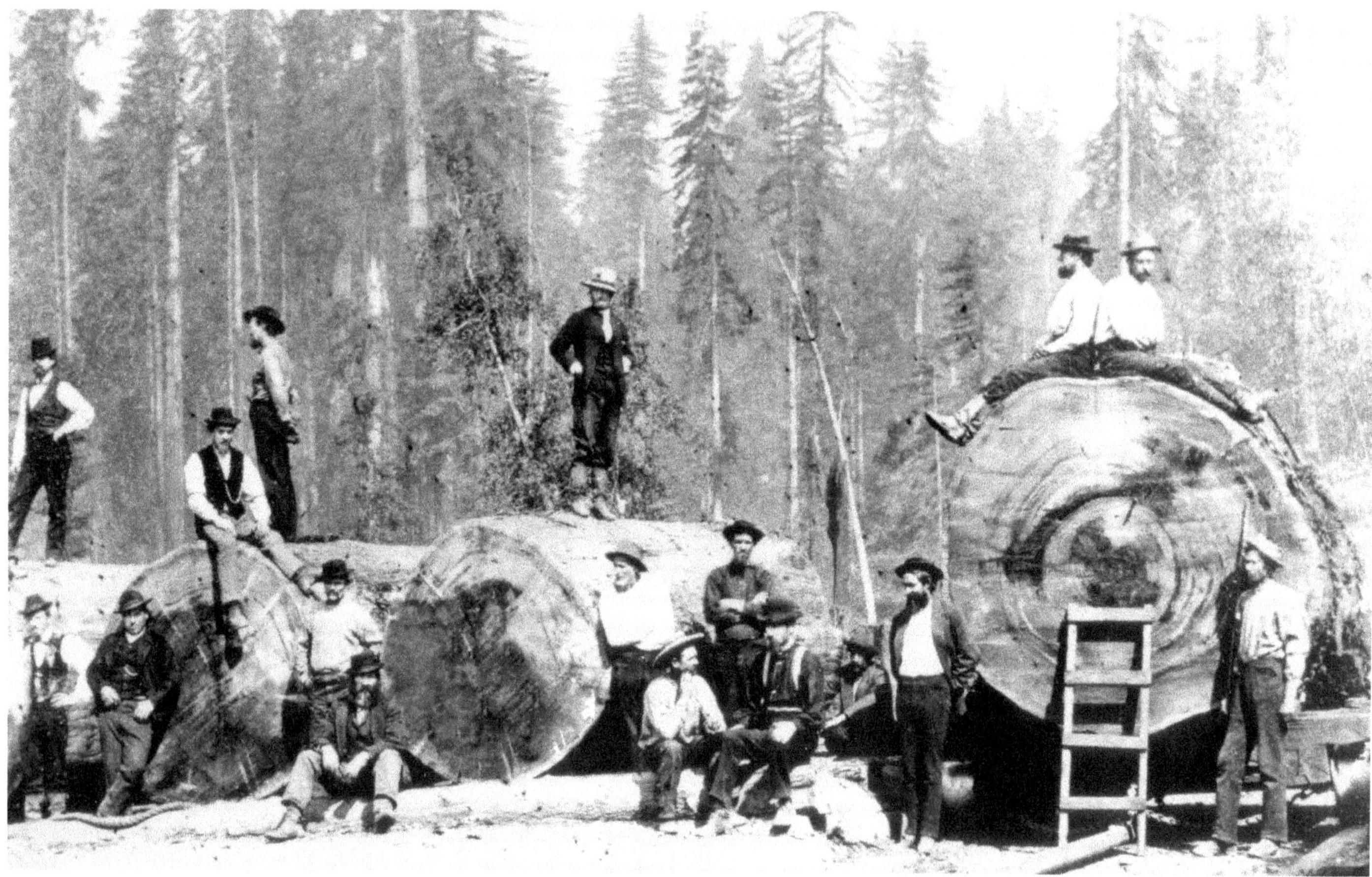

The giant blades at Meeker's Sawmill in west Sonoma County loomed over the crew that daily prepared lumber for the market. Harvesting of redwood and other woods was a major economic stimulant around Guerneville and Occidental. Joe Palmer is third from left and Eva Palmer, the woman with the tall hat, is fifth from left.

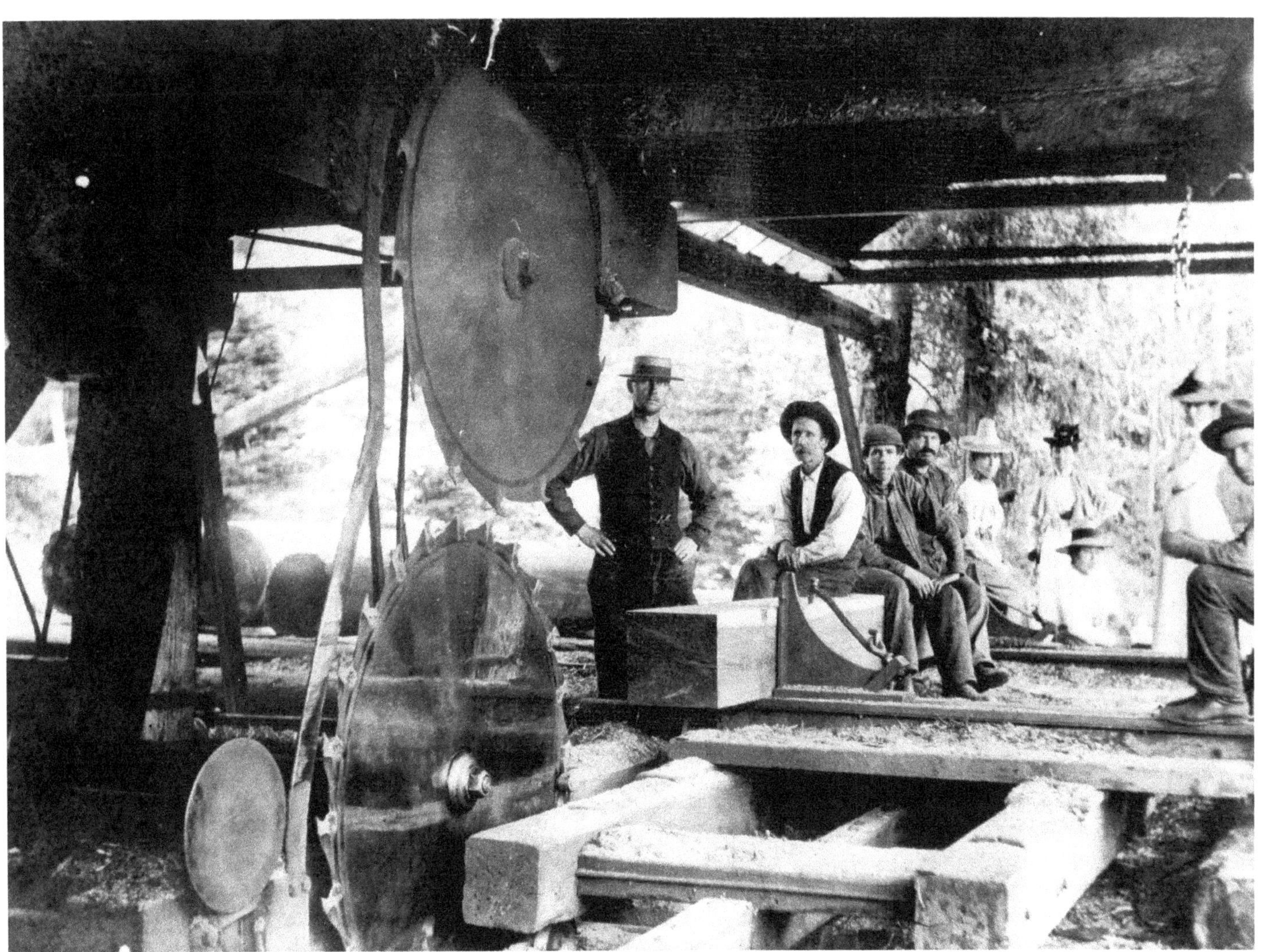

Come rain, sleet, or snow, the prompt delivery of mail was given a high priority. Fortunately, the weather was generally mild in Cloverdale, and by 1870 the city had its first post office, located on West Street between 2nd and 3rd streets. Incorporated in 1875–76, Cloverdale boasted a dozen stores, two good hotels, and prompt mail delivery.

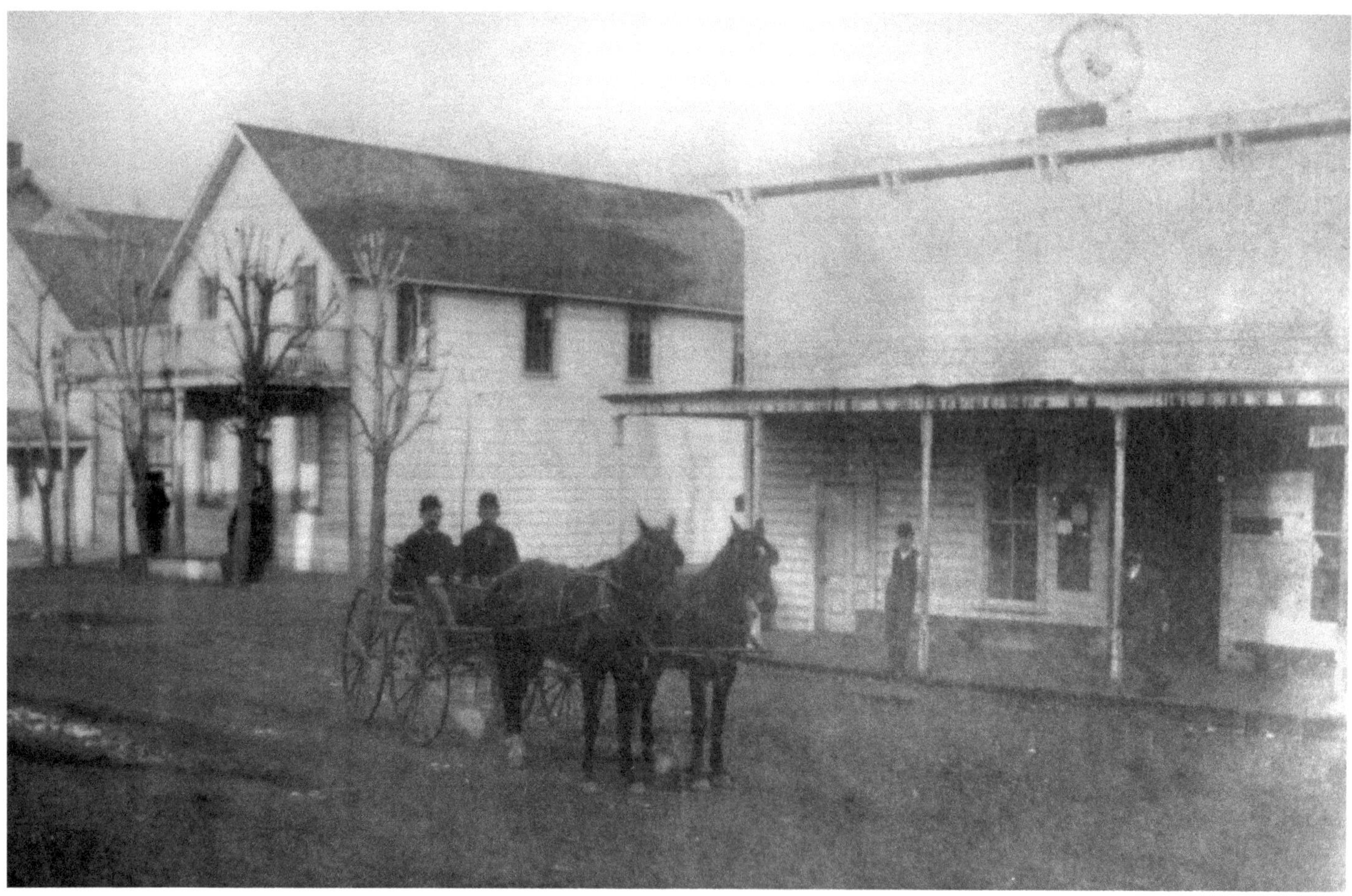

Although a small community, Cloverdale was the northern anchor of Sonoma County in the 1870s. This scene shows the town viewed southeast from the north end of town. It got its start in 1856 when R. Markle and a man named Miller bought 850 acres of land, which included the site of the future city. In 1857, Santa Rosa merchants J. H. Hartman and F. G. Hahman opened a trading post on Markle's land, essentially creating the town.

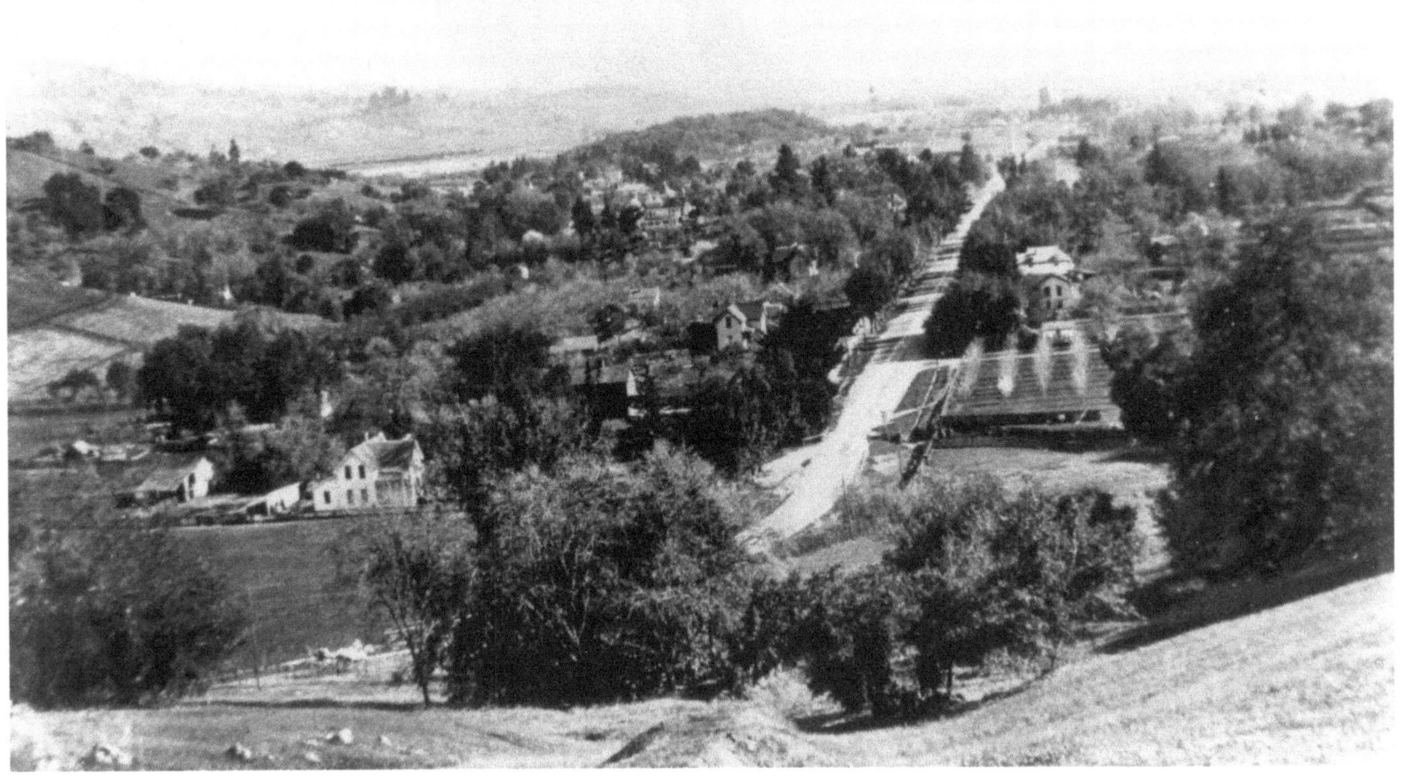

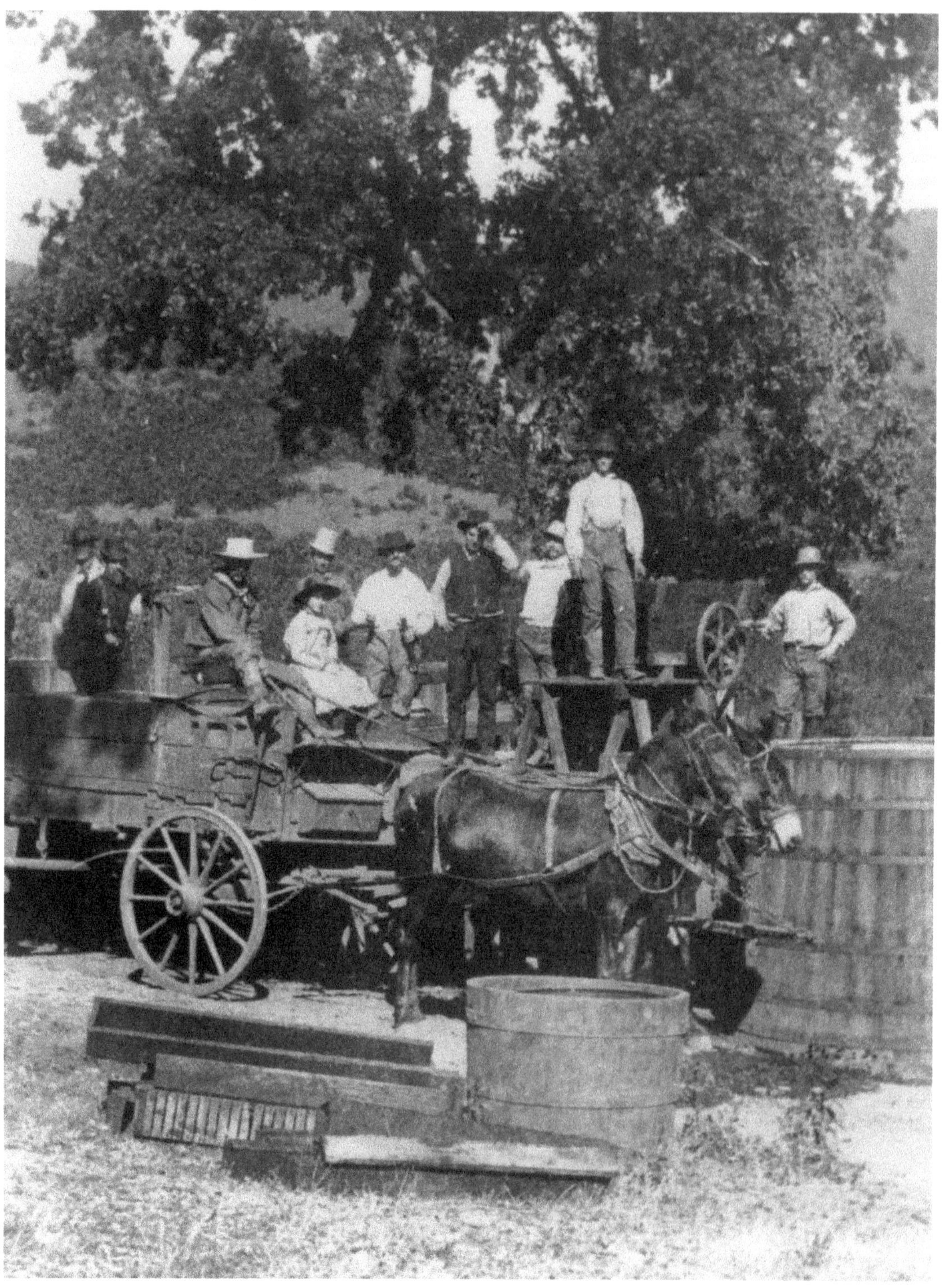

Sonoma County has been synonymous with fine wine since the 1850s when Hungarian Count Agostin Haraszthy brought grapes to Sonoma. Many of the early wineries were small ones, such as the J. Shaw outdoor winery in Rincon Valley, Santa Rosa, shown here in the 1870s. Shaw produced 5,000 gallons of wine in 1877.

In 1880, Cloverdale was enjoying its new status as a city. New buildings were going up, as can be seen looking north on West Street near the IOOF (Odd Fellows) Hall. Male residents had a choice of joining the IOOF, the Masonic Lodge, or the Grange, all of which held regular meetings.

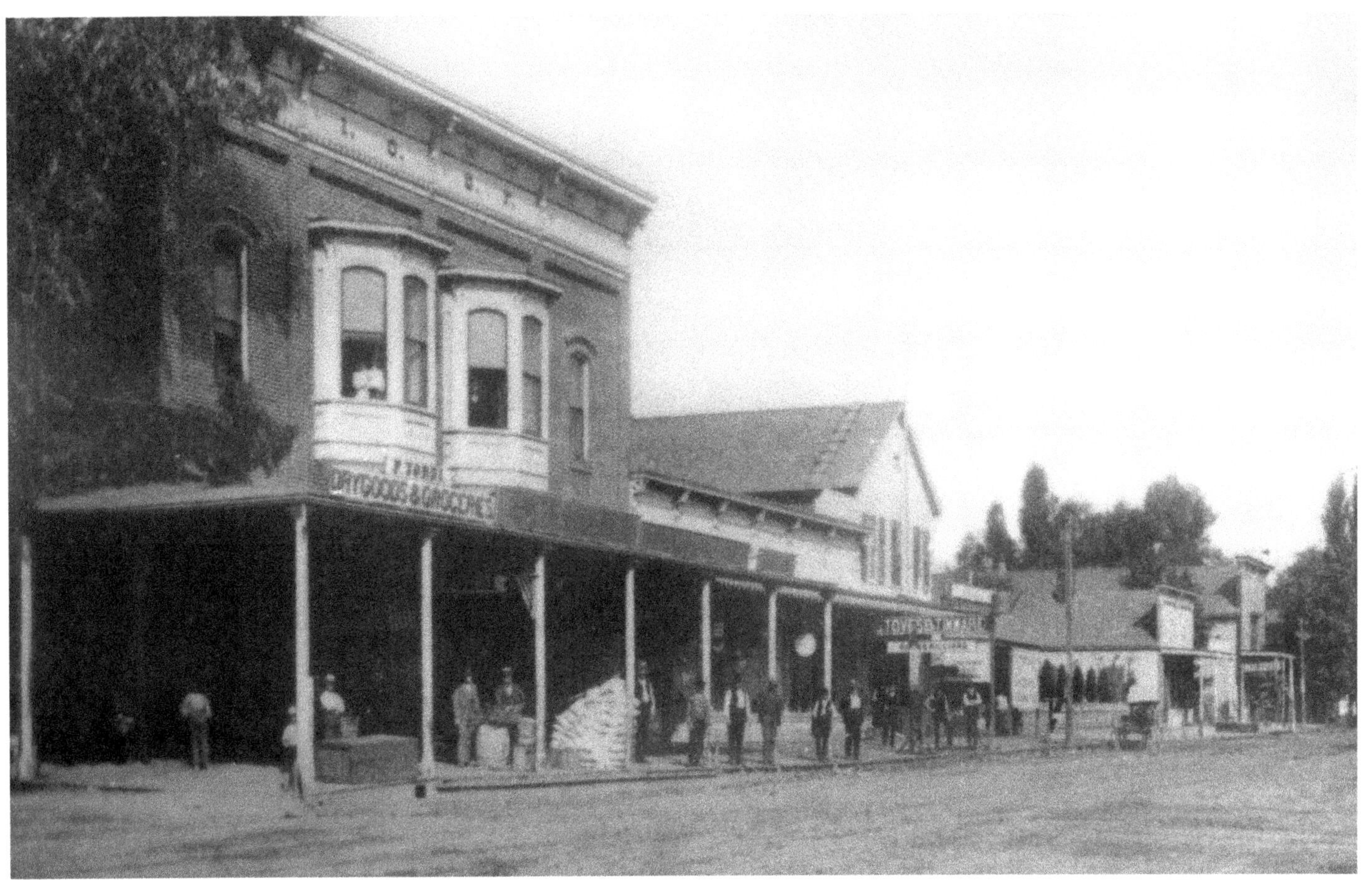

The Windsor and Trenton Winery was the biggest of seven wineries in the Windsor area in 1880. Owners J. Miller and W. J. Hotchkiss had it torn down early in the twentieth century.

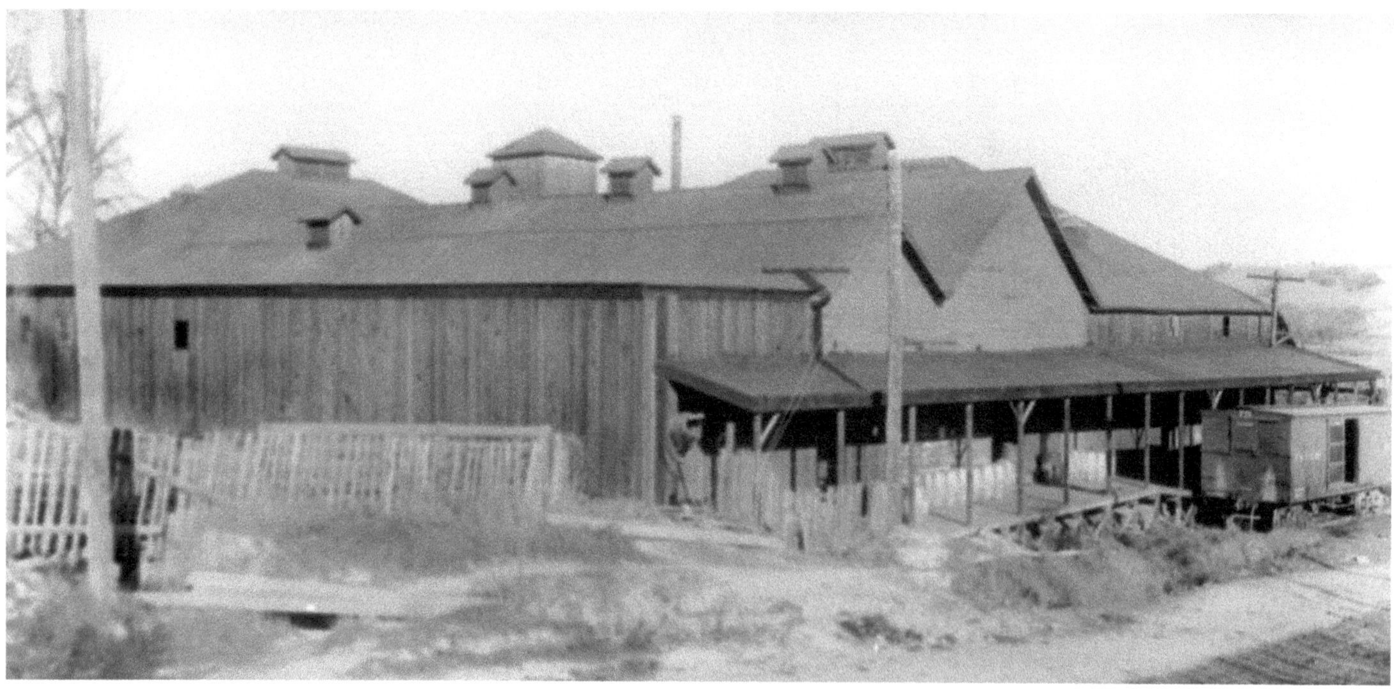

Stables were the service stations of the nineteenth century, providing assistance to weary travelers in Sonoma County communities. This street scene shows the California Livery and Feed and Martin and Holman Stables in the 1880s.

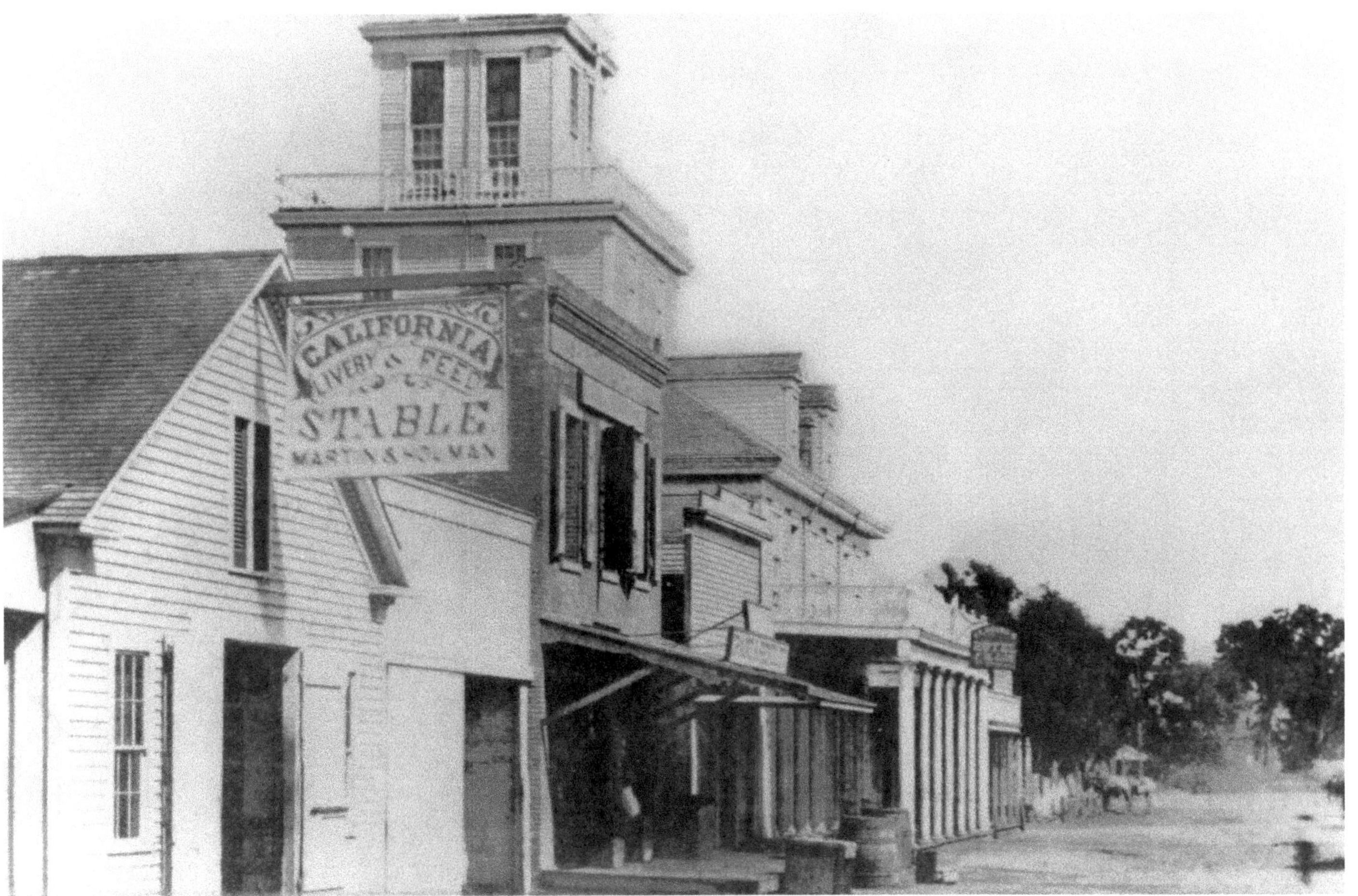

The lobby of the United States Hotel in Cloverdale offered solid comfort for travelers. The facility, located at the corner of West and 2nd streets, was built by H. F. (Fred) Gerkhardt in 1859, two years after he arrived in the city. Proprietor M. M. Menihan made numerous additions in the 1860s and '70s, including a restaurant that accommodated one hundred guests. It was considered one of the two "good hotels" in the north county in the 1870s and was still a popular spot in the 1890s.

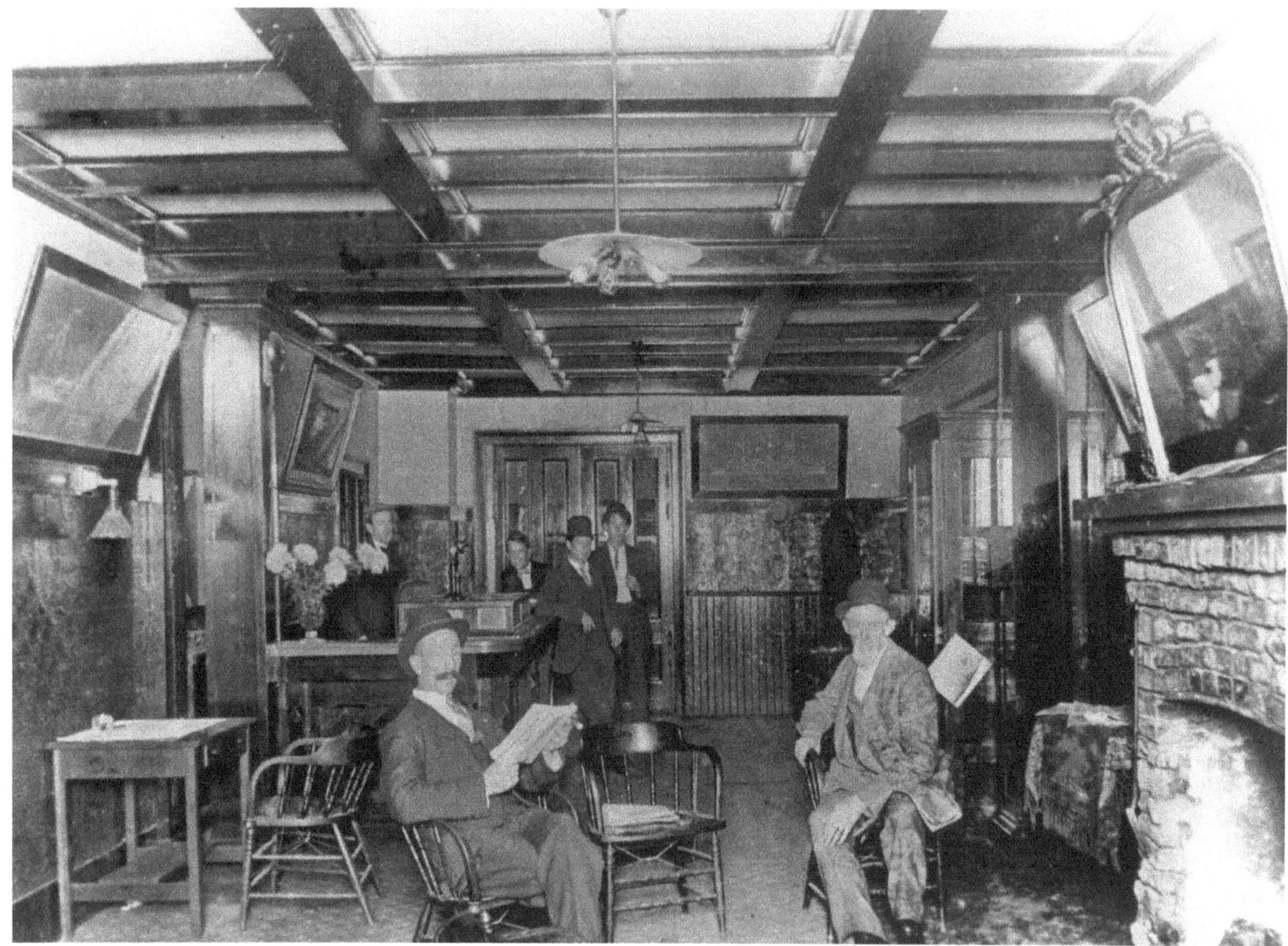

Shaw, Bowman and Co. hardware store was operated in Cloverdale around 1880 by Isaac E. Shaw, a native of New York who came to Cloverdale in 1871, and Mrs. F. J. Bowman. Shaw was also a postmaster and Wells Fargo agent. Among those listed in the photo are J. H. Bowman, E. Shaw, Wynn McCray, E. D. Miner, Mr. and Mrs. J. L. Sedgley, C. L. Sedgley, Ella Shaw, Dr. R. S. Markell, C. B. Shaw, J. M. Hixson, John B. Elliott, W. D. Sink, and Frank Shaw.

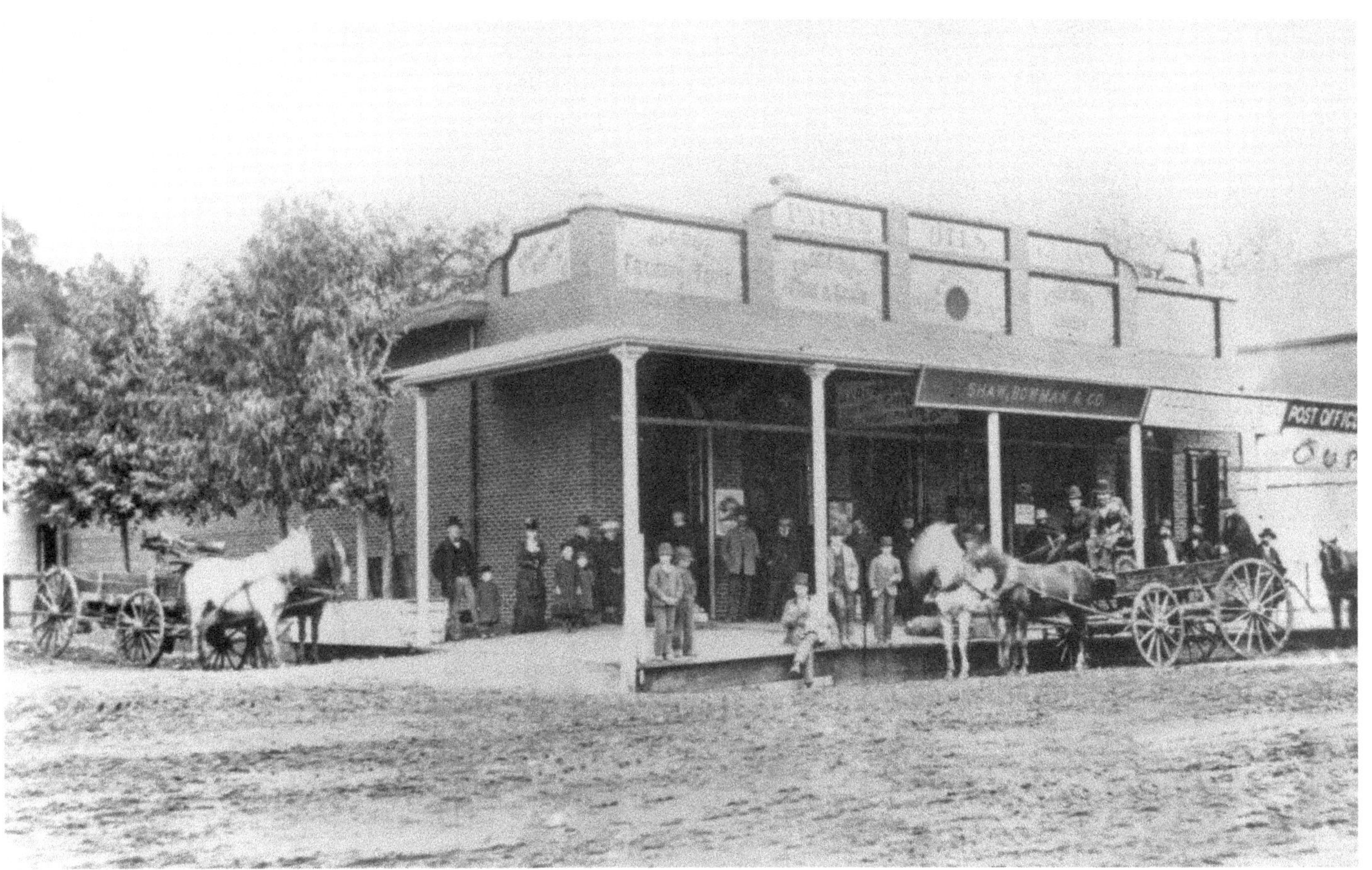

Logging was hard and dangerous work, but it was a major factor of the nineteenth century Sonoma County economy. The redwoods on the lower Russian River near Guerneville worked "beautifully under the plane" and had "the merit of retaining its place and shape without warp or shrinkage." These workers did their logging in the Guerneville area around 1880.

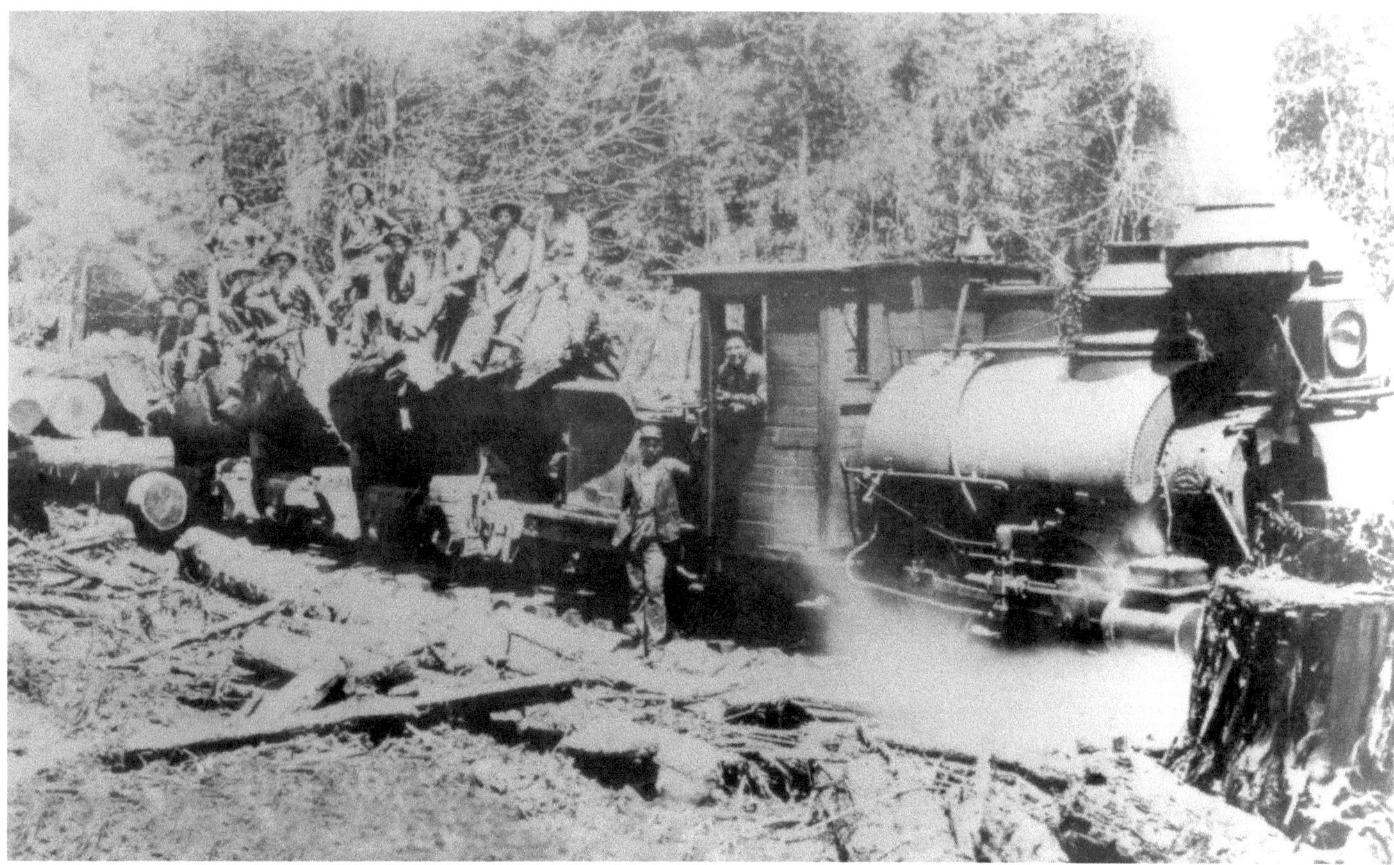

From accordion solos to Irish jigs, musical performances became a major part of the tradition of Sonoma County early on. Immigrant groups brought their musical spirit with them and introduced a wide variety of melodies, providing home-spun entertainment. This band was active in Sonoma County in the 1880s.

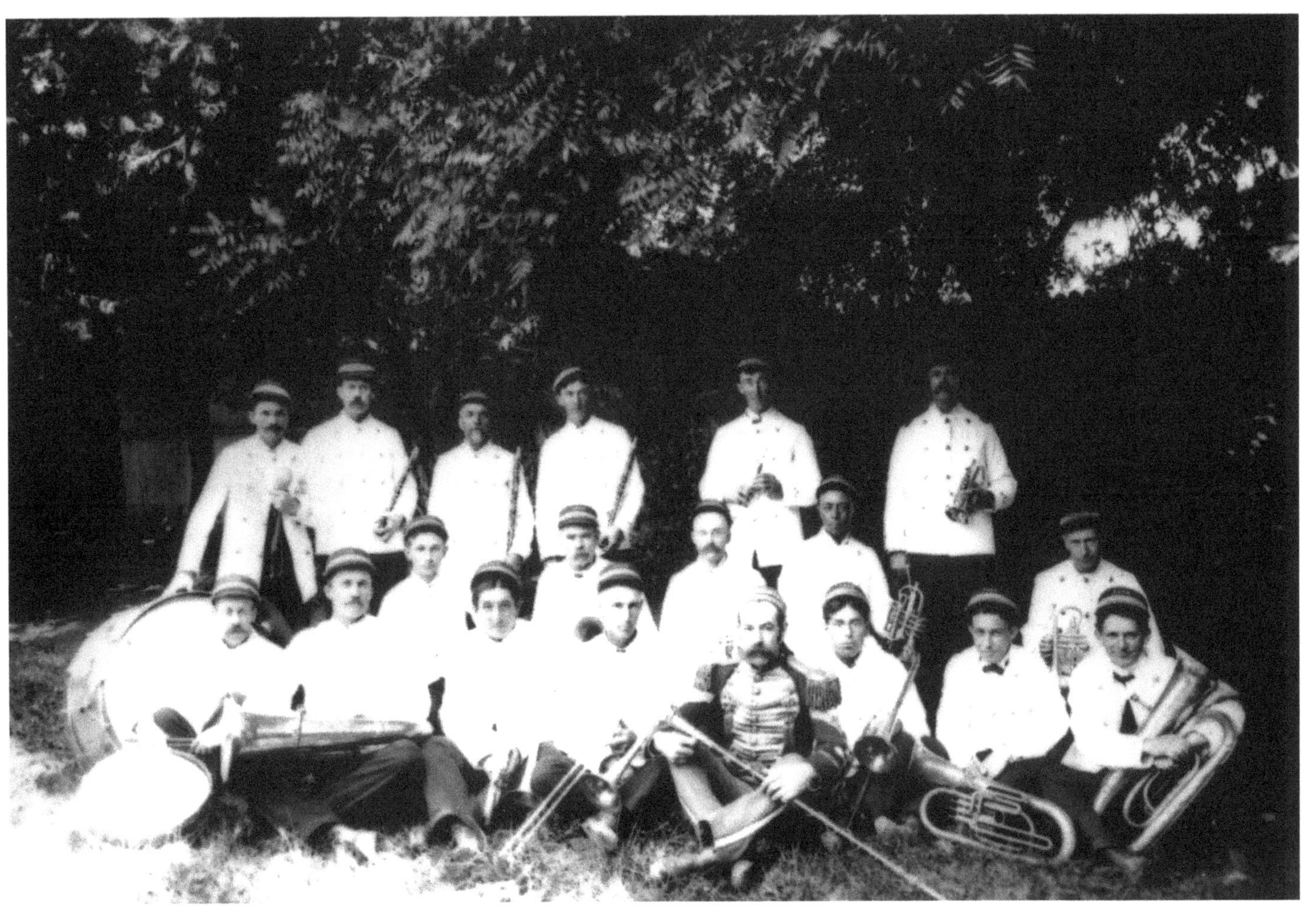

Blacksmith F. G. Varner and G. P. Benville, agent for Studebaker wagons, offered their services to travelers and ranchers in the 1880s.

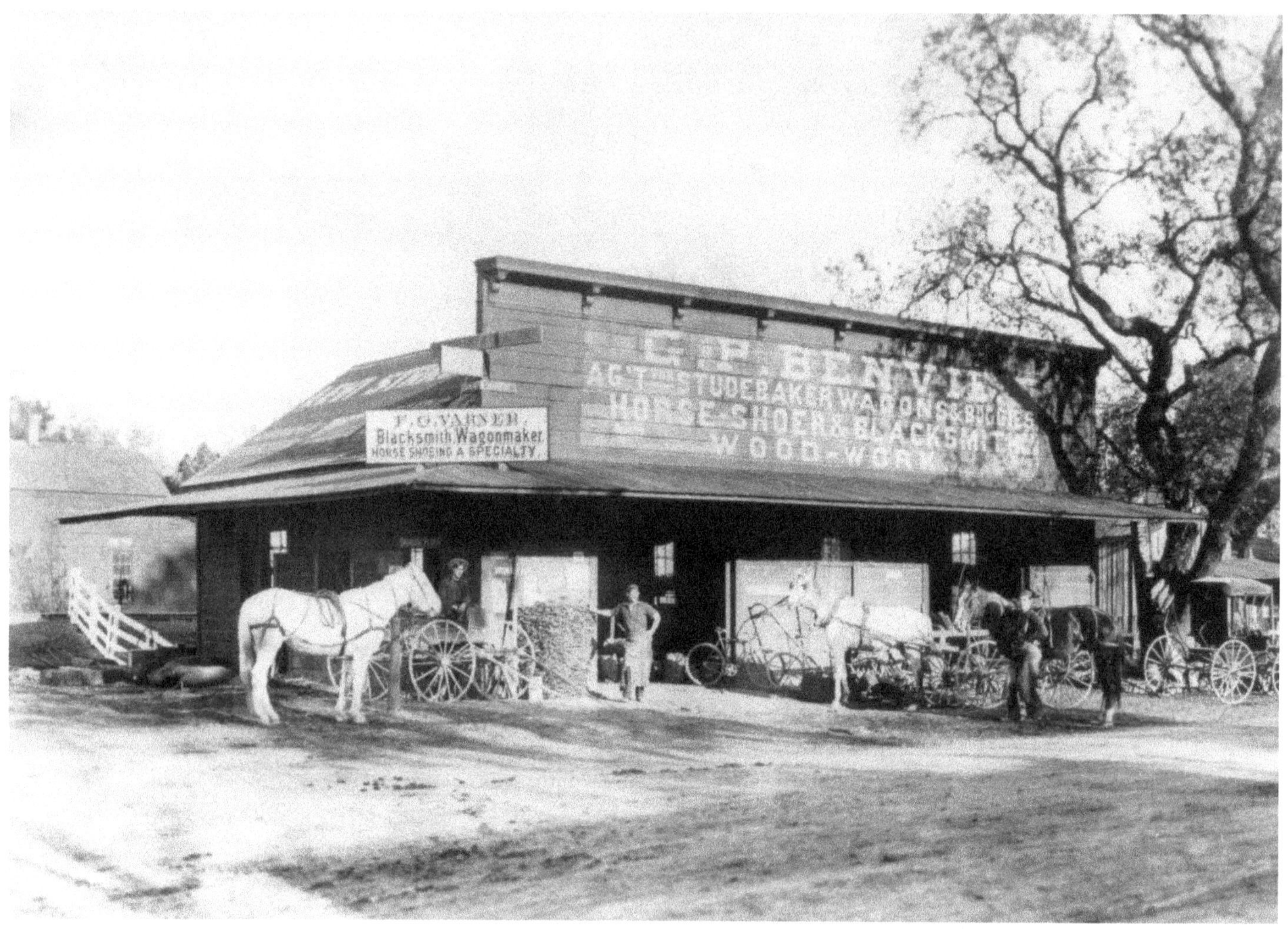

At the western corner of Main and Washington streets in Petaluma, the Derby Block was constructed, offering the services of a cigar and tobacco retailer.

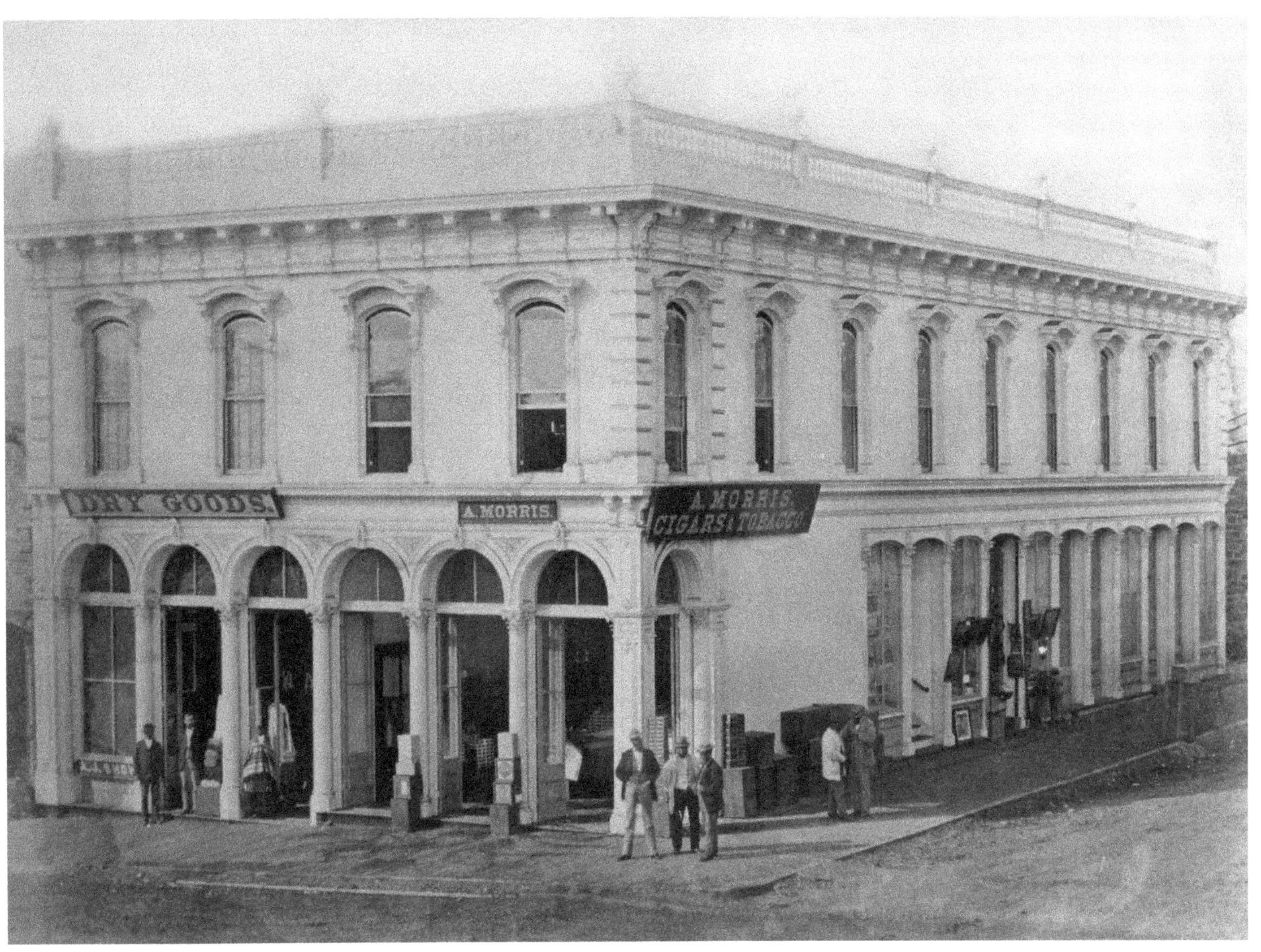

Inspired by French immigrants, Icaria School, at the corner of Asti Road and Old Redwood Highway south of Cloverdale, served the Icaria-Speranza utopian colony set up in 1881 and disbanded in 1886. The Armand Dehay and Leroux families led the experiment, one of four nineteenth century utopian communities in the county. When the colony disbanded, the schoolhouse was deeded to Sonoma County.

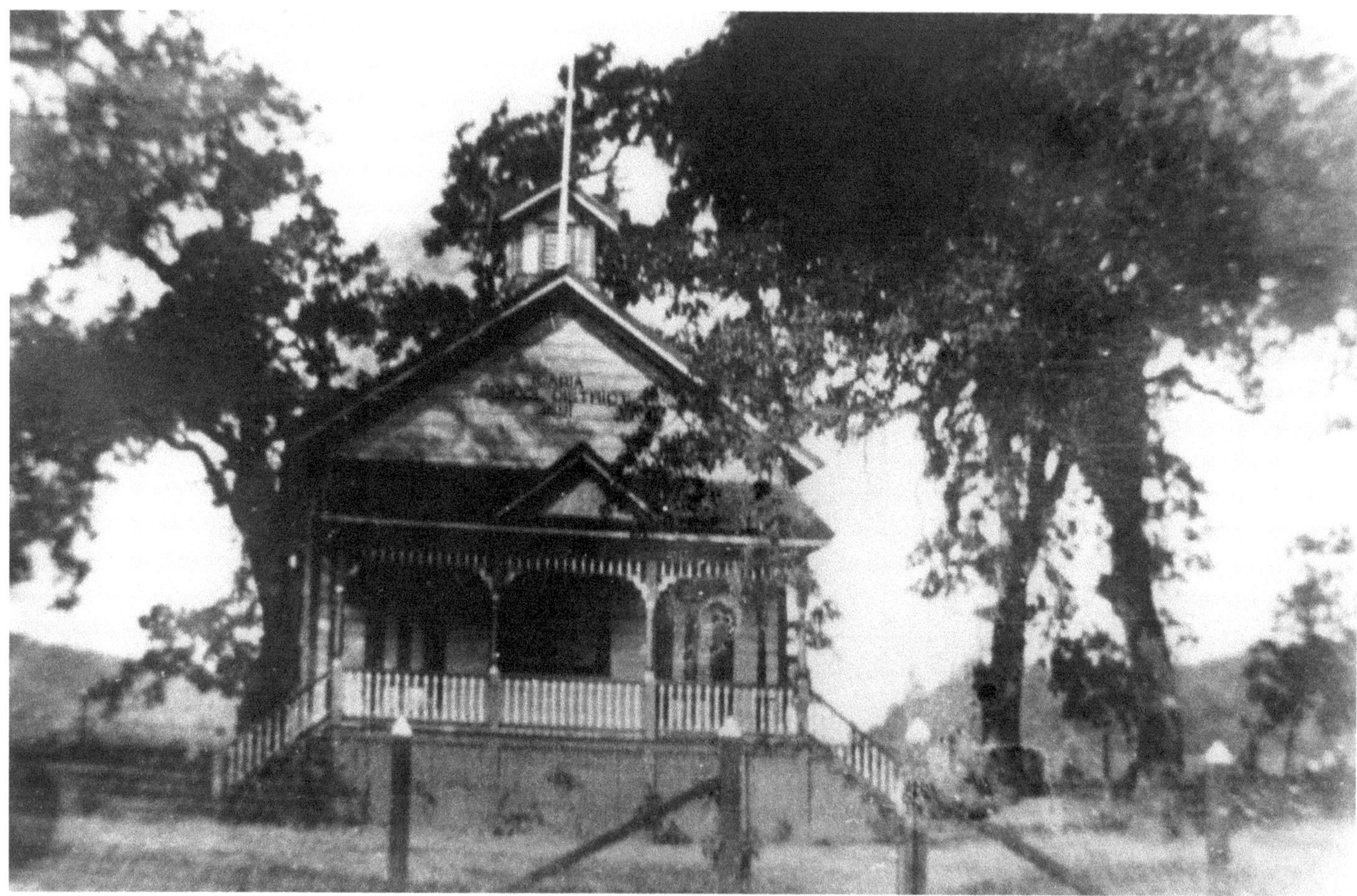

Traveling in Sonoma County took real ingenuity. Whether maneuvering a big wagon with a load of hay or a smaller vehicle, smart riders periodically pulled into the Russian River to soak their wheels. Dry wheels were more brittle and likely to break on bumpy, rural roads, such as those around Cloverdale in the 1880s.

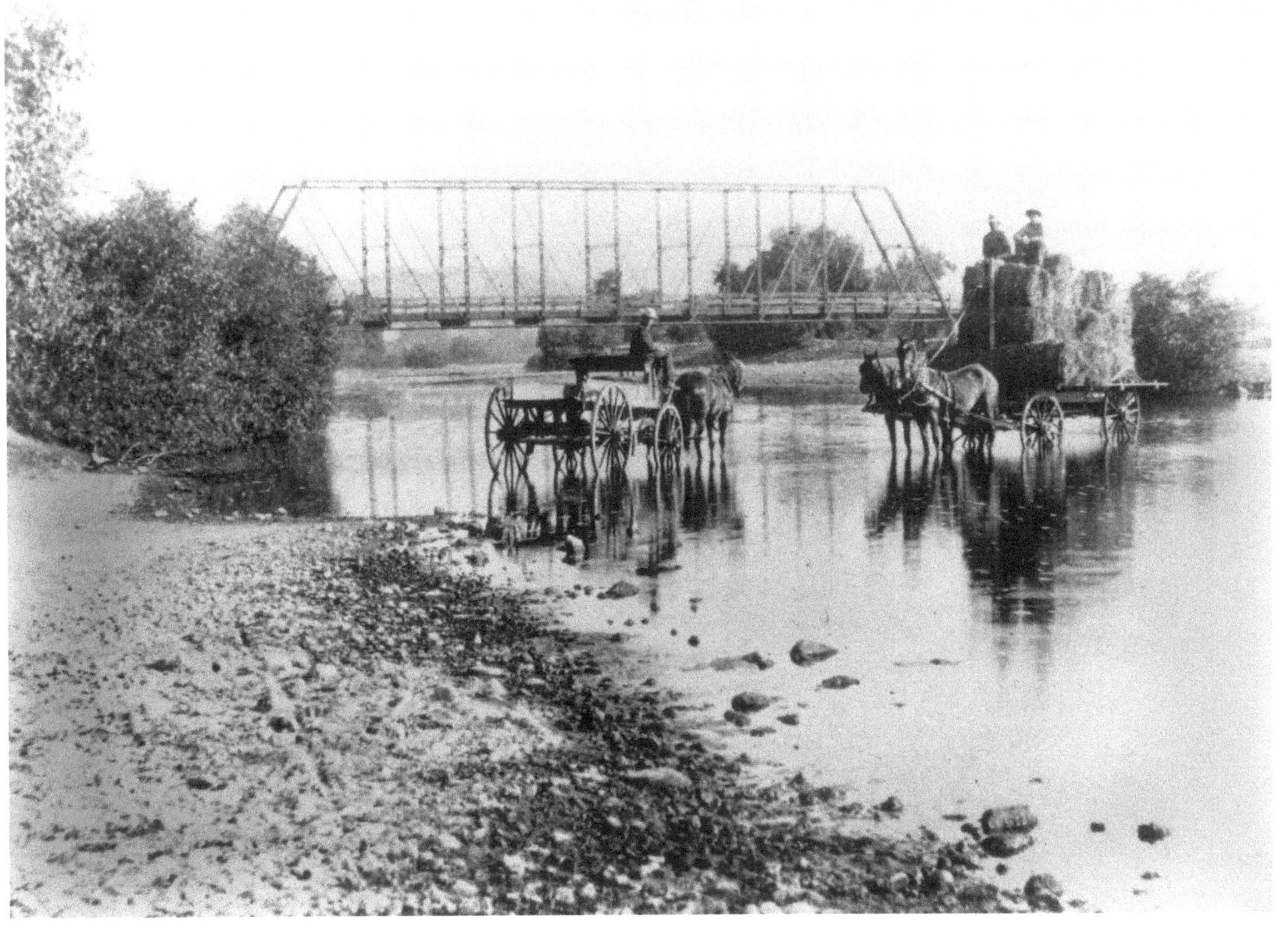

Men halted their wagons at the B. F. Cox Express Stable at Oak and Main streets to do business and trade gossip. The business was later renamed the Petaluma Express Company.

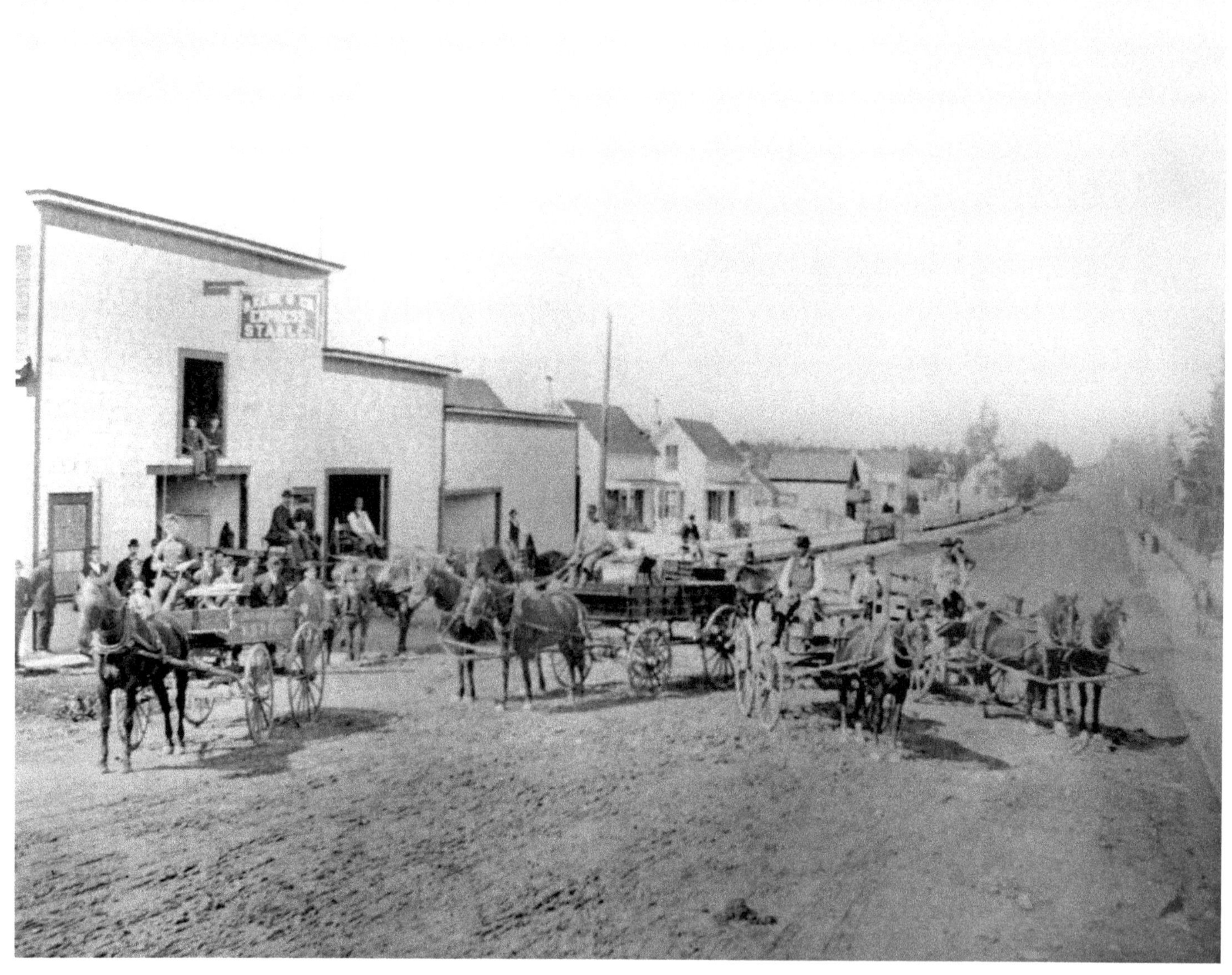

When farmers came to Petaluma to shop, they often caused mini-traffic jams with their horses and buggies. Near the end of the nineteenth century, the buggies pulled in and tied up at a railing at Hill Plaza Park at the corner of Main and Mary streets. A water trough is visible on the right.

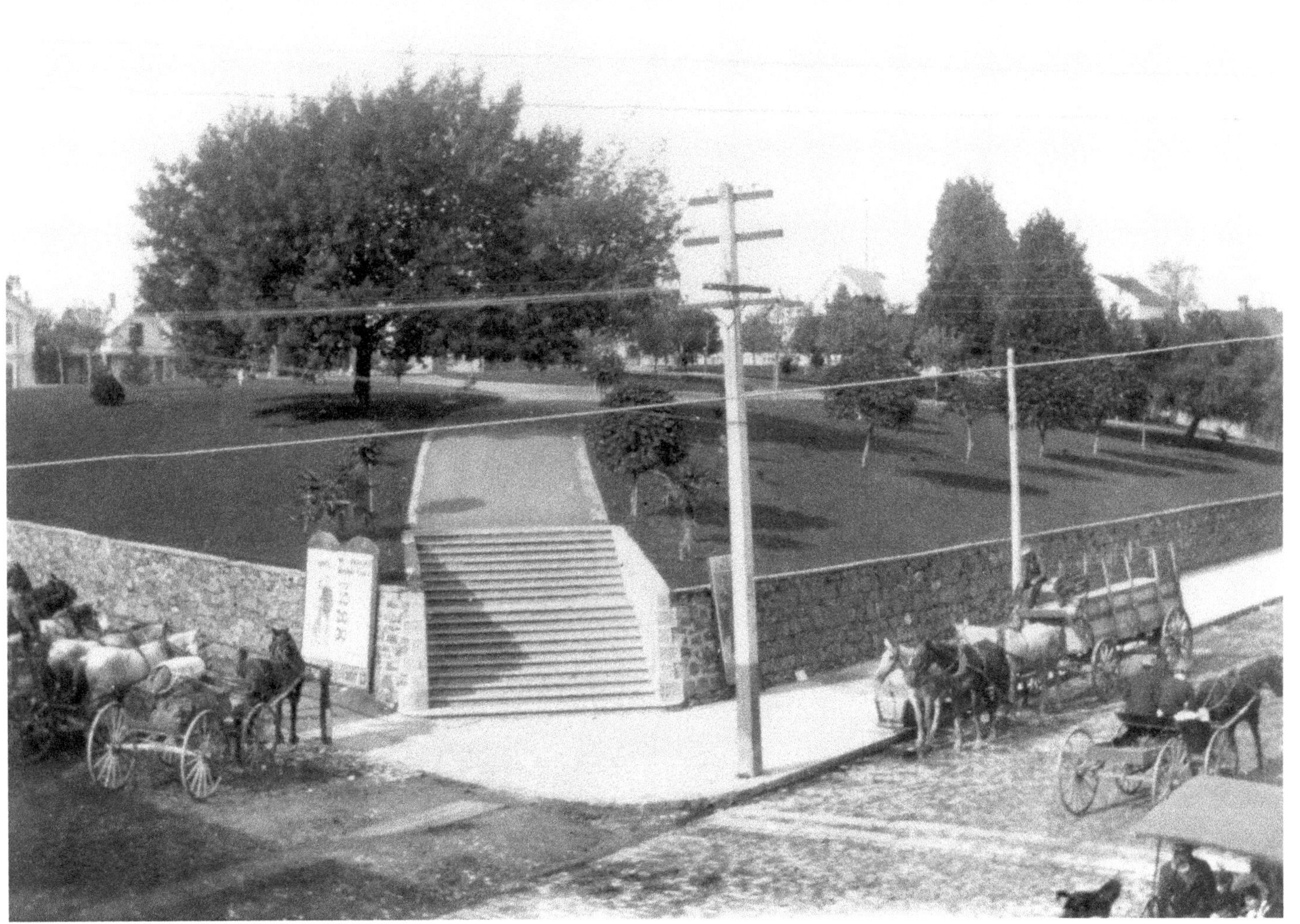

The Windsor Hotel was a popular overnight stop in the 1880s. Sevier Lewis opened the first hotel in Windsor in 1856 but within two years sold the business to Samuel Emmerson. The hotel, on the east side of the road between Santa Rosa and Healdsburg, burned in 1911.

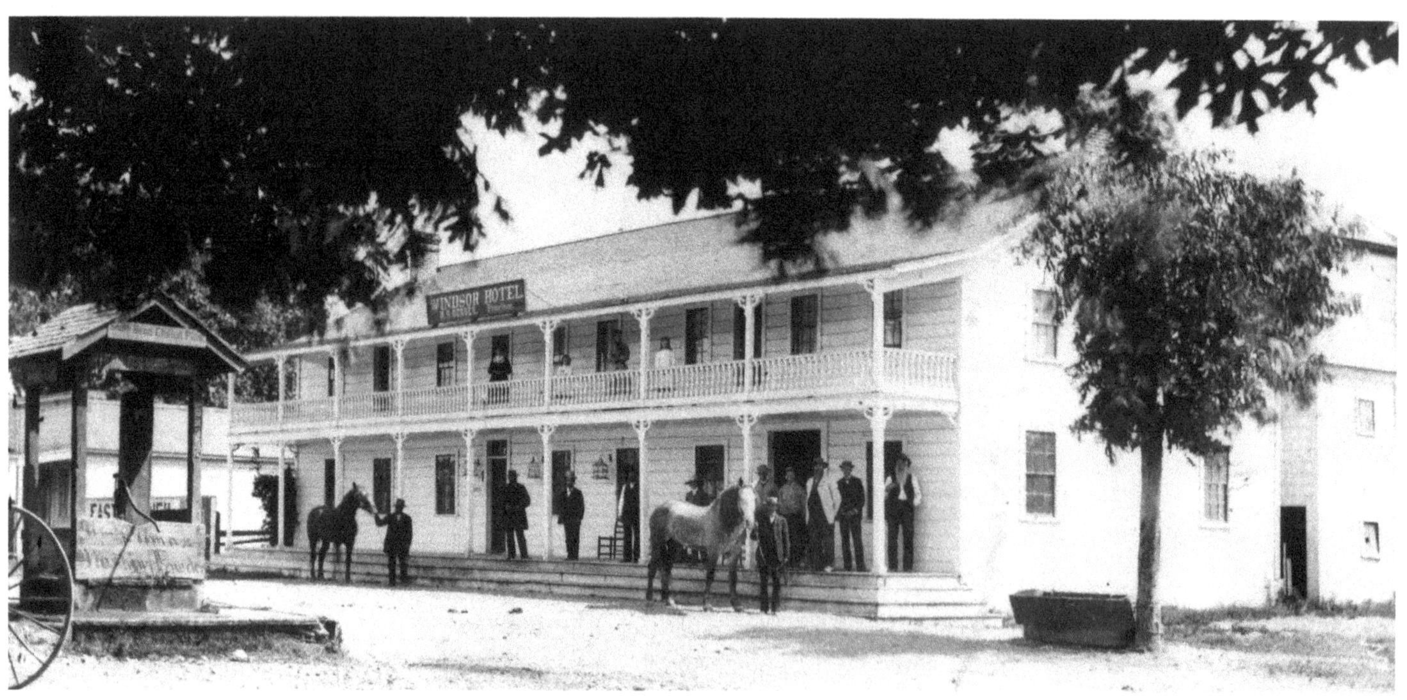

Settlers in fertile Bennett Valley southeast of Santa Rosa learned early how to live off the land. They built their own homes and churches and created a powerful Grange organization which stressed family values. Children from the area gathered for a Spring picnic in May 1892 at the Bennett Valley Grange Hall. Participants, not in order, were: Mary Davis, Parker Talbot, Mamie Strong, Fred Clark, Joe Strong, Ella Badger, Nell Keppell, Fred Bruggemann, Luke Bremmer, George Morrow, Leslie Talbot, John Ahl, Minnie Hielman, Mabel Ahl, and Margaret Bruggemann.

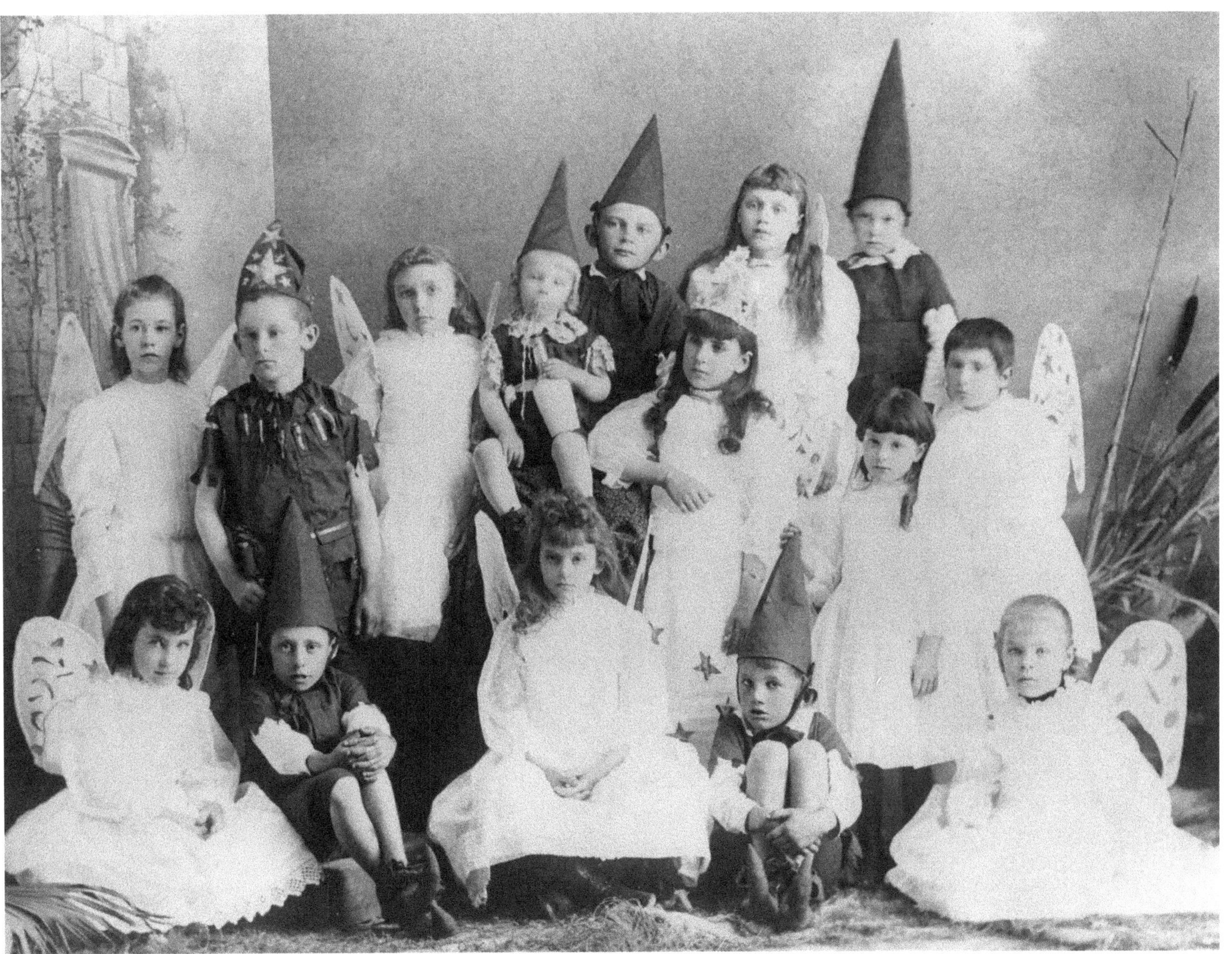

Major celebrations on the Fourth of July and other holidays were common in the nineteenth century and have continued to the present. The Young America Hose Company, a volunteer fire-fighting group, marched in a Petaluma parade in the 1890s. The firemen, often prominent members of the community, risked their lives fighting fires but also enjoyed the camaraderie of socializing with their fellow volunteers.

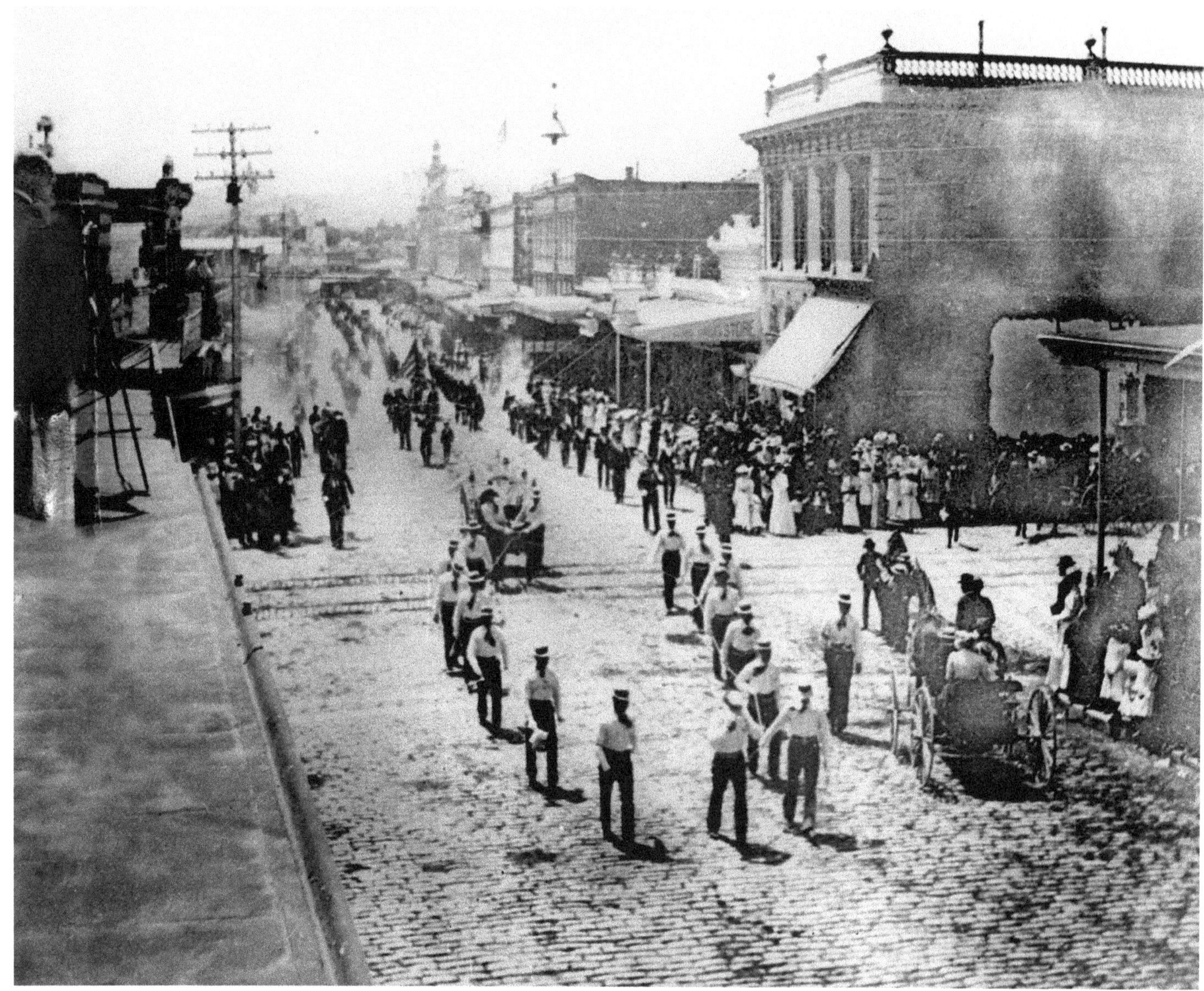

Rural schools dotted the Sonoma County landscape through the nineteenth century. The Windsor schoolhouse about nine miles north of Santa Rosa was built around 1863 at a cost of almost $2,000. In 1890, students from the school took a break and posed on the porch. The school shared space with the Masonic Hall, which was upstairs.

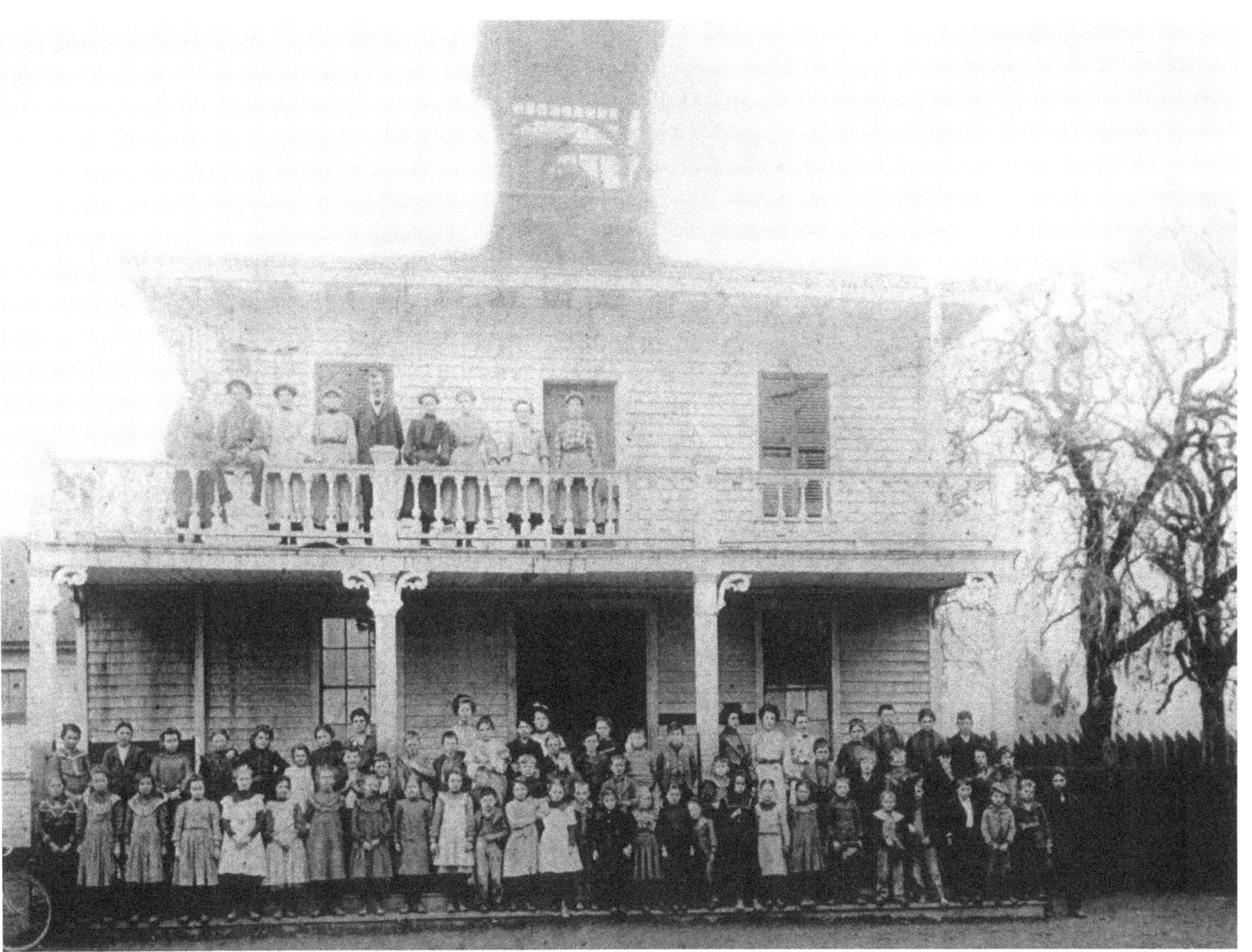

Early residents couldn't enjoy a stop at a coffee shop or fast food restaurant, but they could sometimes find liquid refreshment in the nearest well. In this case, a group of men gathered at the well in front of the Windsor School, one energetic fellow doing the pumping and the other three waiting their turn. The Windsor Hotel was located across the street.

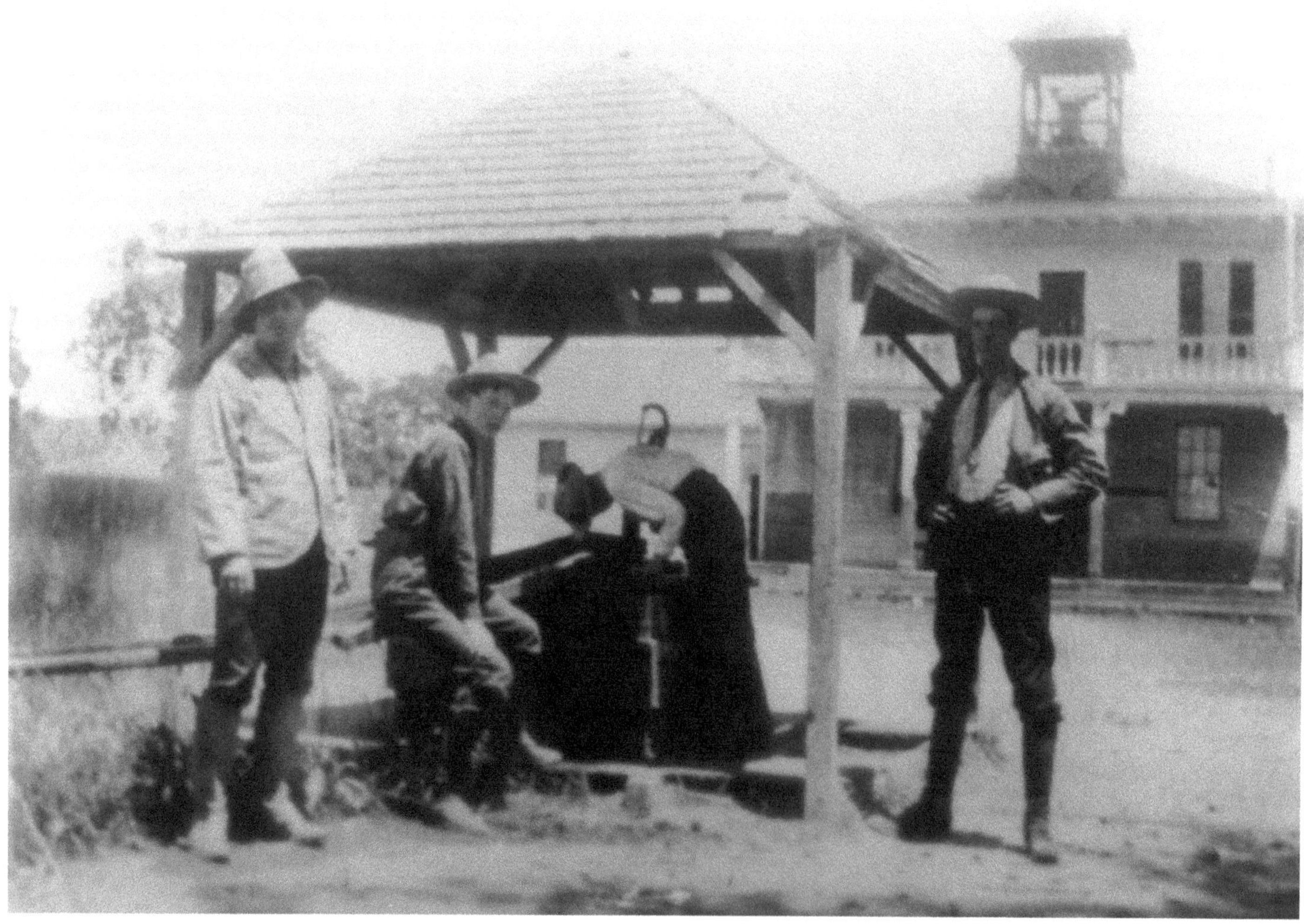

Sorting mail was a "hands-on" job in Cloverdale in 1890. Tom Wilson did the sorting in an office that was very much "open to the public."

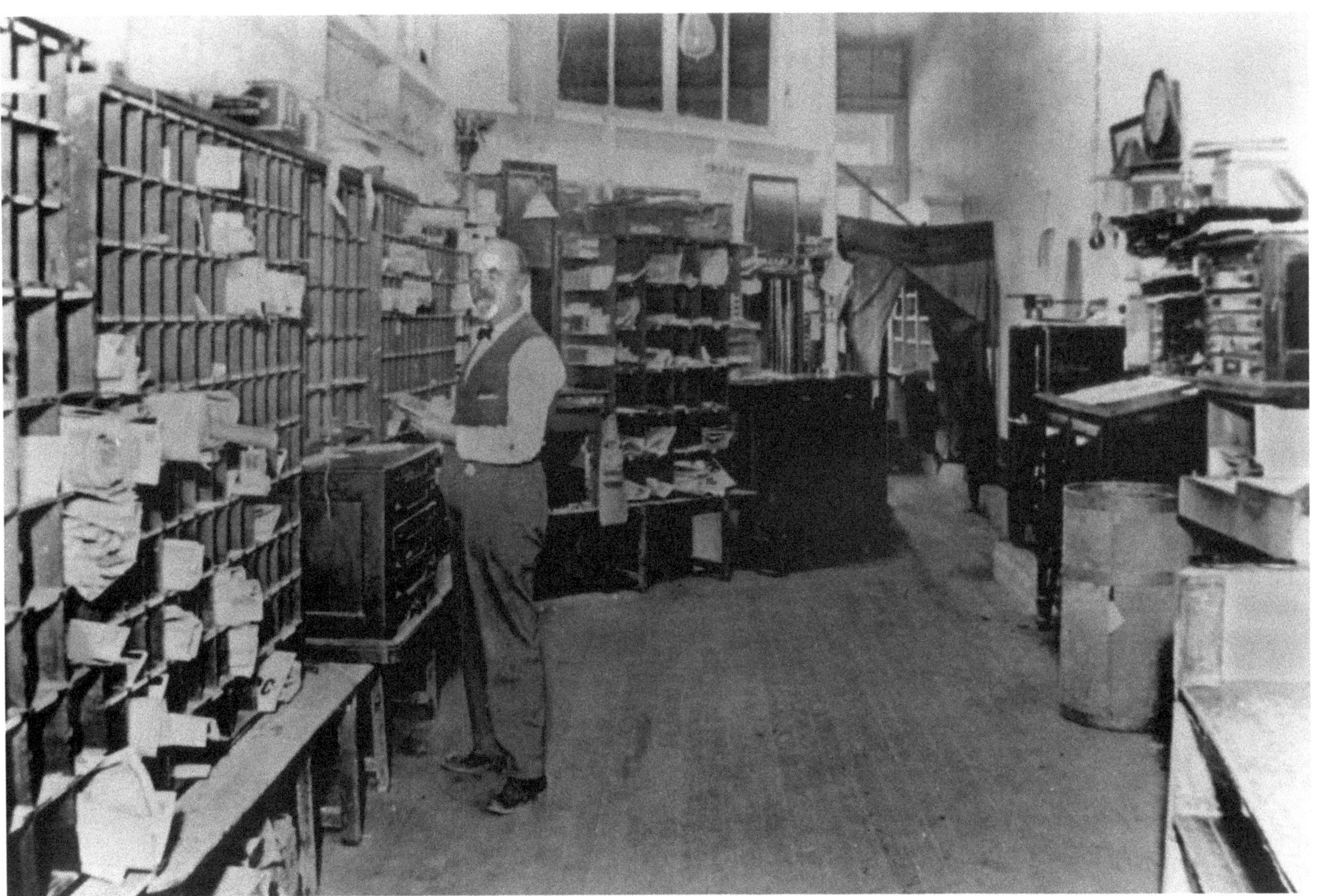

A crowd turned out for a bit of local celebrating in Windsor in 1893. Local residents, many of whom did hard work in the fields on workdays, enjoyed parades, picnics, and other community celebrations.

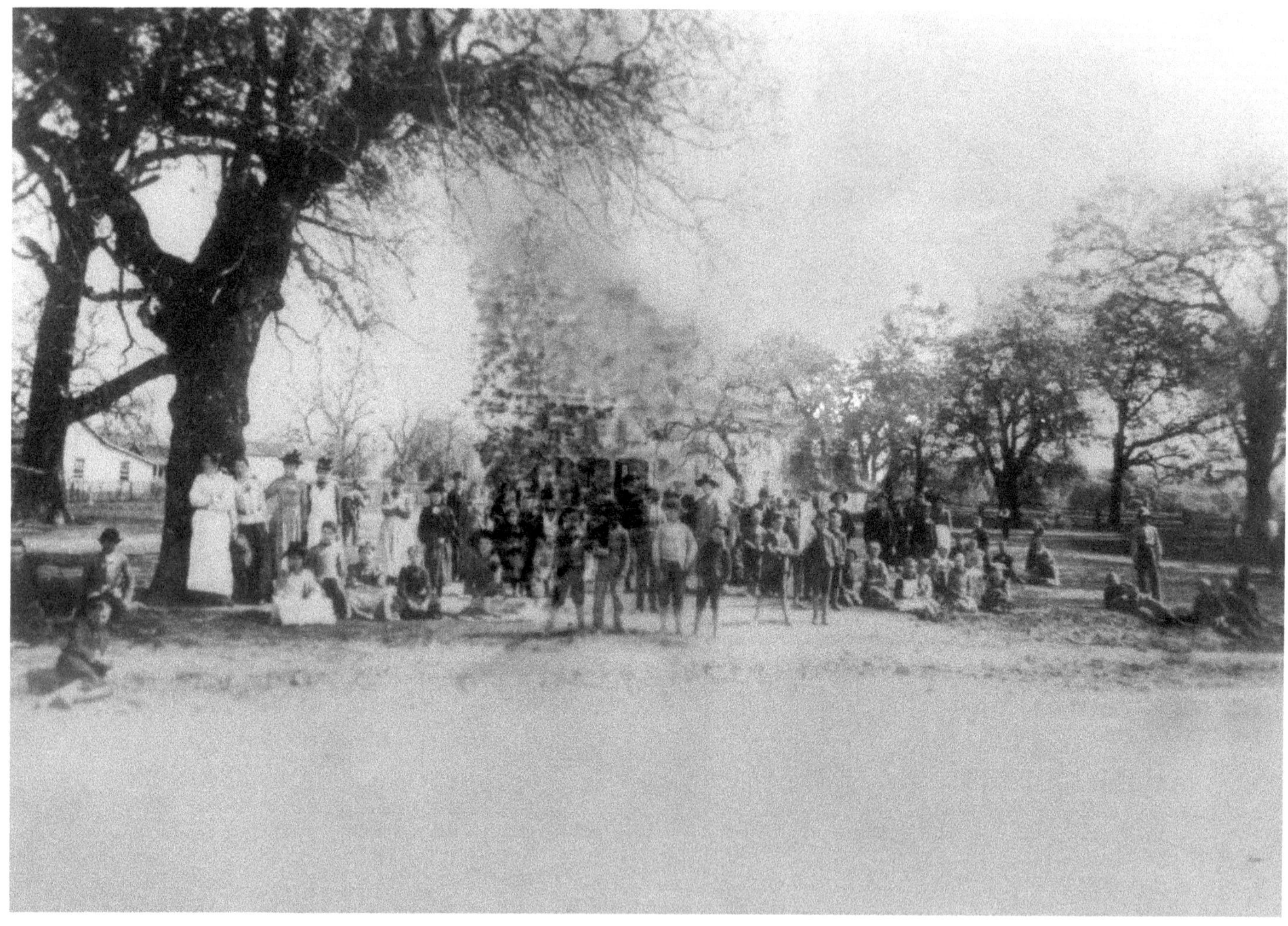

In small-town America, it was not unusual for a person to hold down two or three jobs at a time. Henry Bell, owner of the Windsor General Store in 1891, was such a person, doing double duty as owner of the general store and as Windsor's undertaker. Bell came from New York in 1852 and built a home on River Road, which doubled as a funeral parlor. Later owners of the store were William McCutcheon and L. E. Packwood.

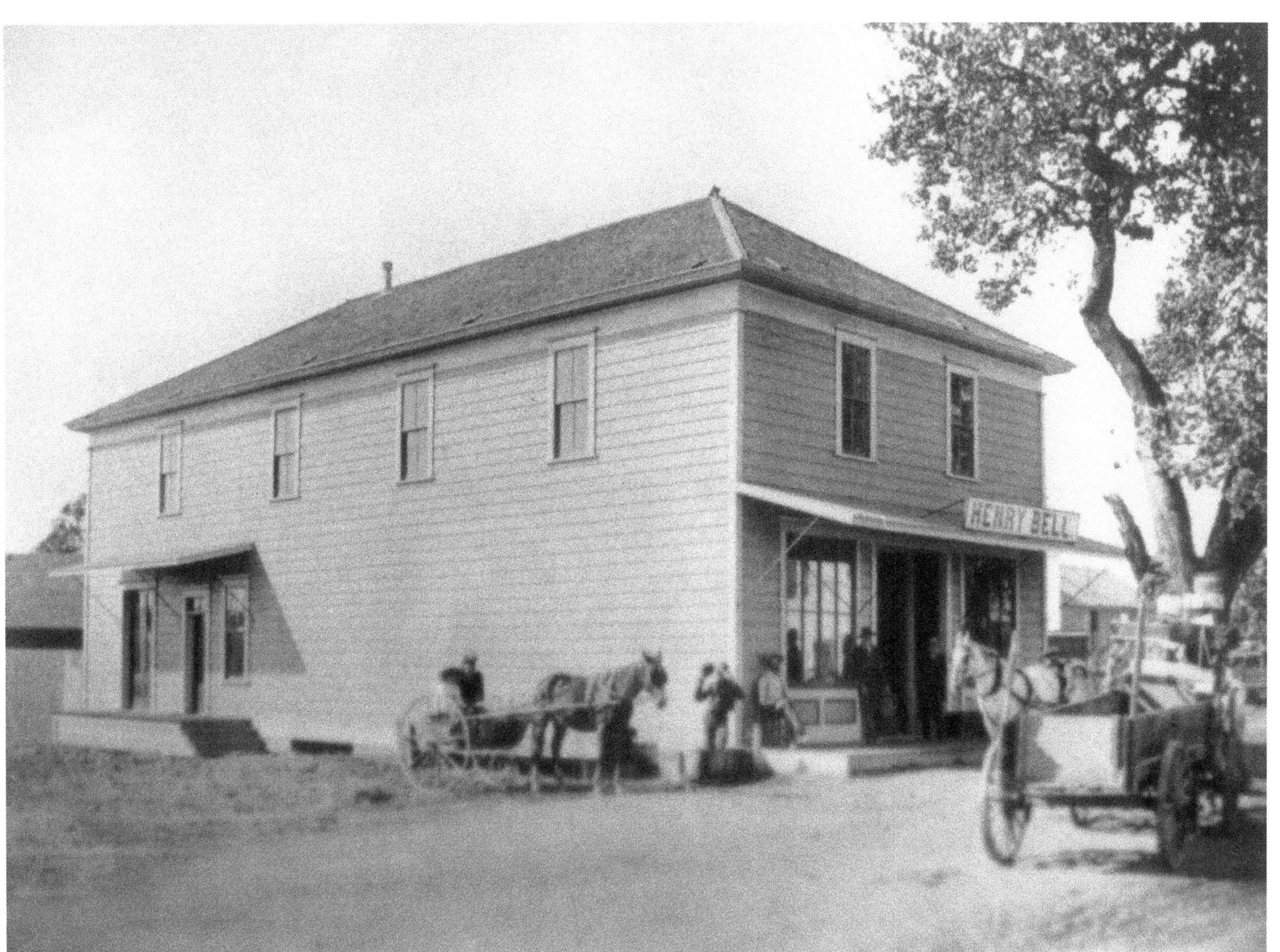

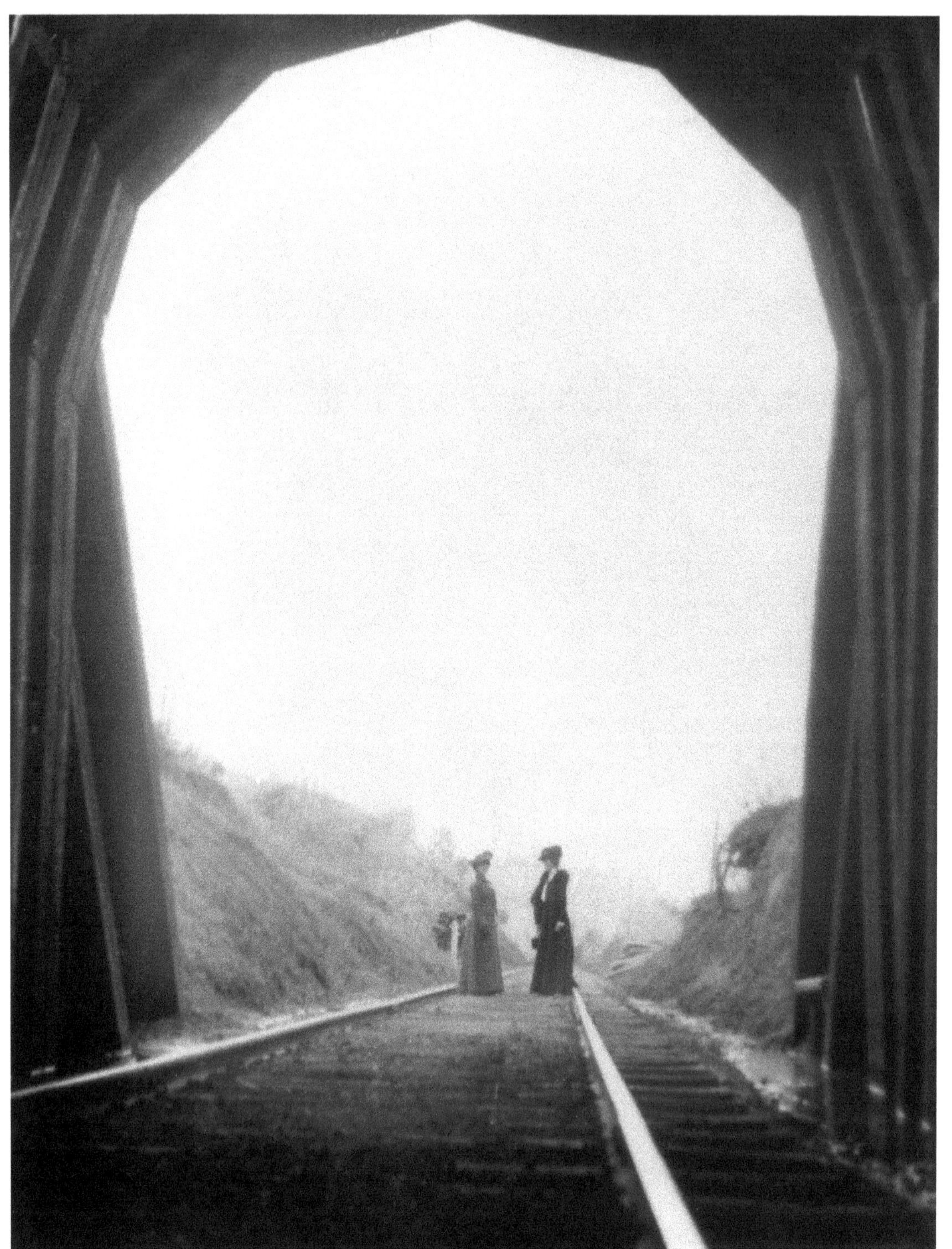

A railroad tunnel above Cloverdale helped speed traffic in the 1890s. Cloverdale served as the gateway to Mendocino and Lake Counties and to the Geysers, the popular tourist spot to the east.

Louis Arata and a woman in a buggy looked rather cheerful considering they were stopped in front of the dental office of H. F. Perkins in Windsor around 1890.

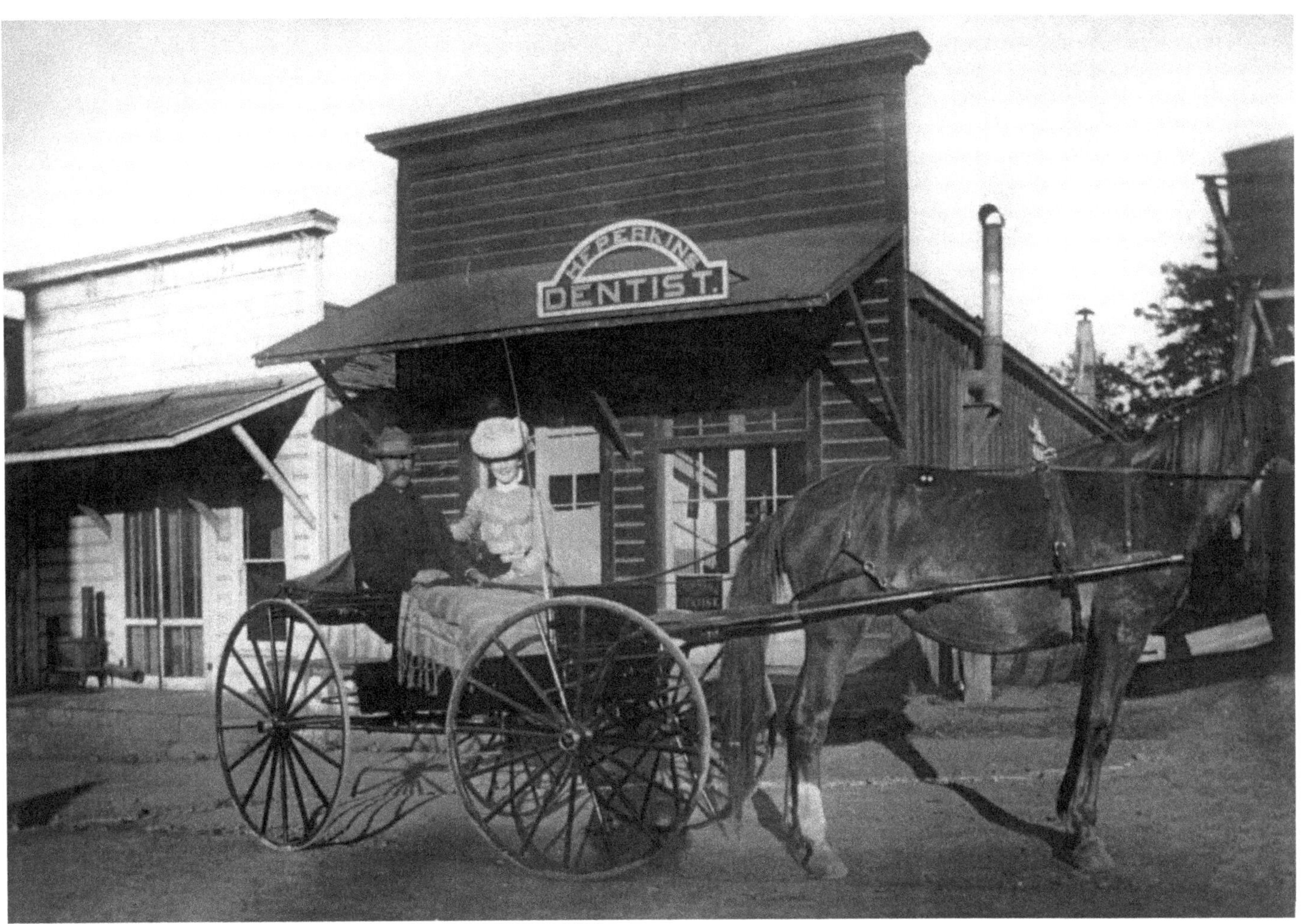

A small boy pulled a flower-decorated wagon at the intersection of busy 3rd and Main streets in Santa Rosa in 1895. In the background were the Grand Hotel and the Central Market operated by the Veirs Brothers. The Grand Hotel, opened in 1873 at the corner of Main and 3rd streets, was equipped to take advantage of the upswing in the economy in the 1890s. It had forty rooms with thirteen suites, running water, and marble washstands.

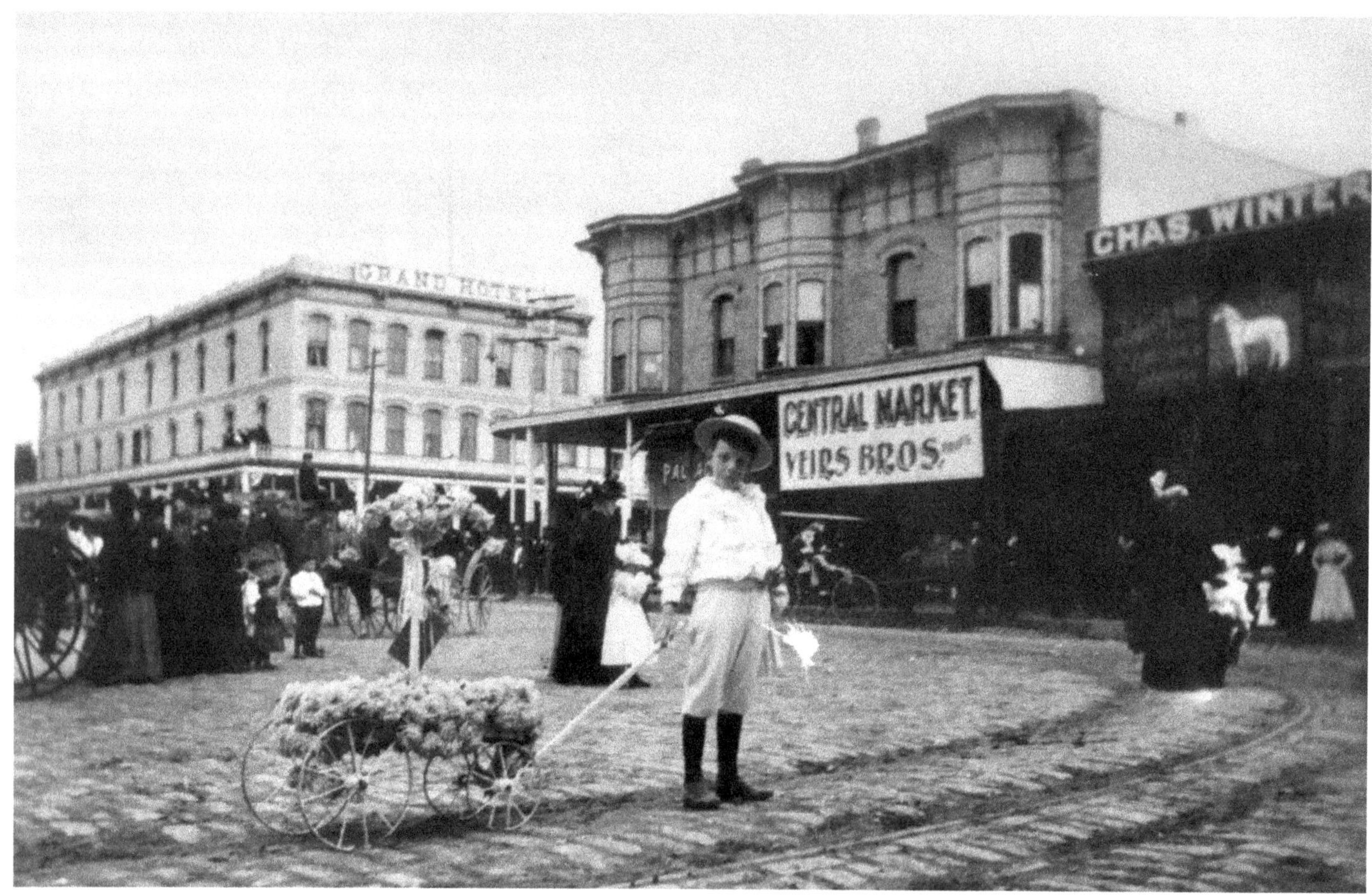

In nineteenth-century Sonoma County, church was a place for worship and also a good place to meet neighbors and share local gossip. The Methodist Church in East Windsor, built by Billings and Company carpenters in 1865, remained a community fixture when this photo was taken in 1893.

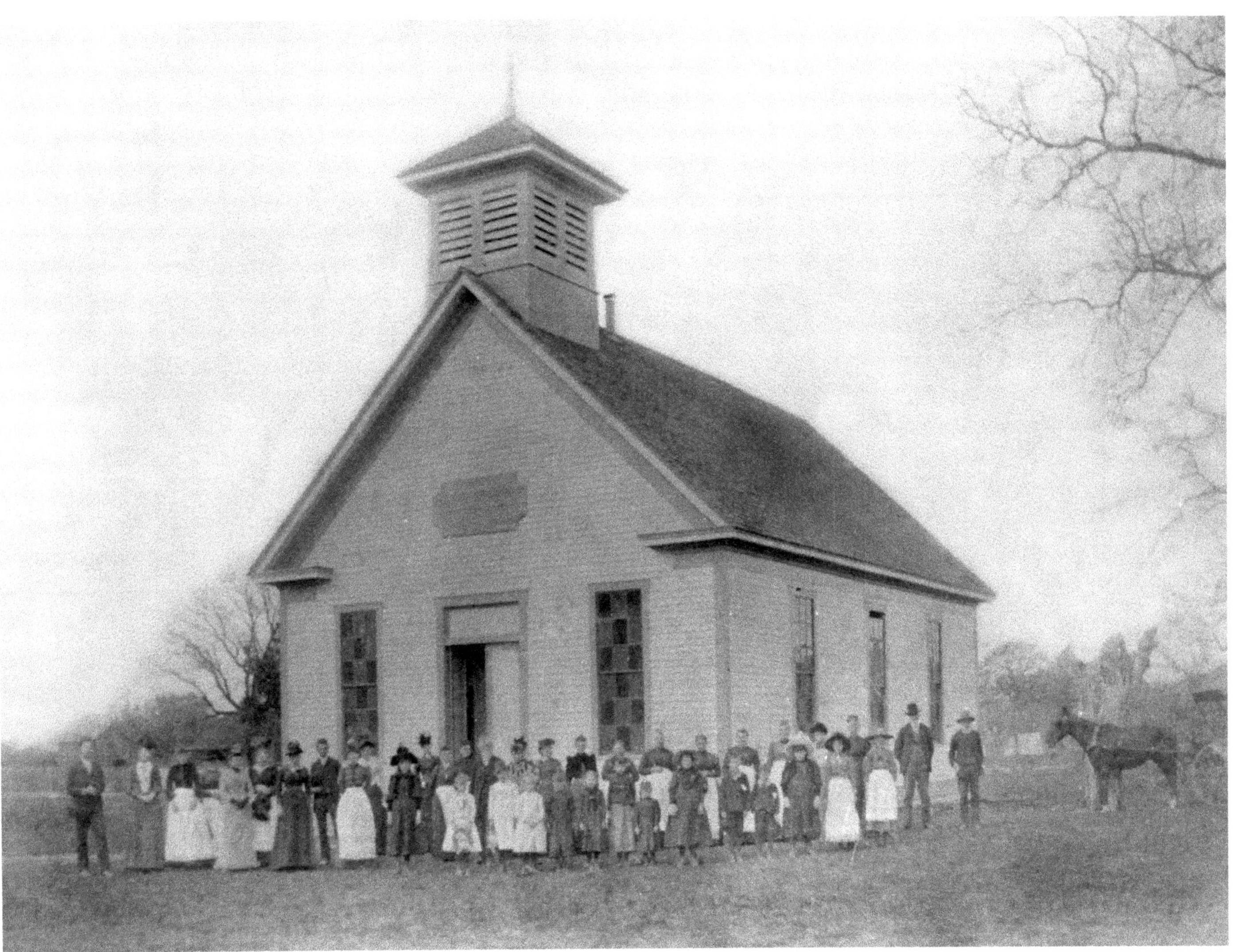

Members of a road crew took a break during repair work near Windsor in 1895. Rainy weather and heavy wagons took a heavy toll on the area's transportation system, even before automobiles came along to complicate the problem.

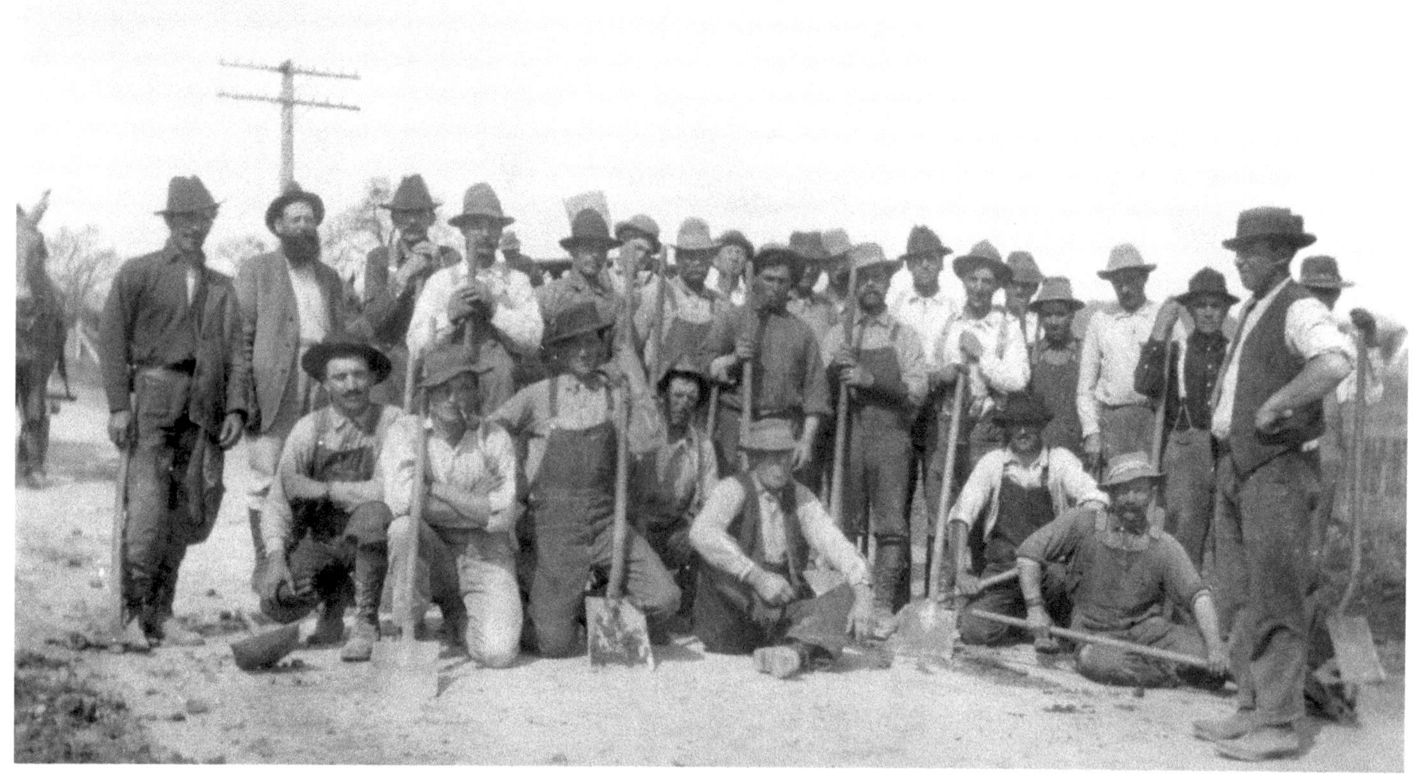

For farmers, what it all came down to was planting the seed, caring for the crop, and getting it to market. Luther Bell, son of Henry and Catherine Bell, got the job done using the first gang plow in Windsor in 1891. A gang plow allowed farmers to cut parallel furrows at a rapid rate.

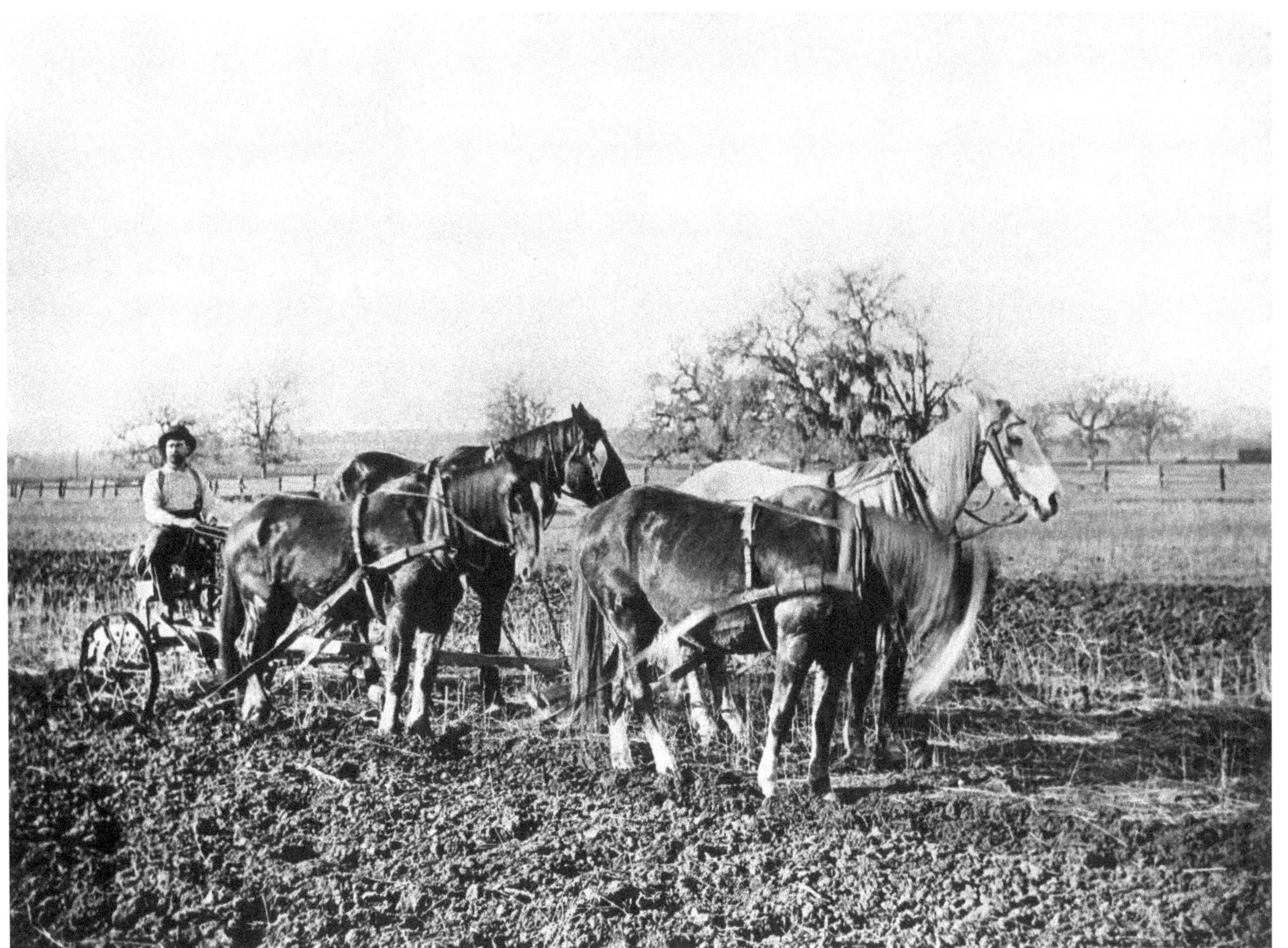

In 1896, as the Spanish-American War neared, soldiers from Company C marched north on Main Street in Petaluma. Identified were Maj. James Armstrong, the white-bearded man in front; Rita Long, on the hotel sidewalk under the flag, and Sgt. Albert Cassidy, third row back on the outside. In the background were the Cosmopolitan Hotel and M. J. Hickey, Greengrocer. The soldiers were called to active duty in 1898 during the Spanish-American War but never got farther than camps in the Bay Area.

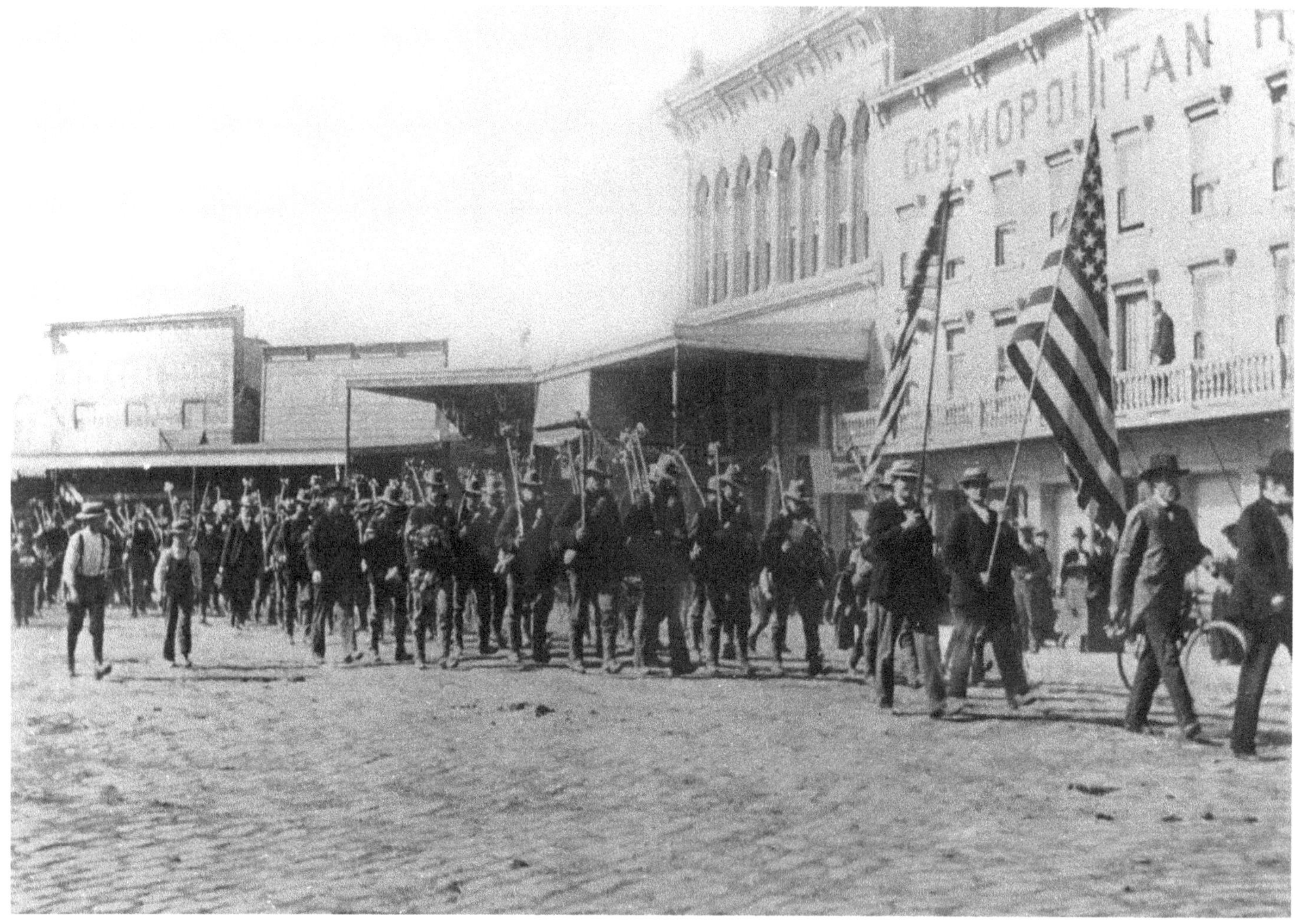

To get a perfect view, a group of four people edged out onto a roof of a Main Street building to watch a military unit march crisply by during a parade in Petaluma in 1898. Sonoma County units, Co. E from Santa Rosa and Co. C from Petaluma, were called to Bay Area training camps during the Spanish-American war in 1898, but the conflict ended before they could be sent overseas.

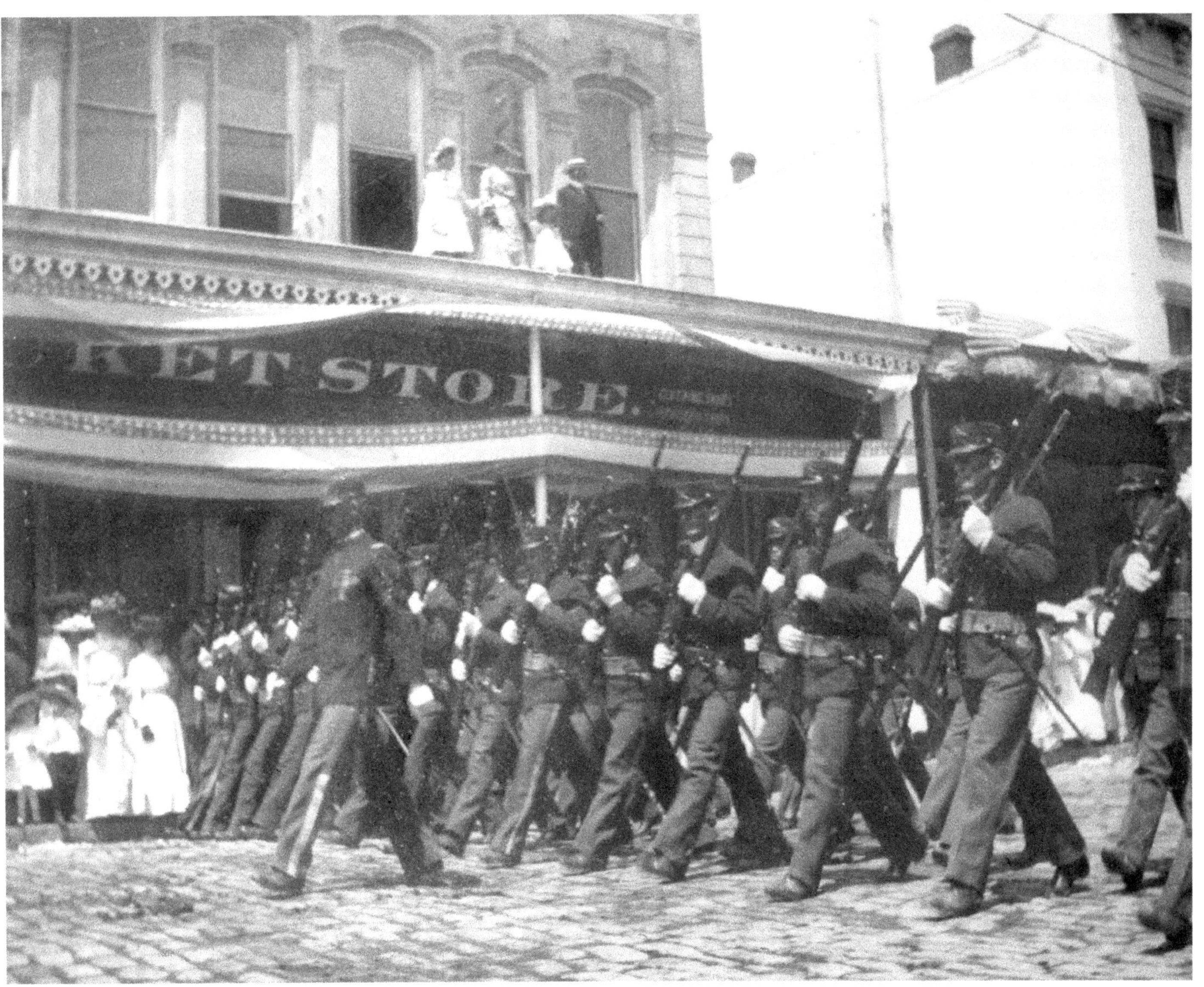

Wanderers following the dusty trails of Sonoma County often looked for a place that provided a touch of liquid refreshment. One of Occidental's finer establishments in the late nineteenth century was the Montreal Saloon operated by Lazare Pere. Far left was Nelson Drago; second from left, C. J. Chenoweth; fifth from left, Lee Carrillo; and sixth from left, saloon keeper Pere.

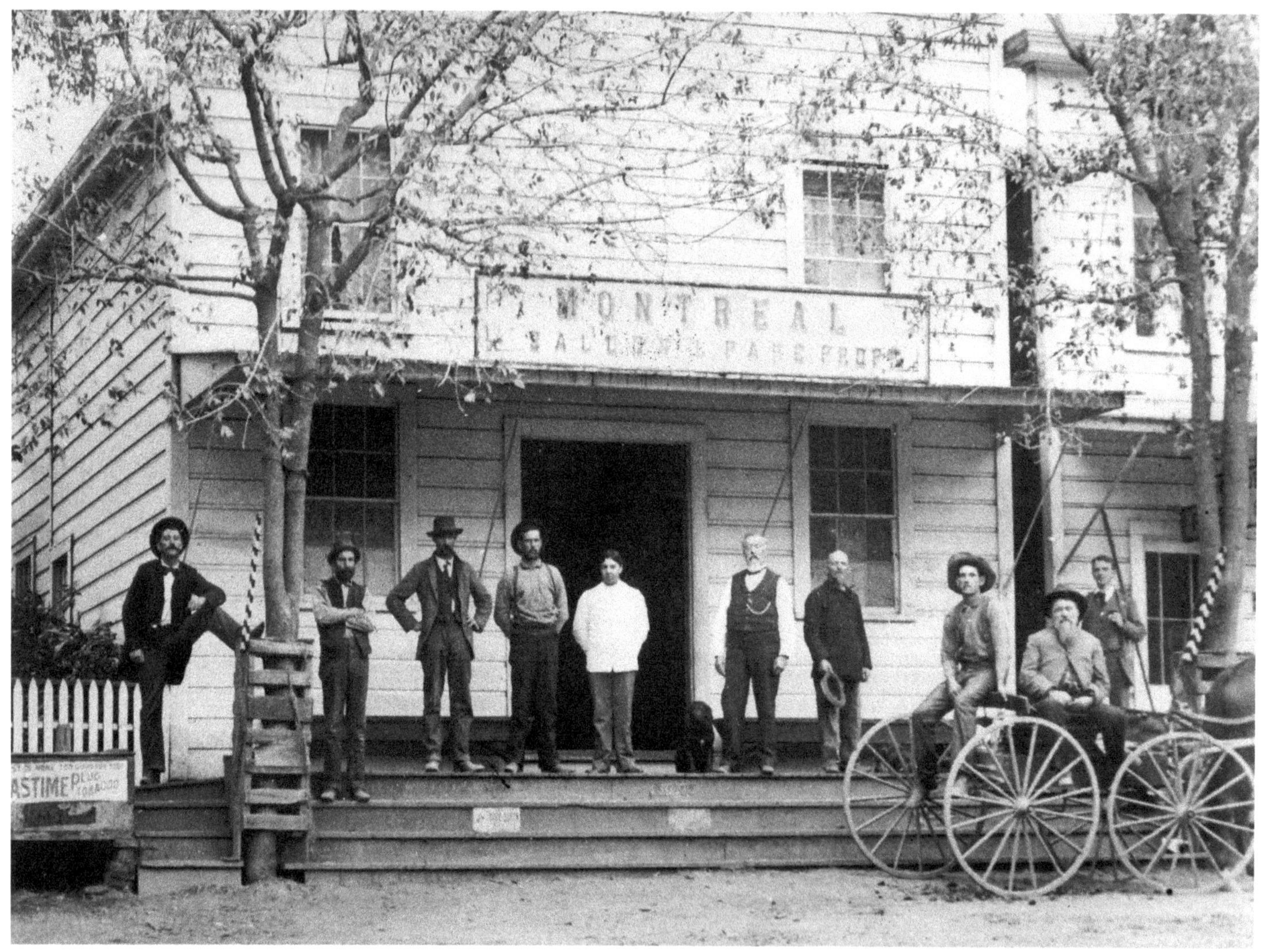

Fresh asparagus? Squash? Green beans? In the days before supermarkets, women shoppers checked out the supply of fresh vegetables available from "green thumb" farmers like Ed Passalacqua. His popular garden was located on Ward Street in Healdsburg in the 1890s.

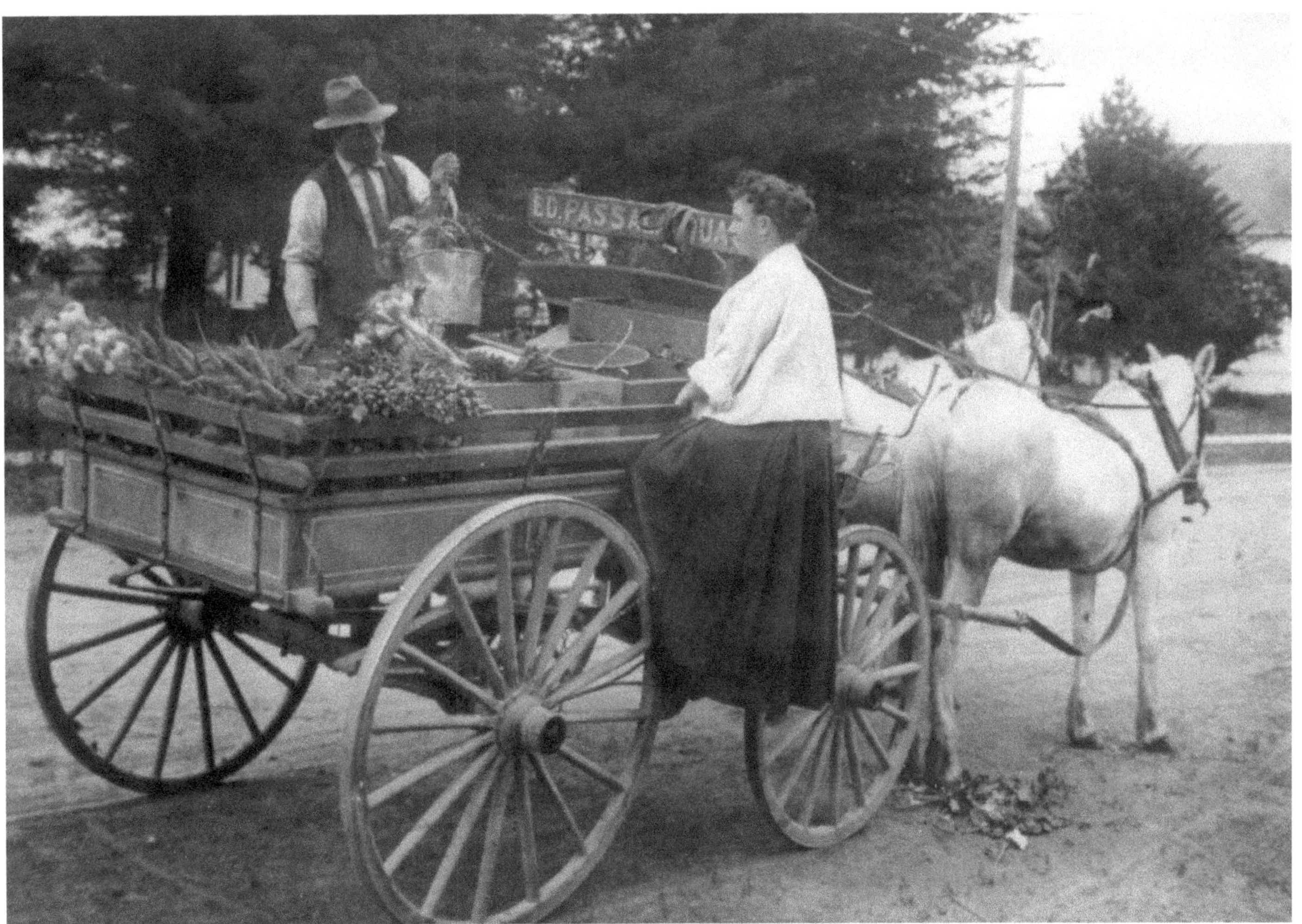

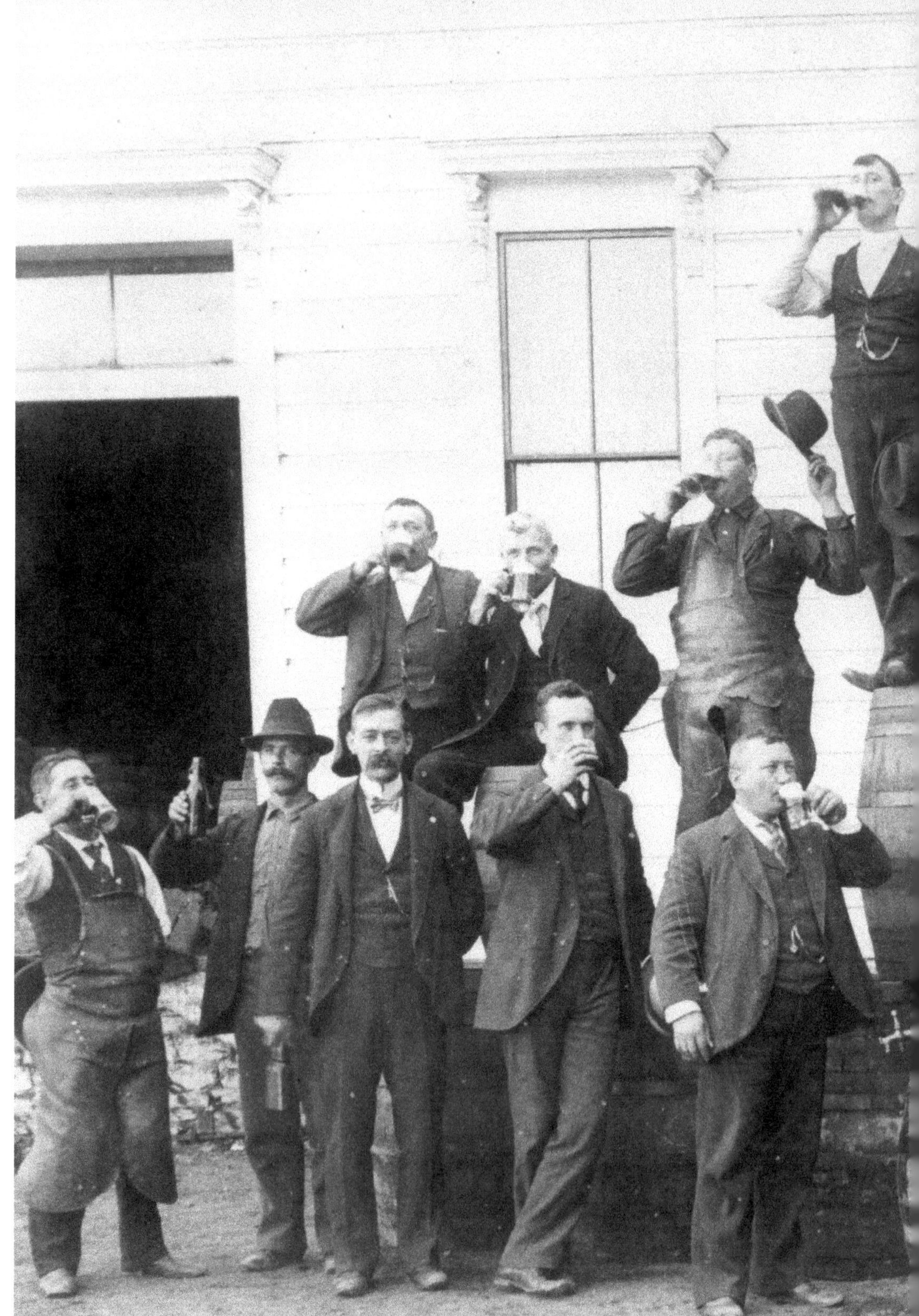

There's nothing like a boss who lets his workers take a break to sample the finished product. In this case, the samplers were employees of Grace Brothers Brewery, founded in 1872 as Santa Rosa Steam Brewery and taken over by brothers Frank P. and Joseph T. Grace in the late 1890s. The brewery became one of Santa Rosa's main enterprises, turning out almost fifty labels before closing in 1966.

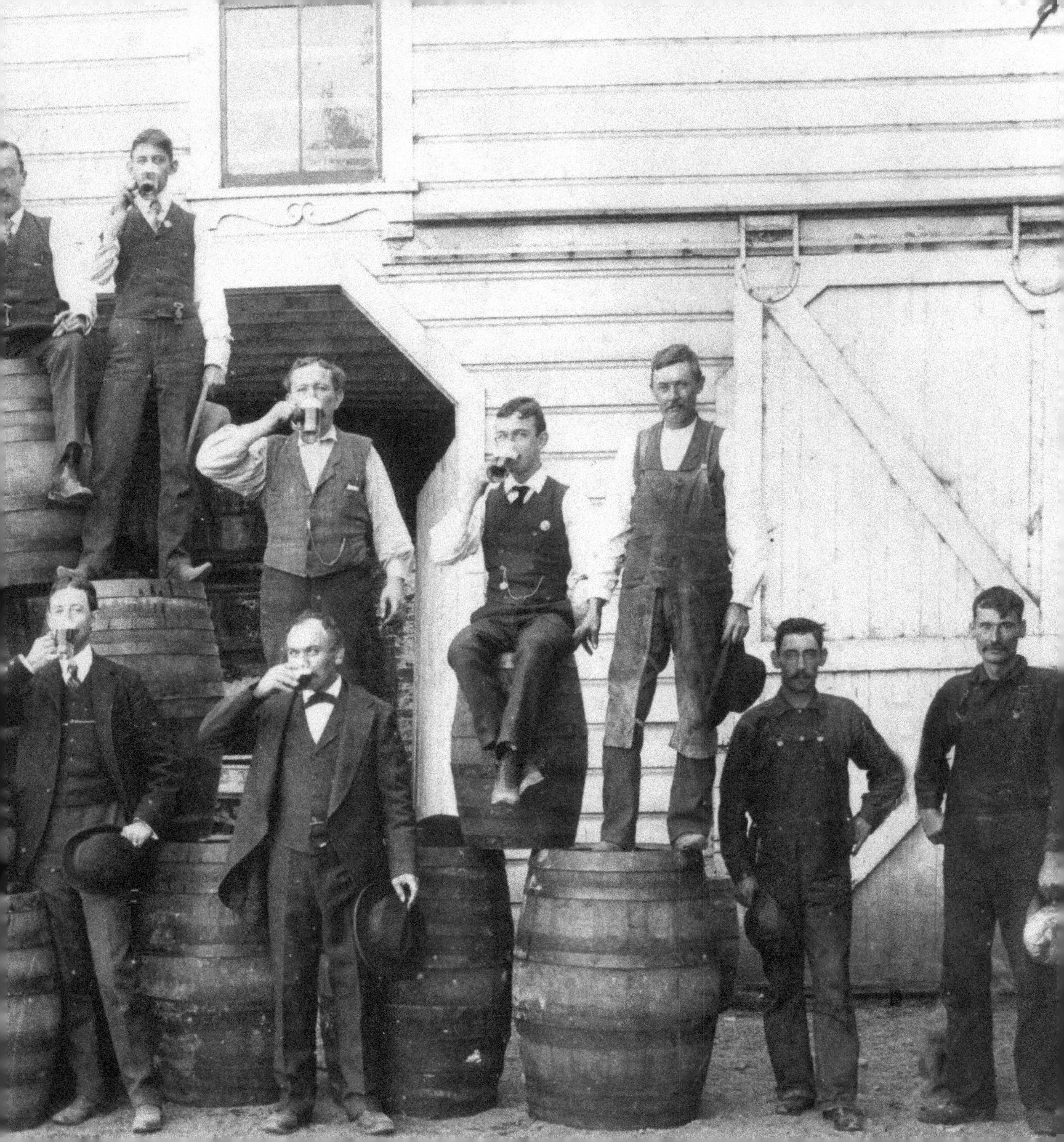

Often forced to work on the hottest days of summer, families set up their tents and picked hops, the key ingredient in the brewing of beer. After the picking, the drivers pictured below took two wagon loads of hops for weighing at the broker's scales in Santa Rosa. Hops were introduced by Amasa Bushnell and Otis Allen, who brought roots from the San Mateo area.

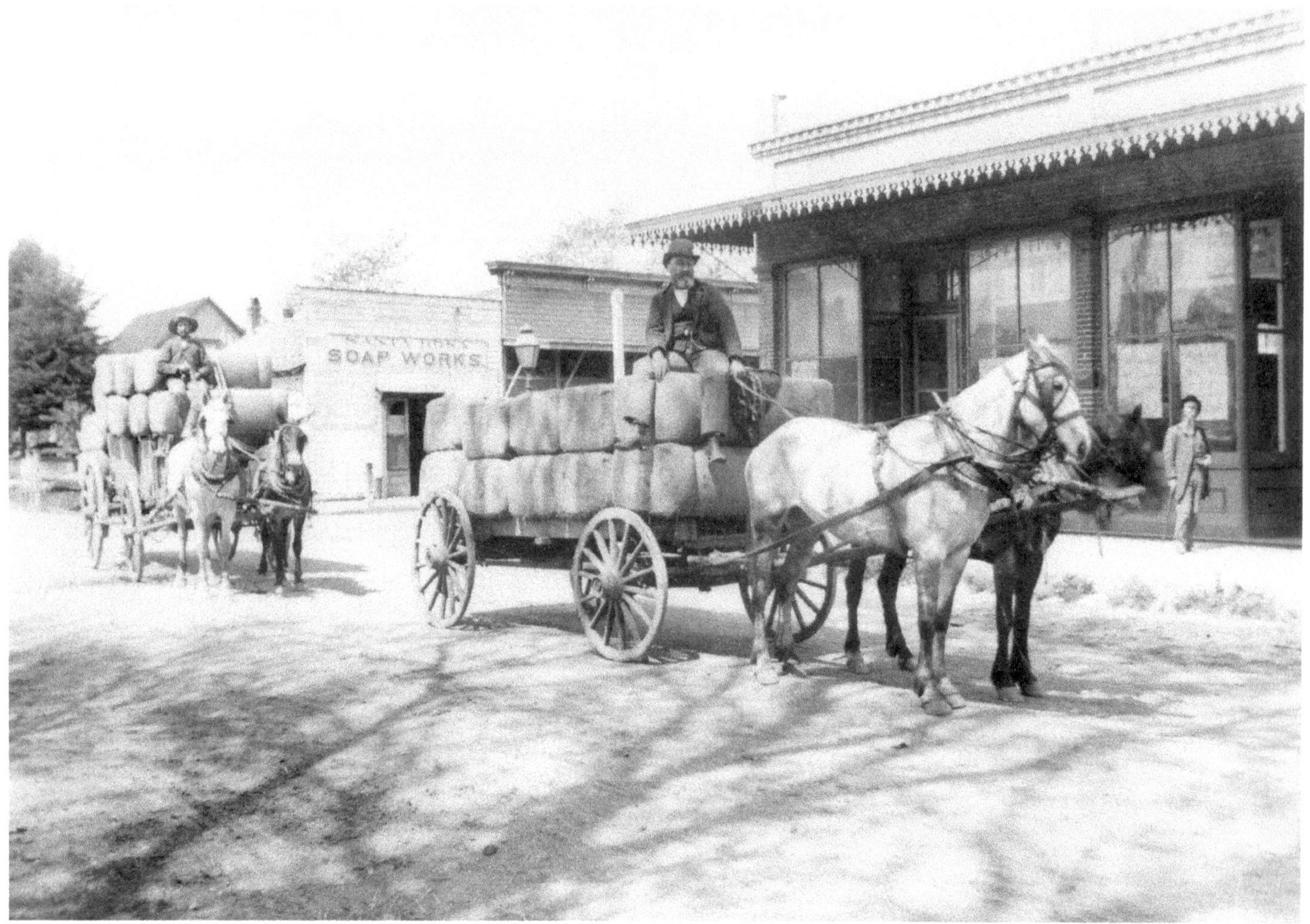

Hop picking was a financial and social endeavor. Many people not ordinarily occupied in agricultural activities participated in the harvesting of the crop for extra money to get through the cold winters. The leaves and stem can irritate the skin and cause a lot of scratches. The woman in this picture was a lady named Brand from Rincon Valley in east Santa Rosa. She was the mother of Alice Austin Hall.

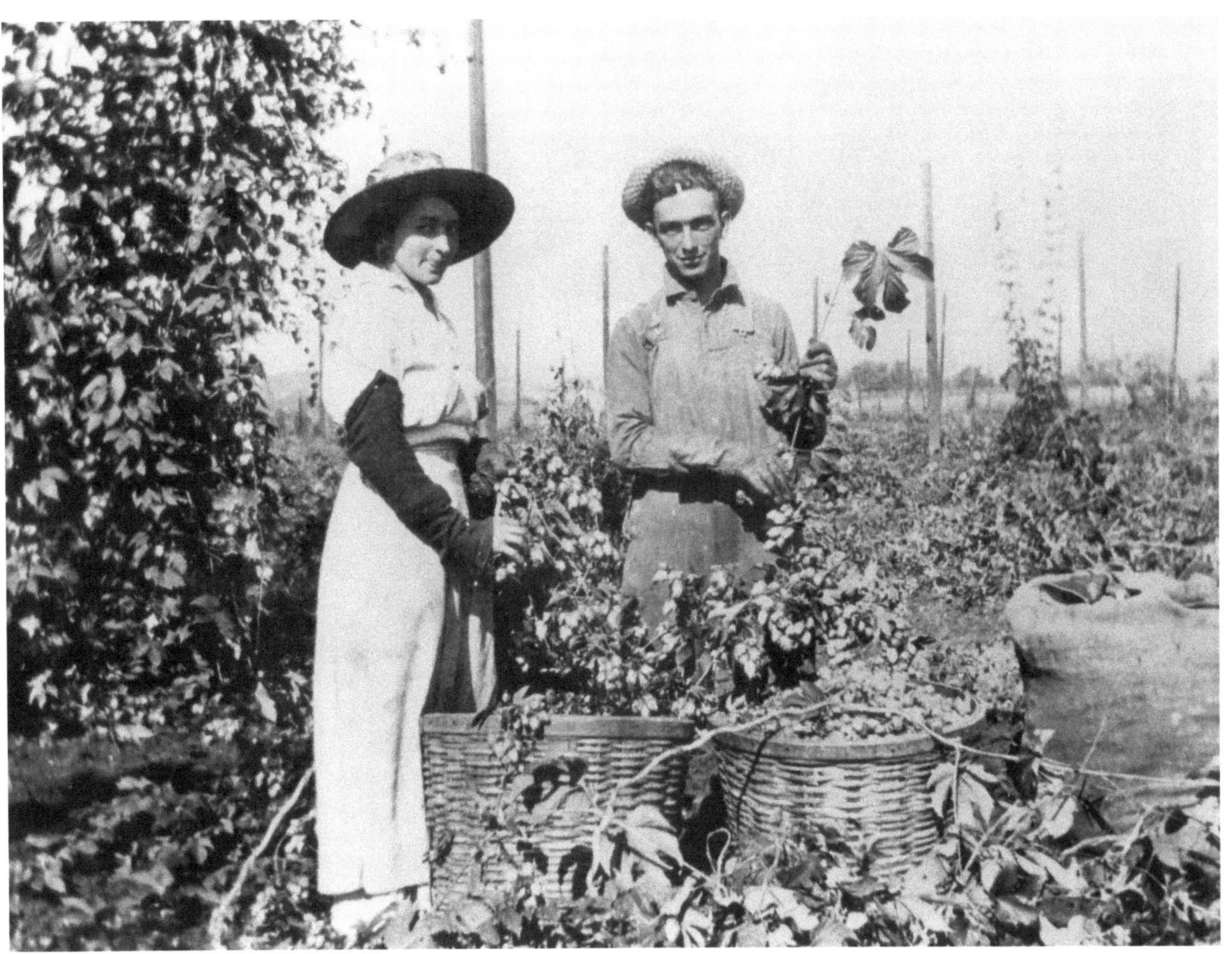

For the energetic young people who wanted to conquer a steep hill or explore Mother Nature, the back roads of Sonoma County beckoned. Healdsburg riders, who organized as the Healdsburg Wheelmen in 1895, gathered on West Street for a long-distance ride to remote Skaggs Springs in the 1890s. Up to 1,000 fans showed up to watch bicycle races in that era. Santa Rosa and Petaluma also had active riding groups.

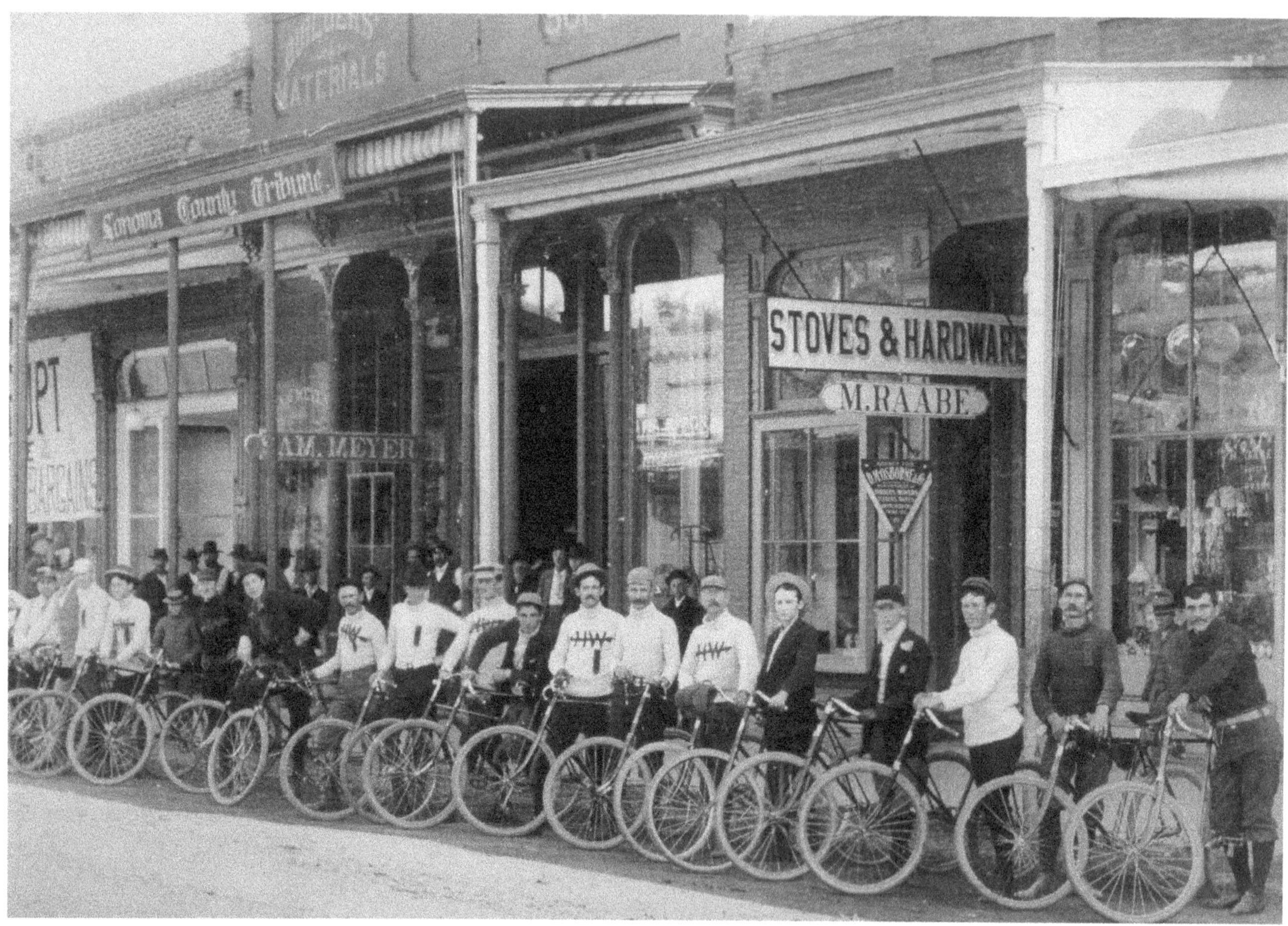

The view north on Main Street in Petaluma around 1900 showed the Ark, the McNear Building, and the Cosmopolitan Hotel. The McNear Building proved useful to the family when the McNear feed store burned down in 1902. The business was moved from North Main Street to the site farther south at Main near B Street. The Cosmopolitan Hotel, with forty rooms for workingmen, charged thirty-five to seventy-five cents a night for rooms early in the twentieth century.

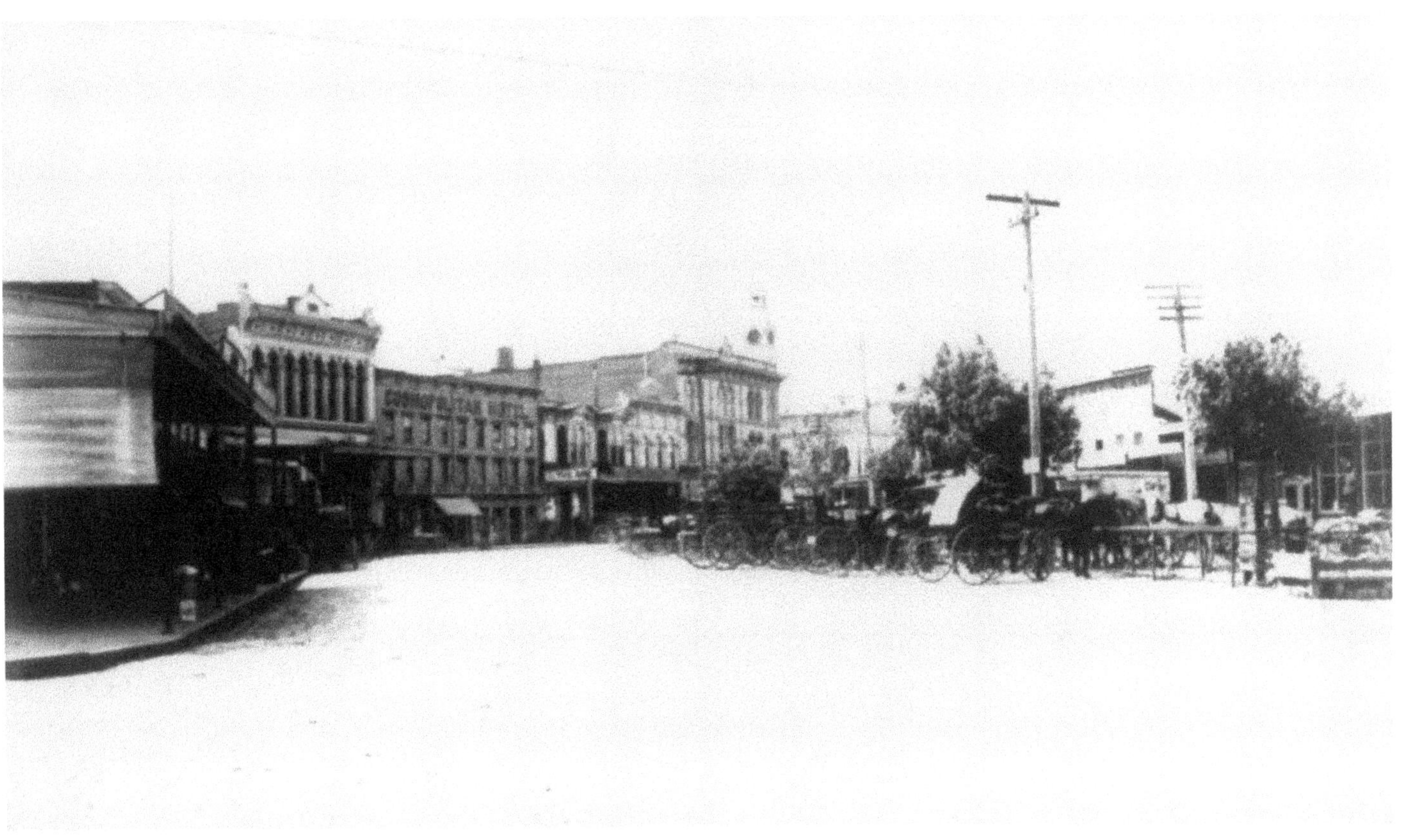

The Prescott Mansion was one of Cloverdale's most impressive structures, shown here around 1900. Mr. Prescott, owner of the Union Ironworks in San Francisco, built the house at Main and 4th streets from the profits he made building the battleship *Oregon*. The house was destroyed in a fire on October 20, 1953.

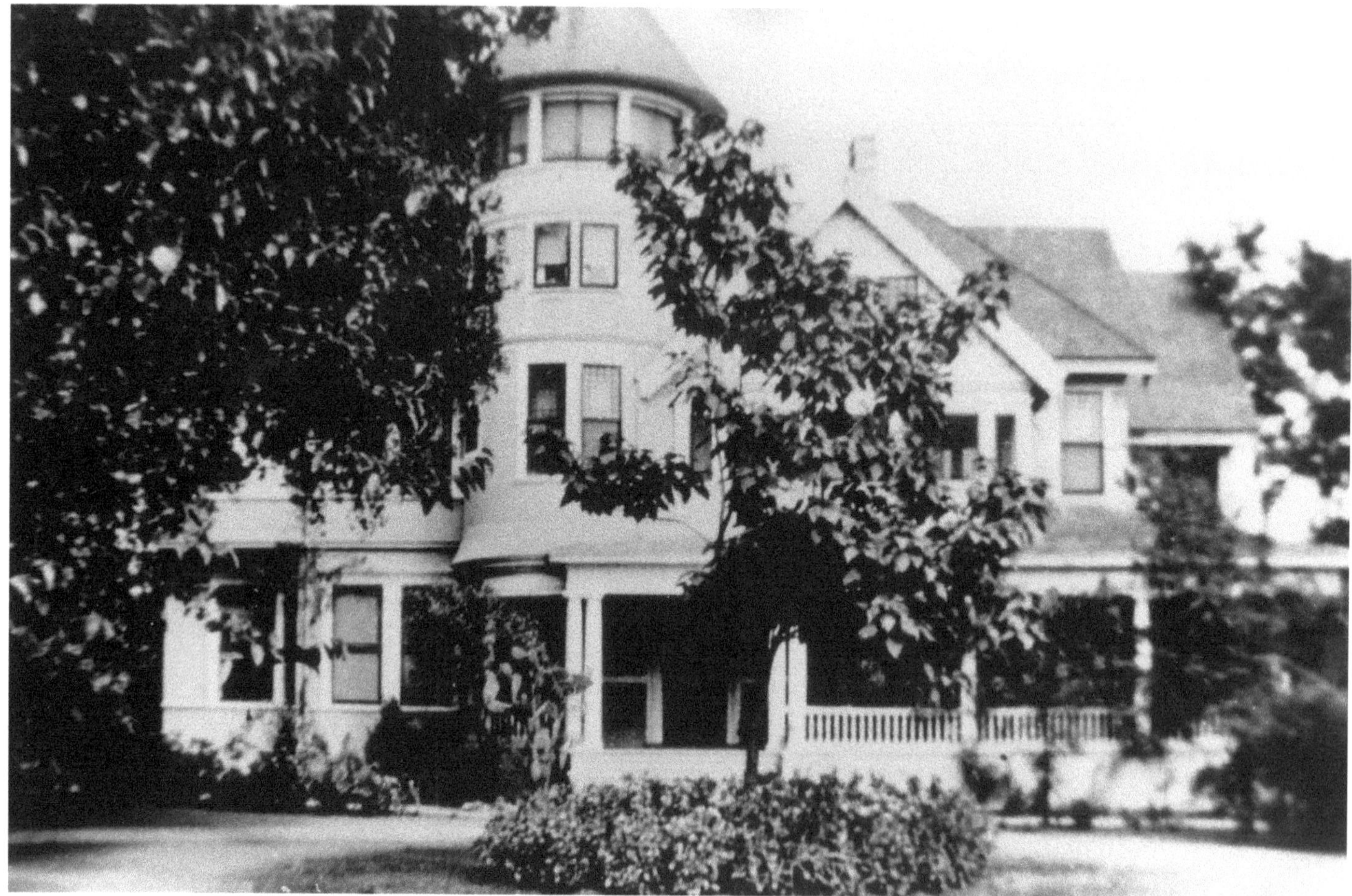

The fall harvest was a time for hard work and the rewards that came with a successful crop. Wagon loads of grapes were moved through the Geyser Peak Vineyard in Geyserville in 1900. The Dry Creek Valley winery was established in 1880.

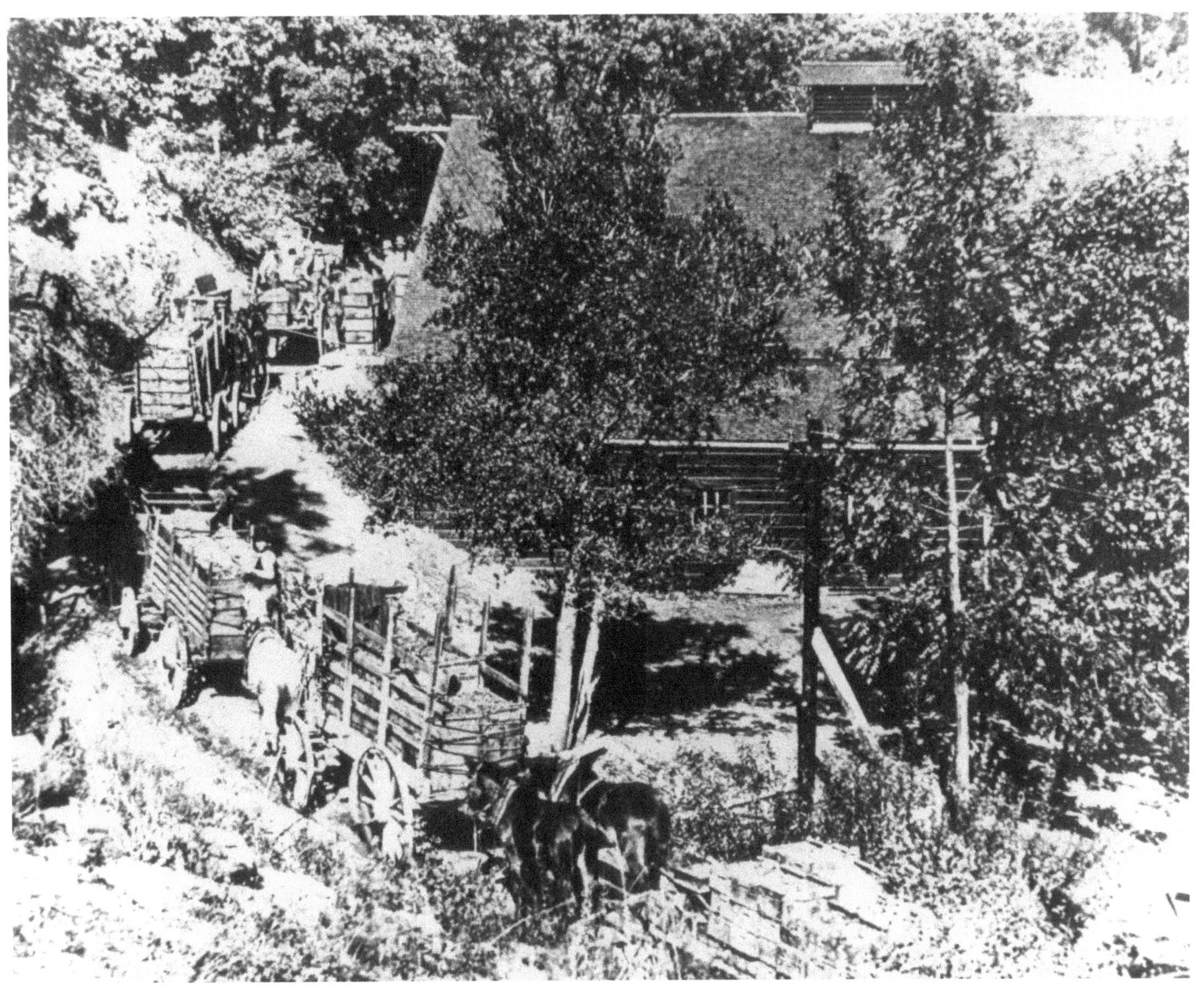

As a new century arrived, trains played a major role in moving people and goods, including the lumber of the west county. On Christmas Day 1901, Engine NPC-21 hauled its cargo southbound. William Roix was the young man looking up at the engineer. By 1902, the town had changed names and the main depot sign read Occidental with a small Howards sign above it.

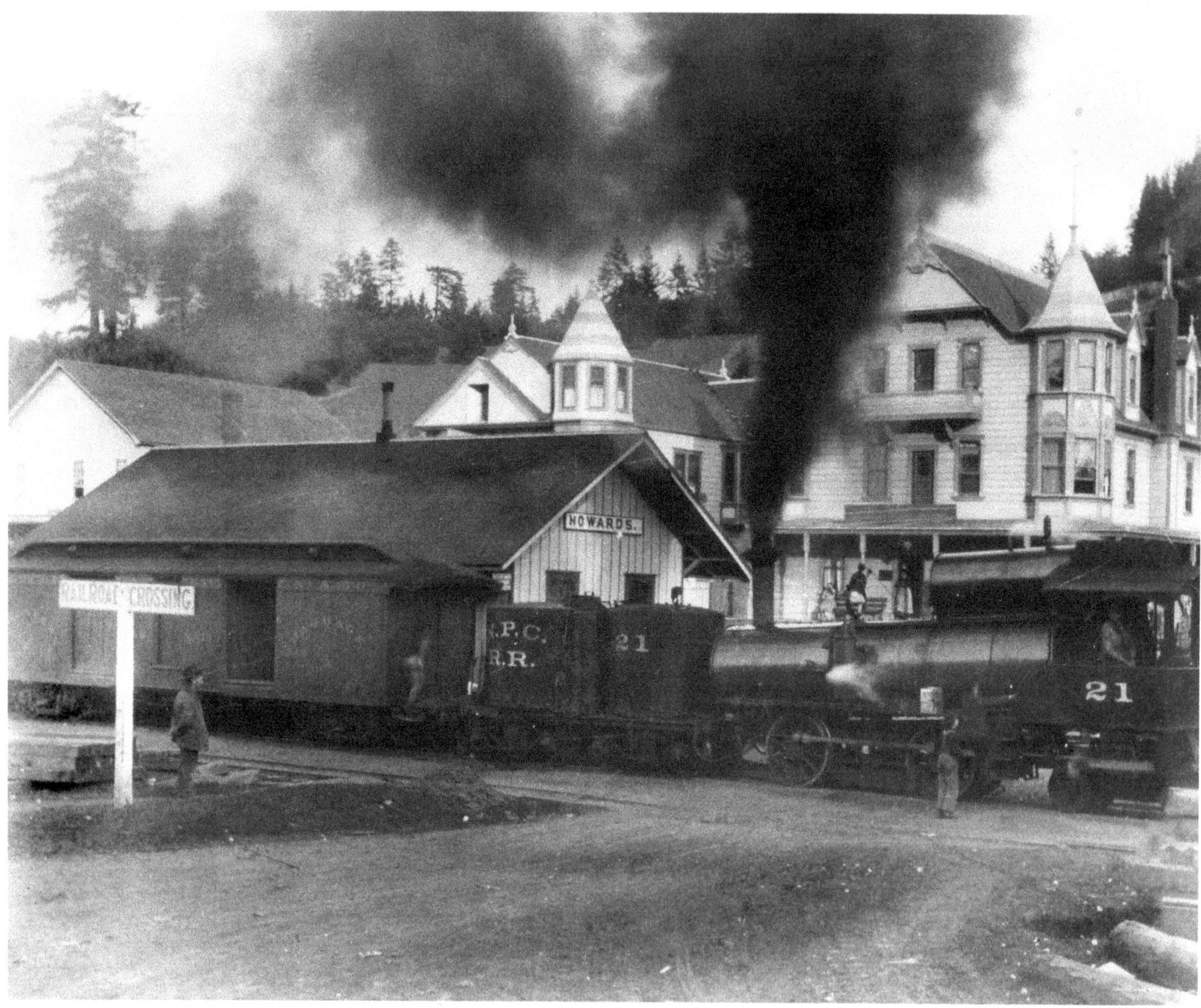

As cities grew, the demand for government services expanded. Santa Rosa made its first efforts to create a library in 1859, but setting up a system took time. The Carnegie Foundation provided funds to build a Romanesque-style library that opened in 1904, with a large crowd attending the dedication. When the building suffered extensive damage in the 1906 earthquake, Carnegie provided funds for repairs. The beloved old building was demolished in the 1960s. Carnegie libraries were also located in Petaluma, Healdsburg, and Sebastopol.

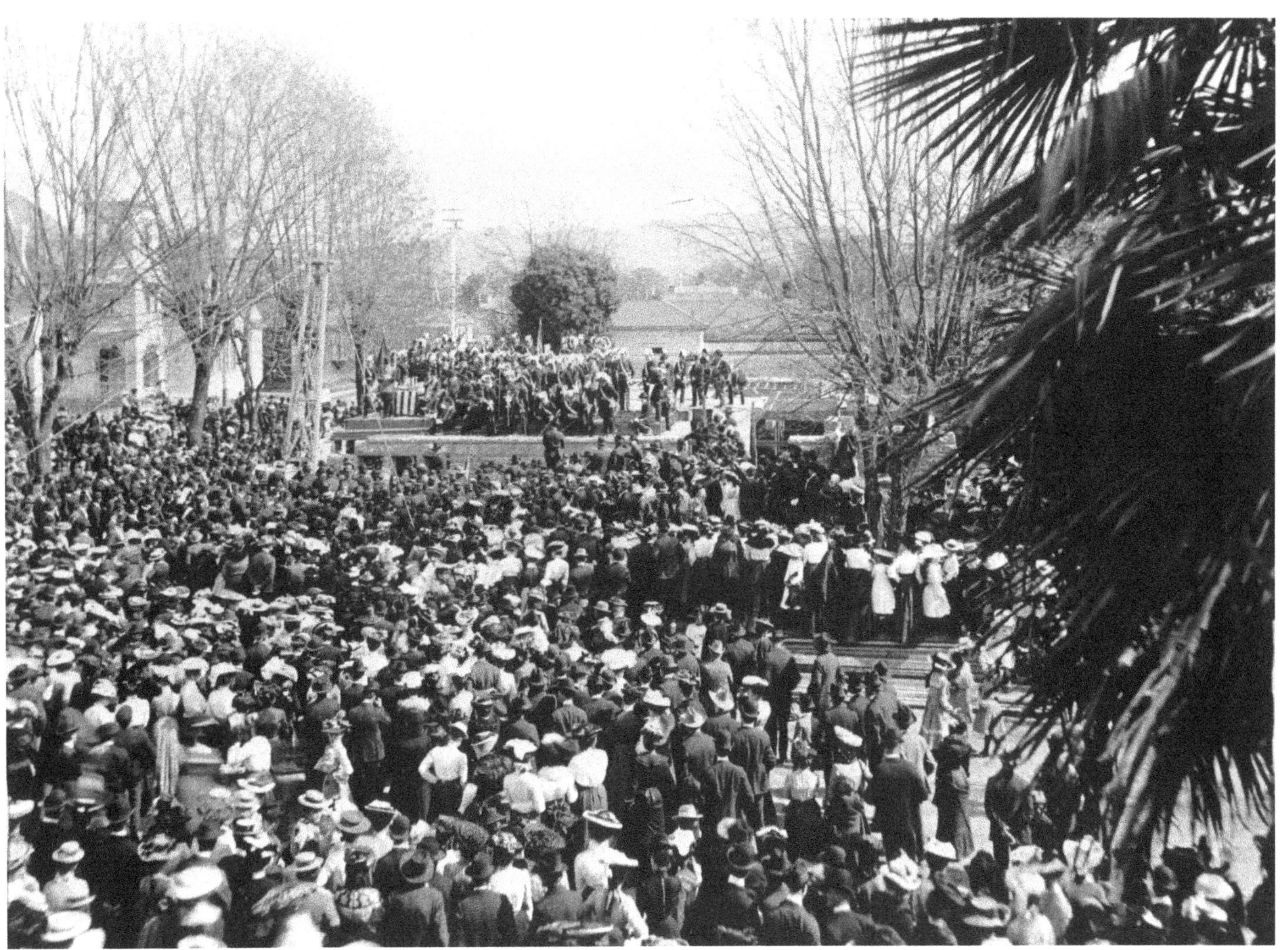

A look down 4th Street in Santa Rosa the year before the 1906 earthquake showed a slow-moving horse providing the power for a streetcar. Major buildings included the Imperial Order of Red Men's Hall and the Atheneum Building. The 2,000-seat Atheneum Theater, financed by Isaac DeTurk and other leading businessmen, was built in 1884 to provide a venue for prominent performers. It was destroyed in the 1906 earthquake.

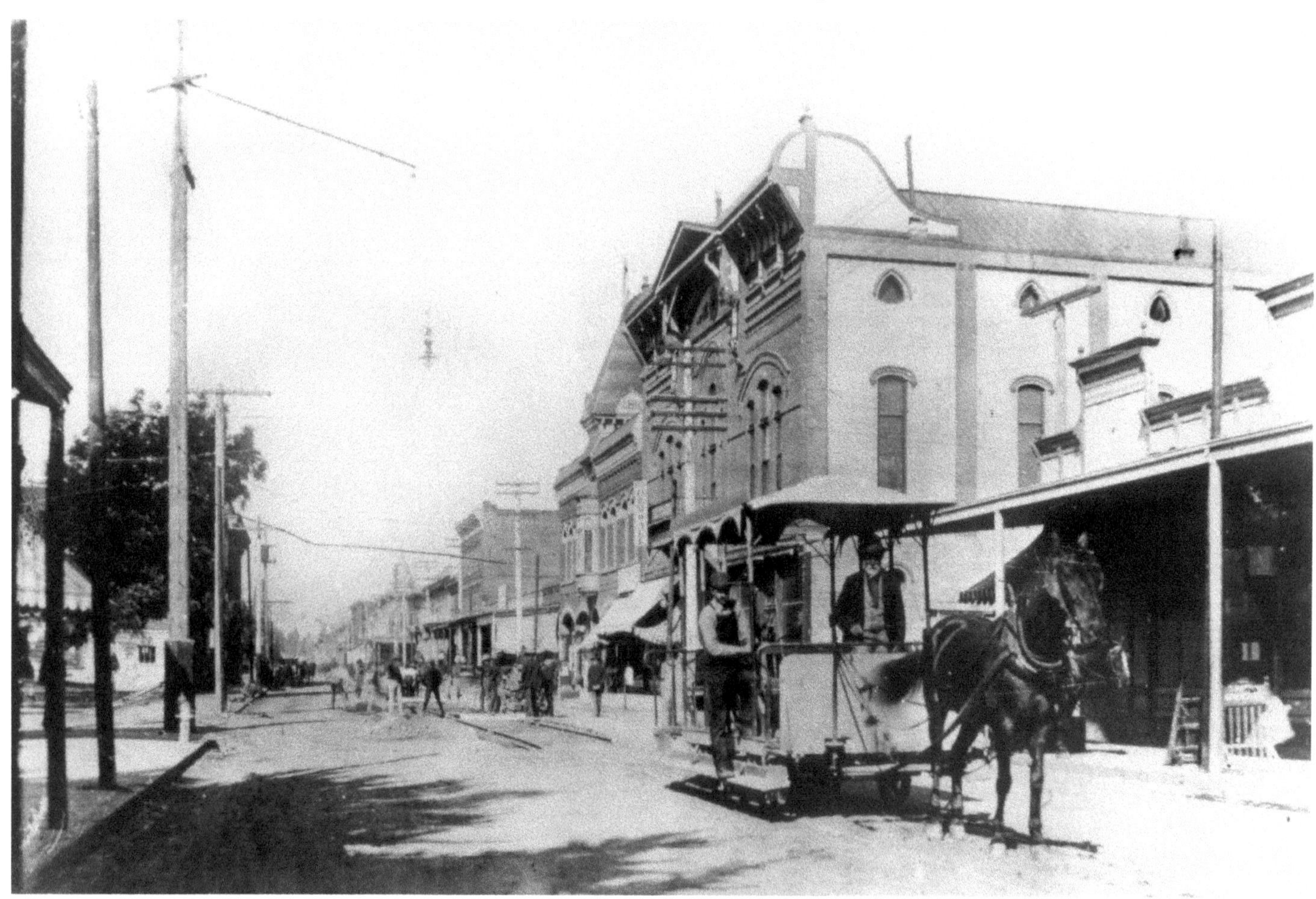

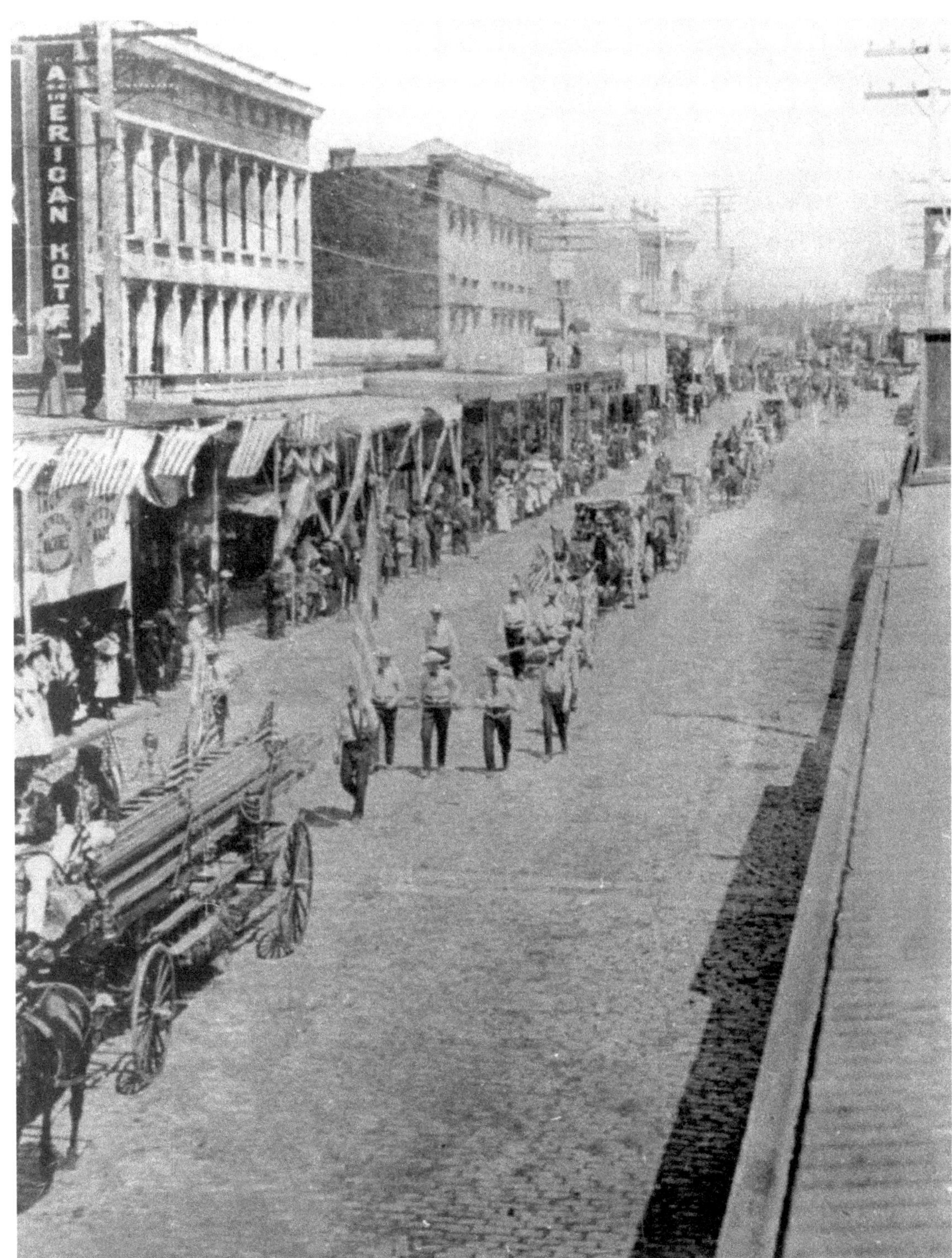


Members of the Young America Hose Company marched behind their pumper in a much-anticipated appearance in the Fourth of July parade in Petaluma in 1905. From the 1850s onward, volunteer firemen gathered to fight fires, compete in holiday games with other community groups, march in parades, and enjoy the camaraderie of being with their own special bunch of men.

April 18, 1906, was a day of doom in Sonoma County. The giant earthquake that severely damaged San Francisco left Santa Rosa and other parts of Sonoma County "a total wreck." Brick structures were generally the first to go, leaving flattened buildings downtown on Hinton Avenue between 3rd and 4th streets.

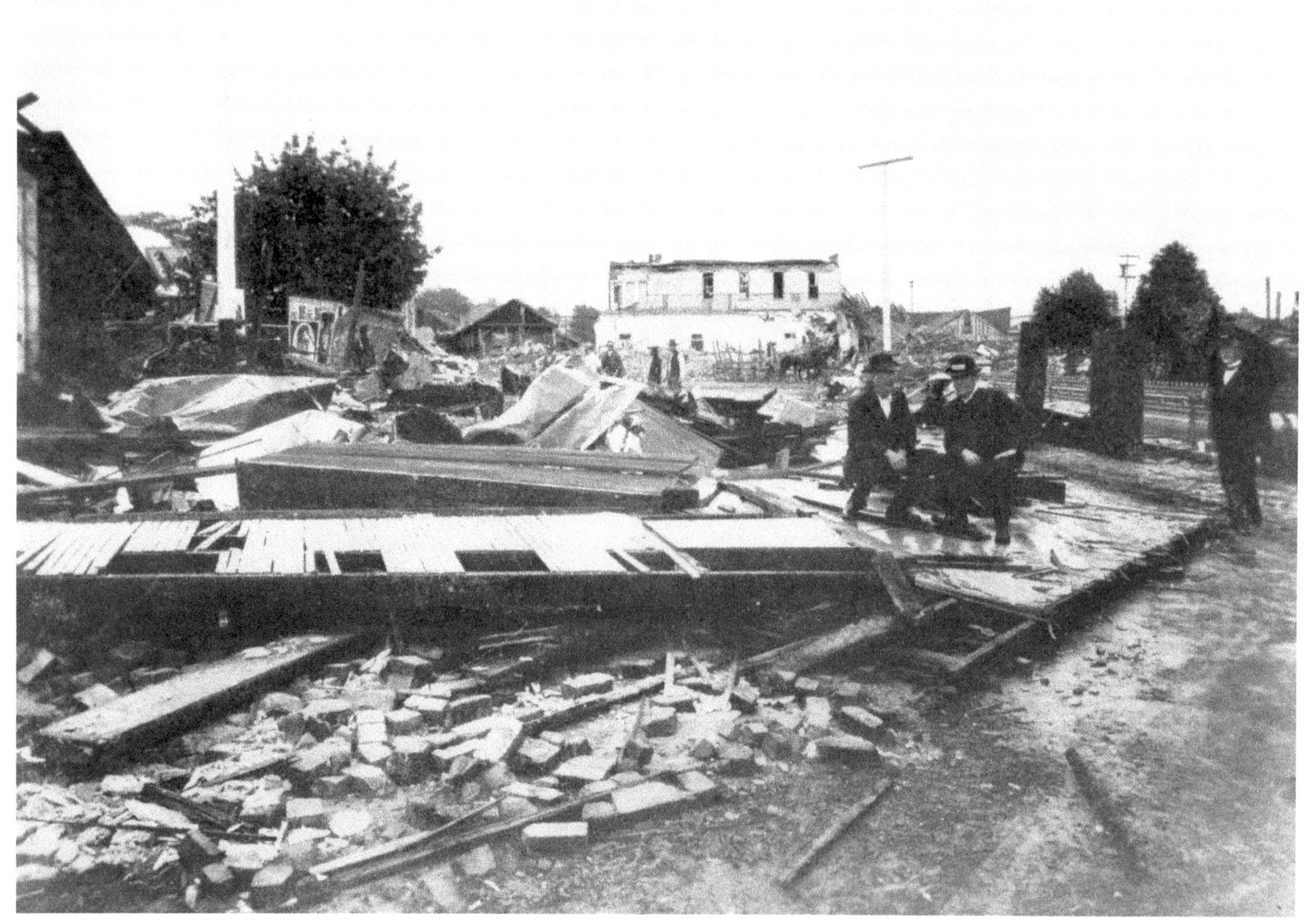

An injured survivor, his arm in a cast, looked blankly from what had been the Occidental Hotel at 5th and B streets in Santa Rosa. The Saint Rose and the Grand Hotel were also destroyed. The Carnegie Library, the county courthouse, the Press Democrat building, and many other structures suffered heavy damage.

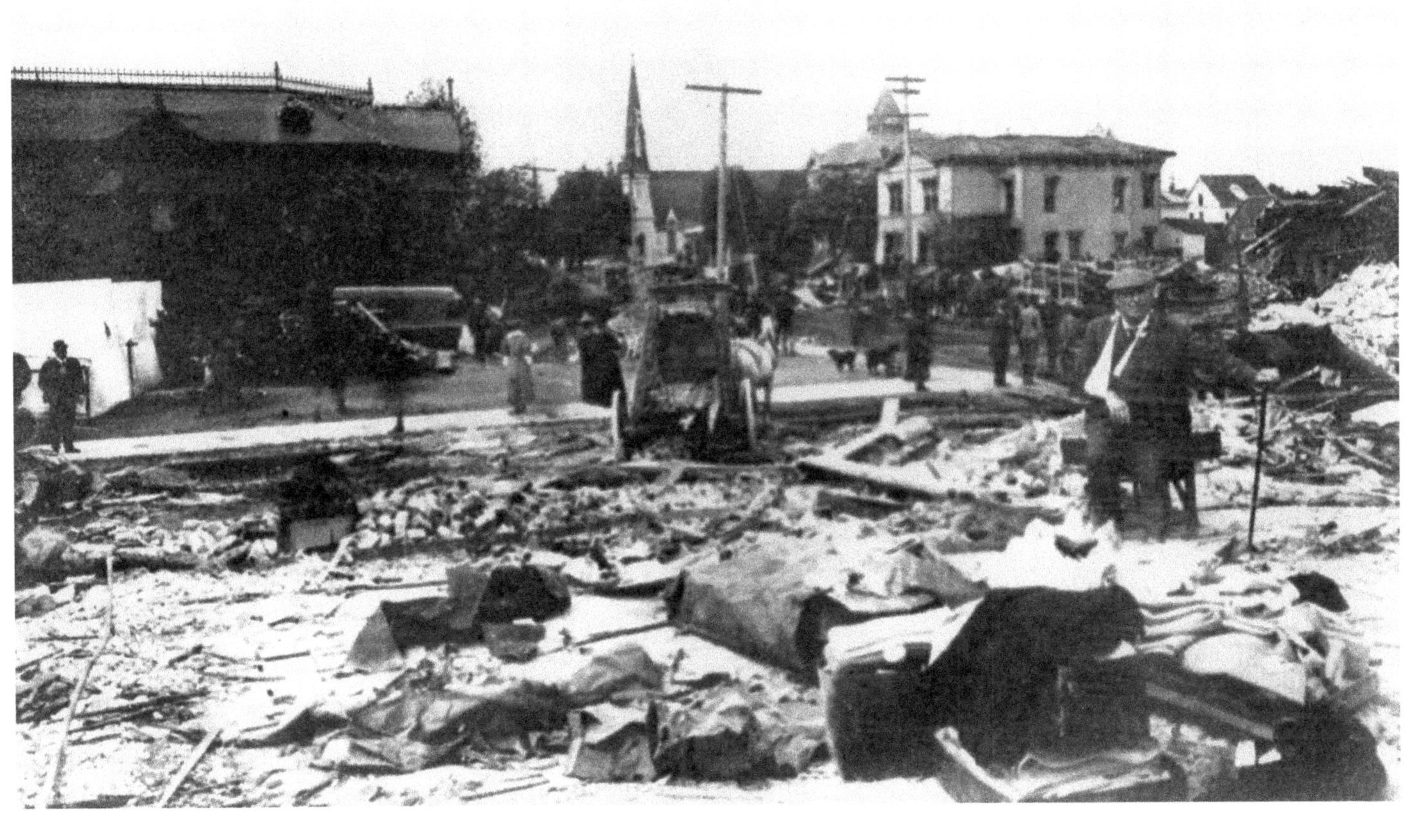

There weren't many unbroken bottles left at Sam's Rendezvous Tavern at Main and Washington streets in Petaluma after the 1906 quake. Sam's rebuilt, but the building came down in 1968 as part of a road-widening and bridge project. The quake did relatively little damage to Petaluma.

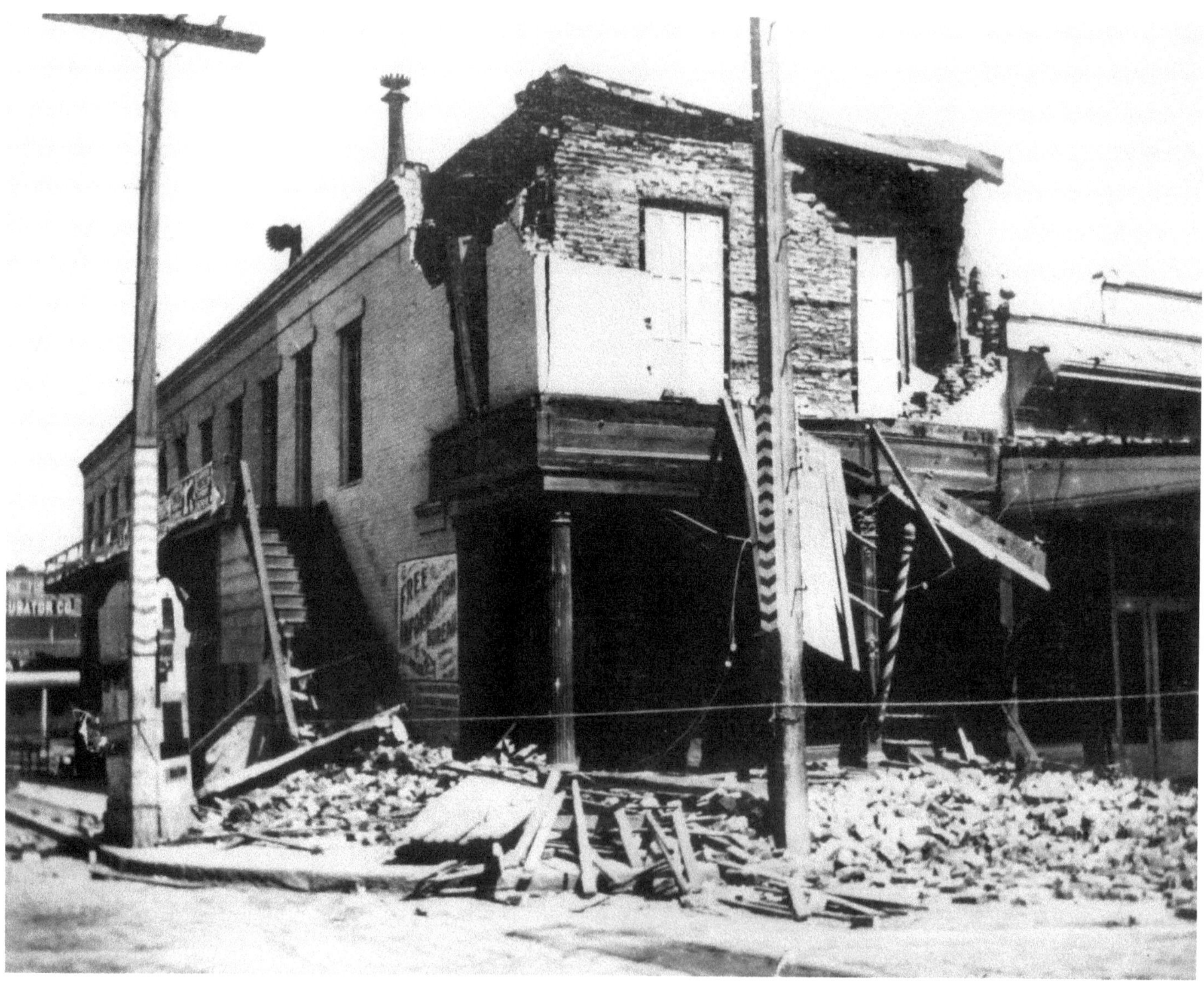

Although accurate figures were hard to come by, the death toll of the 1906 earthquake reached more than one hundred in Santa Rosa, a city of less than 7,000 people. This view from 3rd and B streets shows the tilted courthouse dome in the background.

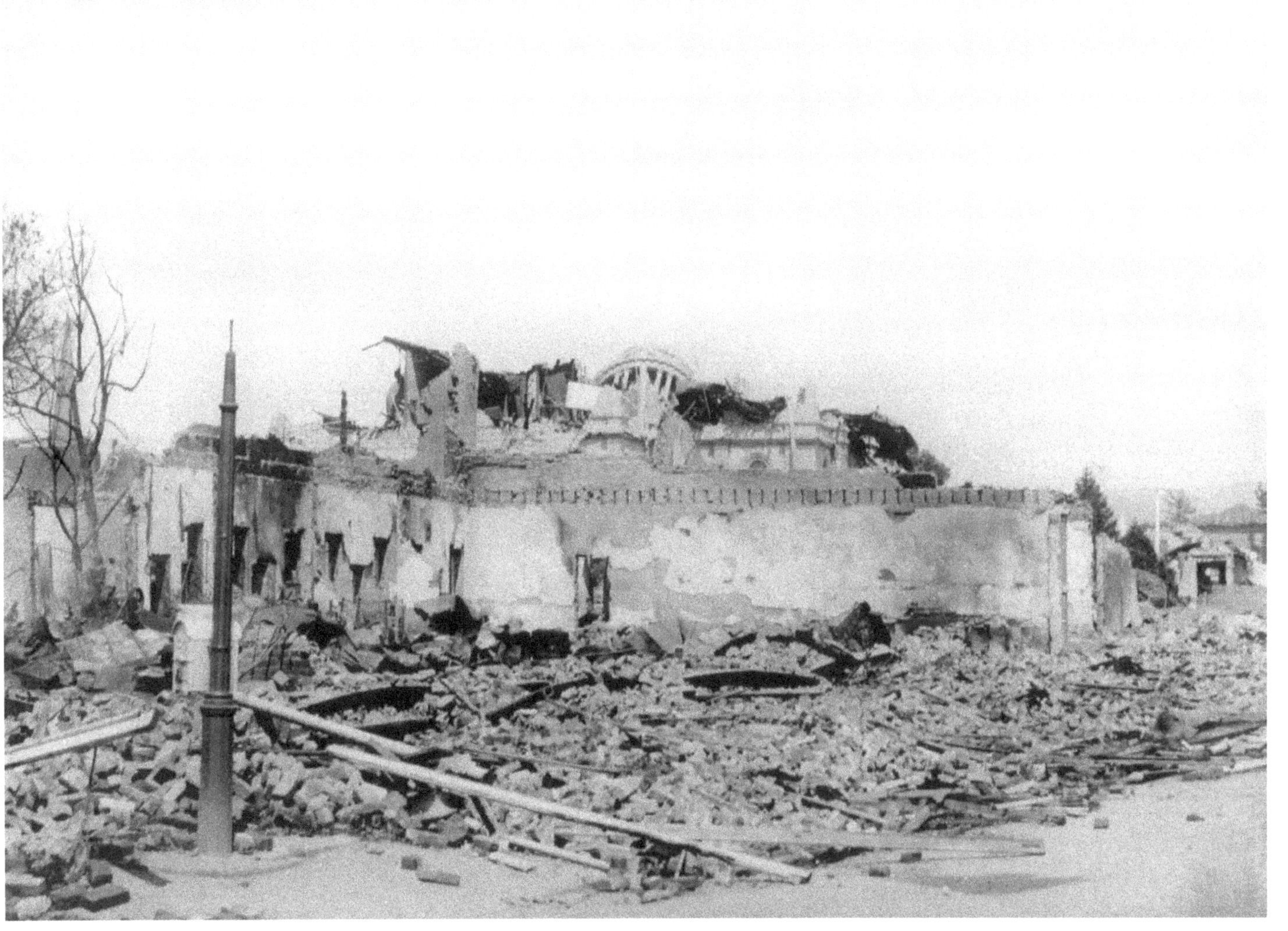

The Methodist Church (left background) at 5th and D streets survived the giant tremor, although many downtown buildings turned into a pile of bricks.

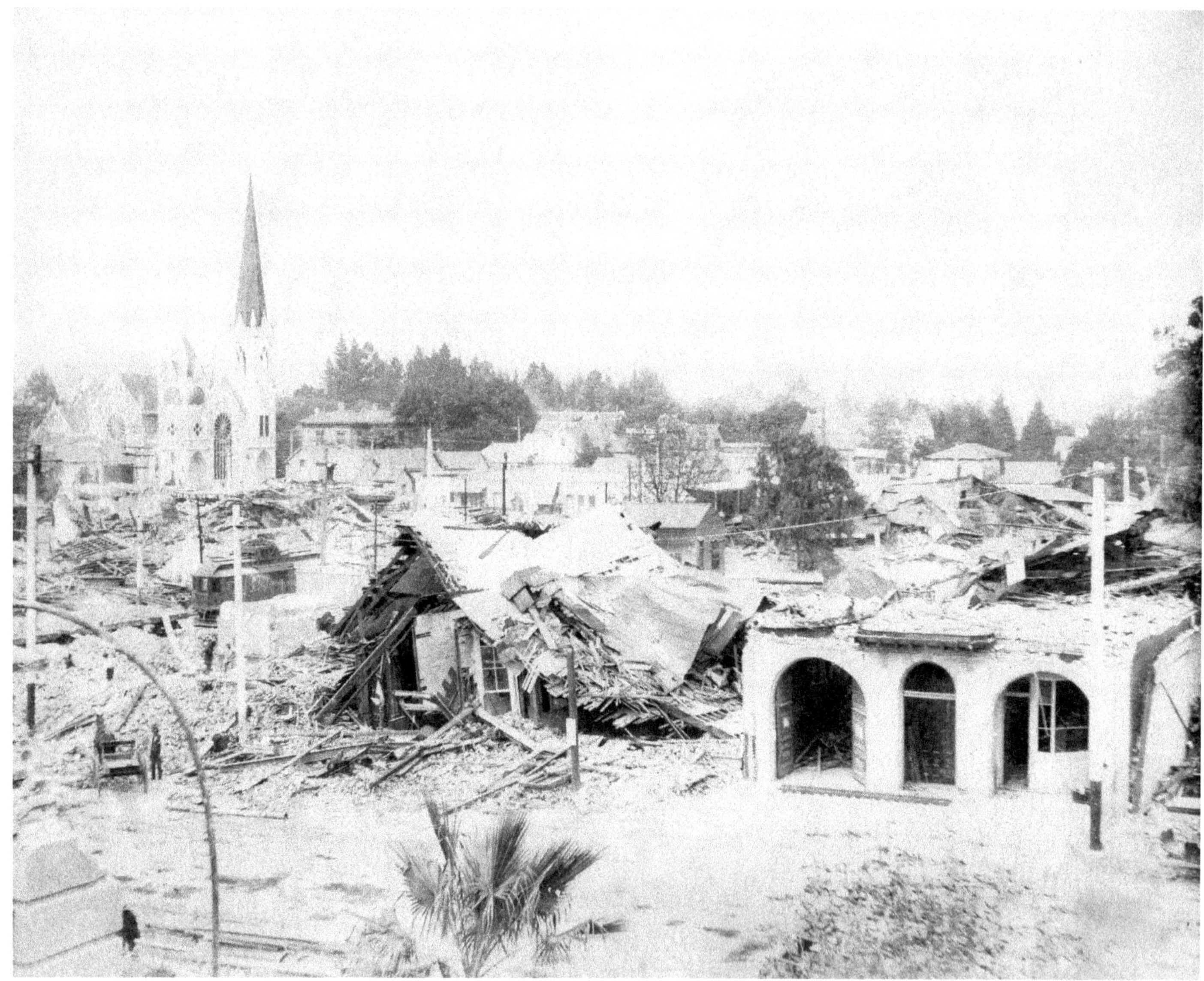

A view south on Main Street from north of Washington Street in Petaluma shows minimal earthquake damage. Buildings still intact included the Sonoma County Bank, C. R. Winfield Real Estate, and Scott Hardware. The expressmen on the left were hired by Andy McPhail of Ayers and McPhail Express and Transfer.

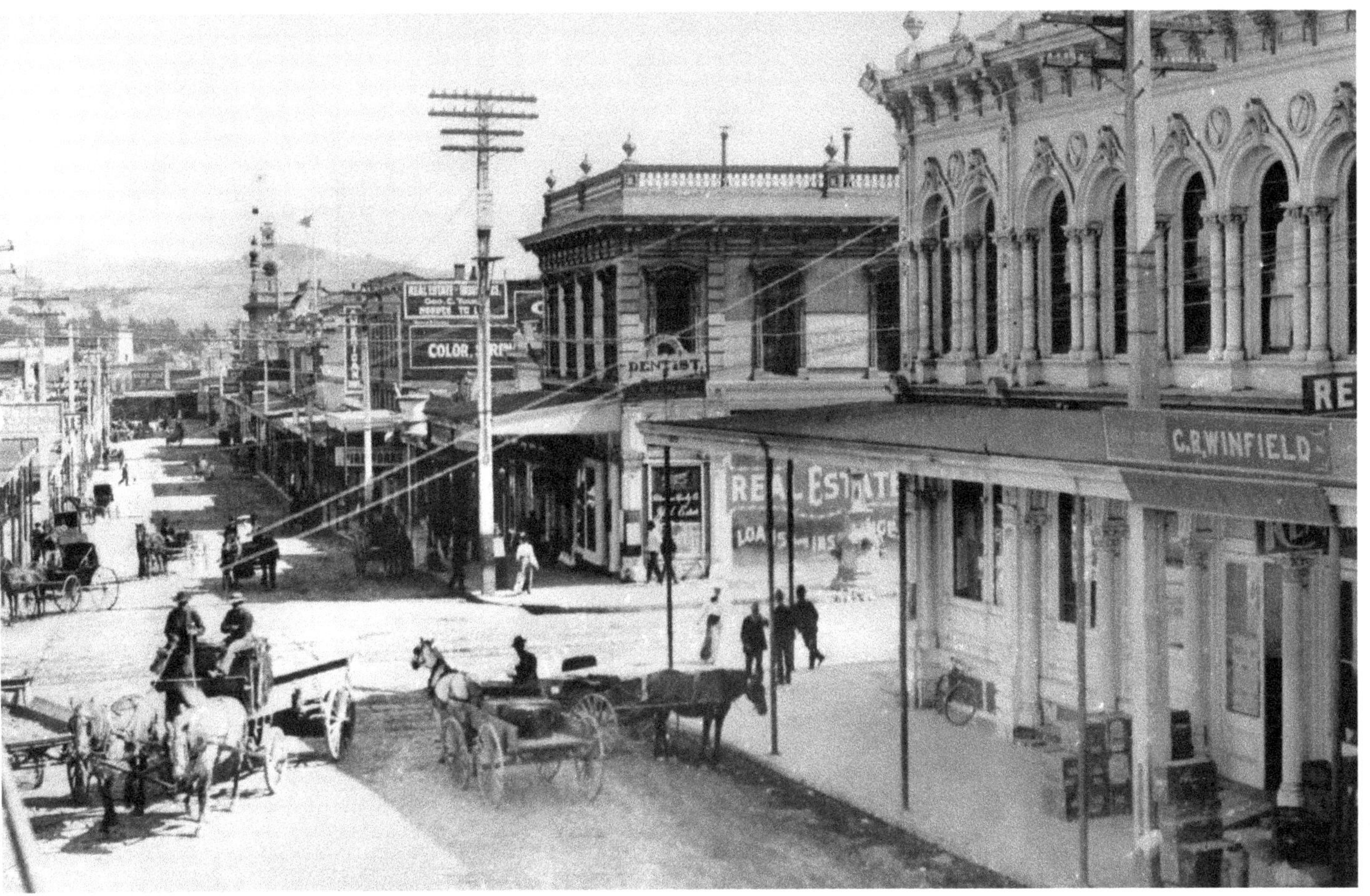

It is believed, though not certain, this small building covered with ads was used as a temporary police station and city tax collector's office in Santa Rosa after the great quake. For a time, city and county officials were forced to set up "street offices" to do business.

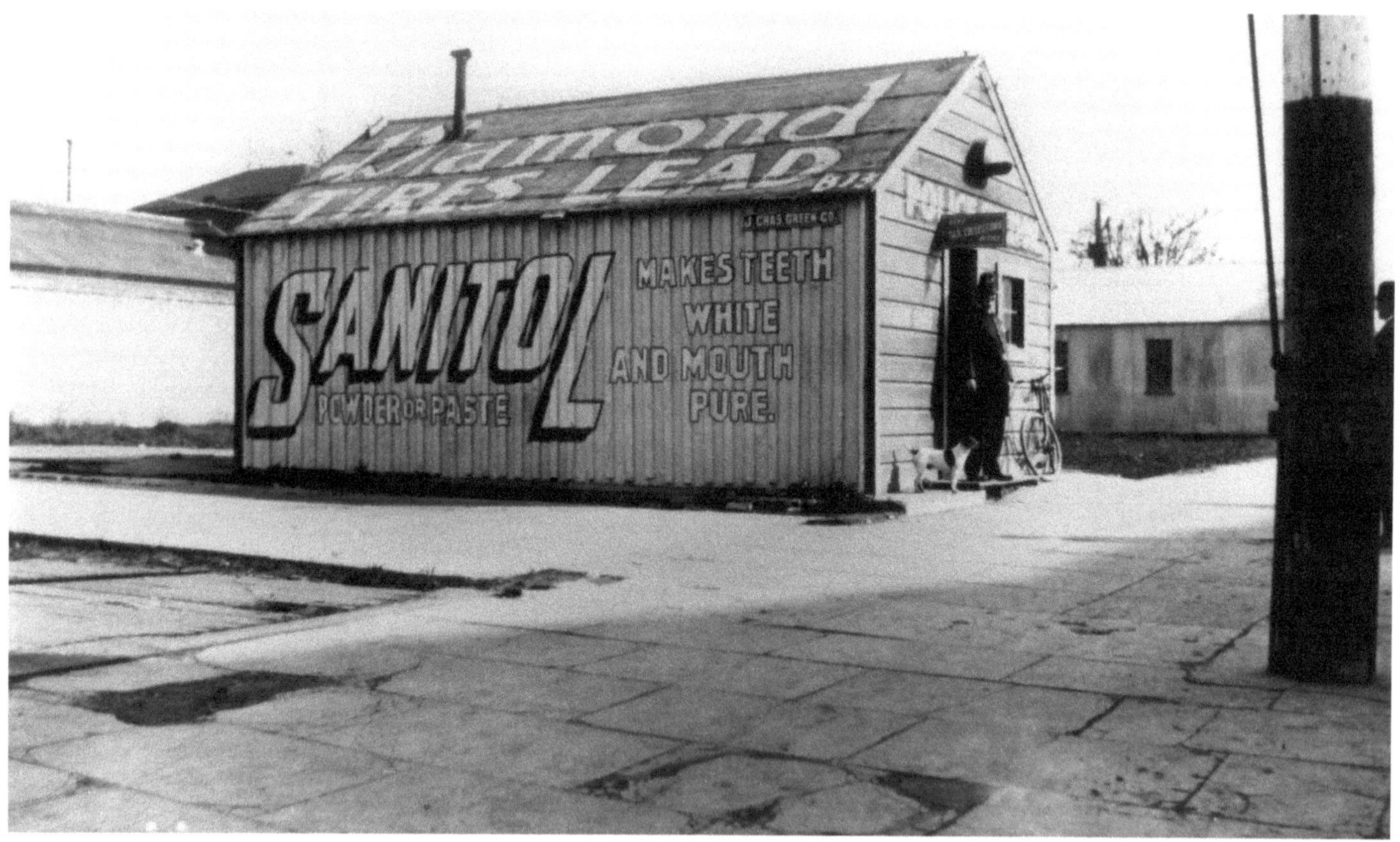

The policeman in this photo was George W. Matthews of the Santa Rosa force, who was watching several men taking up squatter's rights on a ladder. The picture probably shows the opposite side of the small police building pictured on the previous page.

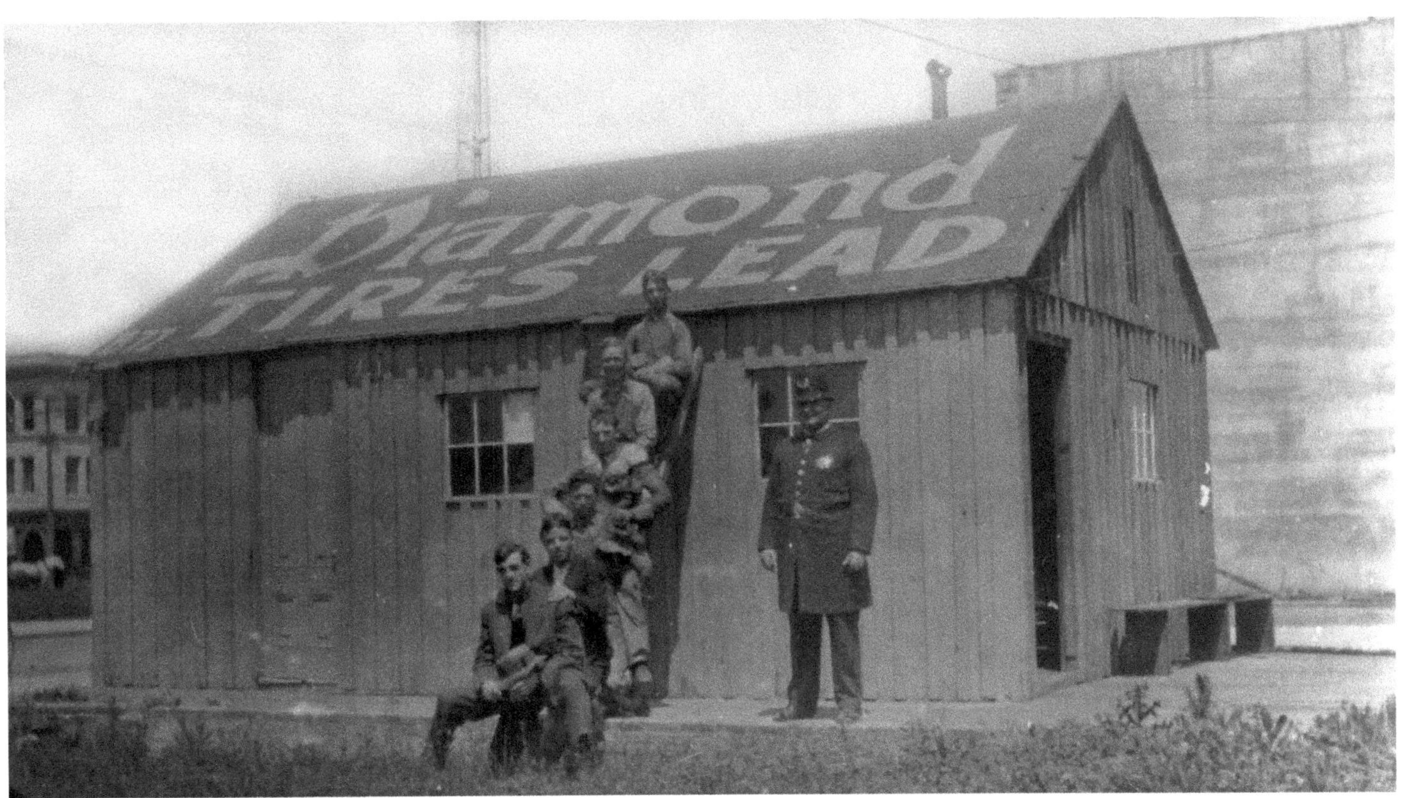

When the earthquake rattled the merchandise, owners of the White House Department store in Santa Rosa quickly adapted, selling dry goods, fancy goods, cloaks and suits from a quickly built temporary structure. By avoiding any mention of bad news, community leaders were able to keep people focused on rebuilding their battered city after 1906.

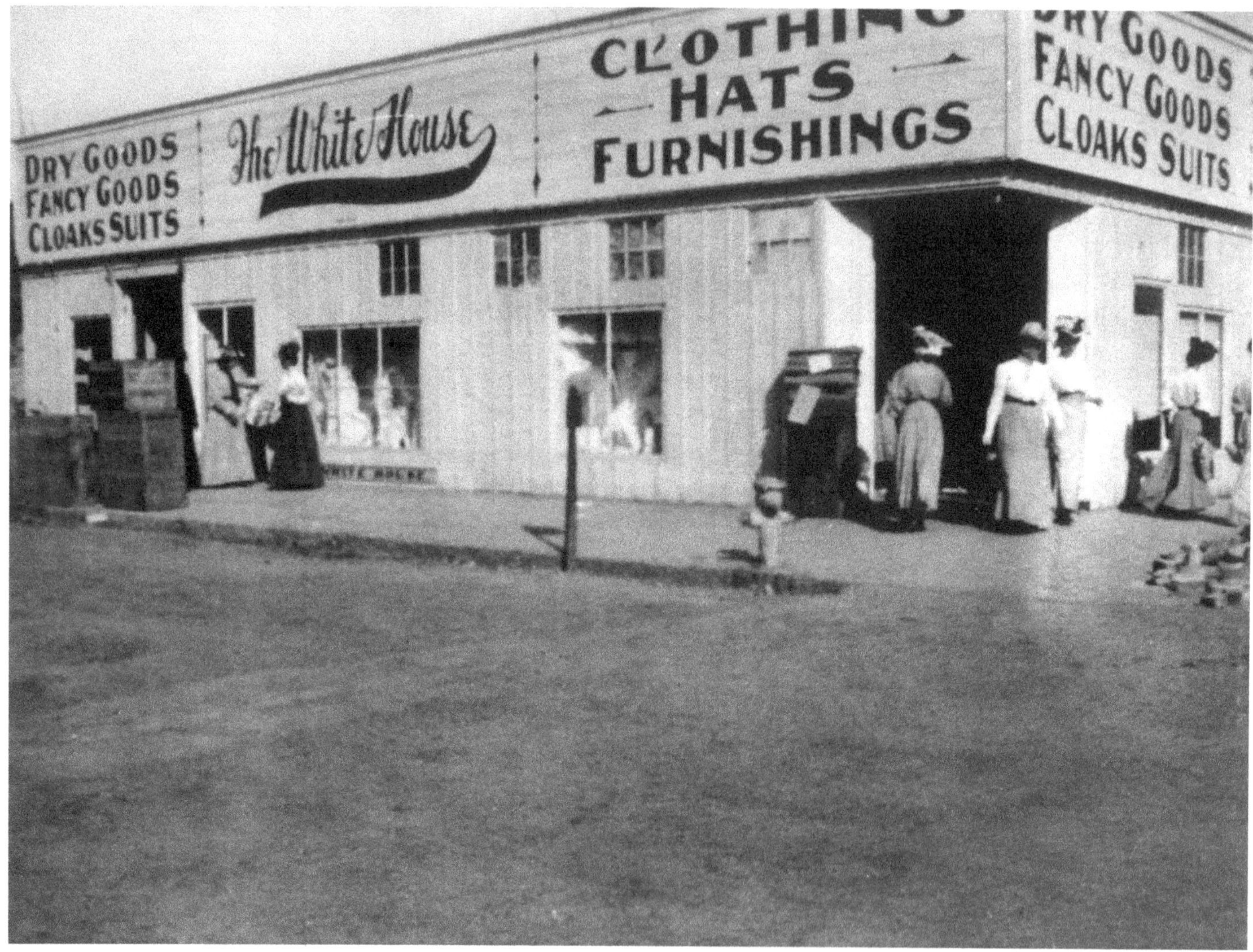

# Earthquake Recovery in a 'Growing' Economy

## (1907–1919)

Part of the legacy of the north coast of California is the reality of living with deadly shifts of terrain—major earthquakes. The great earthquake and fire of April 18, 1906, had shaken not only San Francisco but much of Sonoma County as well. Many rural areas suffered major damage but the heaviest hit was Santa Rosa, where vulnerable brick buildings crumbled almost instantly. The county courthouse, the city library, the Press Democrat newspaper building, and many other structures crumbled. More than one hundred people were killed, but communities quickly rallied to defy the forces of nature and rebuild.

Meanwhile, the area showed its growing interest in liquid refreshment. Hungarian Agostin Haraszthy brought wine grapes to the Sonoma Valley in the 1850s. Fed by the demand of immigrants such as the Italians who came in large numbers, winemakers found the area a fertile place to develop their tasty product. Names like Sebastiani, Simi, and Korbel became well-known. The "Japanese Wine Baron" Kanaye Nagasawa grew his grapes on the slopes of Santa Rosa's famed Fountaingrove estate. Grace Brothers Brewing Company established its beer empire by the late 1890s and survived well through the first half of the twentieth century. In the following decade, prohibition of alcoholic-beverage manufacturing would have a profound effect this region.

Numerous communities took formal action to celebrate their agricultural heritage. Santa Rosa inaugurated its Rose Festival in 1894 and held agricultural fairs before World War I. Sebastopol held its first Gravenstein Apple Show in 1910.

The pace of transportation picked up with the introduction of automobiles and airplanes. Dr. James Jesse bought what is believed to be Santa Rosa's first automobile around the turn of the century. An adventurous young bicycle shop owner named Fred Wiseman wrote himself into the history books by making the first airmail flight, a two-day, fifteen-mile trip between Petaluma and Santa Rosa in February 1911.

Among the most prominent men of the early twentieth century was botanist Luther Burbank, who opened his Santa Rosa home to Thomas Edison, Harvey Firestone, and Henry Ford during the Panama-Pacific Exposition of 1915. World-renowned author Jack London lived on a splendid rural estate in Glen Ellen he called the Beauty Ranch.

World War I intruded as troops marched off to fight the "War to End All Wars." Returning soldiers brought back the deadly Spanish flu which took a heavy toll in Sonoma County and caused a rush to buy protective gauze masks.

The 1906 tremor did great damage to many of the old Victorian-style homes in Santa Rosa, but some of the distinguished buildings survived, such as these homes around Benton and Slater streets.

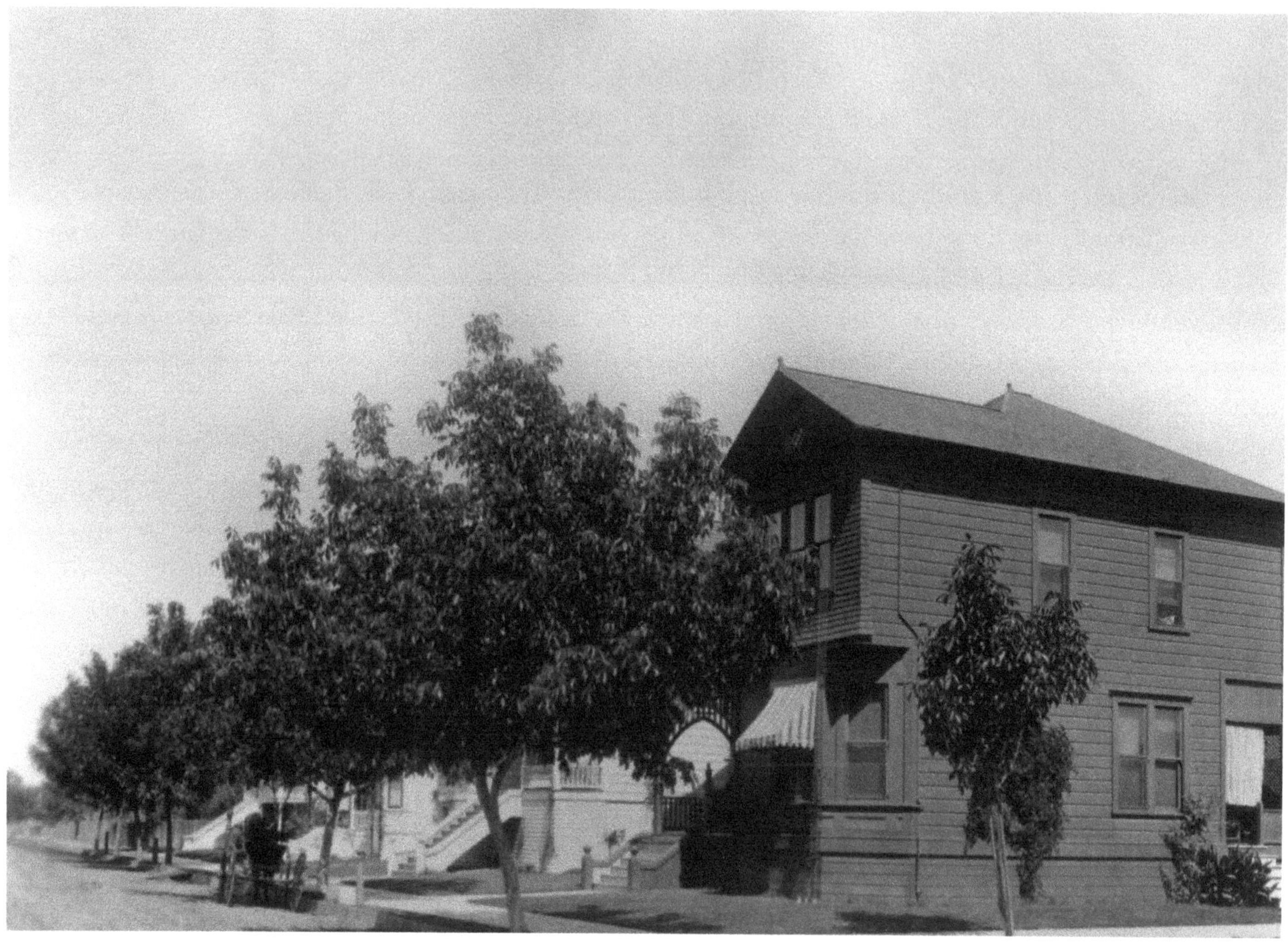

A group of students and adults used the pump house and well at Hill School near Windsor as the backdrop for a group photo around 1903. The first Hill School, located on Chalk Hill Road east of Windsor, was built in 1892. A fire destroyed it, but it was later rebuilt and stayed in operation until 1937.

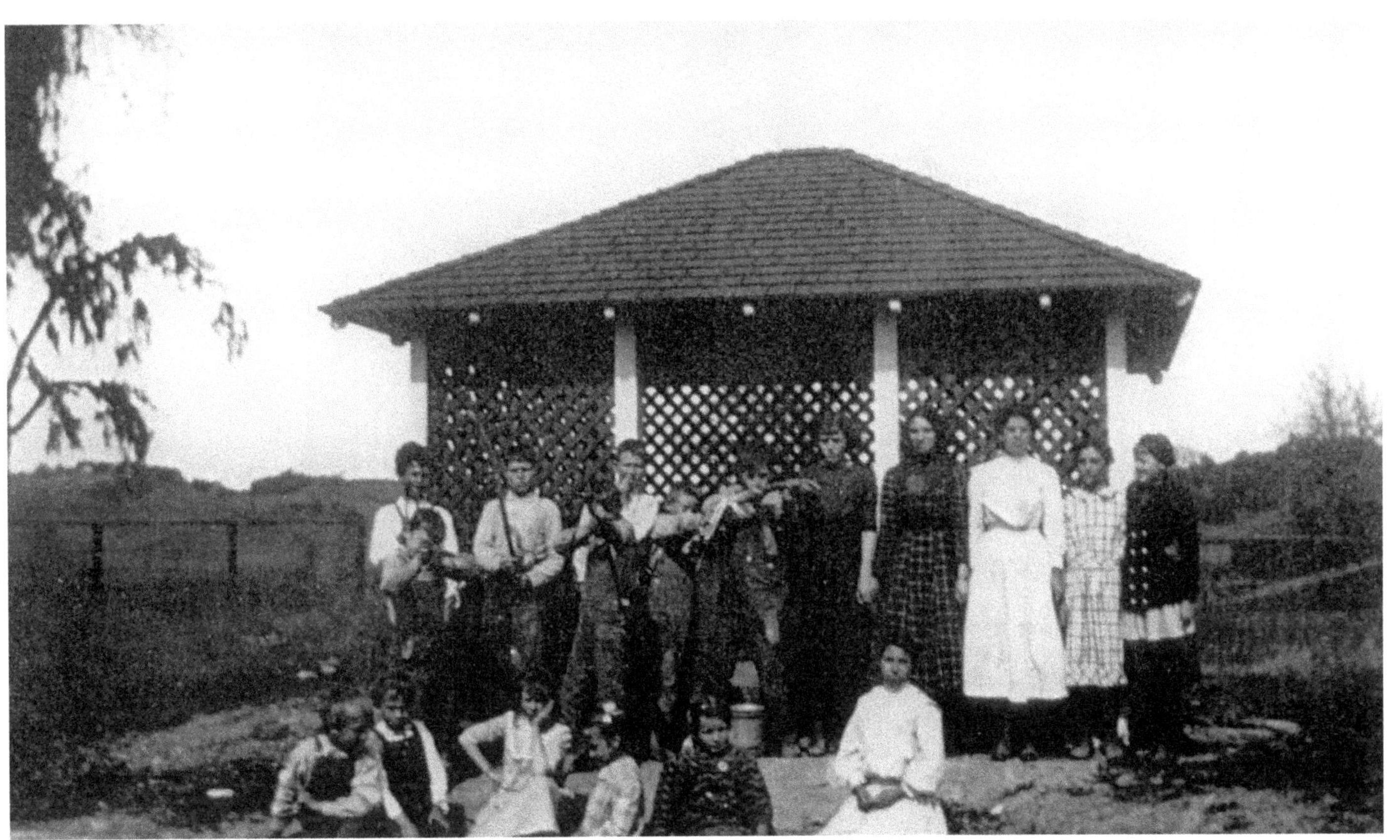

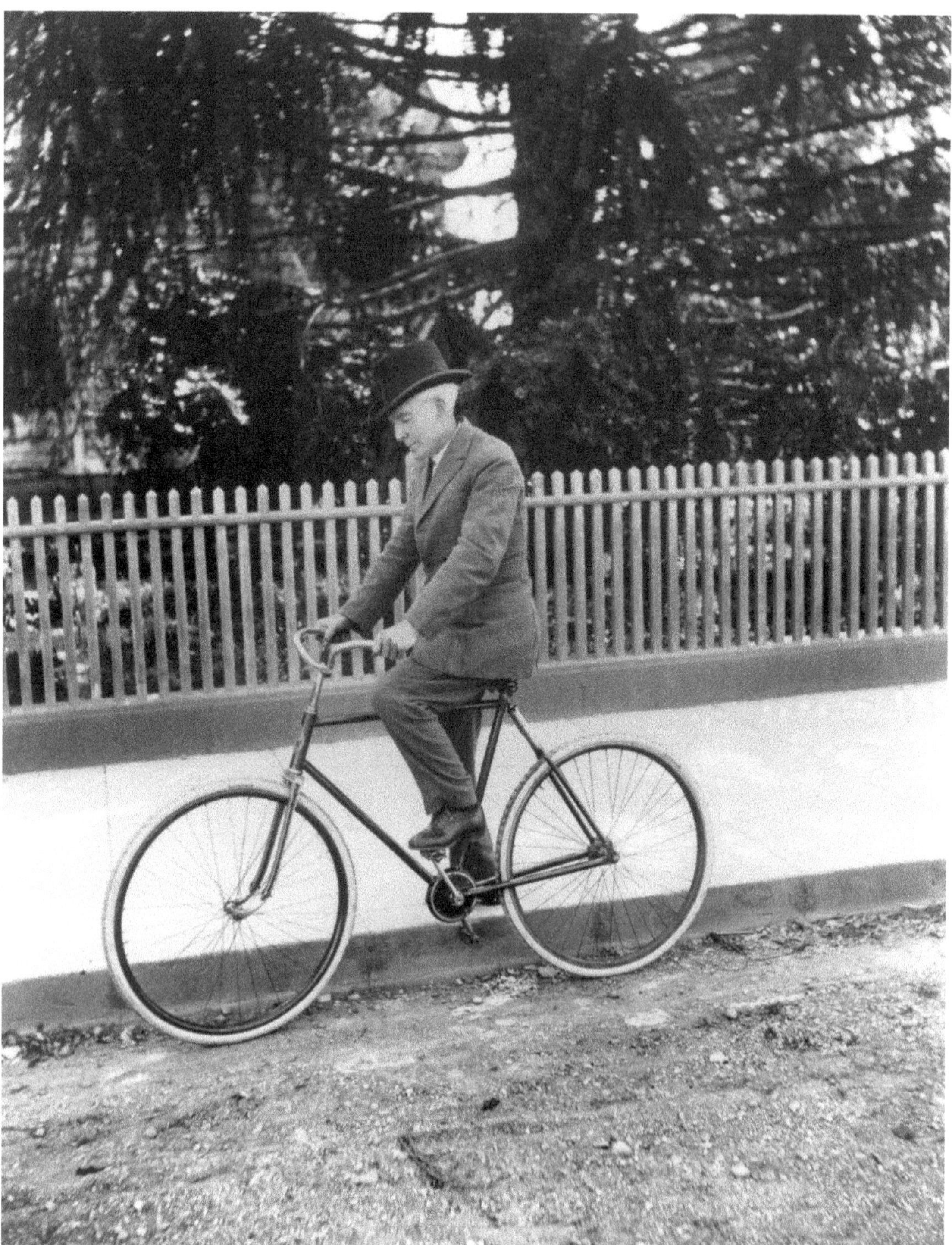

Writing about the 1906 quake, famed botanist Luther Burbank said he did not realize at first how powerful it was, but then "I arose . . . but was thrown back on the bed and found it impossible to stand even by holding onto objects usually stable, receiving such a shaking as I never before experienced." Here, he is shown riding a bicycle in 1908.

Although numerous of the prominent old Victorian homes had been destroyed, tree-lined streets continued to provide an inviting welcome to visitors in the City of Roses. While the destruction of hotels left many people homeless, a good number stayed on to rebuild the city and find new homes in the residential parts of towns. These photos show upper Third Street and upper College Avenue in 1909.

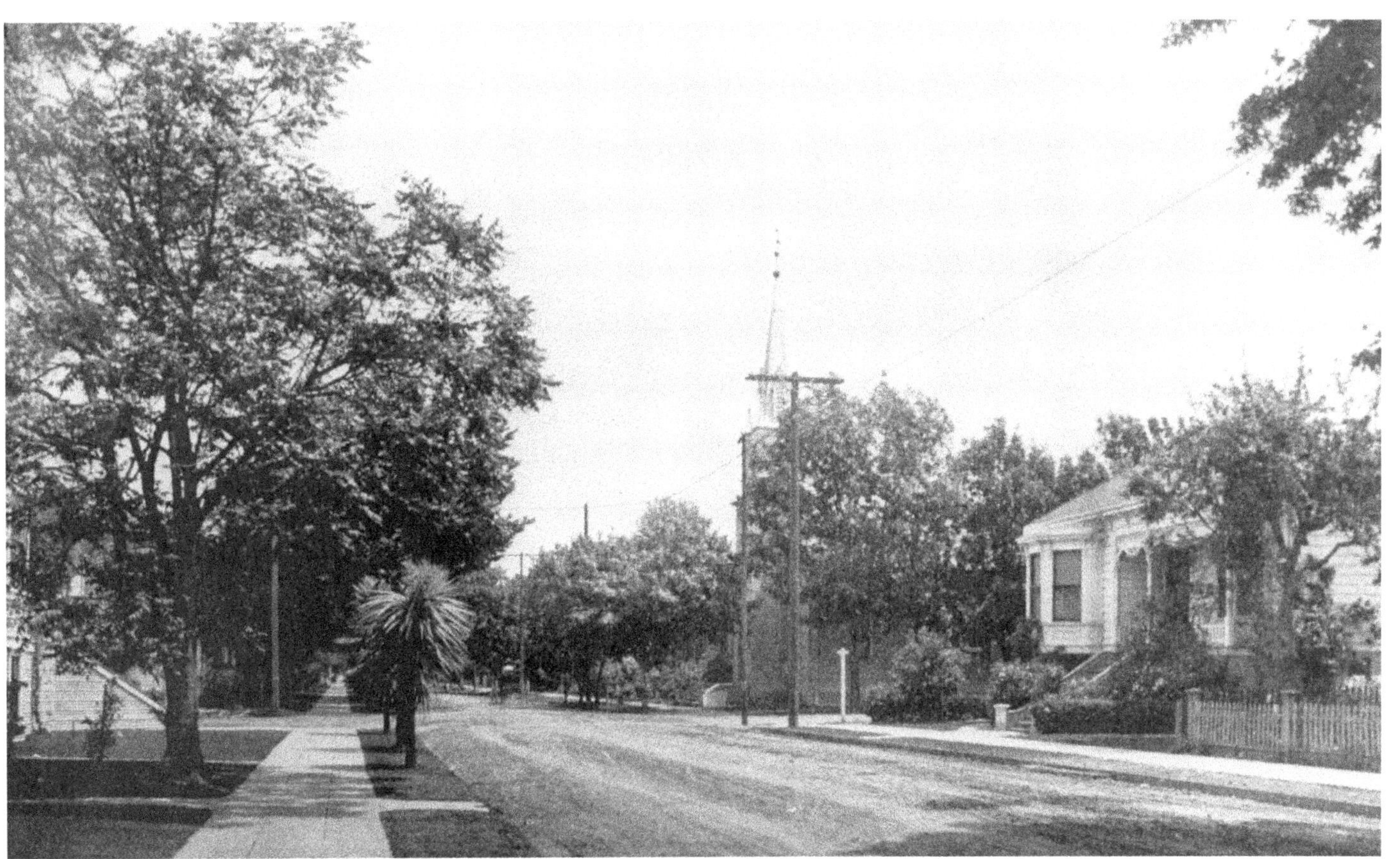

A survey of the downtown streets of Santa Rosa by Temple Smith in 1909 showed the rebuilding effort of Santa Rosans after the earthquake. Among the most significant was construction of a new courthouse. In spite of local bickering, a courthouse building was started by 1908 and dedicated in 1910.

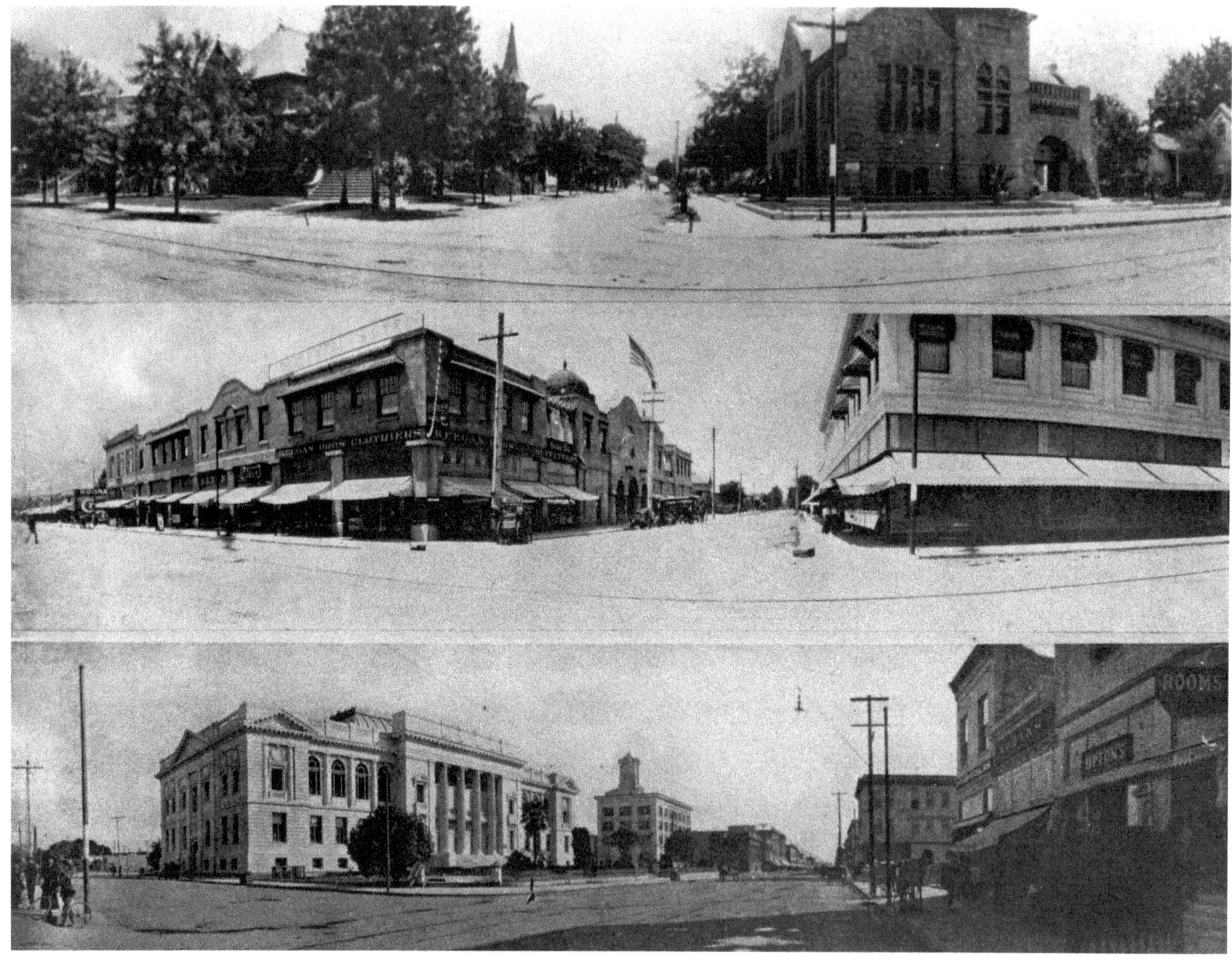

As the cities of Sonoma County grew, many residents fought to retain their independence and familiar rural life style. A wagon meandering down River Road near Windsor in 1908, toward the Methodist/Episcopal Church on the right, was a reminder of earlier times. Wine grapes, eggs, poultry, apples, hops, and similar products kept the agricultural spirit alive.

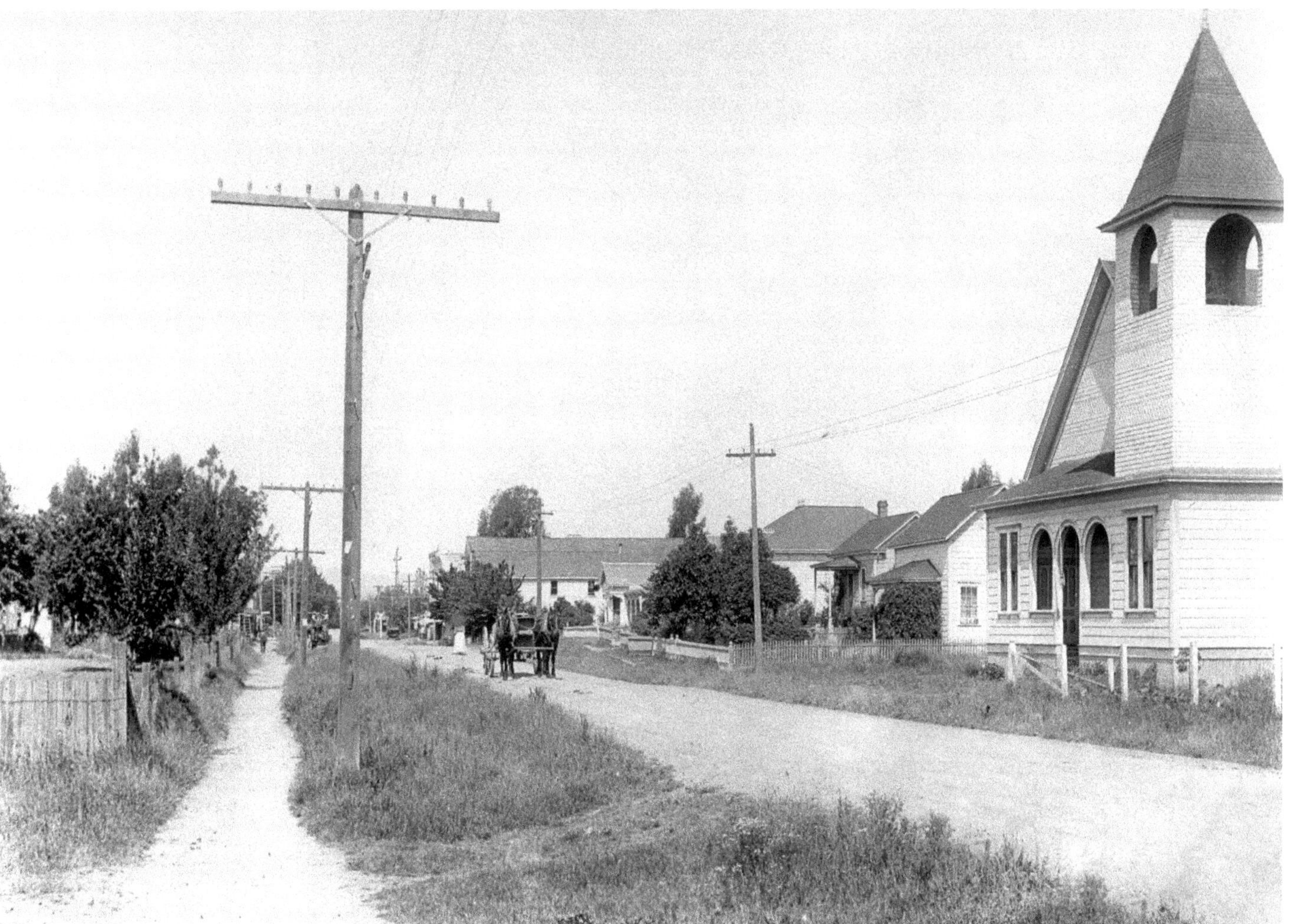

The wine business, even with occasional economic setbacks, has remained a major element in the county's prosperity. Scenes such as this one in Geyserville were familiar—a team of horses hauling a wagon loaded with wine barrels. By 1875, Sonoma County led the state in wine production by a wide margin. By 1900, there were more than one hundred commercial wineries. Sebastiani, Seghesio, Foppiano, and Pedroncelli were among the many pioneers and their names remain familiar today.

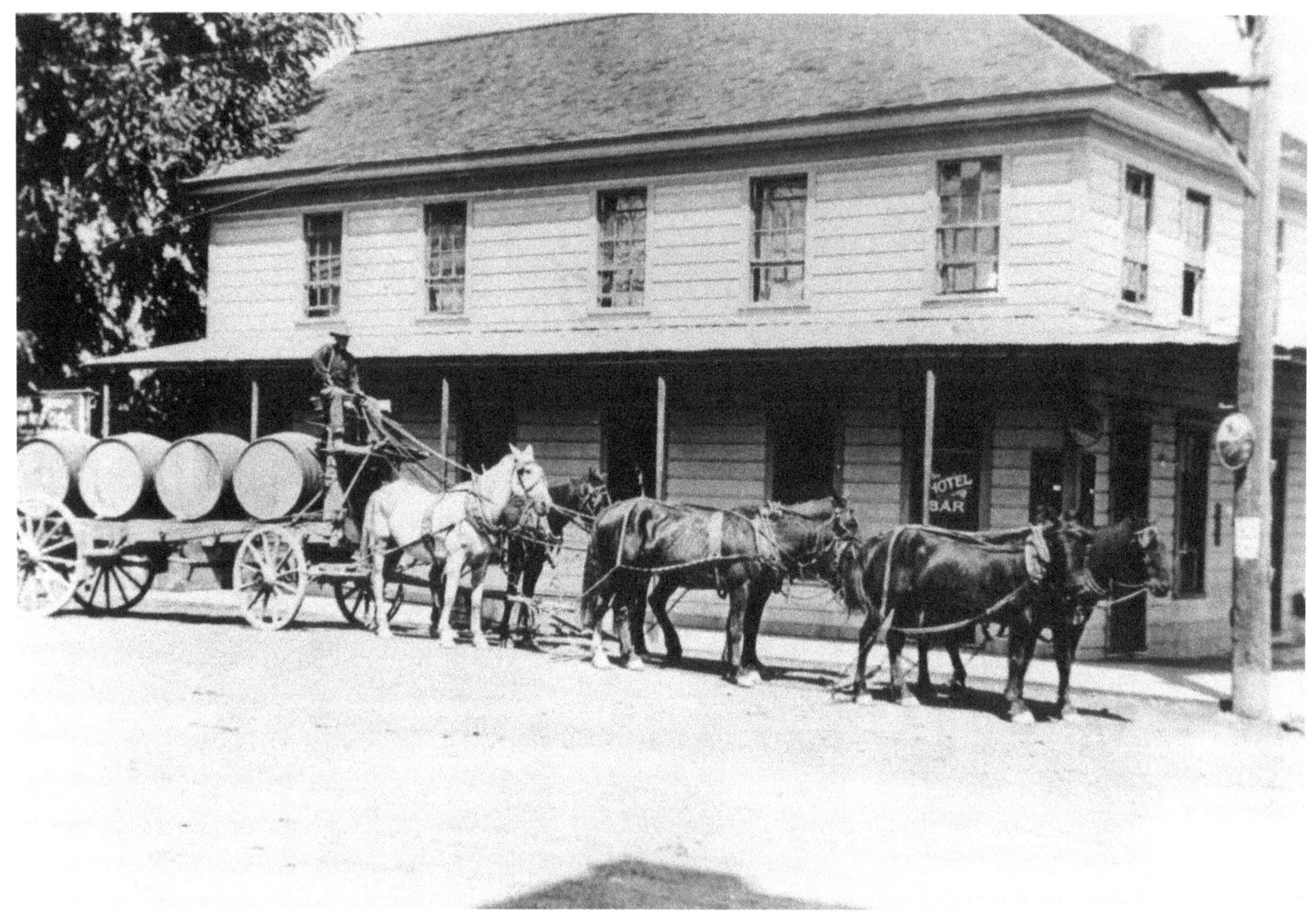

A typical Sonoma County scene was provided at the Geyserville Winery and Vineyard a few years into the twentieth century, but the business was unpredictable. Vineyards were hit hard in the 1890s by an economic depression and the presence of the dreaded tiny insect phylloxera that can harm plants, drastically affecting grape yield and quality. After an upswing, Prohibition put many wineries out of business in the 1920s.

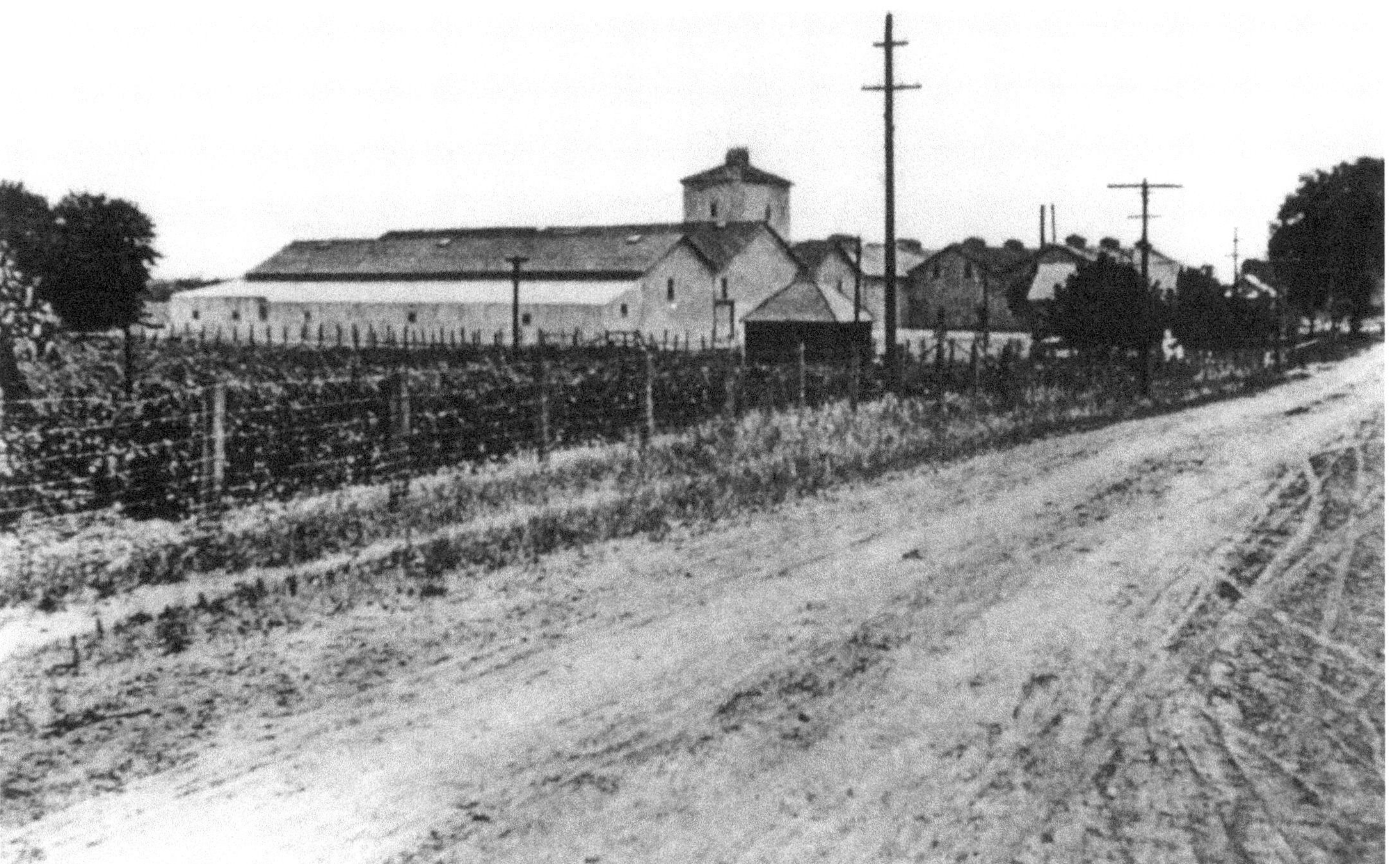

In 1908, Windsor celebrated the opening of its new schoolhouse, considered one of the most attractive school buildings in rural California. The district acquired the property in 1897 but didn't get the three-room facility built until more than ten years later. A fourth room was added when student numbers swelled.

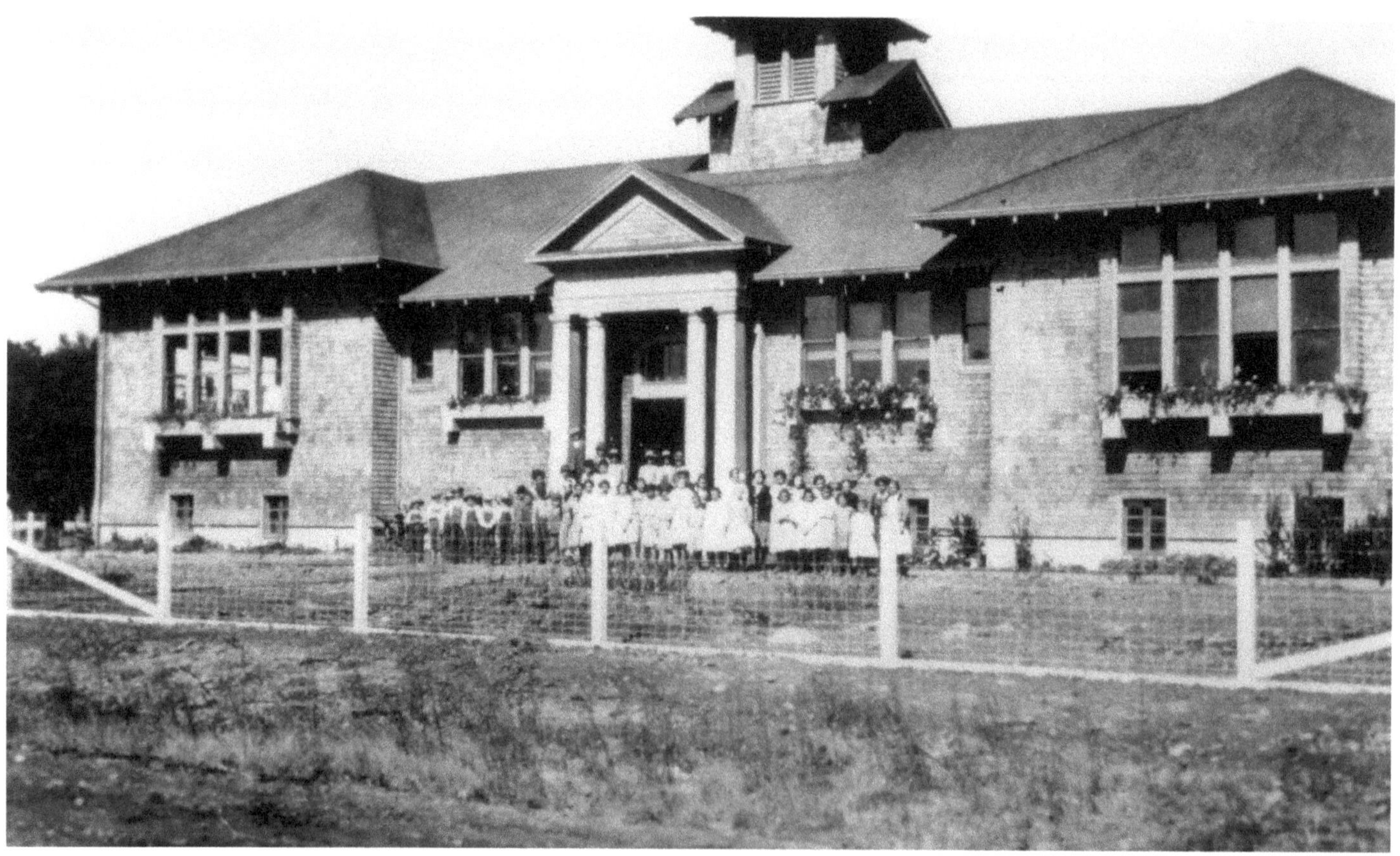

Northwestern Pacific Railroad tracks ran through a vineyard near the utopian community of Preston in 1908. The colony, founded by Emily Preston in the 1880s, was located two-and-a-half miles northeast of Cloverdale near the border with Mendocino County. A health-oriented religious community, the village reached a population of 150 in 1895 but took a sharp decline after the death of its leader in 1909.

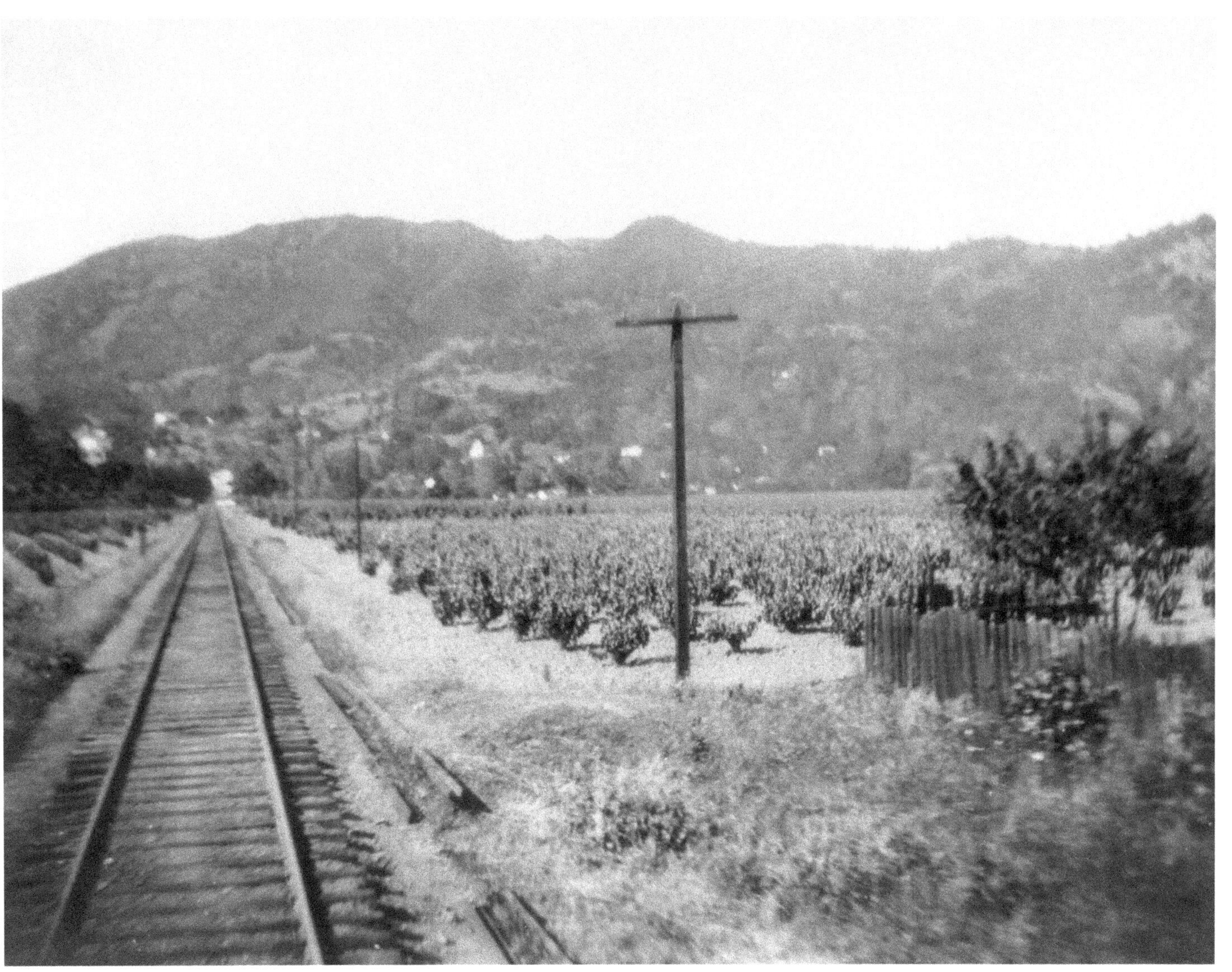

J. C. Scott Hardware was one of the numerous businesses operating on Main Street in Petaluma in 1910. The store at 806–808 Main Street featured plumbing, windmills, stoves, ranges, and cutlery. This view is from Washington Street looking south down Main.

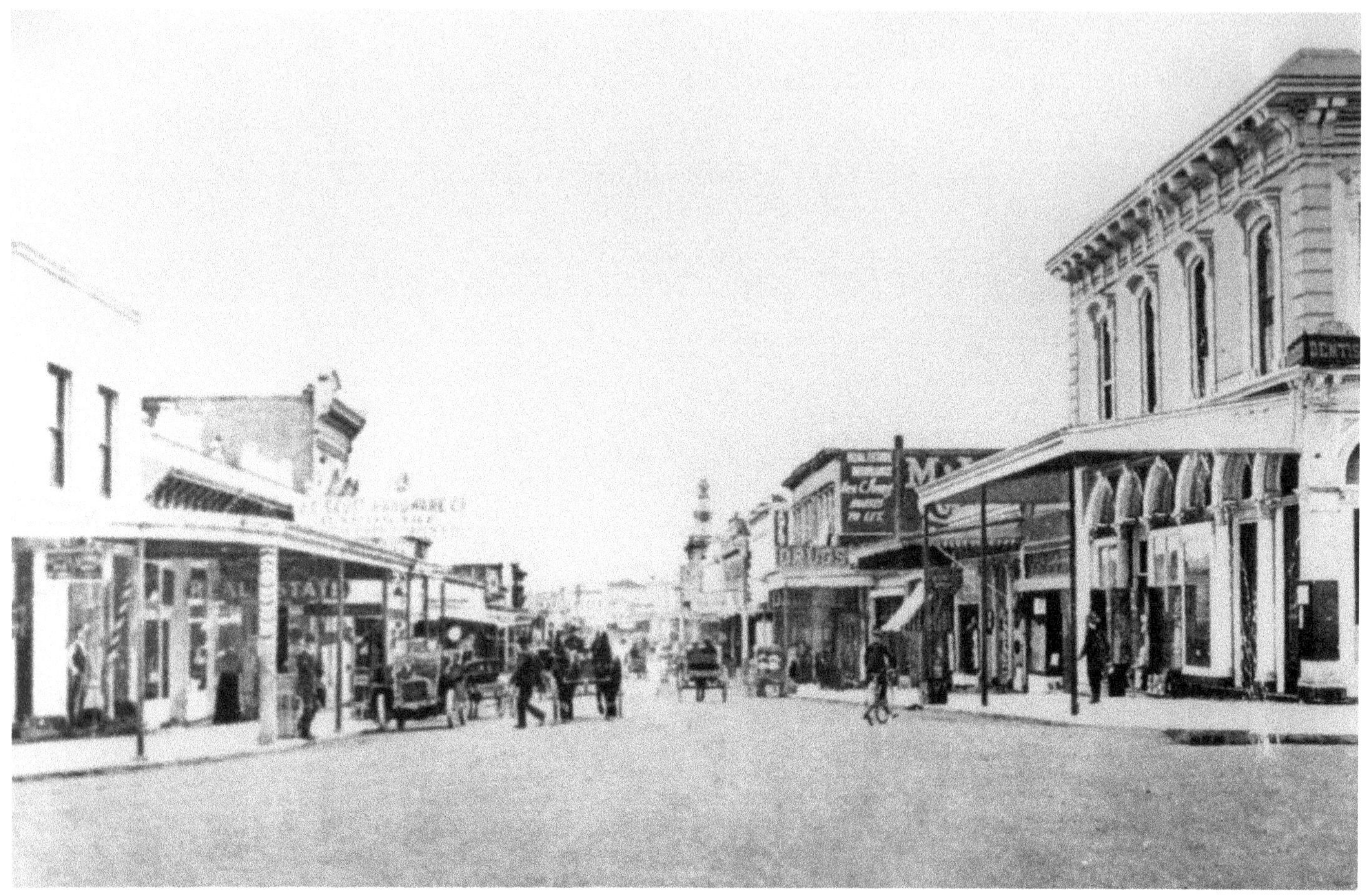

In spite of heavy odds, the City of Roses was almost back to normal by 1911. To the west from the corner of Hinton and 4th streets, the new courthouse could be seen in the left foreground with the domed Empire Building behind it. The Exchange Bank was across the street on the right. Other major rebuilding successes included a post office at a new location at 5th and A streets, a swimming pool, and a skating rink.

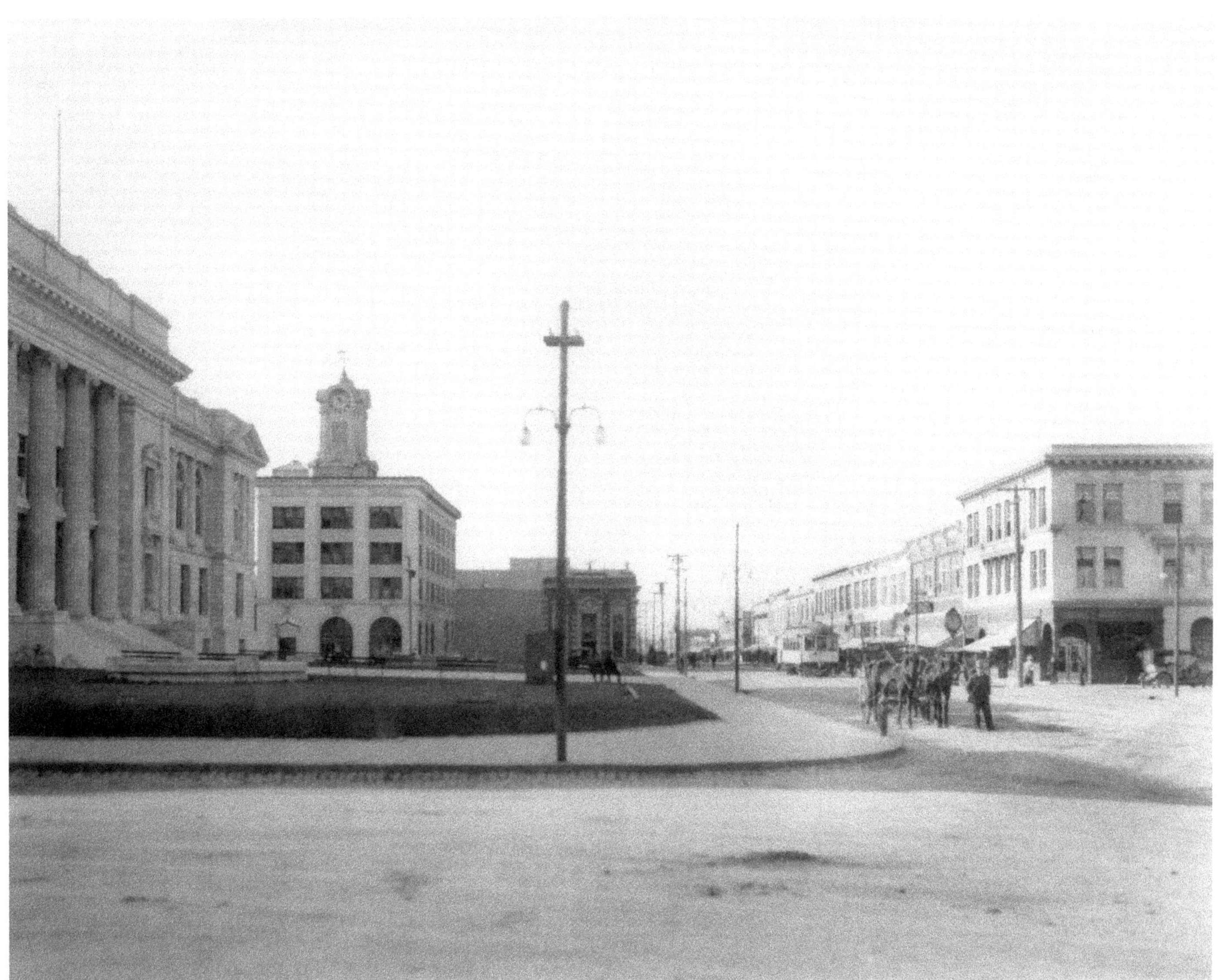

As the harvest took place, workers unloaded barrels at an unidentified winery around 1910.

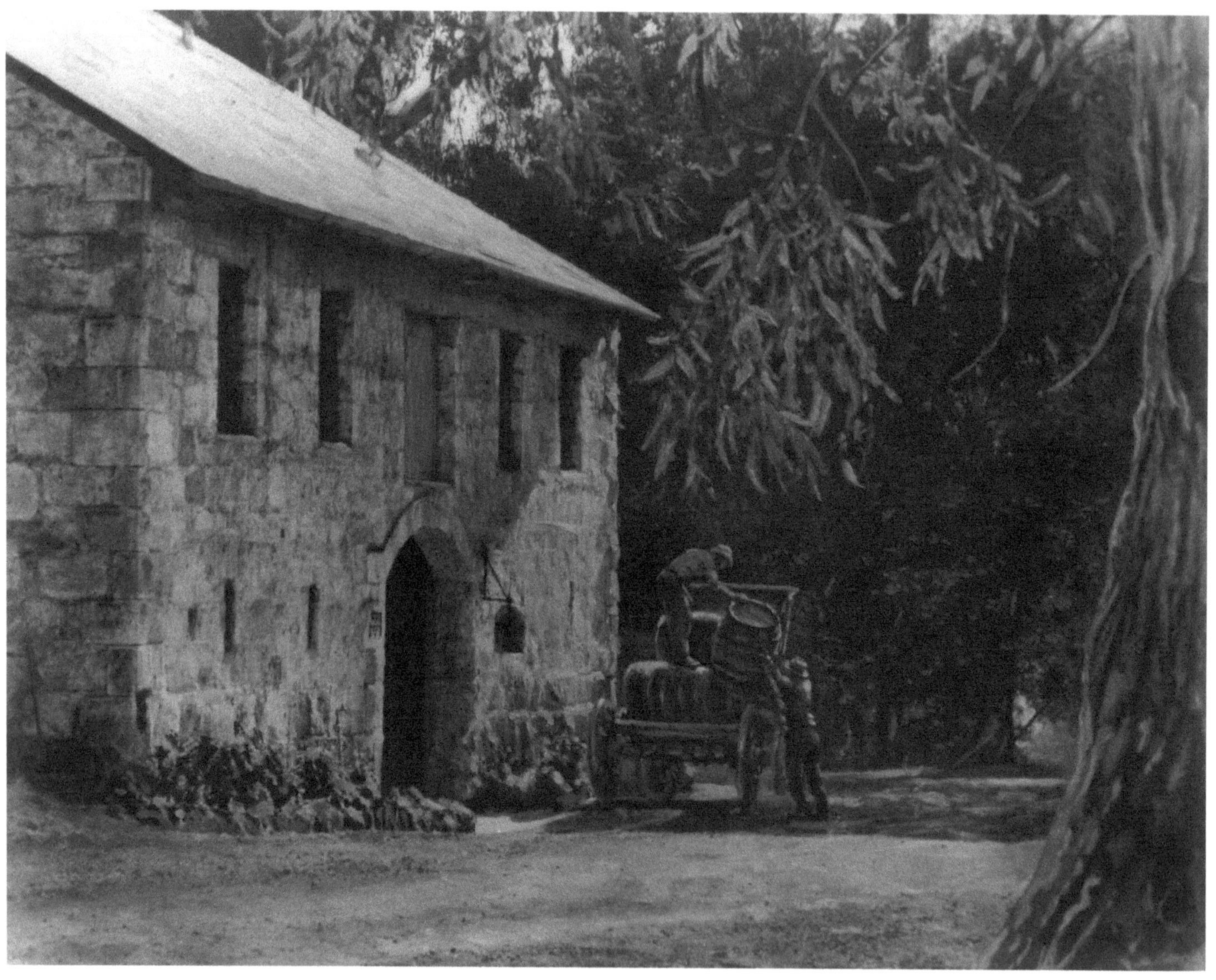

Young Fred Wiseman brought Sonoma County into the aviation age in 1911 when he made what is believed to be the first air mail flight in history—six months before the Postmaster General officially authorized air delivery—weaving his way to Santa Rosa in a trip that took two days. In a flight that caused great excitement all along the way, Wiseman flew at an altitude between 100 and 200 feet, carrying three letters and a package from a Petaluma firm. He landed in a muddy field at a dairy near Santa Rosa and walked away uninjured.

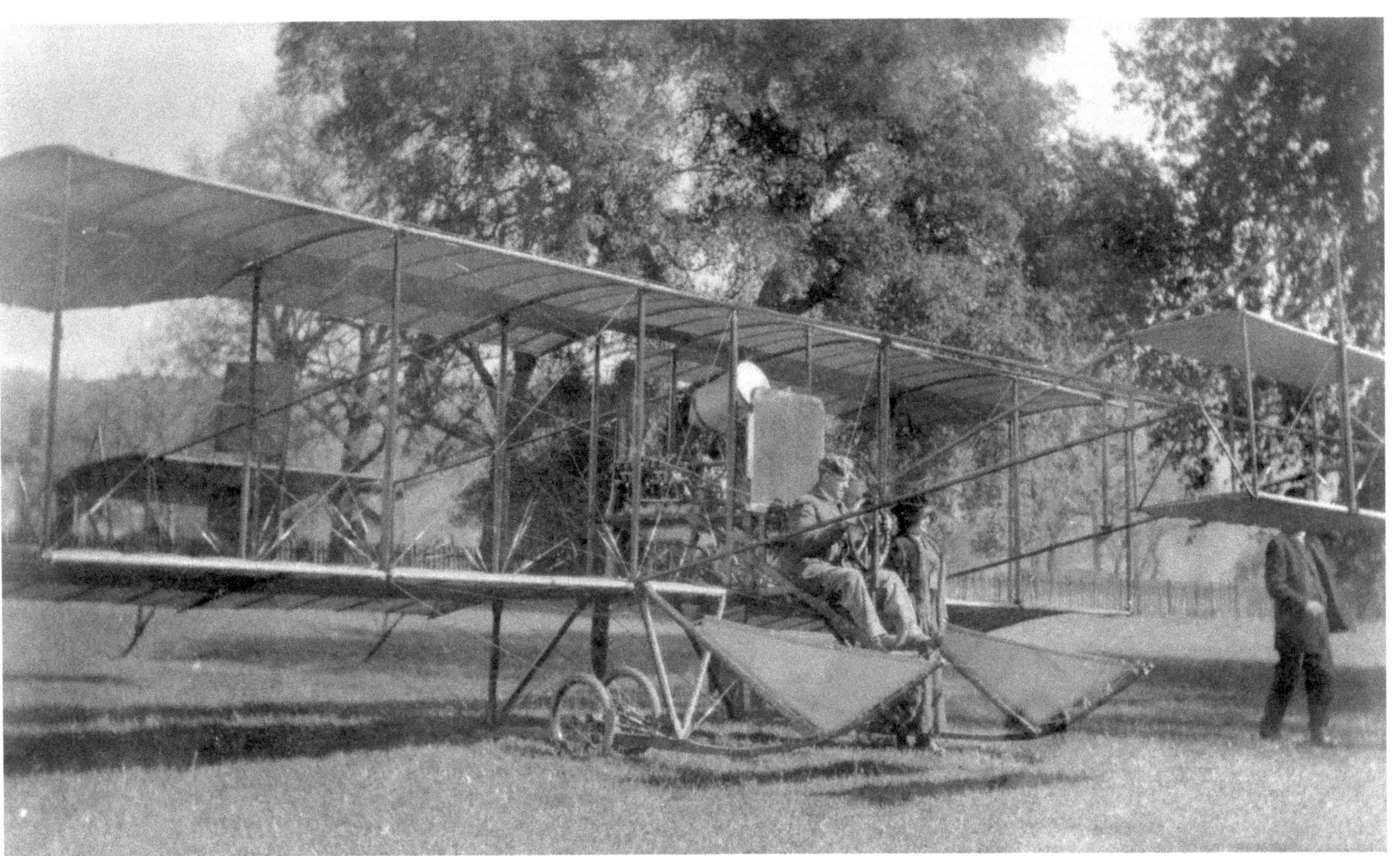

The White House Department store was first known as Carithers and Forsyth, operated at Fifth and B streets by William R. Carithers and Henry M. Forsyth. By 1911, the name had been changed to the White House. Lined up in front of the store in 1911 were Forsyth (left), Carithers, and young Billie Carithers (sitting on his father's lap). The staff fell in behind the owners.

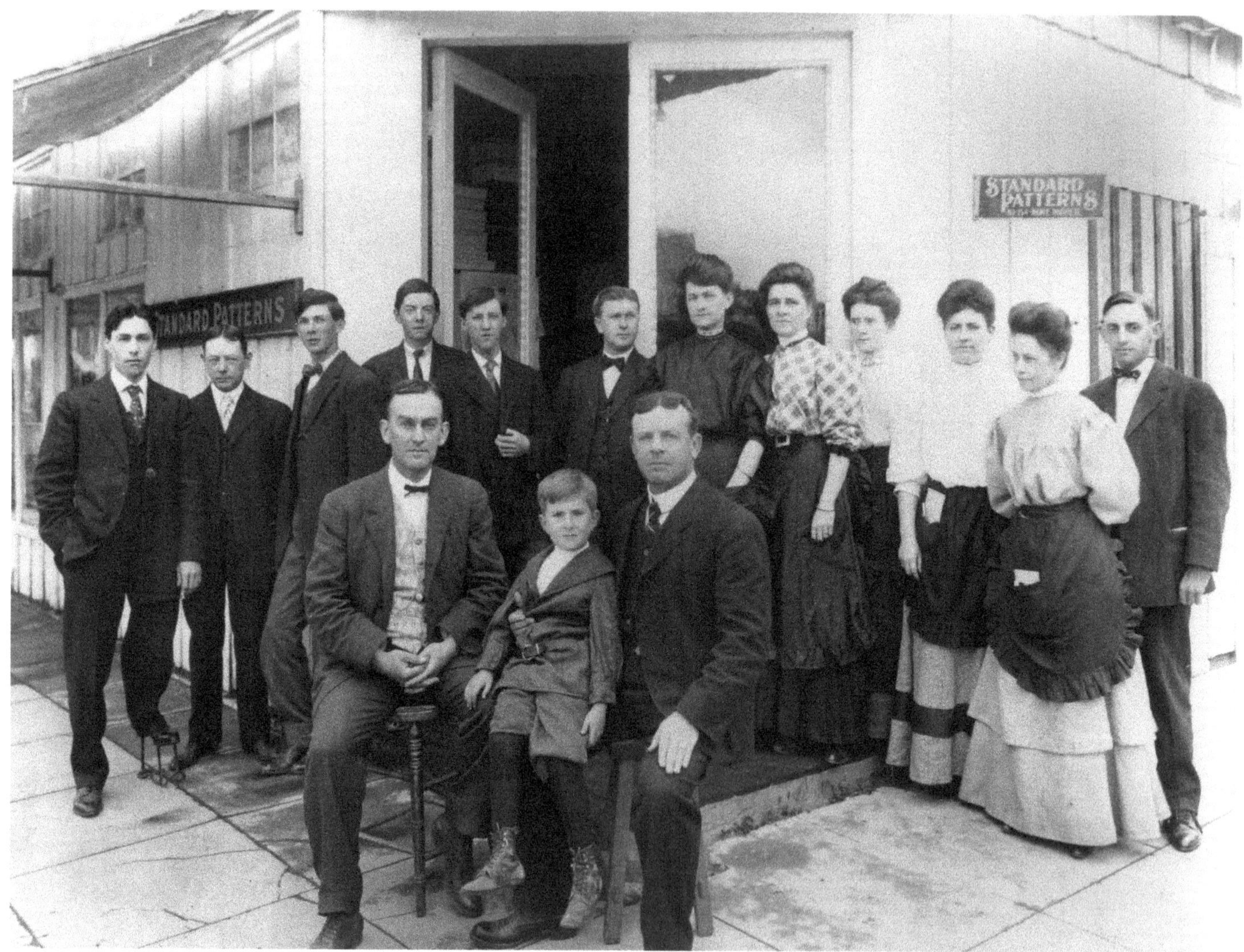

Author Jack London and his wife Charmian made a dynamic team, traveling the world in search of adventure. They settled into the "Beauty Ranch" at Glen Ellen southeast of Santa Rosa, where London worked to build his dream home called The Wolf House. Charmian relaxed on the sleeping porch of their cottage at the Beauty Ranch. The area is now a much-frequented state park and museum. Fire damaged the Wolf House, and London died before it could be completed.

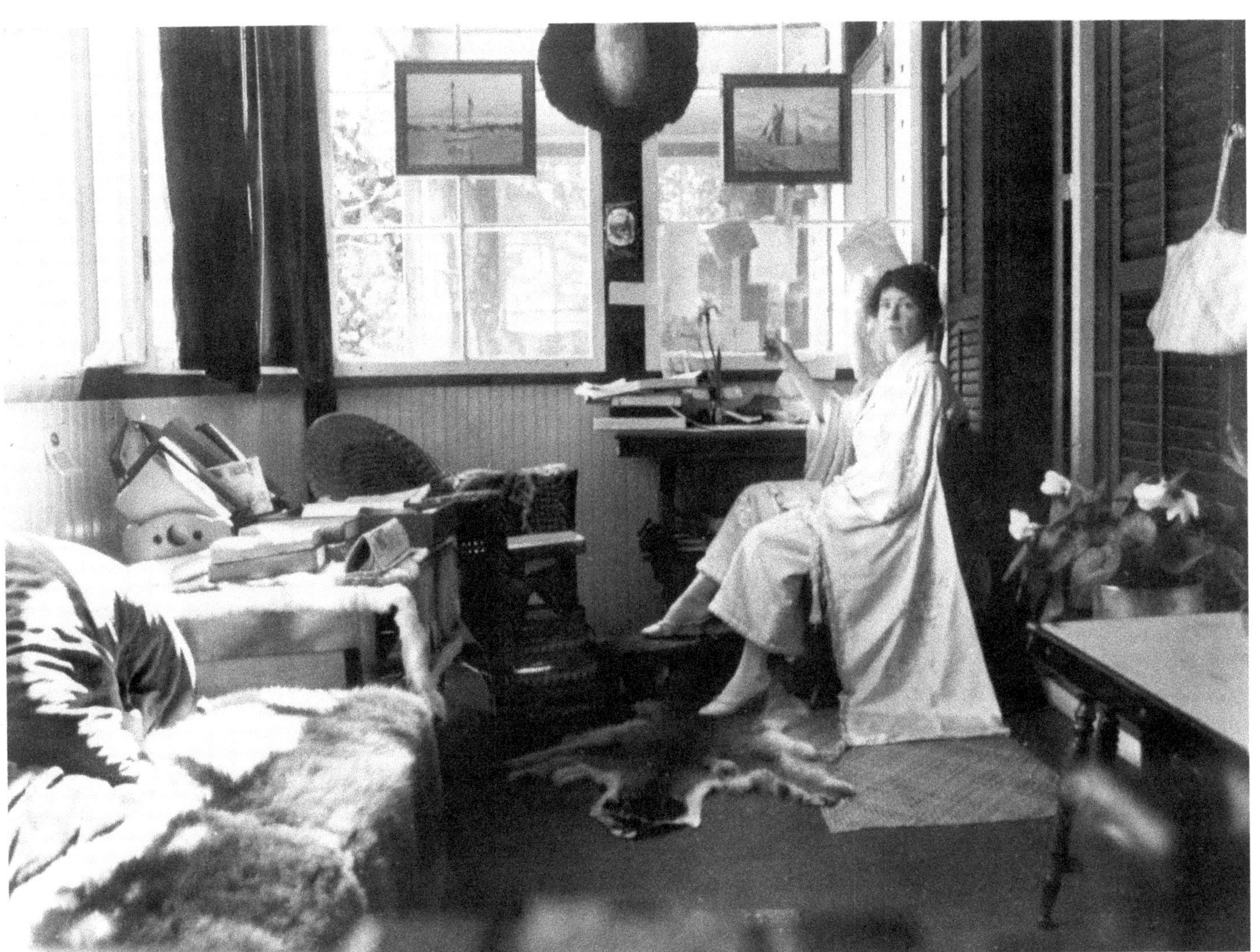

The Catholic heritage was strong in Santa Rosa where a large group gathered in front of the St. Rose Church in 1910. A church had been built at the B Street location in 1880, but it was not until 1900 that the famous stone building was constructed on the same site under the direction of stonemason Peter Maroni. Father John Cassin presided over the project and was credited with strong leadership during his forty-two years as pastor of St. Rose.

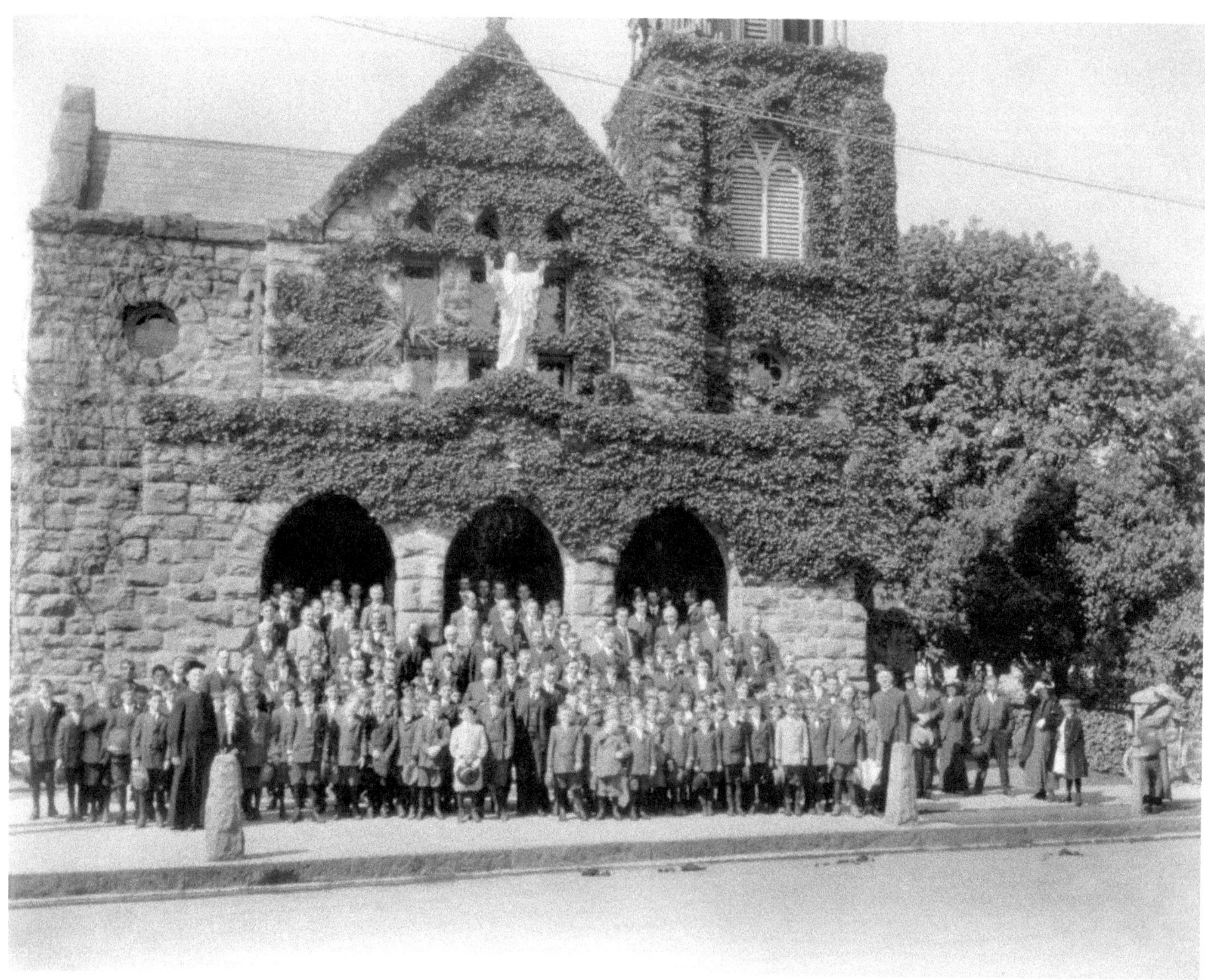

The St. Vincent's Catholic Parish in Petaluma, founded in 1857, has served the needs of its community into the twenty-first century. In 1910, this church was located at Liberty and Howard streets. In the mid-1920s it was moved and became the Elim Lutheran Church at 220 Stanley Street. Around that same time, Pastor James Kiely built a new church on the Howard Street site, which remained a center of Catholic activity in Sonoma County.

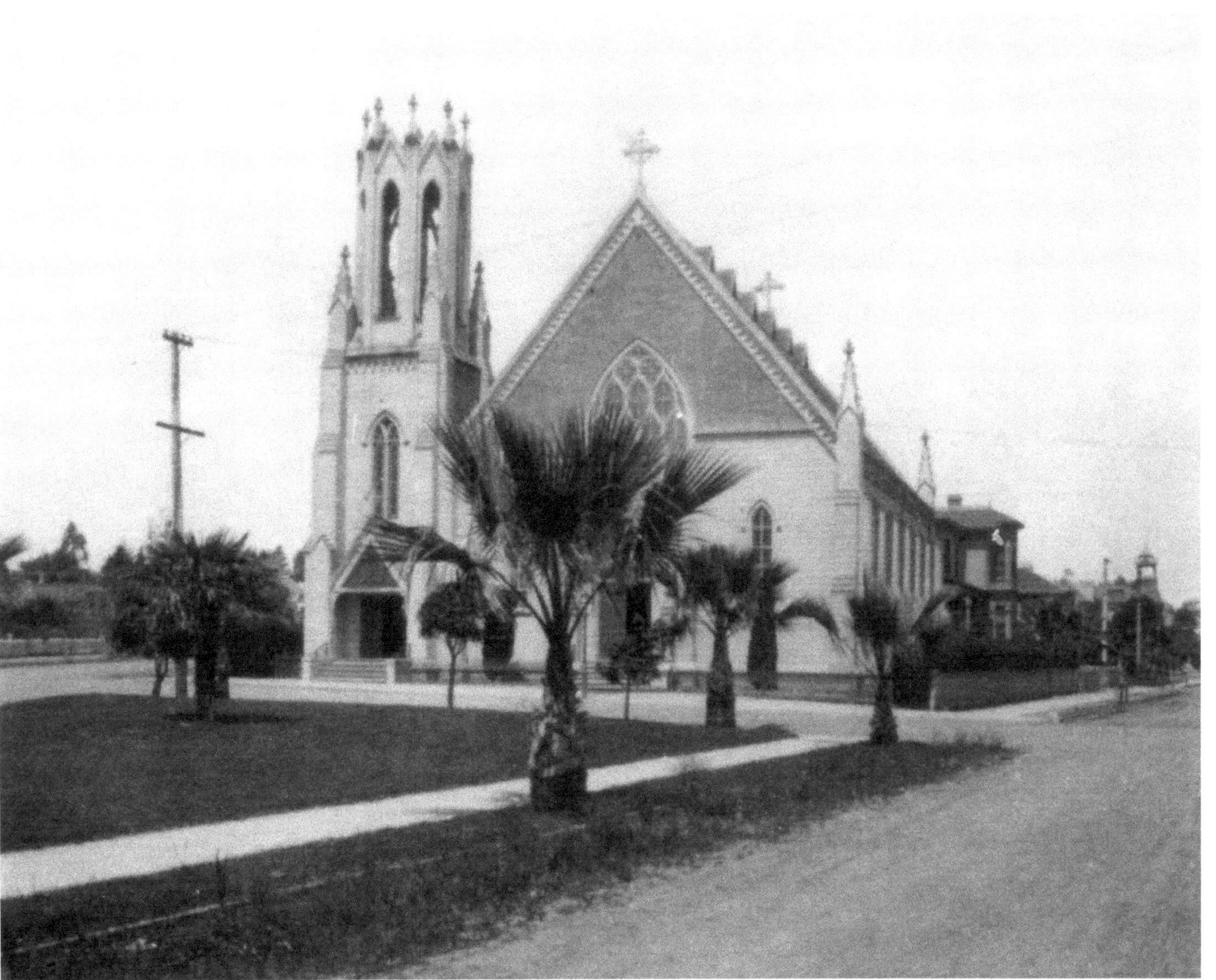

Businesses were prospering on Washington Street in Petaluma in 1909. Peek and Wilson grocers were located at 8 Washington Street and Petaluma Lodging House was nearby at number 16. Photo was taken from the intersection with Main Street, looking west.

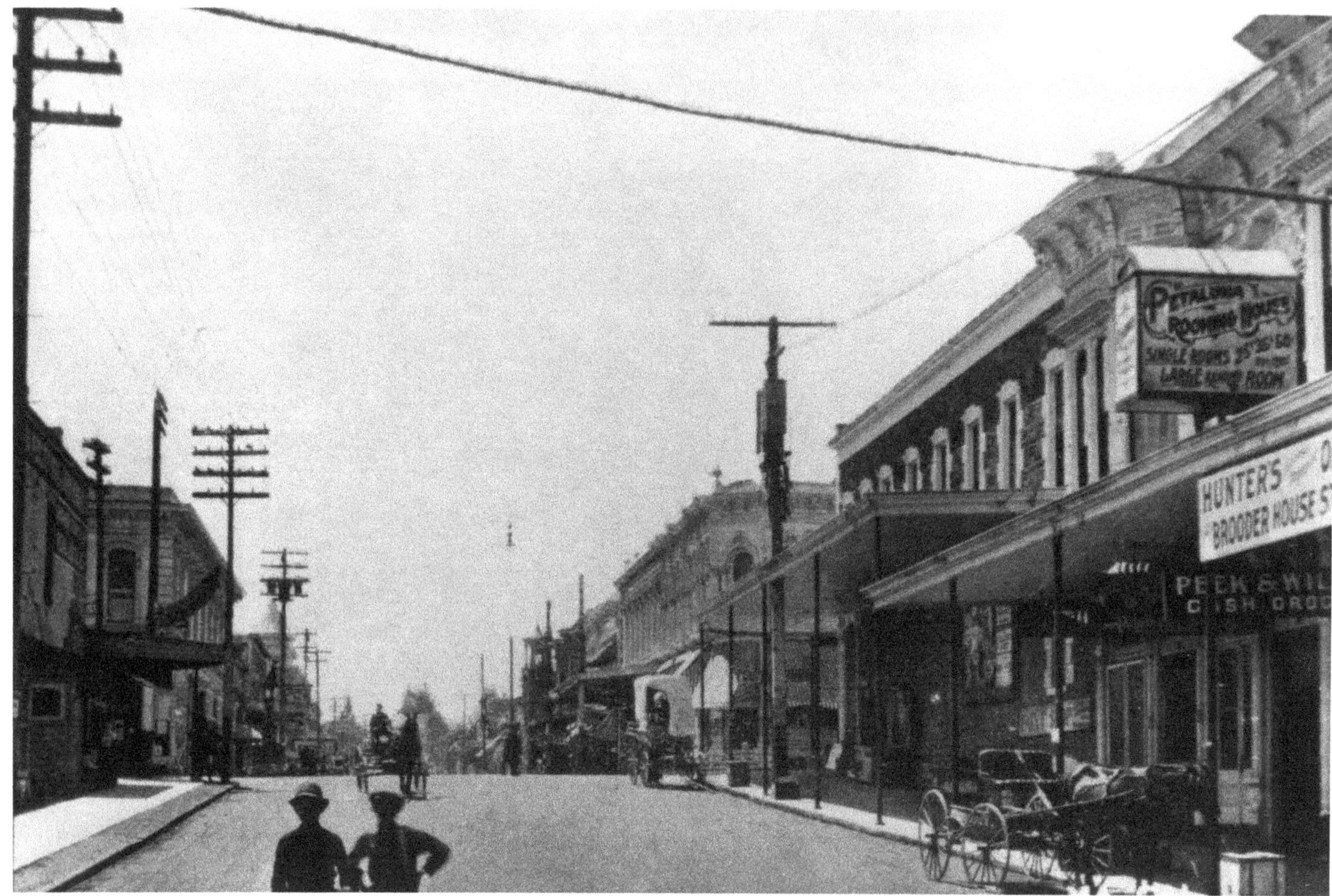

By 1910, autos competed for space on Petaluma's streets, although many travelers were more comfortable moving about by horse and buggy. In this view to the north on Petaluma's Main Street, the Ark and American Hotel were among the major businesses.

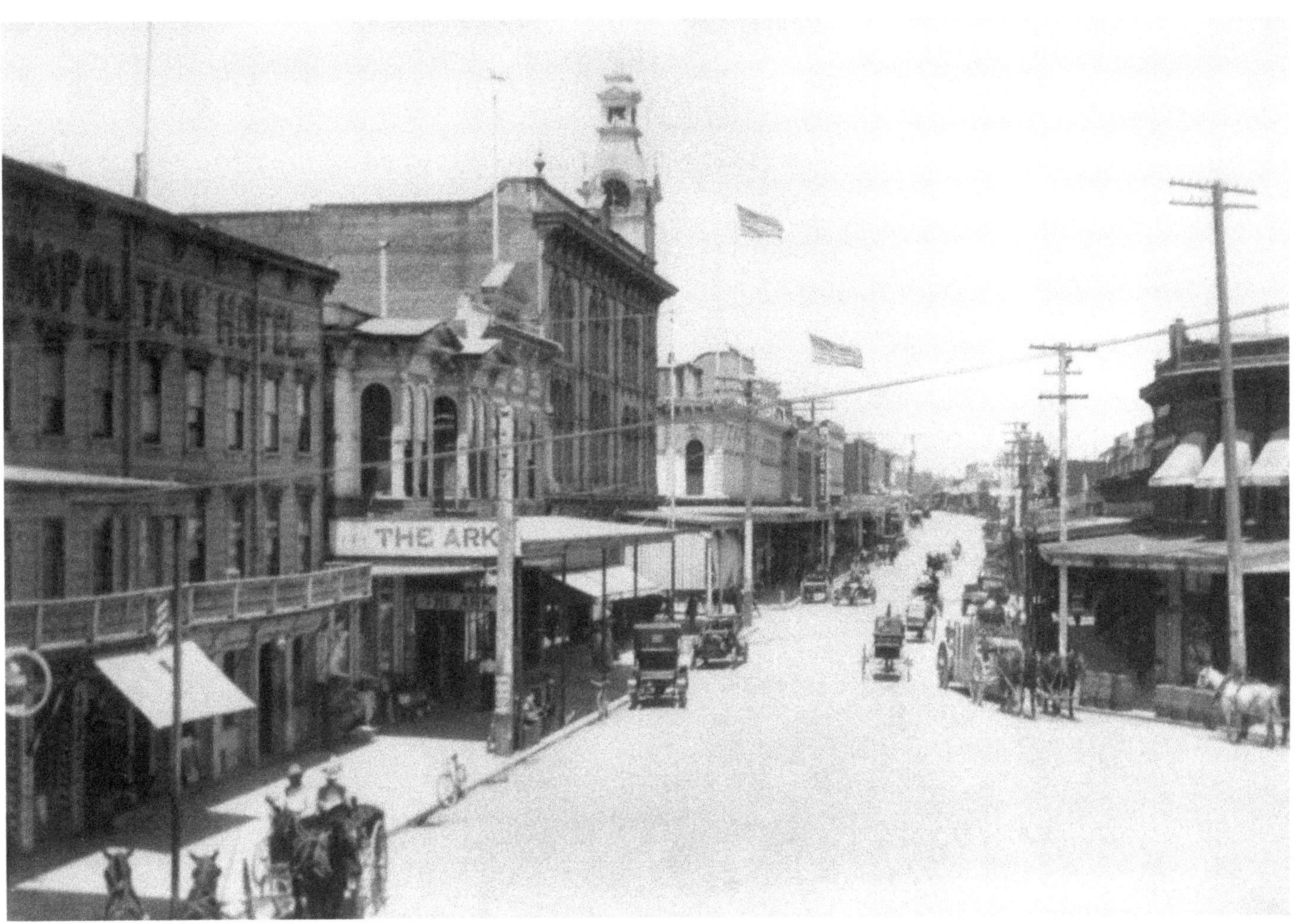

Horse and buggy fans did not give up easily. The defenders of transportation's "good old days" found safety in numbers as they gathered at a "parking lot" on Petaluma's lower Main Street in 1910. Nearby firms included the Unique Theatre and McNear Feed and Grain.

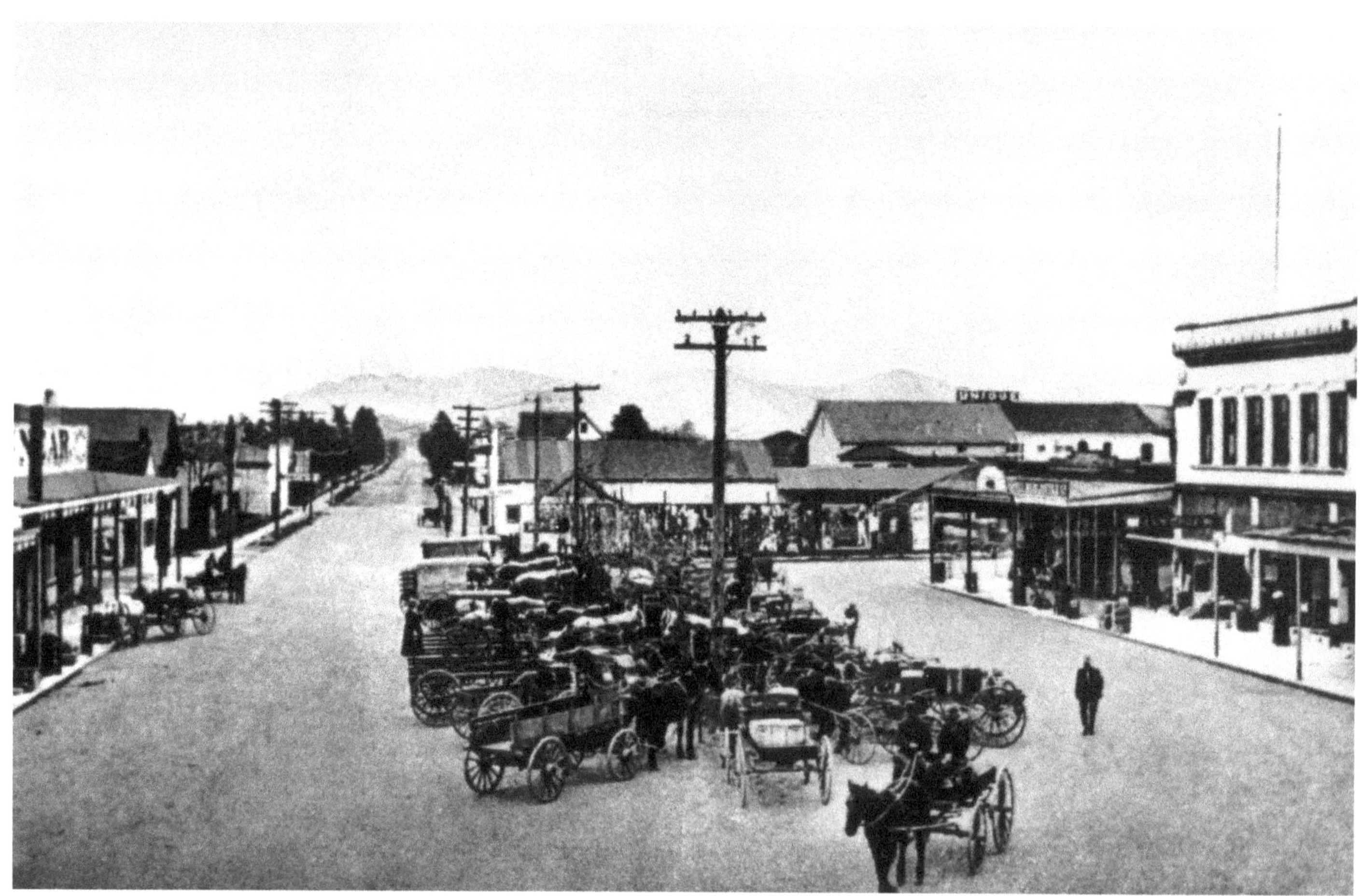

It was a bit of a trip in from the country, but the Two Rock band seemed happy to be in a Petaluma parade early in the twentieth century. Two Rock Station was the terminus of the branch line from the Liberty District of the Petaluma and Santa Rosa Railroad. The area was named after two rocks of unusual shape that stood a few feet apart on a gentle rise above the Petaluma–Bloomfield Highway near Two Rock Station.

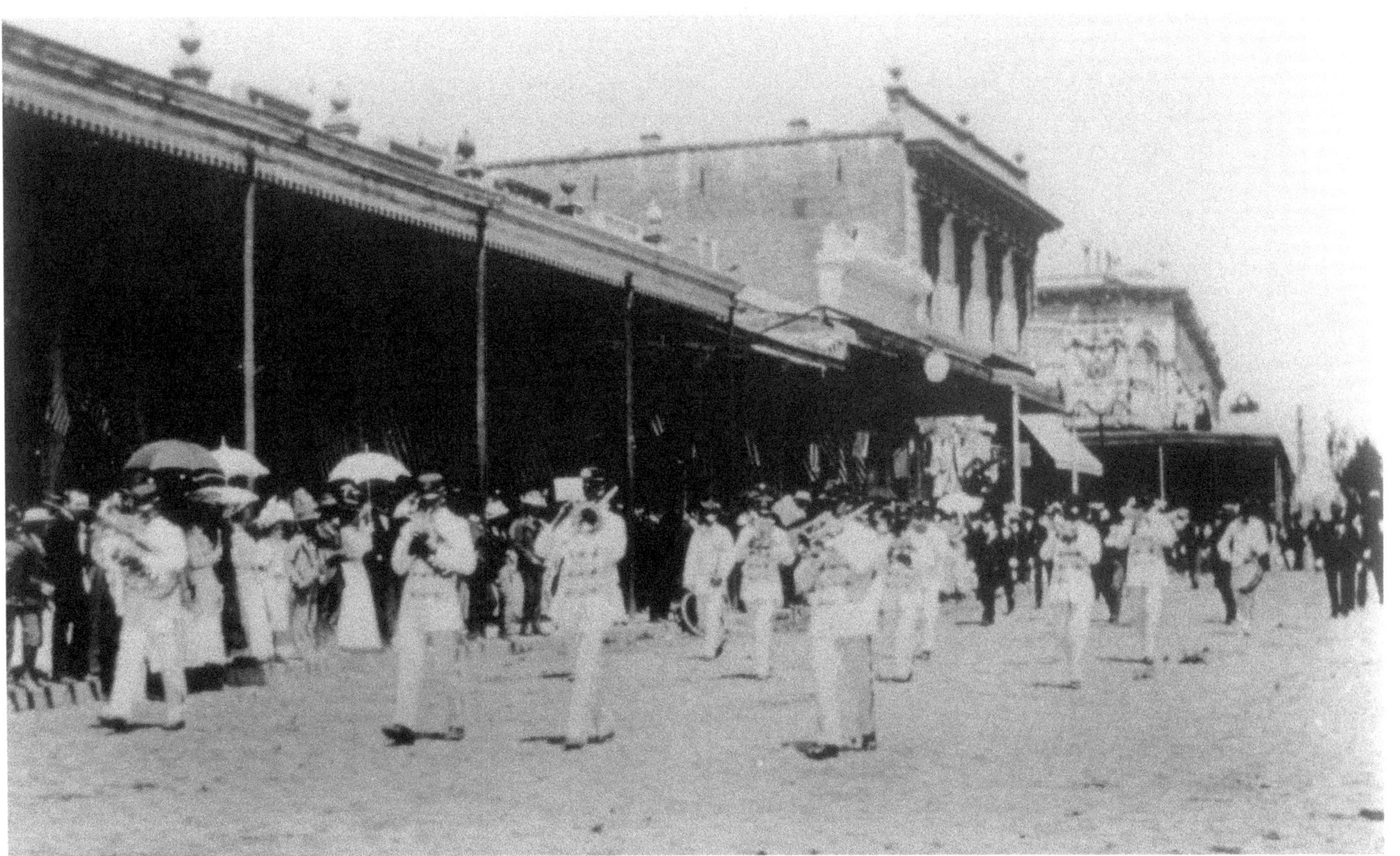

The Healdsburg Chamber of Commerce sent an exhibit for the Sebastopol Apple Show in 1912. While Healdsburg was known for its prunes, Sebastopol was celebrating its emergence as a center for the tart Gravenstein apple. Sebastopol, population 2,000, held its first apple show in 1910. In that year, the county had 5,700 acres planted in apples, a number that jumped to 27,000 acres in 1920.

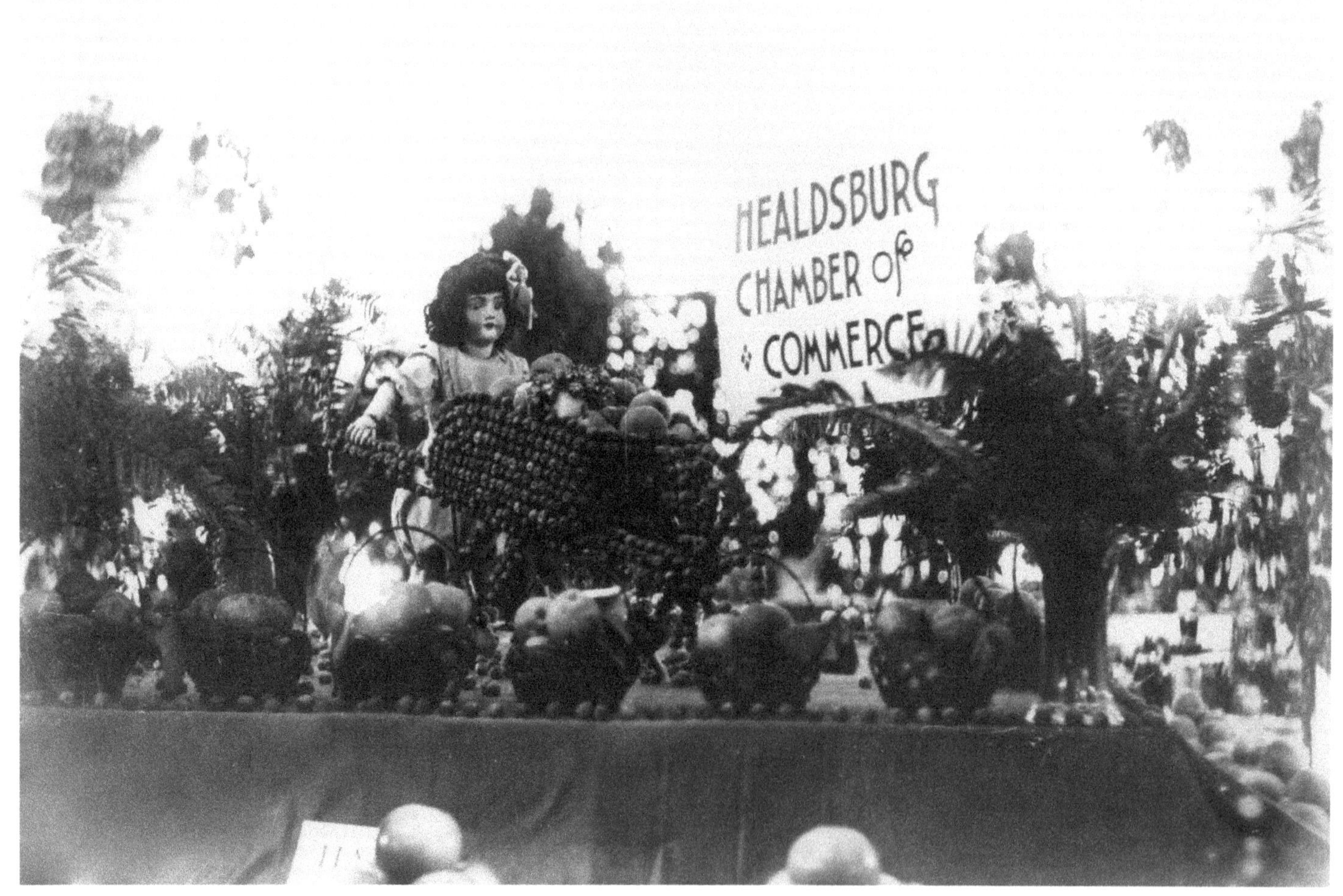

As is well-known in Sebastopol, apples were good for eating but they also could be used to build exhibits, such as this creative entry using the crunchy fruit to create a structure resembling the Greek Parthenon.

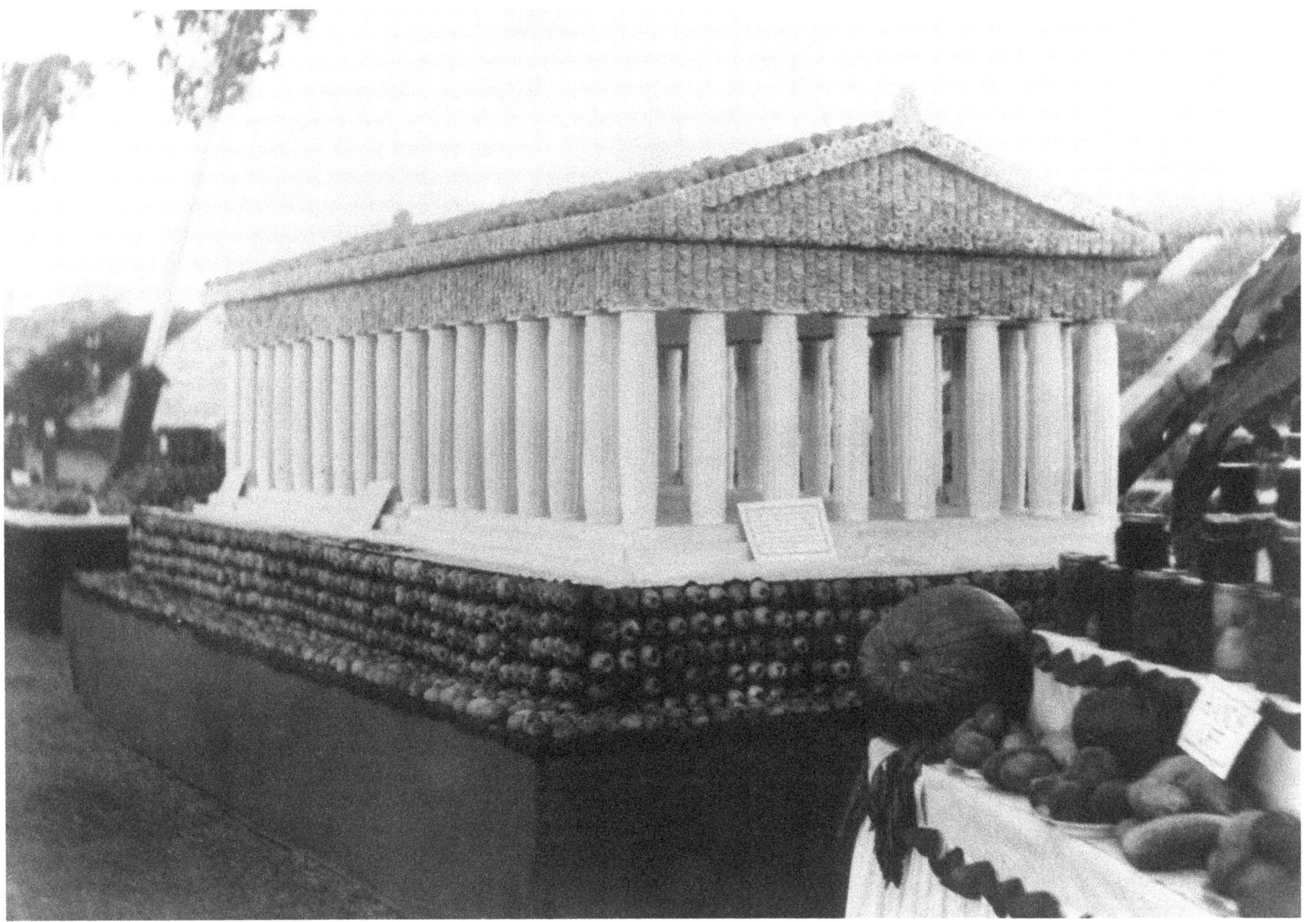

Beer drinkers relied on Grace Brothers Brewery for a thirst-quenching drink. Louis Rizzi and Lee Duckhorn guided the Grace Brothers delivery wagon at 4th and Wilson Streets in 1914. The Santa Rosa Steam Brewery, opened in 1872, was taken over by Grace Brothers Brewery in 1897, and the Grace family held control until 1966. Brothers Frank P. and Joseph T. Grace purchased the steam brewery for $6,750 in 1897.

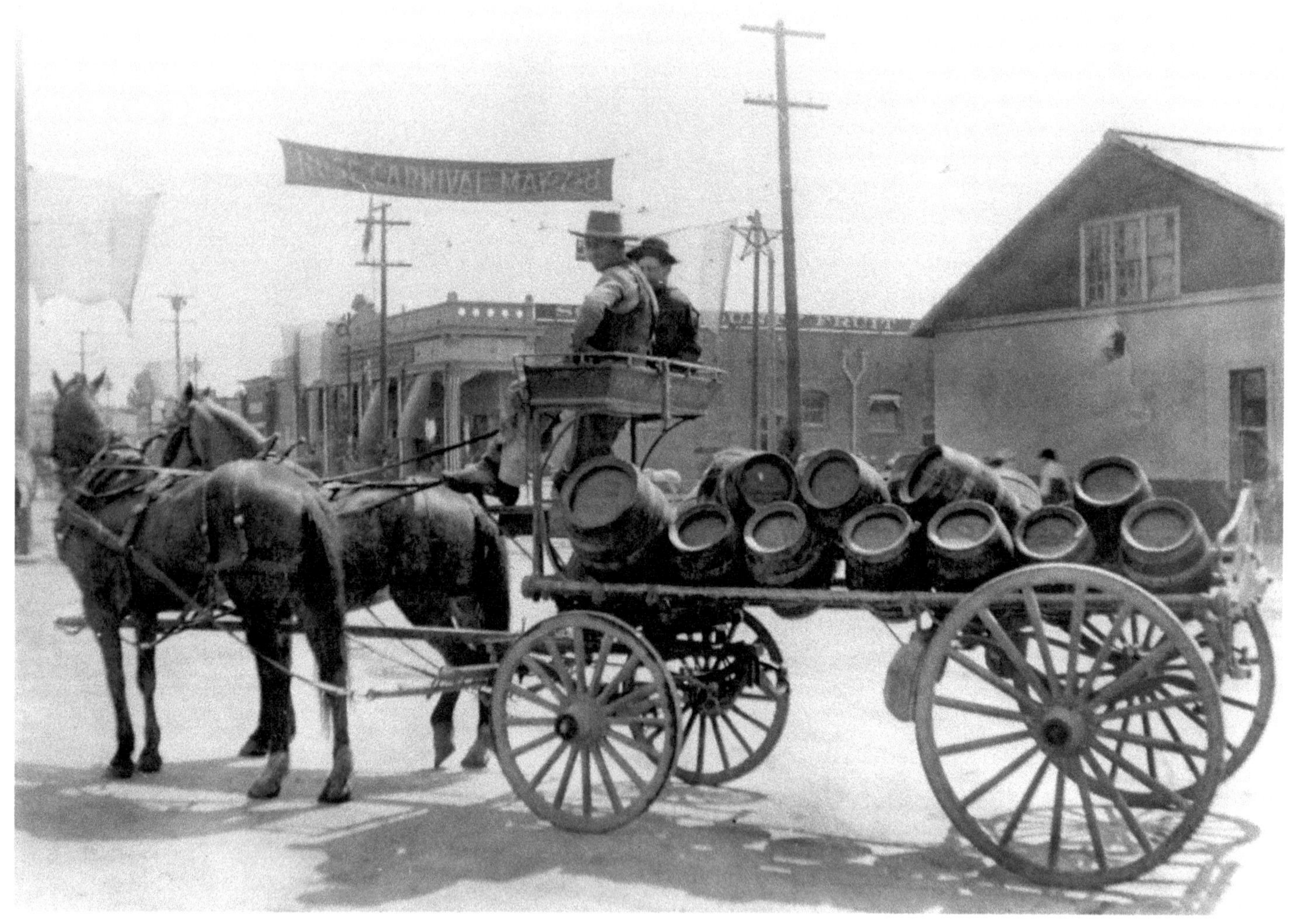

A view of Windsor in 1915 showed the Bell family residence and the Masonic Temple, as well as F. A. Emery's Livery and Feed Stable and, beyond it, a meat market.

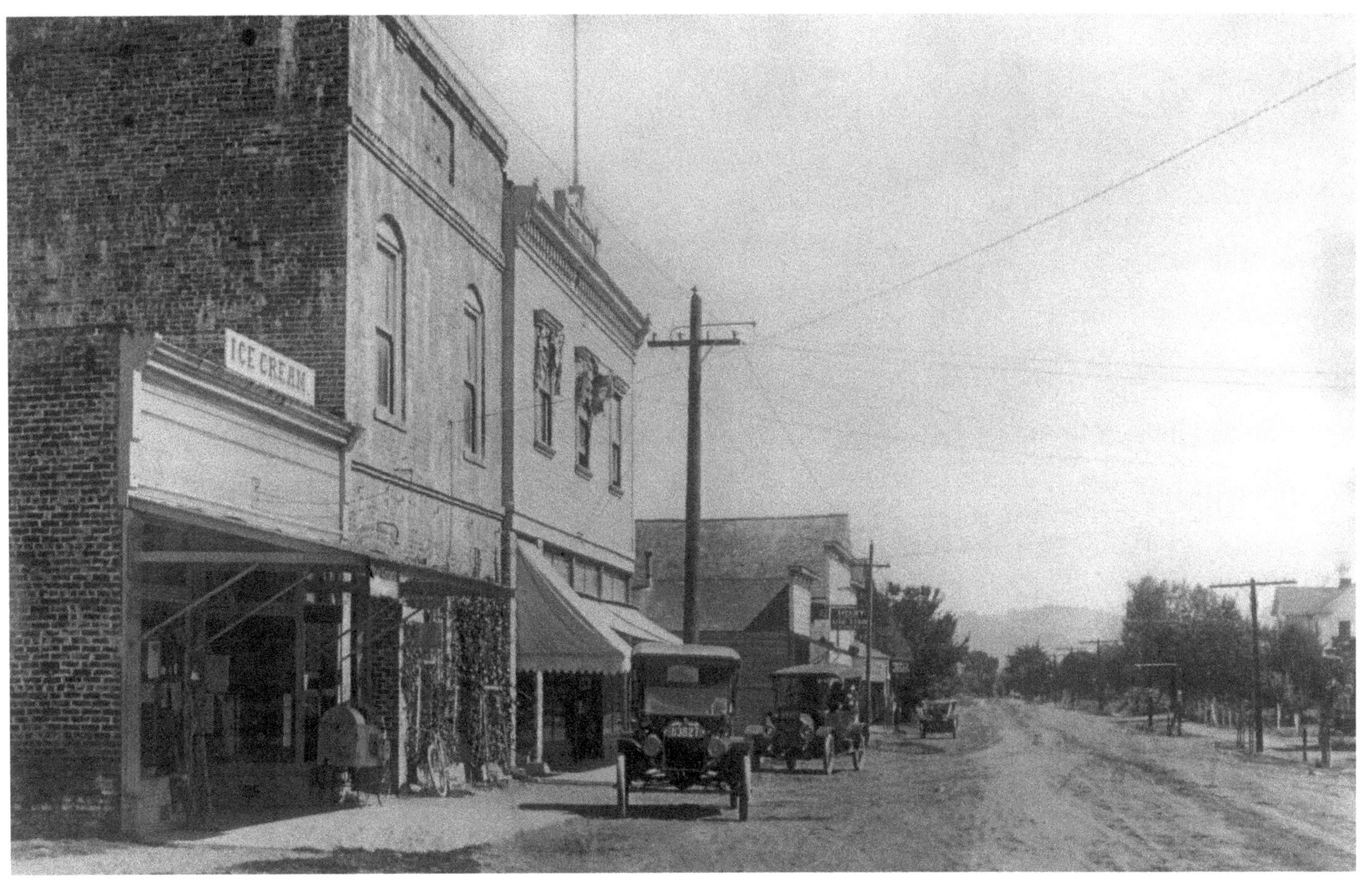

A wood-burner engine helped speed the hauling of redwood logs in the Duncans Mills area around 1915. The man with the beard was William Fraser. Orren Smith was the locomotive engineer, and his wife was beside him.

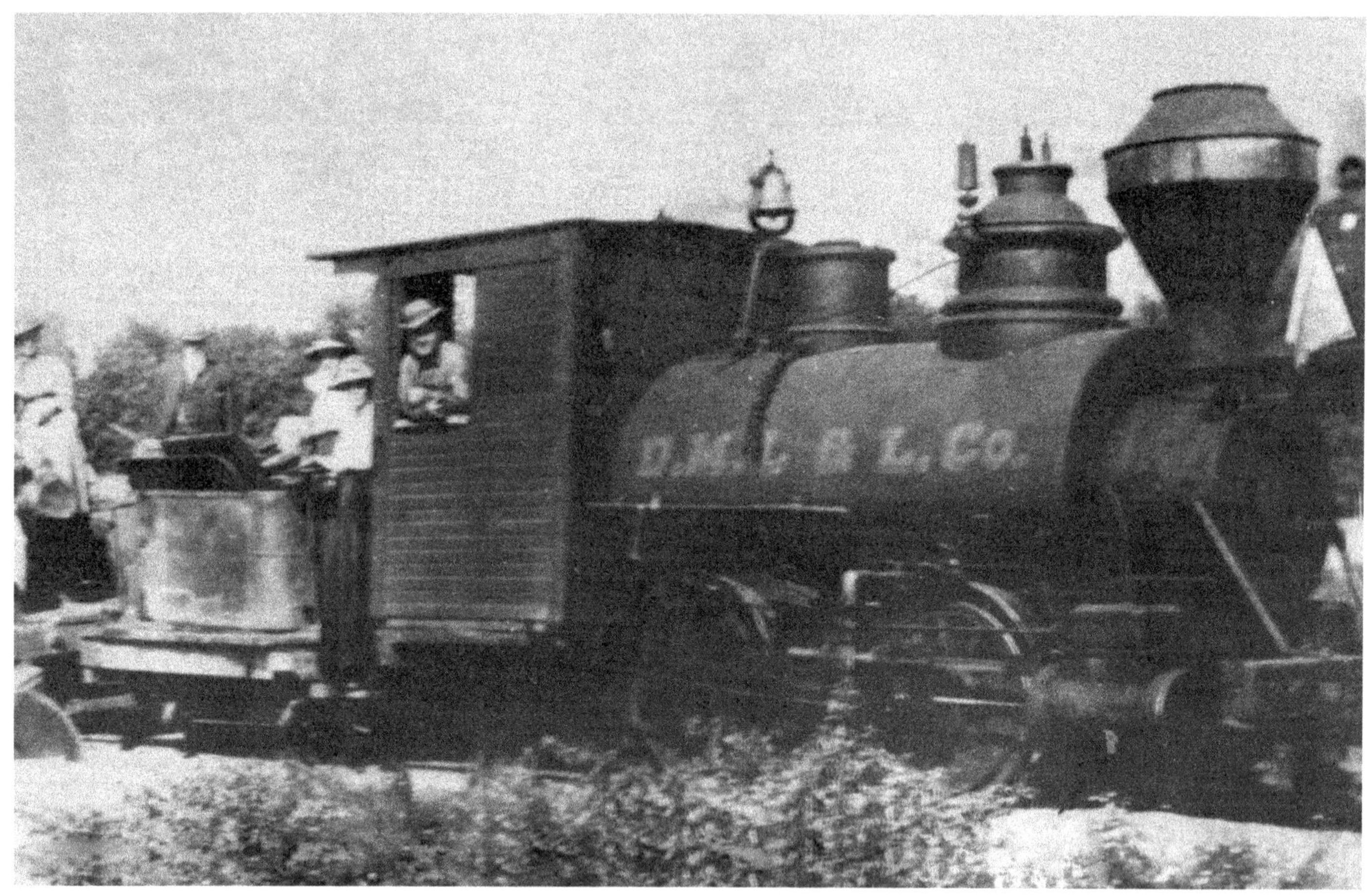

The waterway out of Petaluma carried goods to the heavily populated urban area in and around San Francisco. Flat-bottomed scows were a frequent sight on the Petaluma River, carrying hay and other products. The boats were the workhorses of the bay, moving in the early days on wind and tide, but at a later time they were powered by internal combustion engines. Growth of the trucking industry put the hardy little boats out of business.

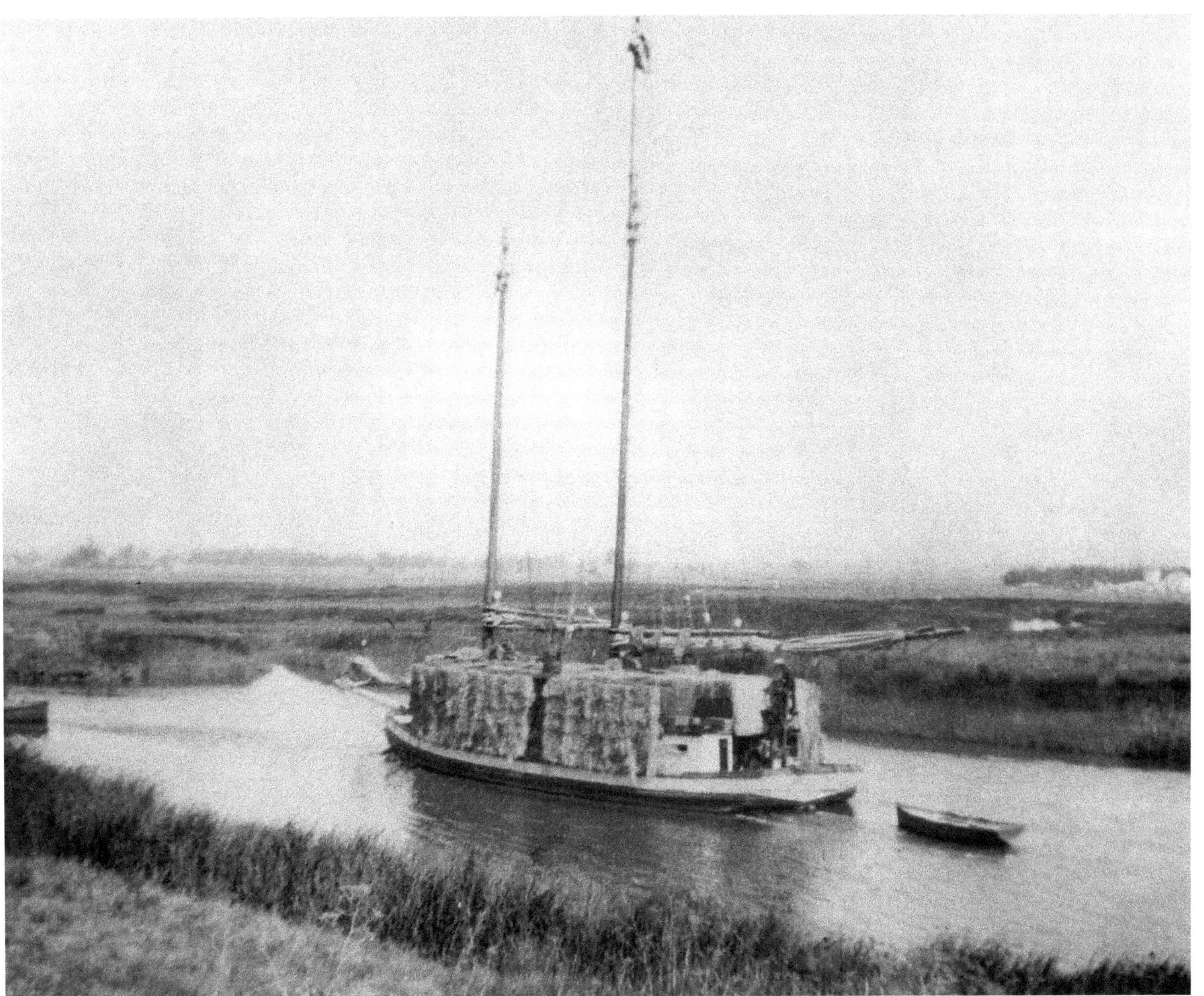

War came and many young men from Sonoma County left to join the conflict in Europe in 1917–18. Lending support on the home front, patriotic Petalumans turned out in large numbers for the Fourth of July parade. The viewers cheered mightily as bands, floats and marchers crossed the Washington Street Bridge, the link between the "east" and "west" sides of the Egg City.

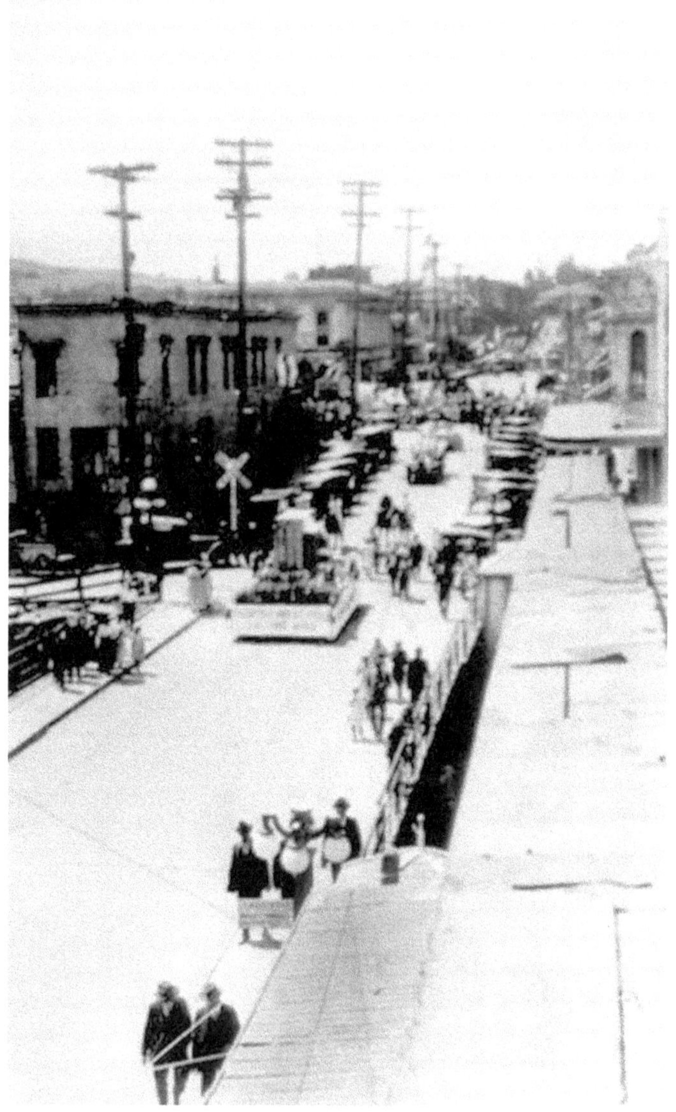

This scene on the corner of 4th Street and Mendocino Avenue wouldn't last much longer. The Rosenberg family, who already operated a department store, decided to construct the biggest office building between San Francisco and Portland, a five-story-high, steel-frame structure that wiped out the Standard oil station and other buildings shown in this picture. The Woolworth Company and more than one hundred other clients moved in after the structure was completed in 1922.

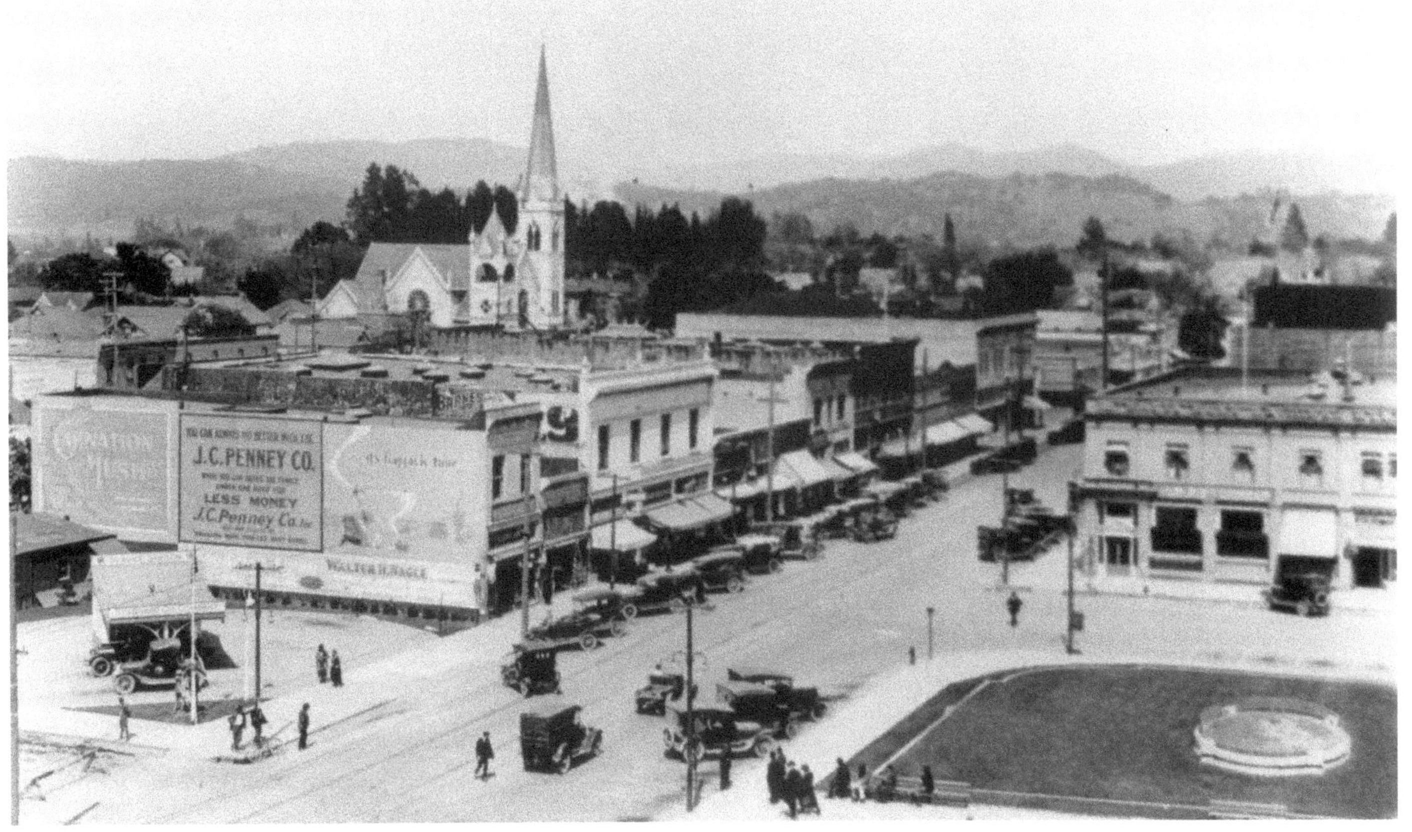

The dairy industry grew rapidly in the coastal areas of Sonoma County. Early in the twentieth century, milkers—often immigrants from Portugal and elsewhere—got up early and fought the persistent fog to tend their cows. The milkers included, from left, Charlie and Leo Gleason.

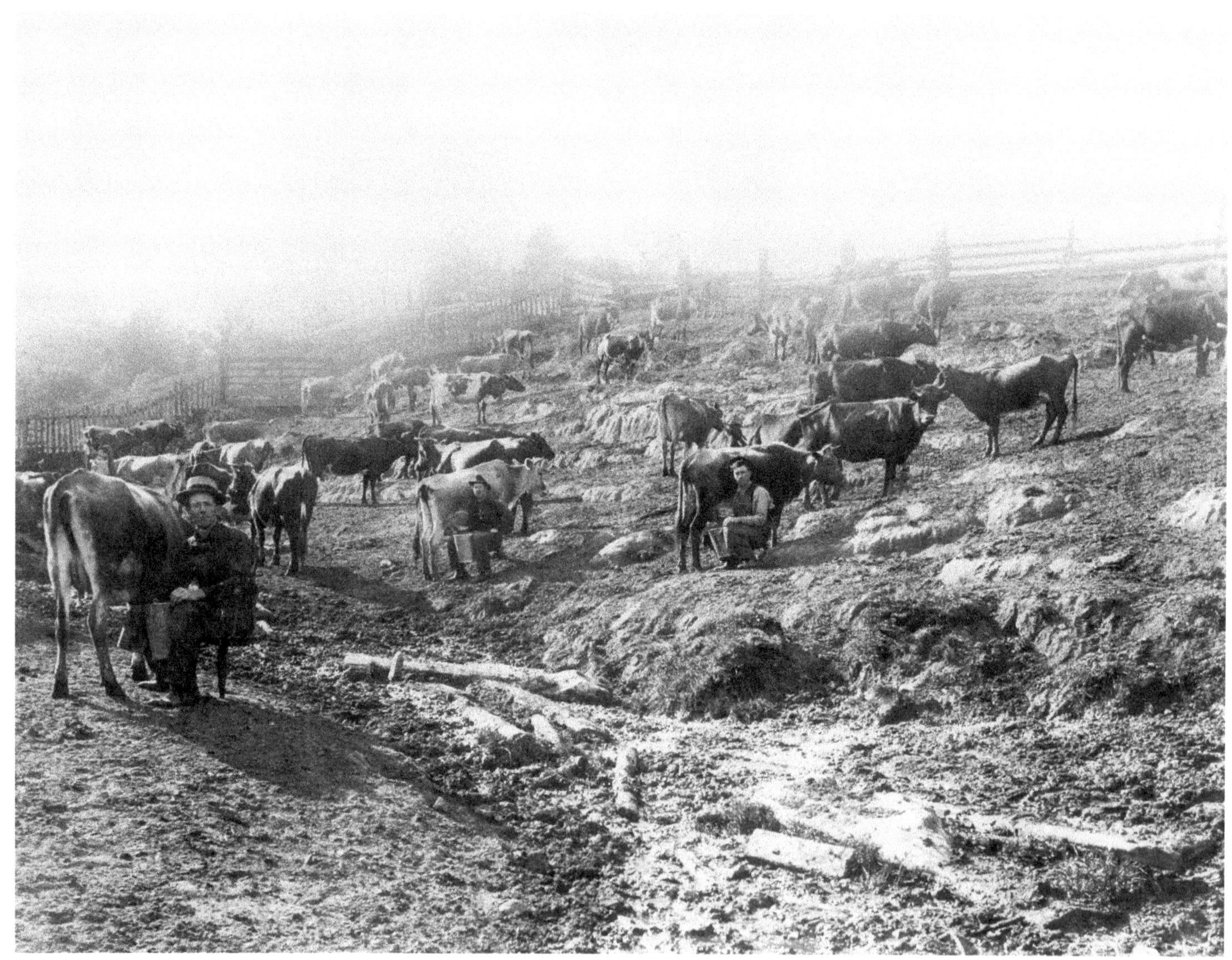

# Prohibition, Labor Conflicts, and a Bridge (1920–1939)

The imposition of Prohibition laws in 1920 was a jolt to Sonoma County's wine industry. While creative individuals worked on ways to get around the law, well over half of the county's wineries went under. The new law may have had a sobering effect on some, but it also triggered pitched battles between law enforcement and rumrunners and deceptive tactics by doctors who prescribed items such as a "hot claret wine gargle." A number of people ingested some foul-tasting liquids.

Razzle-dazzle promoters came along; H. W. (Bert) Kerrigan was one of the best. Small in stature, he made his first mark in the world as an Olympic high jumper, but in Petaluma, he was hired to promote the egg industry, which he did with innovative ideas such as an Egg Day wedding and the hiring of a "human rooster" to crow in a variety of fowl dialects. Charlie "Cash and Carry" Pyle organized Indian ultra-marathons in 1927 and 1928. Native American runners ran, jogged, and trotted 480 miles from San Francisco to Grants Pass, Oregon, spending much of their time on the glorious Redwood Highway that cut through Sonoma County.

Most of the population cheered the repeal of Prohibition in the 1930s. Winemakers set about rebuilding their industry. Still, the Depression hit hard and urban conflicts between business and labor spilled over into Sonoma County. The ugliest incident was the tarring and feathering of two Sonoma County "radicals" in 1935. The list of accused vigilantes included numerous prominent citizens.

Better news came in 1937 with the opening of the Golden Gate Bridge, promoted heavily by Santa Rosa banker Frank P. Doyle. He and his supporters argued the bridge would speed up communication and create progress and prosperity in Sonoma County.

Looking back more than seventy years later, it would be hard to deny the impact that the span has had in shaping life in the northern part of the state.

The Cloverdale Fire Department, located at 2nd and Commercial streets, recognized the need to modernize its operation when it took a major step toward fire safety in 1923. The city bought a used Model T fire engine from the city of Sebastopol. The city hall and jail were located in the rear of the fire hall. Cloverdale, considered in its early days to be the gateway to the north, was a takeoff point for Mendocino and Lake County as well as stage trips to the Geysers recreation area to the east.

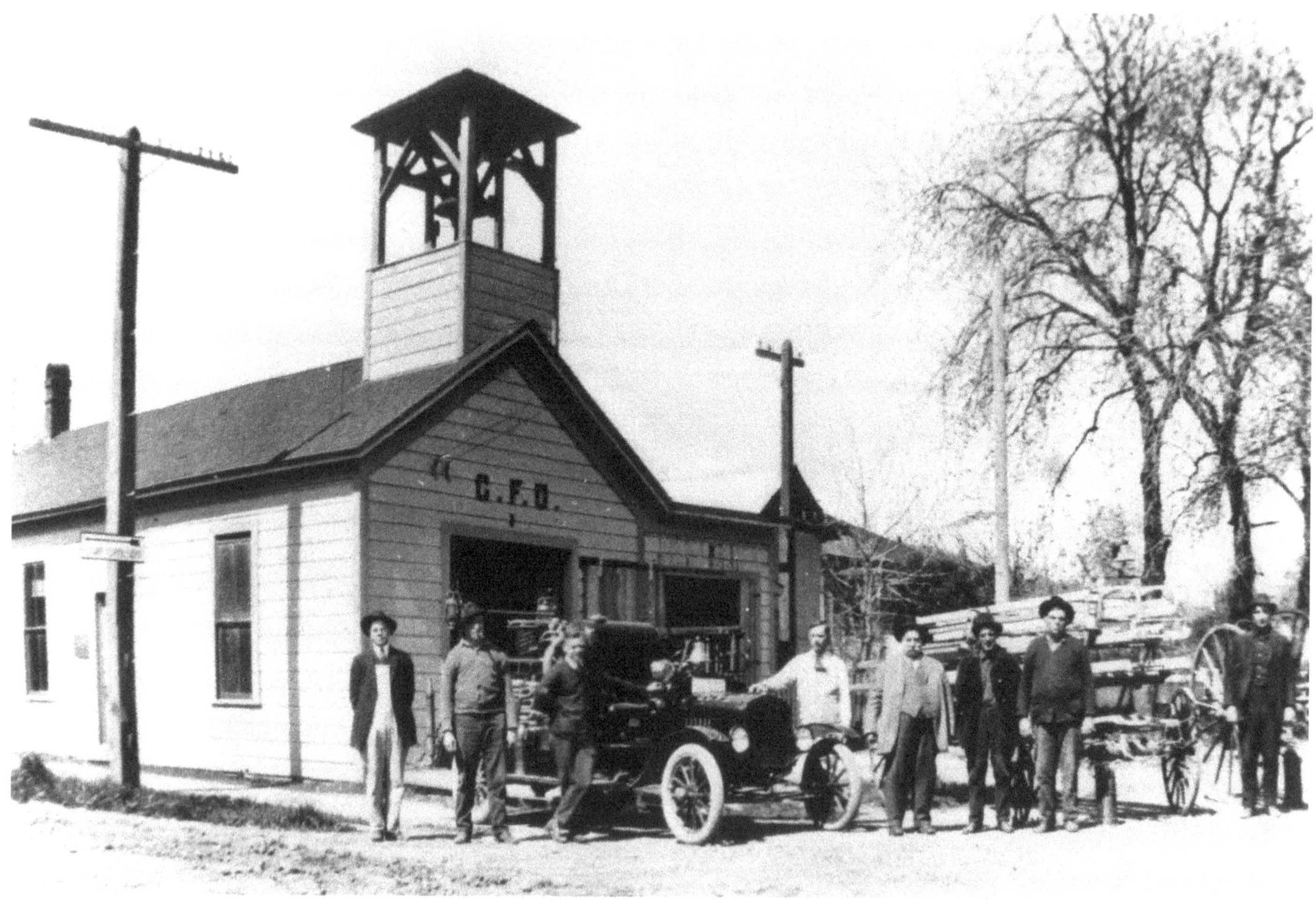

Among the features on West Street in Cloverdale in 1928 were the W. McGrath Grocery Store and Cloverdale Auto Supply. The community's economic strength was bolstered by a major citrus crop and the presence of the nearby winery at Asti, featuring the world's biggest wine vat. A Citrus Fair celebration took place each February.

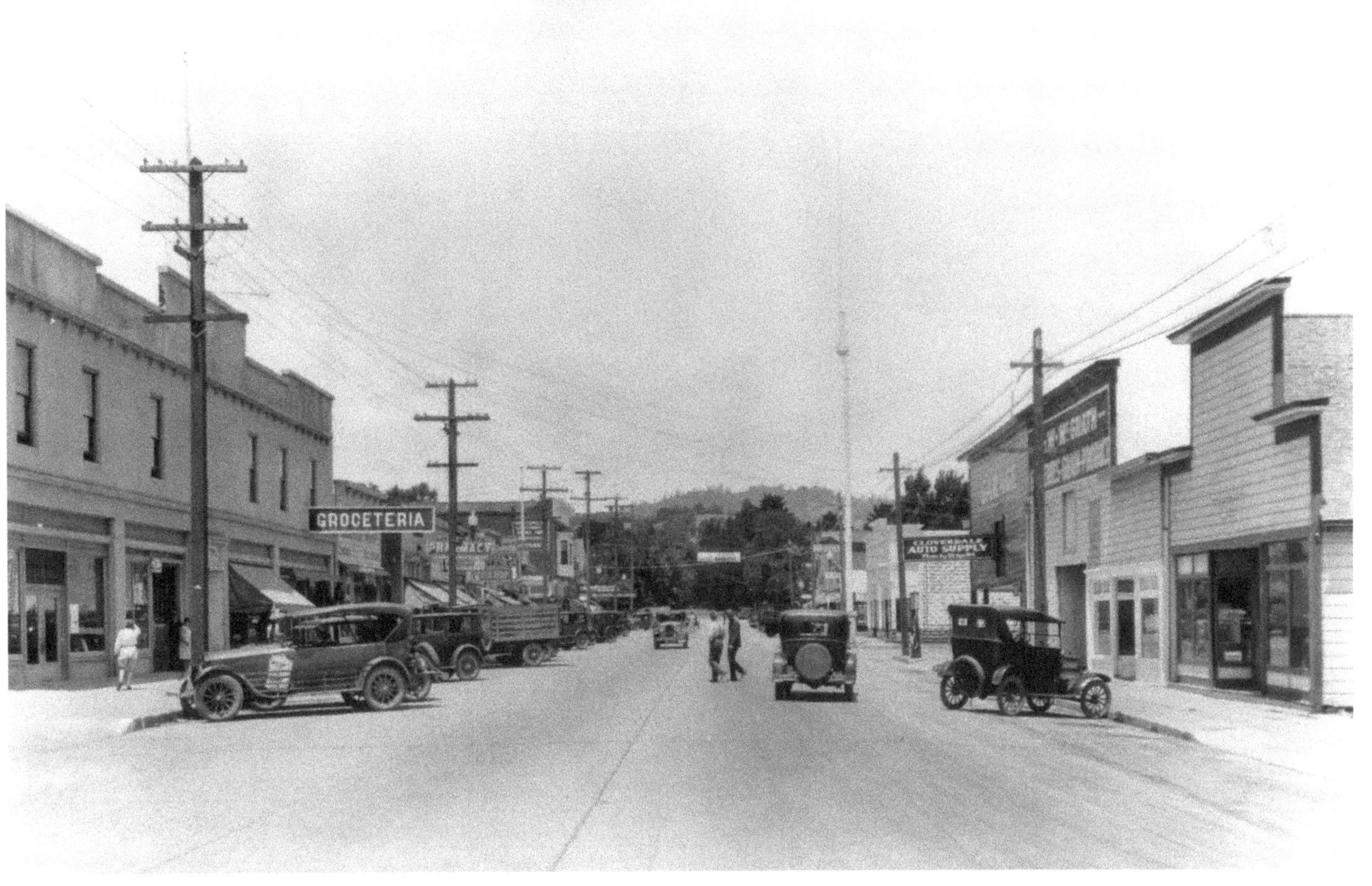

The eighth county courthouse in Santa Rosa, built after the 1906 earthquake, dominated downtown architecture in Santa Rosa in the mid-1920s. After the 1906 quake destroyed the stately courthouse erected in the 1880s, local officials put up two temporary structures before planning for a permanent replacement.

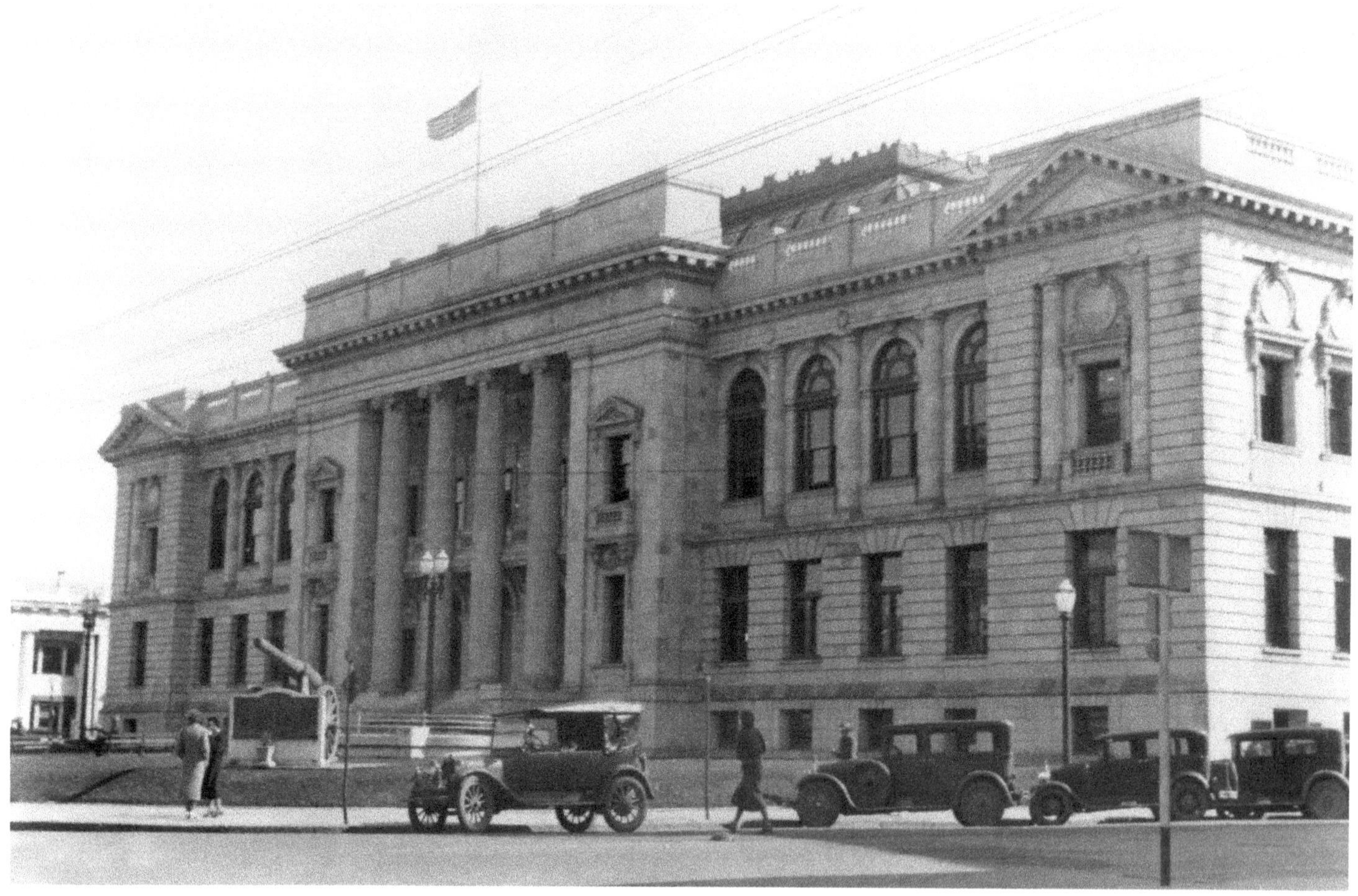

The Occidental Hotel had a one-hundred-year run as one of Santa Rosa's major hotels. It was called the Centennial or Palace in the early days and was owned by George Tupper, one of the most prominent Republicans in town. The Occidental was flattened in the 1906 earthquake but was up and running again under the ownership of Frank, John, and Charles Bane, who bought it in 1911. The Occidental and the Overton (later the Santa Rosa Hotel) competed on opposite corners of 4th and B streets until the 1970s.

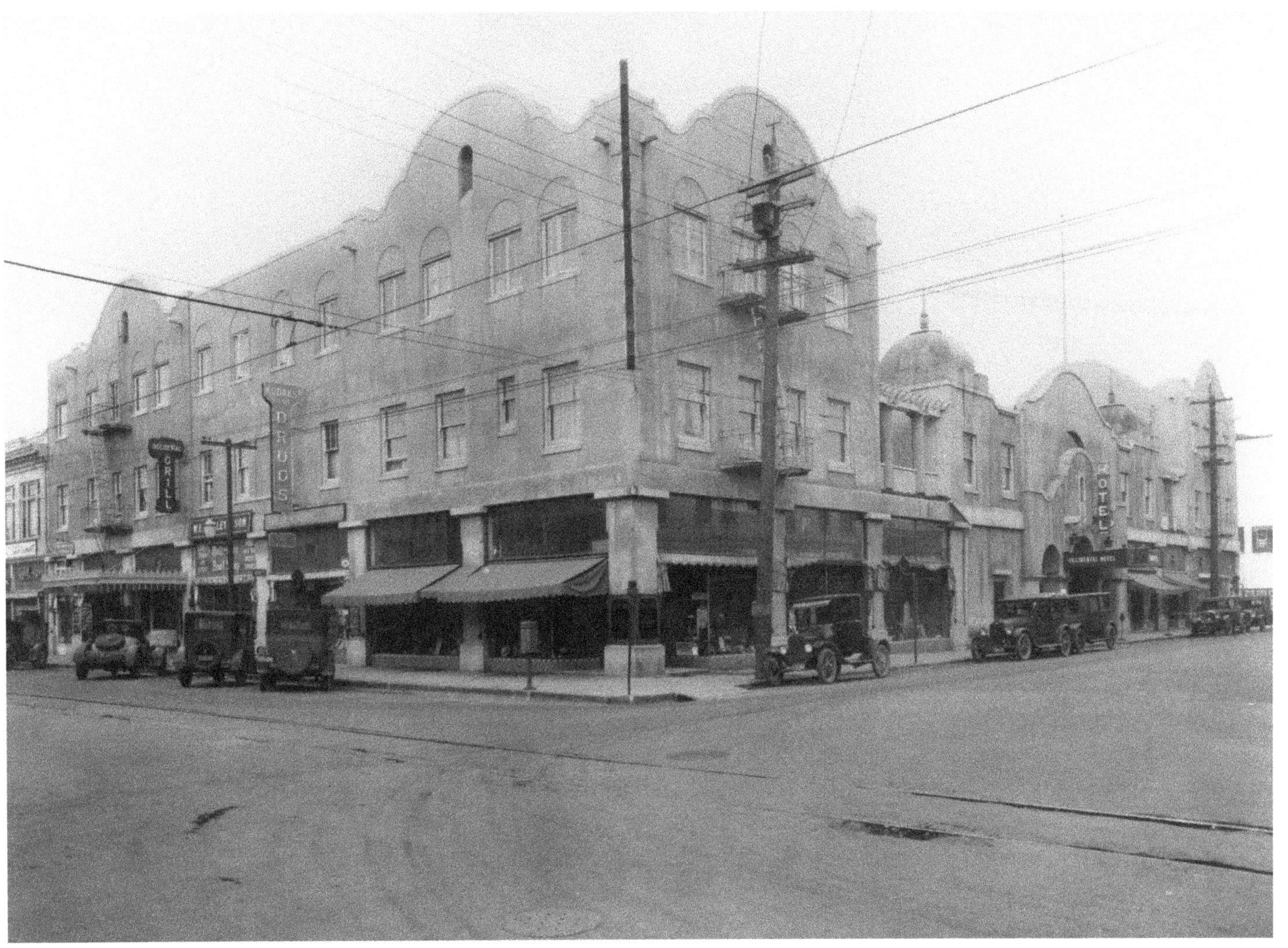

W. E. Barber's Shell Station at 5th and B streets or Richardson and Wendt auto repairs on 2nd Street provided assistance for drivers in the downtown area. M. E. Richardson and D. W. Wendt ran the auto shop. Catron Jackson and J. R. Azvedo worked from Jackson's Neon Sign Co. on 2nd Street.

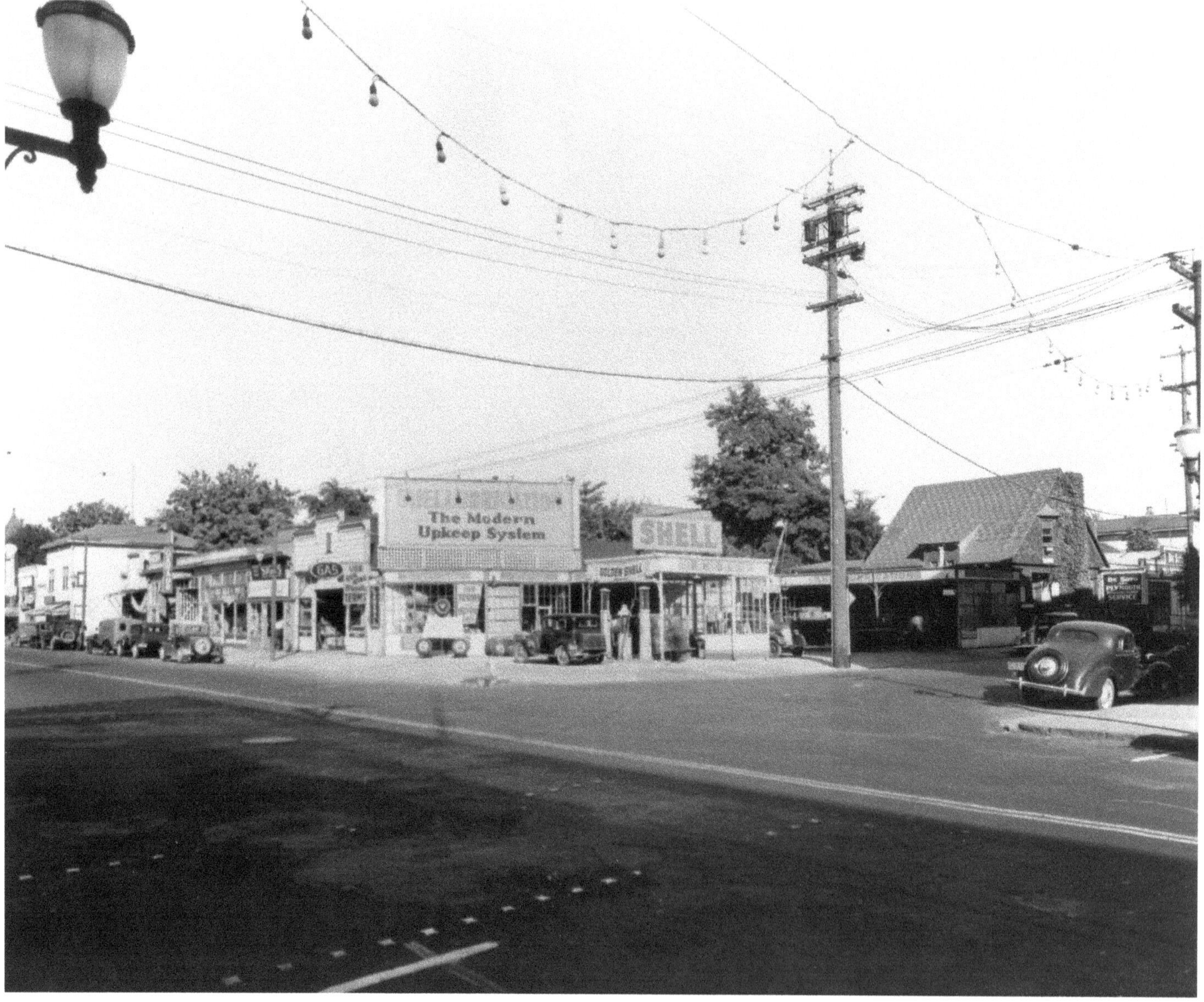

Sonoma County enjoyed the prosperity of the late 1920s with good crops and low prices at the grocery stores. The store pictured here was not identified, but at Skaggs Cash and Carry Markets' two Santa Rosa locations, picnic hams were nineteen cents a pound, potatoes eighty-nine cents per fifty-pound sack, oranges forty-seven cents a dozen, and pork chops thirty cents a pound in those halcyon days of 1928.

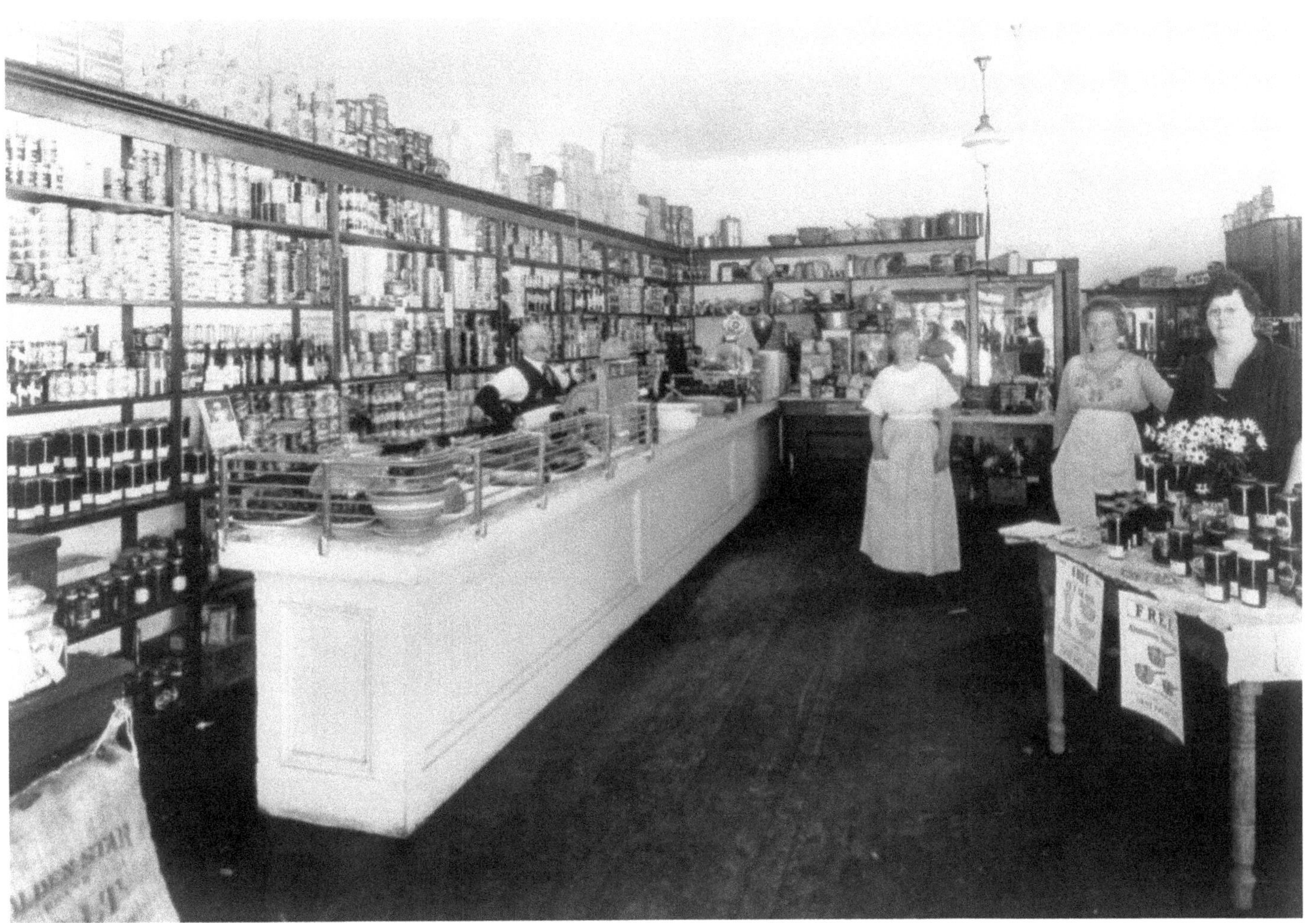

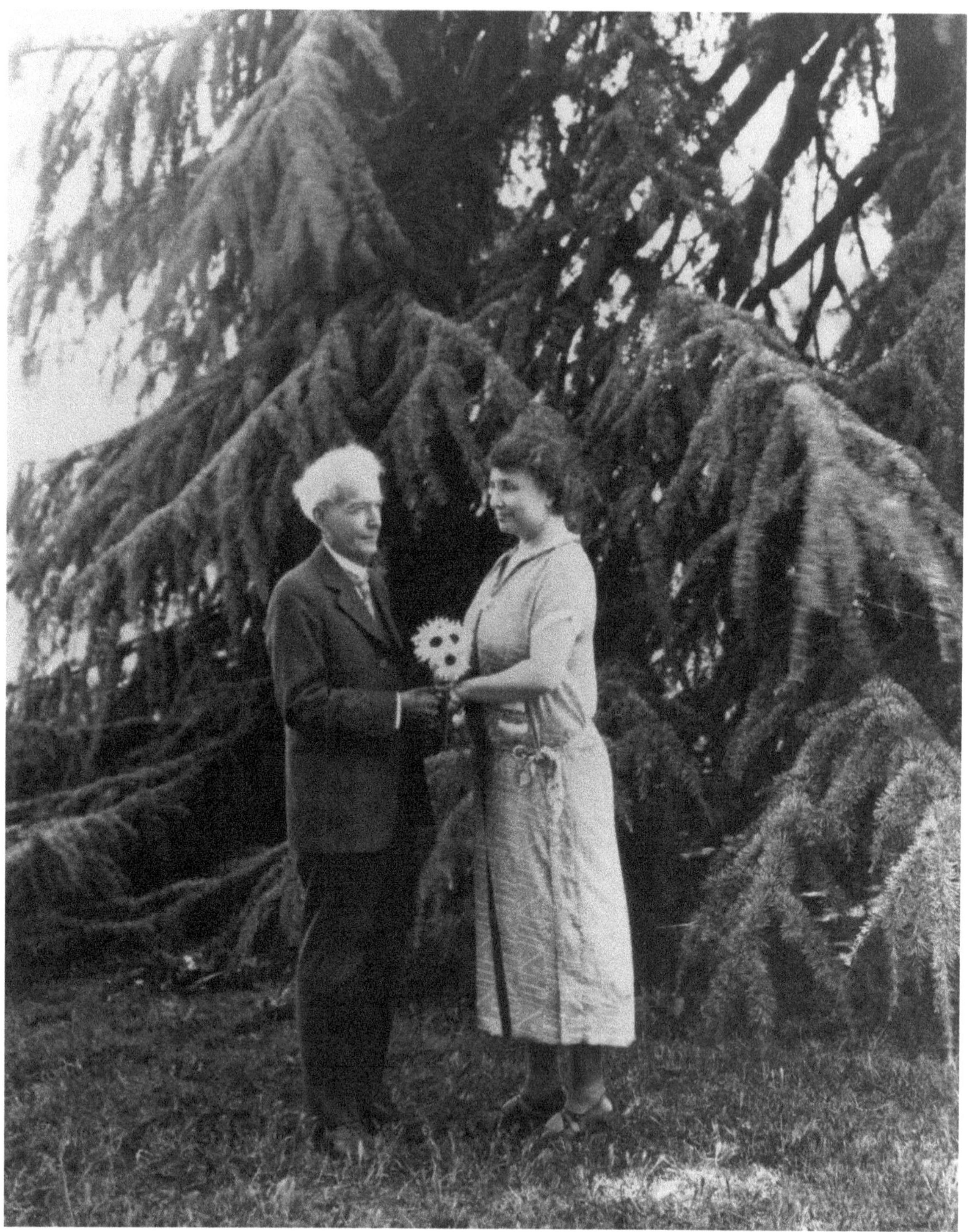

The innovative botanist Luther Burbank tinkered with plants and flowers through much of his life but took time out to meet with numerous people who came to check out the man and his experimental work. Helen Keller, spokesperson for the blind, was welcomed by Burbank during a visit in 1925. In 1915, inventor Thomas Edison and industrialists Henry Ford and Harvey Firestone came to Santa Rosa to share views with Burbank.

Robert "Believe or Not" Ripley went on to international fame after a childhood spent studying in the Santa Rosa school system. He often gave credit for his success to his mentor, the intrepid Frances O'Meara (below, with Ripley), who taught for fifty years in the Santa Rosa schools.

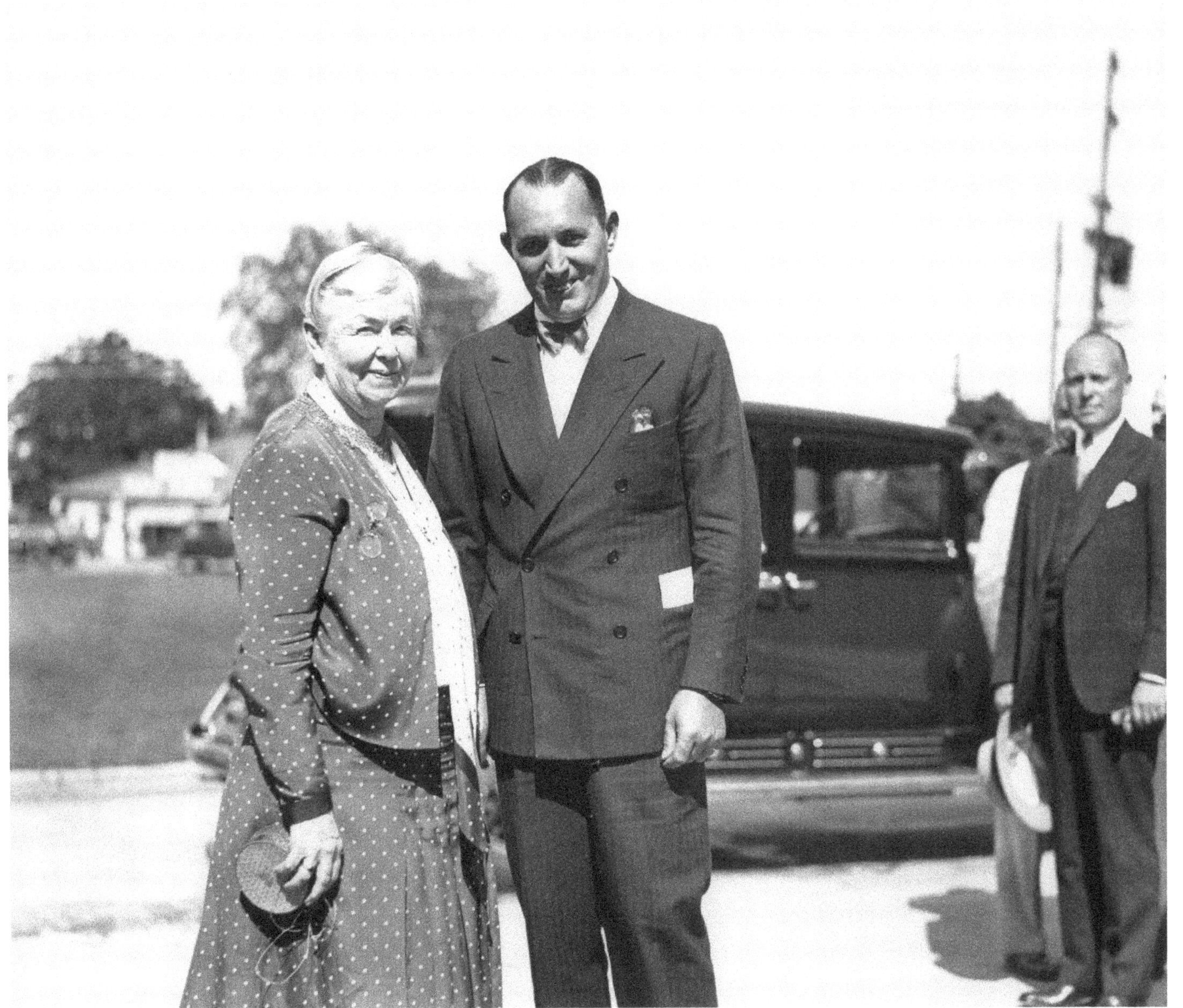

Talking pictures came along in the 1920s, enhancing indoor entertainment for young and old. The California Theater at 434 B Street in Santa Rosa, which presented movies and live vaudeville acts, made a smooth shift from silent movies to talkies. Admission at the time was 15 cents for adults, 10 cents for children. Later, Alfred Hitchcock and other moviemakers picked Sonoma County to film such hits as *Shadow of a Doubt* and *The Birds.*

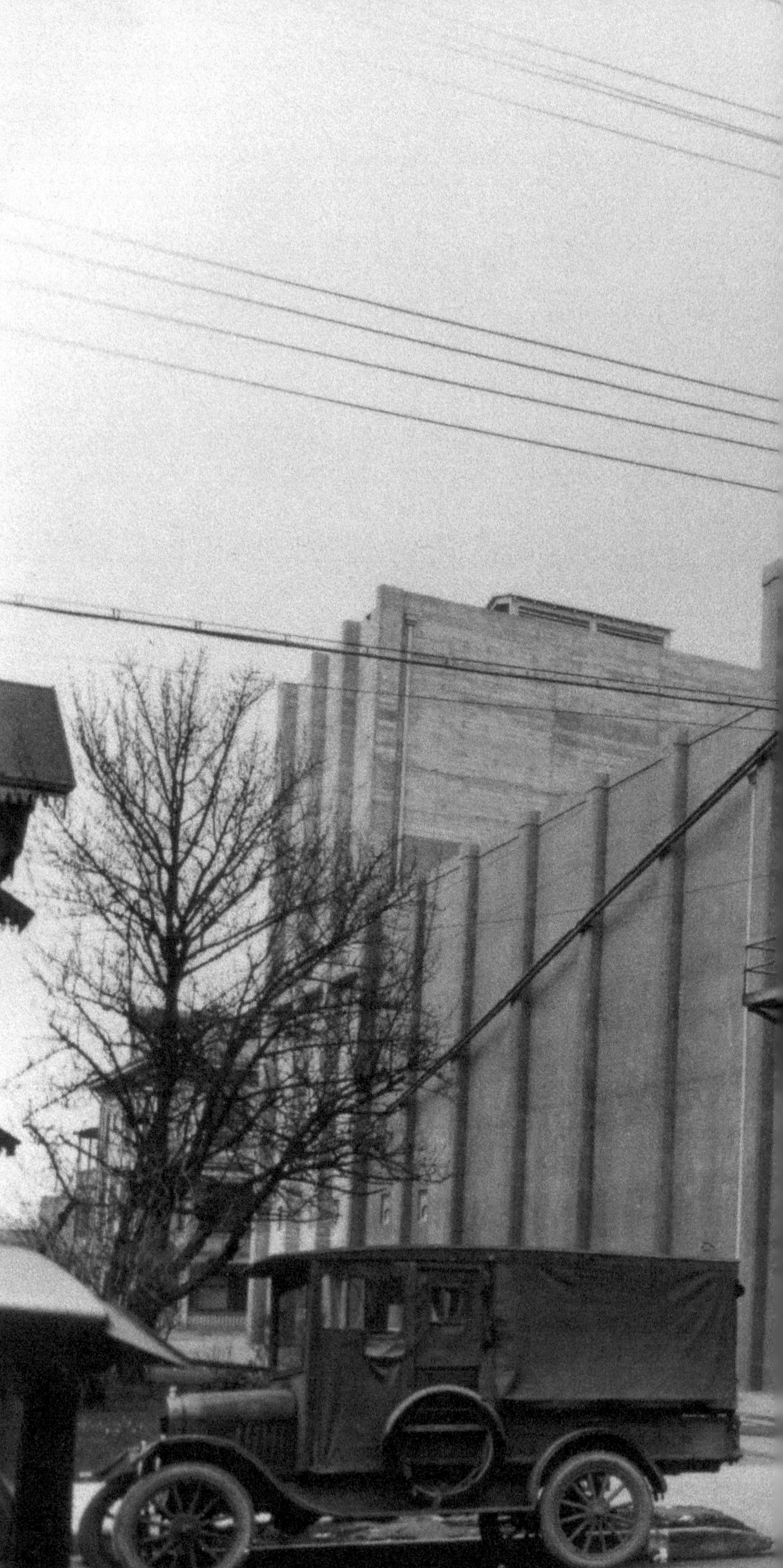

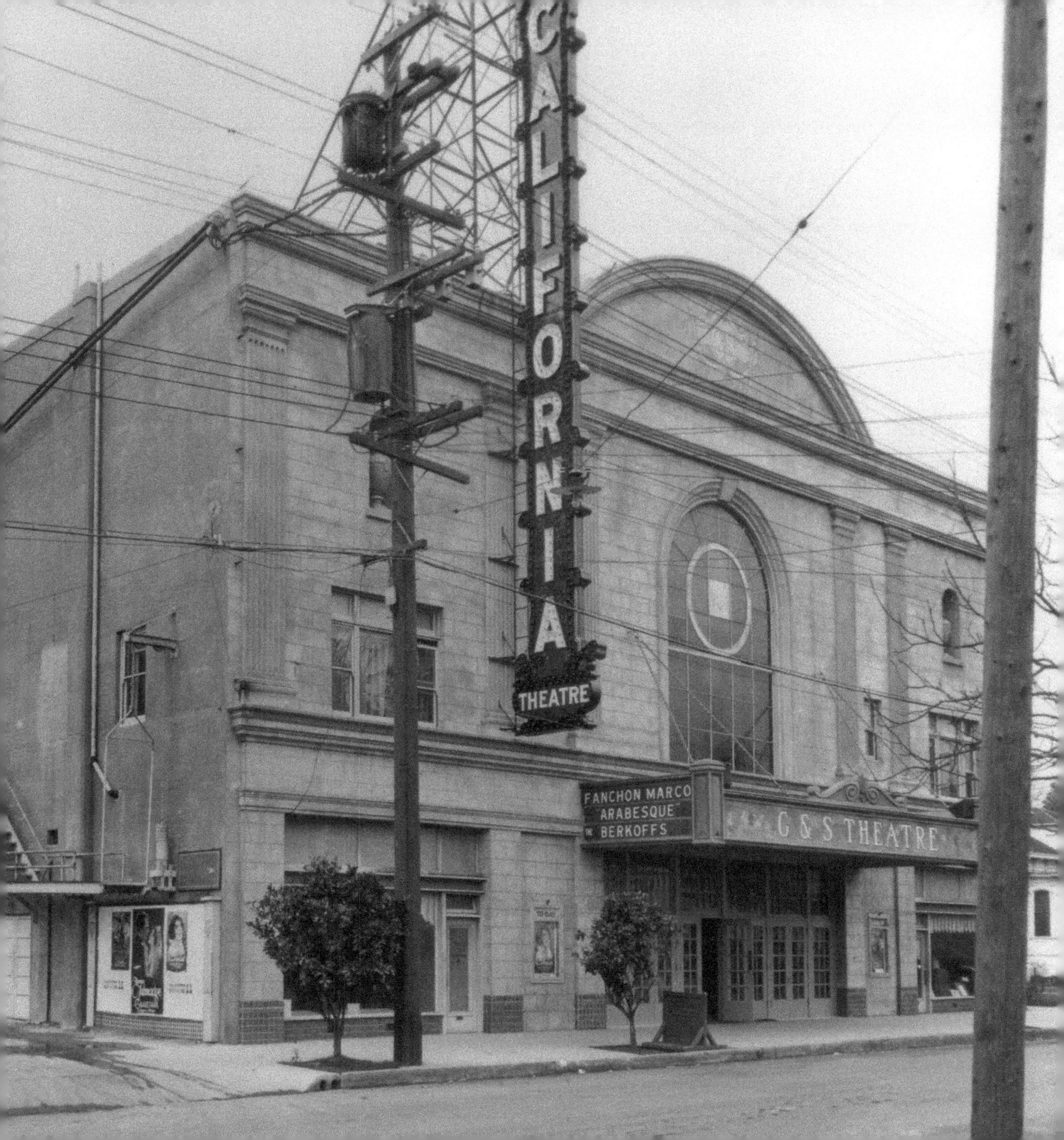
CALIFORNIA
THEATRE
FANCHON MARCO
"ARABESQUE"
BERKOFFS
G & S THEATRE

Petaluma hired H. W. (Bert) Kerrigan to promote the egg industry in the 1920s, and promote it he did. Kerrigan, shown holding his daughter Herleon while at the wheel of a classy Studebaker, concocted numerous stunts to keep himself and Petaluma in the headlines. There were Egg Day weddings, leafleting of San Francisco by plane, young men and women in yellow-and-white chicken costumes, and much more.

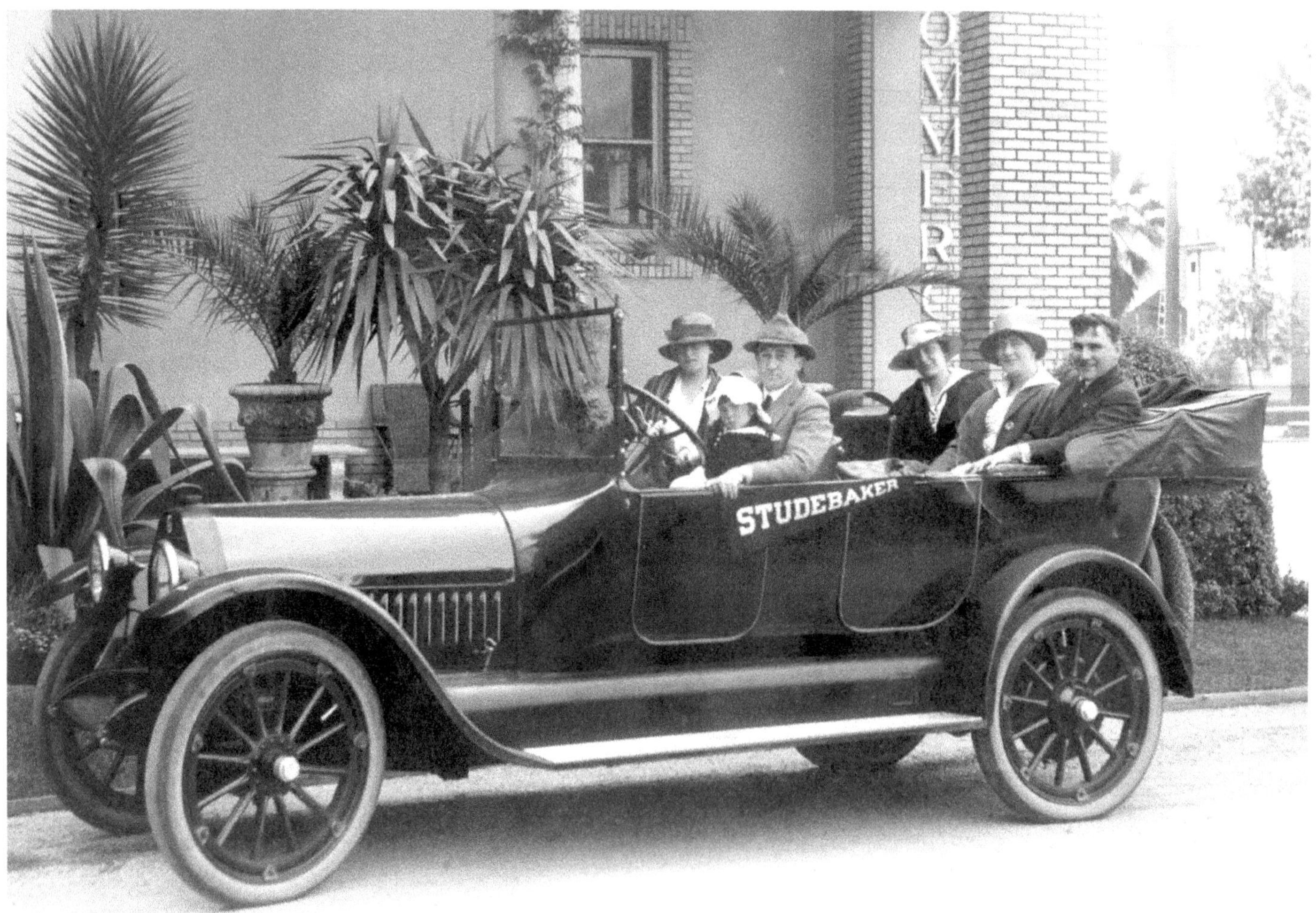

The egg boom centered in and around Petaluma where, in 1921 for example, the number of eggs shipped jumped from 22 million dozens to 26 million dozens in one year. Customers in the 1920s were located in such cities as New York City, London, Buenos Aires and Tokyo. Poultry prosperity spread through much of the county. F. J. Pool and Son, based in Windsor, got in on the good times, operating as a hay, grain, feed, poultry, and egg buyer in the 1920s.

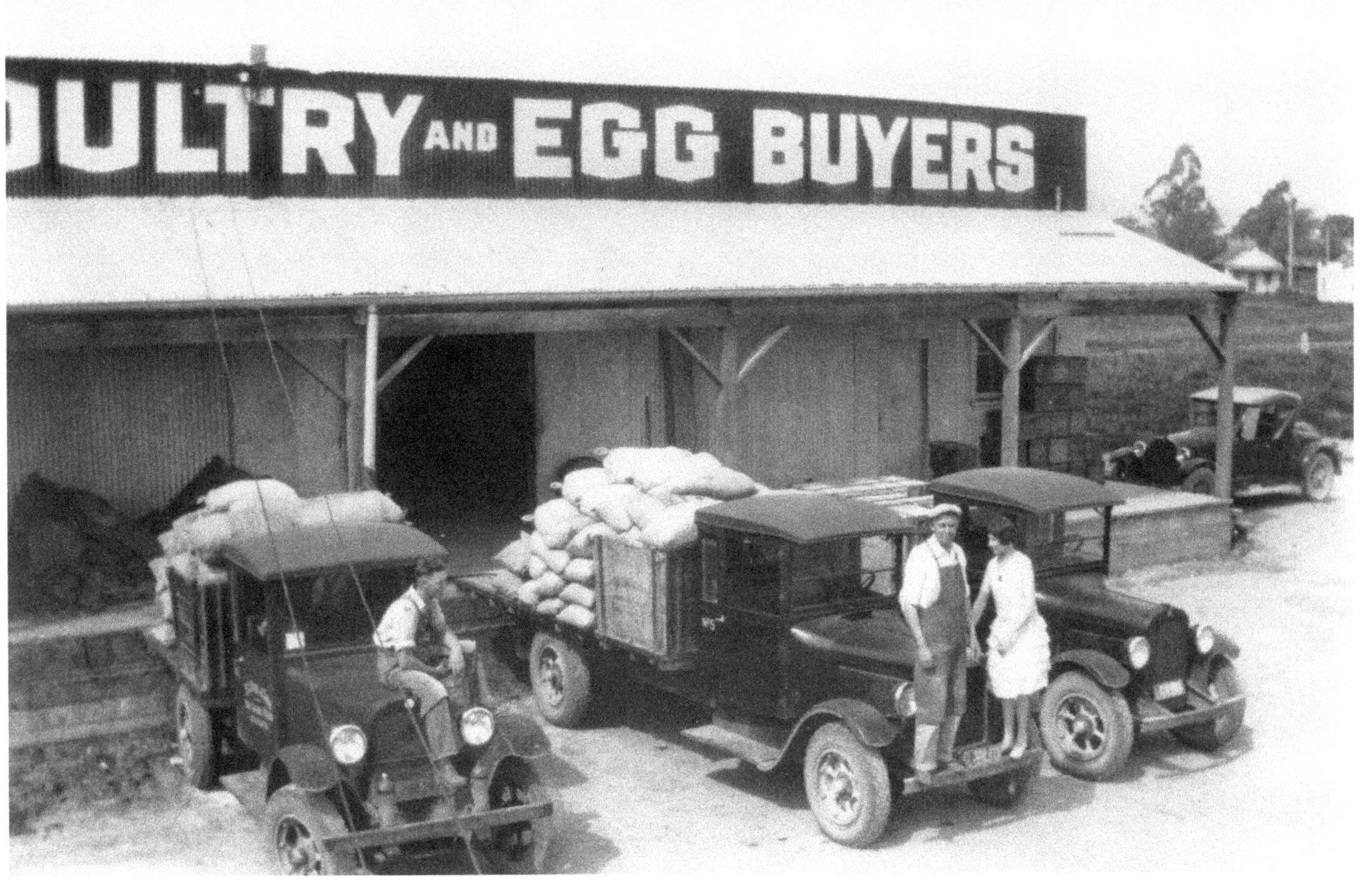

If it was a Kerrigan-created parade, the theme was sure to be chicken and eggs, and the display would be elaborate. In this case, four boys dressed like chickens pulled an egg float on Liberty Street in Petaluma in the early 1920s. Publicity man par excellence H. W. (Bert) Kerrigan helped put Petaluma's major products on the map.

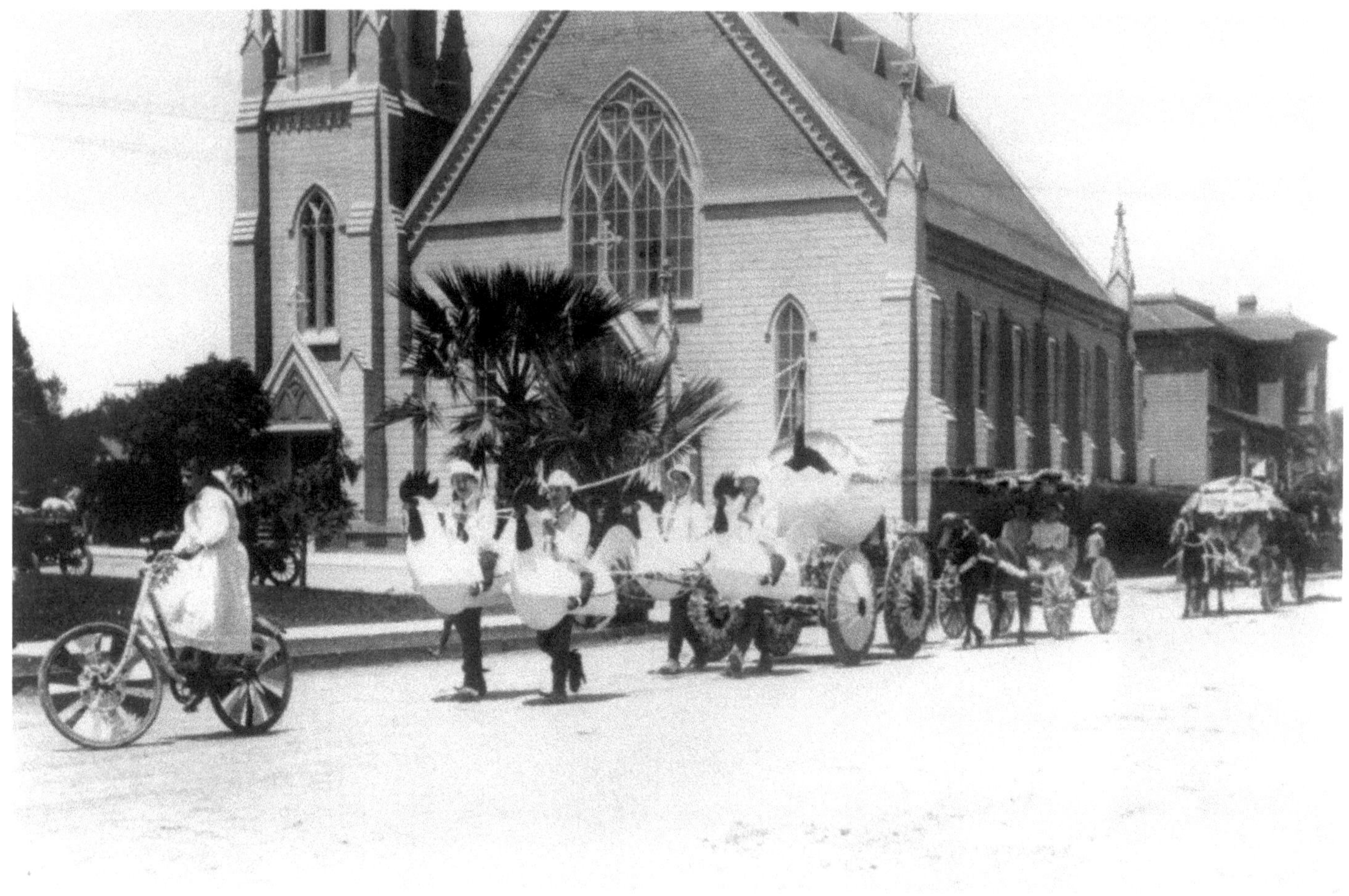

Six comely ladies from Petaluma took the parade route in a roadster decorated with flowers, streamers, and a large set of antlers around 1925.

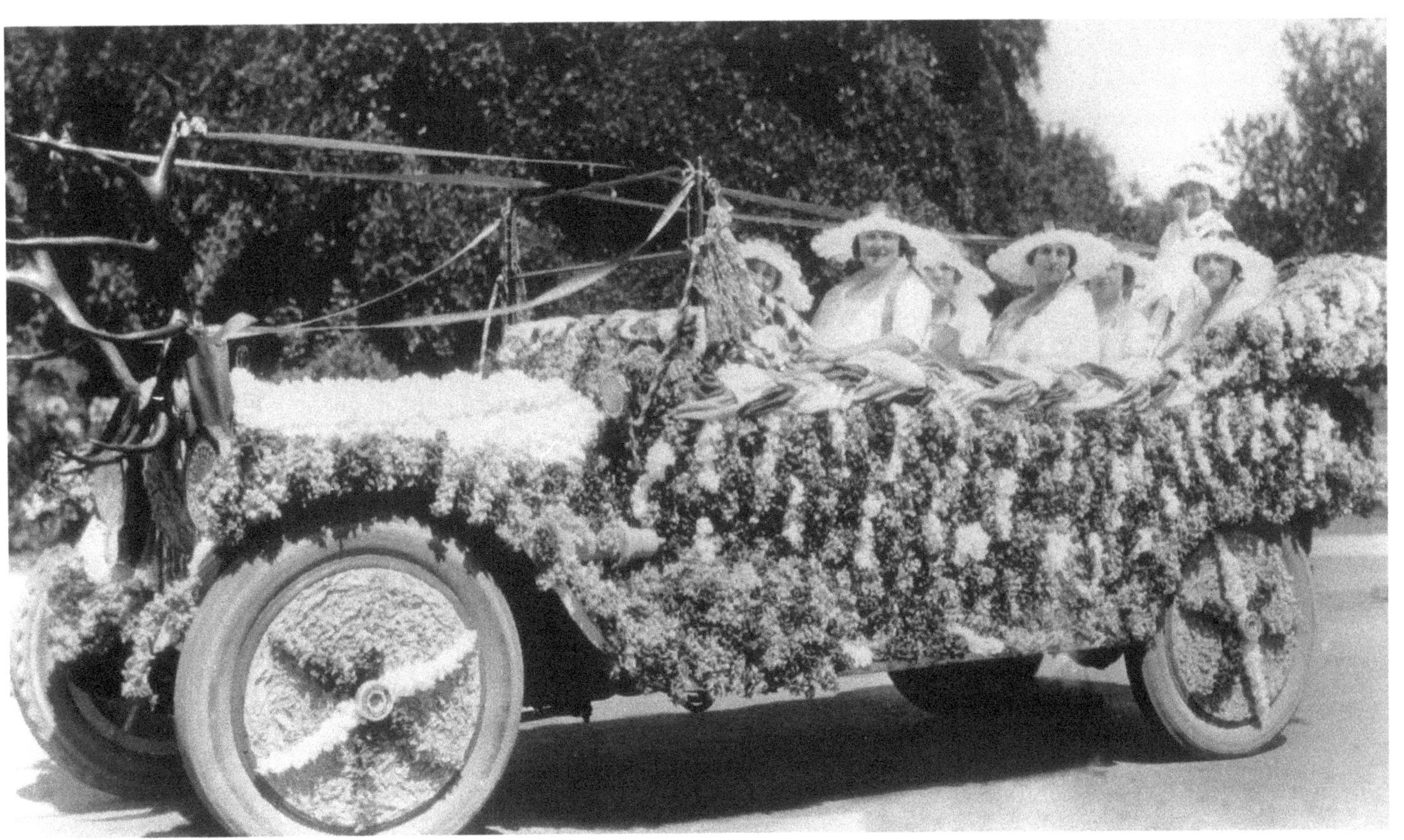

Parades remained a popular form of entertainment in Sonoma County, partly because they promoted local products and partly because they gave people a chance to enjoy a shared experience. Note the location of the license plate just below the windshield on the vehicle in this Petaluma parade of the 1920s.

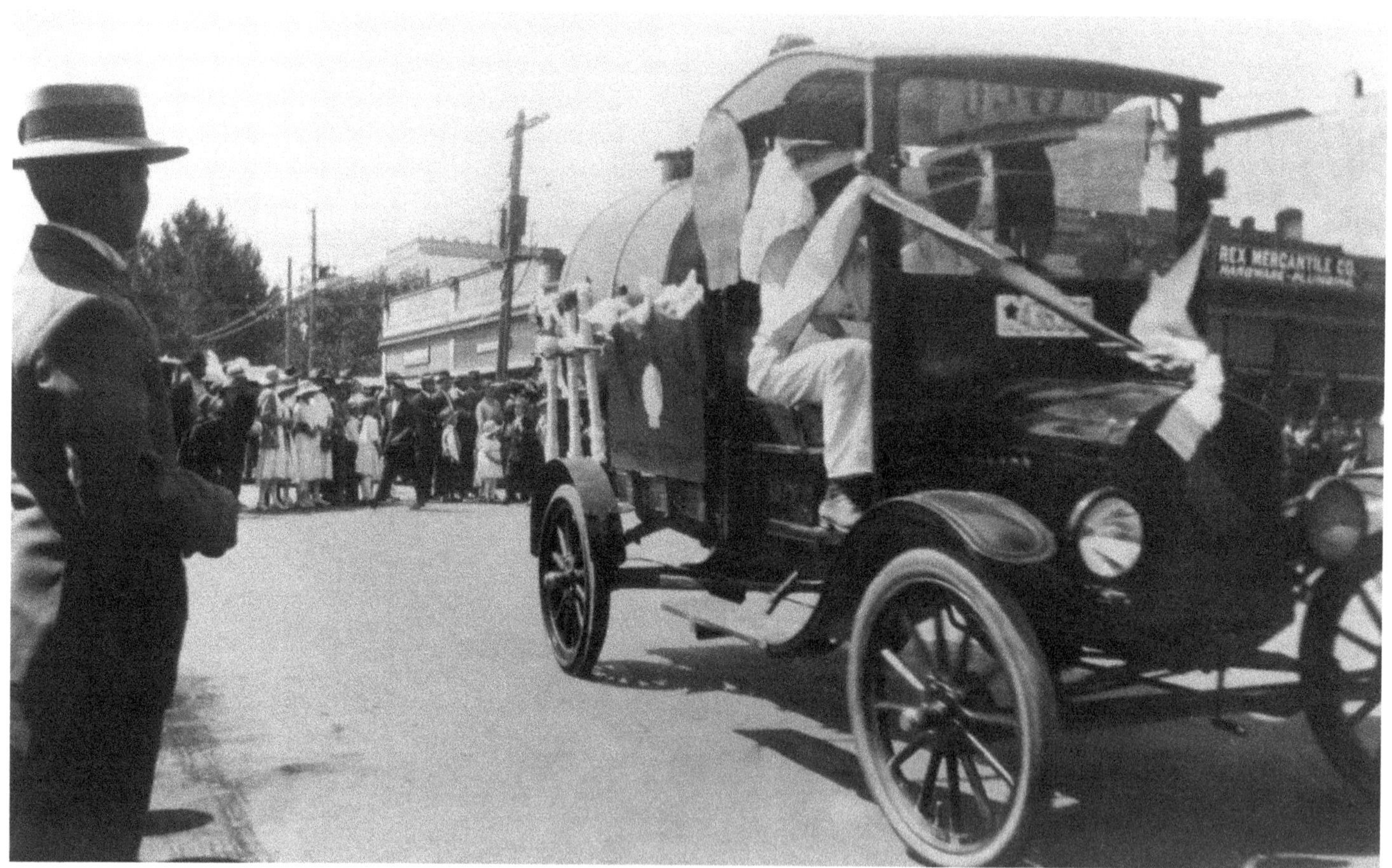

Vehicles didn't have much protection from the wind and rain, but the thrill of highway travel kept people on the roads in the 1920s. Newspapers gave prominent display to stories about bumpy roads, weekend car caravans, trips to the coast, and daredevil drivers. Many drivers, short on gas or plagued by a boiling radiator, made stops at the Shell station in Petaluma at 3rd and I streets, where Charles A. Kelley provided friendly service.

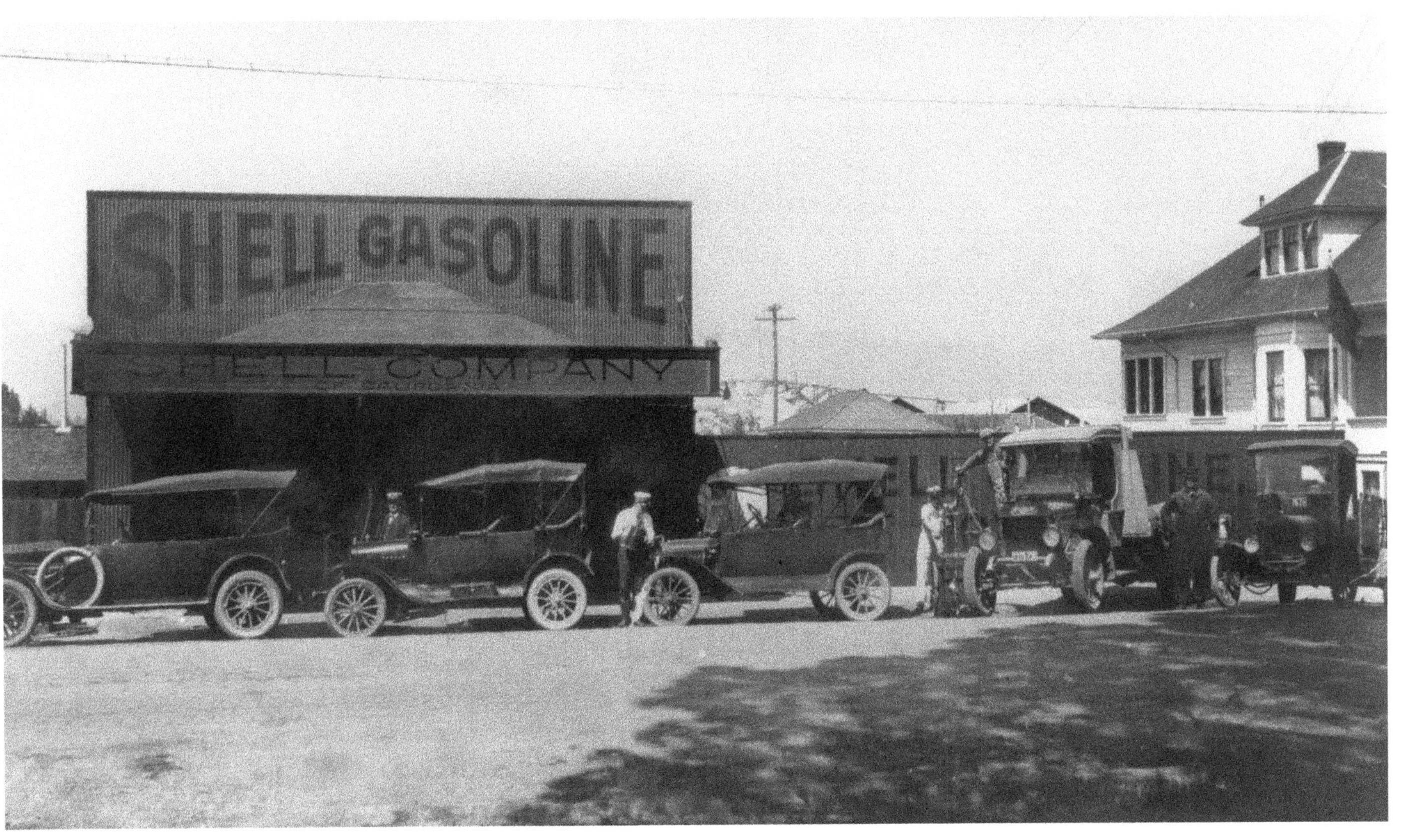

Elegant they weren't, but these trucks and trailers became moving vans in the 1920s for all sorts of items, including furniture, food, and, in this case, work clothes. An unidentified driver, accompanied by a bevy of young models in Western garb, pose near the train depot in Petaluma. Behind them, a sign depicts a similarly attired woman riding a giant chicken as if it were a horse, suggesting this scene may have been part of one of Kerrigan's promotions for the poultry industry. Portions of the historic Tivoli Hotel can be seen in the background.

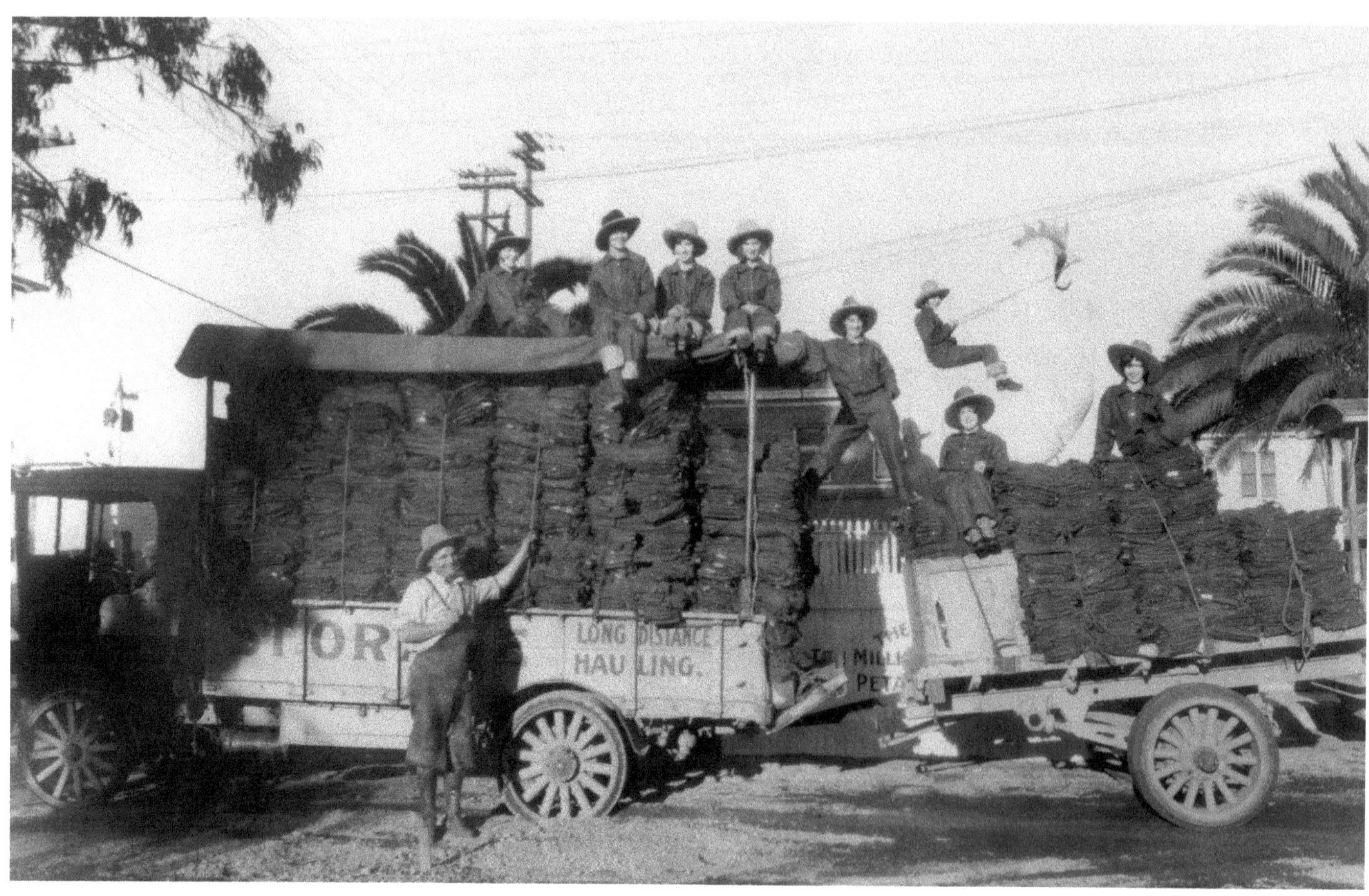

The lower Russian River at Rio Nido was home for many sun worshippers in 1925, who came from as far away as San Francisco to enjoy the sandy beaches, water sports, sunbathing, and evening dancing to popular orchestras.

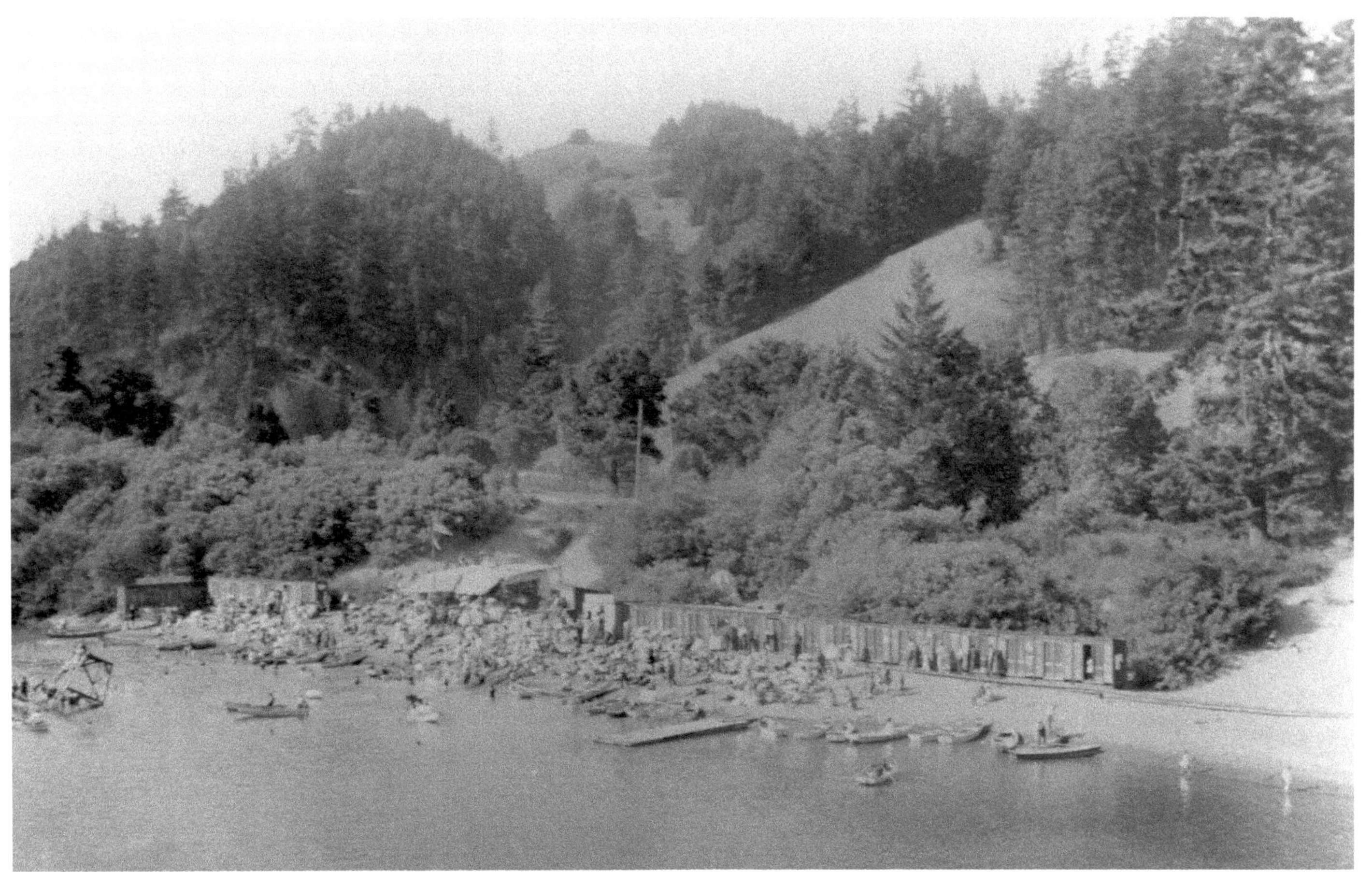

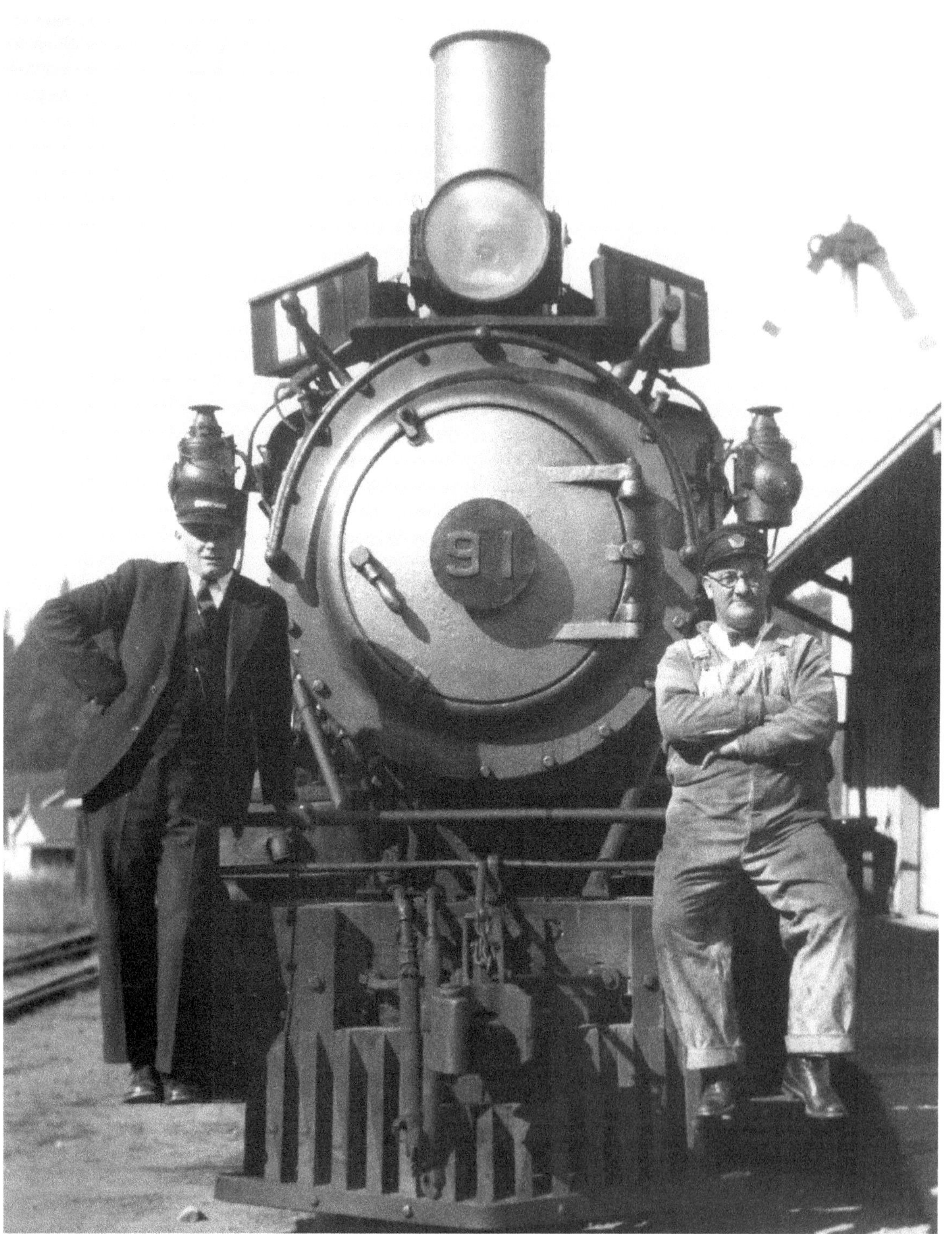


The Northwestern Pacific train # 58 served Occidental in the 1920s, but its days were numbered. Two years after this 1928 photo was taken, this route, which connected with the broad gauge system at Point Reyes, was discontinued. Flanking Engine 91 were the brakeman (left) and the express messenger, a Mr. Beach.

Occidental was a stopover point between the Russian River resorts around Guerneville and the Bay Area. It featured good Italian restaurants with plenty of minestrone, homemade ravioli, and apple fritters. Two of the local characters included Oreste Gonnella and his cousin Ray, members of a large extended family with roots in Italy. Cigars clutched in their mouths, the boys explained that they were just "hamming it up."

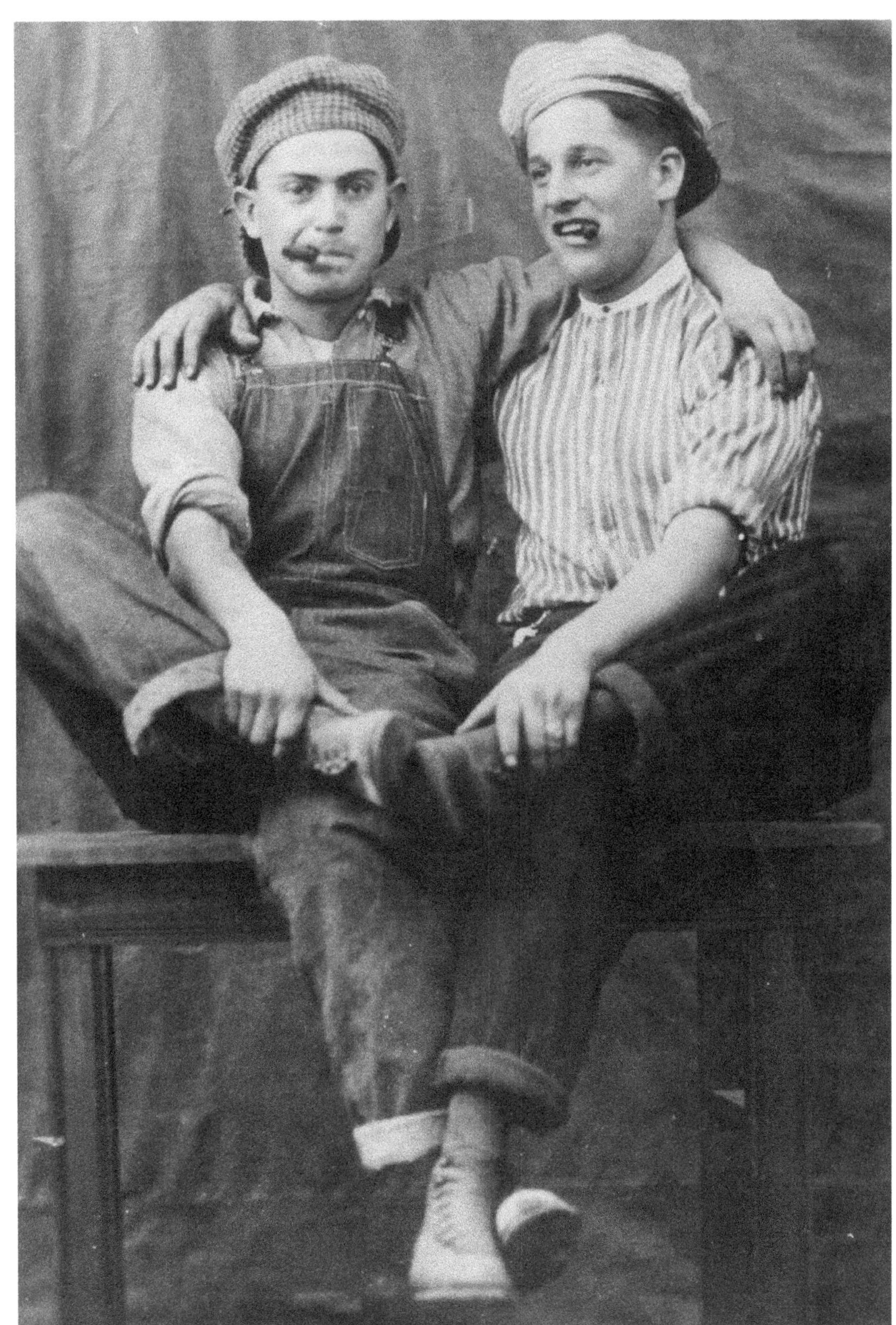

By the mid-1920s, modern technology in the form of sleek new bicycles helped the children at Windsor School put the pedal to the metal and make it home in record time.

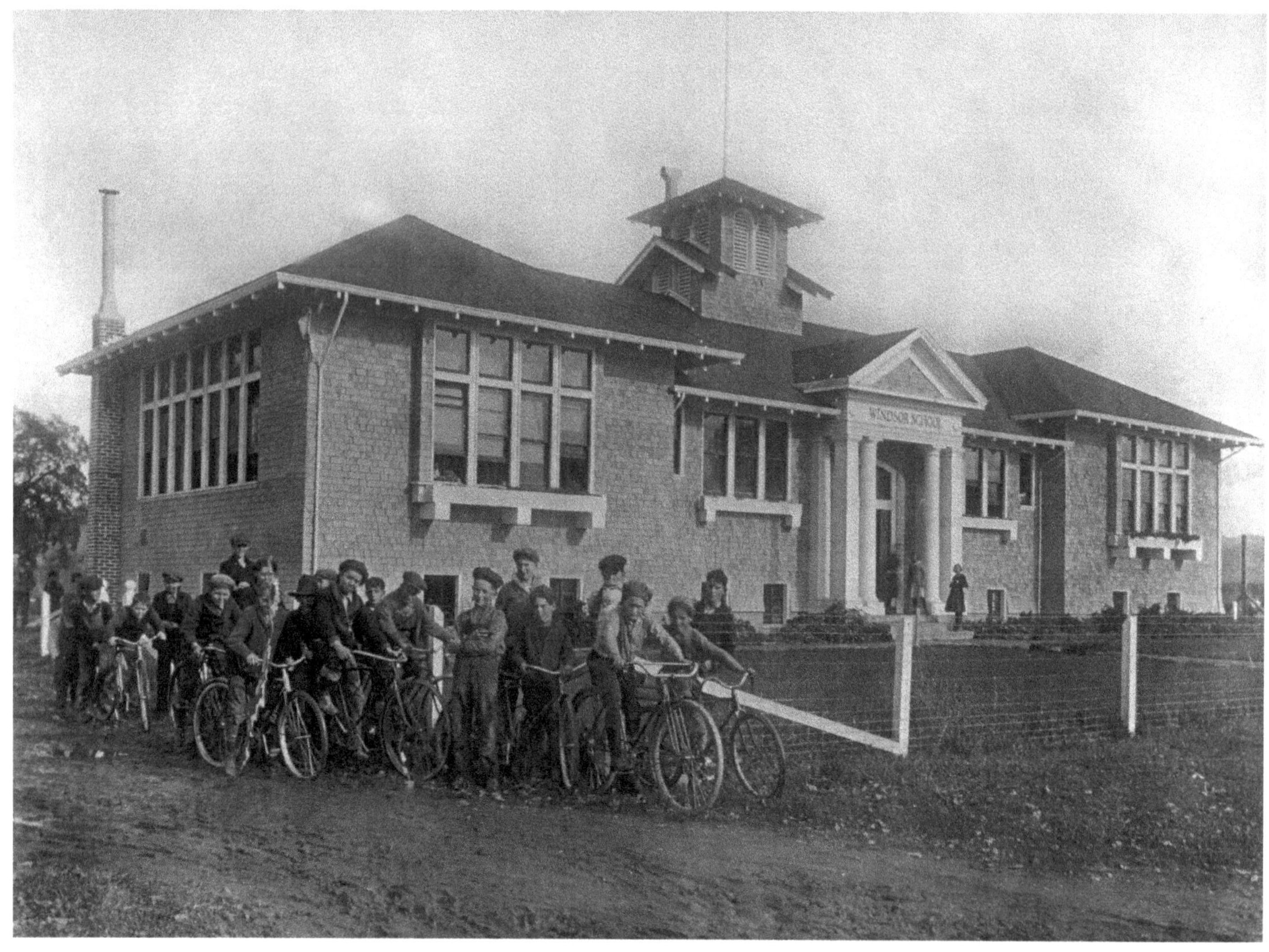

Sunday afternoon was game day in much of Sonoma County in the years before World War II. Towns big and small fielded semi-pro baseball teams and competed to the cheers and catcalls of local fans. This 1925 Healdsburg team included: Villow, Bidwell, McNulty, Watson, Corrick, Dan Alley, Remell Arlett, Shinn, Hitchcock and George Autrey. When young Joe DiMaggio was with the Pacific Coast League San Francisco Seals, he frequently took part in weekend games in Sonoma County.

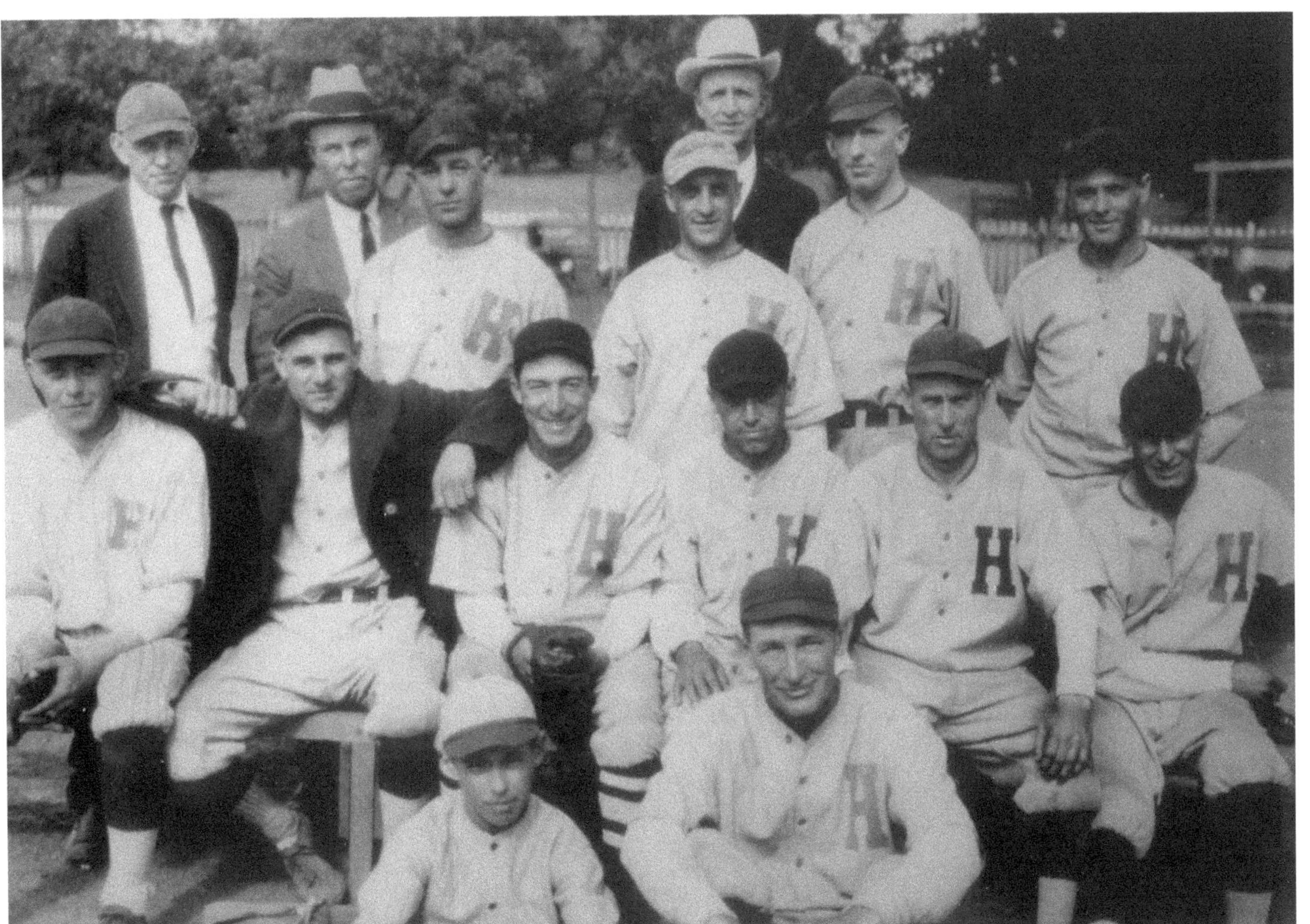

Ernie Nevers, one of football's all-time greats, showed up at Santa Rosa High School in 1920, turning the team into a North Bay powerhouse that year with his powerful running talent. He played for the professional Duluth Eskimos (1926–27) and the Chicago Cardinals (1929–31), but also played on the Santa Rosa Bonecrushers semi-pro team 1928–30, leading them to three state championships. A Bonecrusher team photo shows Nevers in the second row from the bottom, sixth from the right.

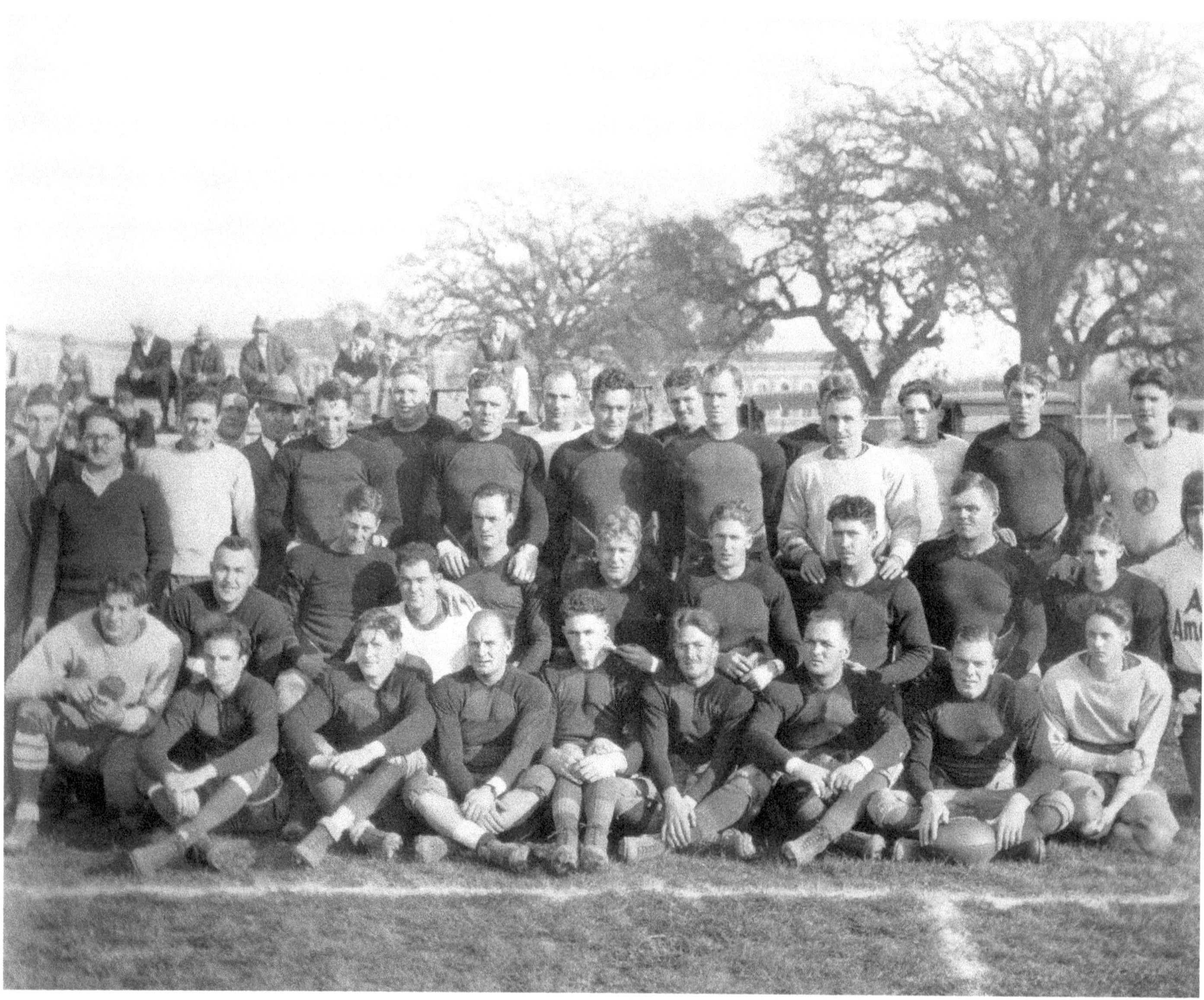

In the 1920s, a boom in chicken and eggs put Petaluma on the map internationally. The new prosperity triggered the building of the upscale Hotel Petaluma on the corner of Washington and Kentucky streets, at the then-spectacular cost of $250,000. The papier-mâché chicken, on display in 1938, advertised the downtown hotel with its prestigious Lanai Lounge. The chicken was a favorite target of out-of-town "rowdies" bent on blowing it up the night before local football games.

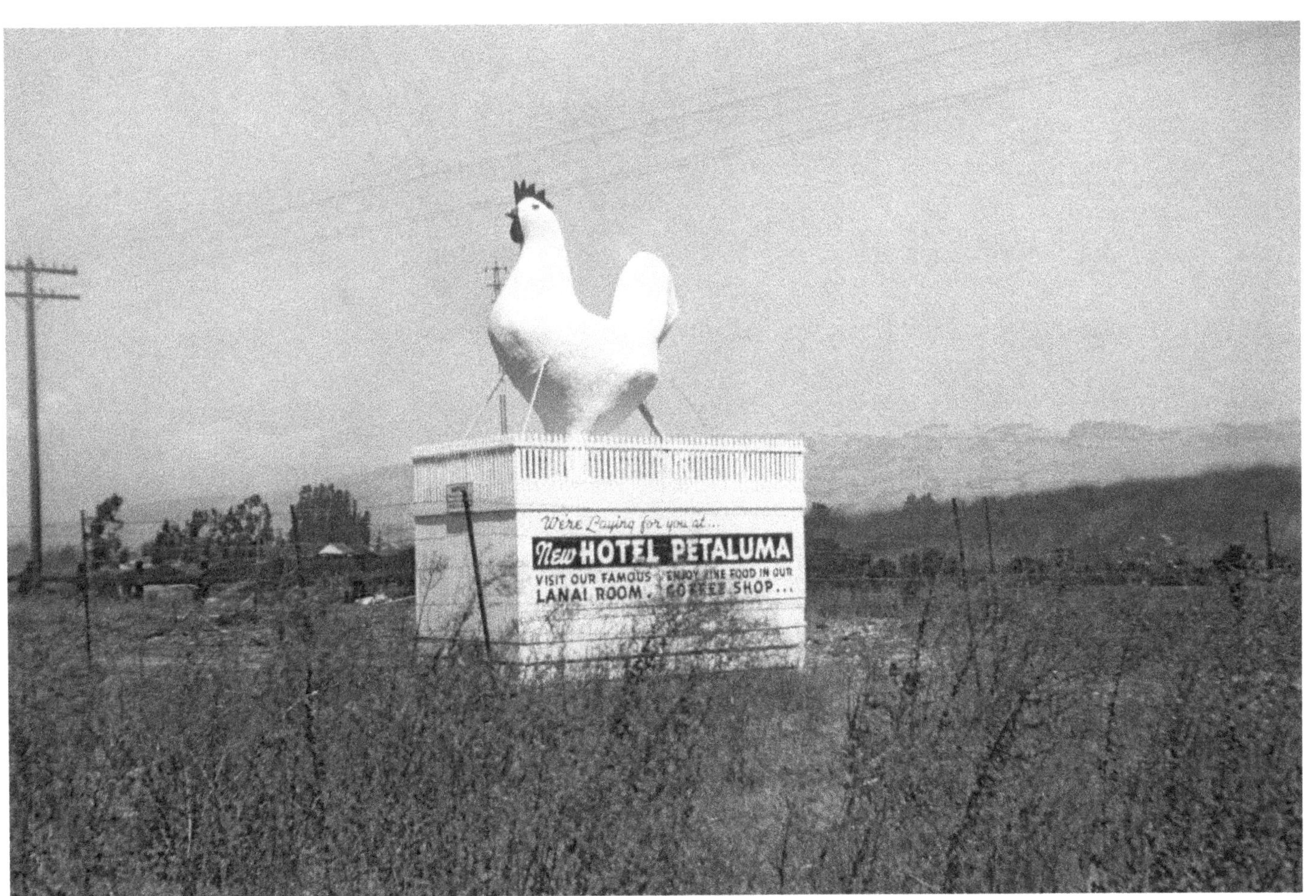

"Look Ma, no hands." What better way to impress a lady friend than by taking a "death-defying" ride on a water slide high over the Russian River? The river, which runs through Healdsburg, was a recreational magnet when temperatures rose each summer. The beach at Healdsburg around 1930 provided a challenging slide for devil-may-care youngsters. A nearby store provided snacks for survivors.

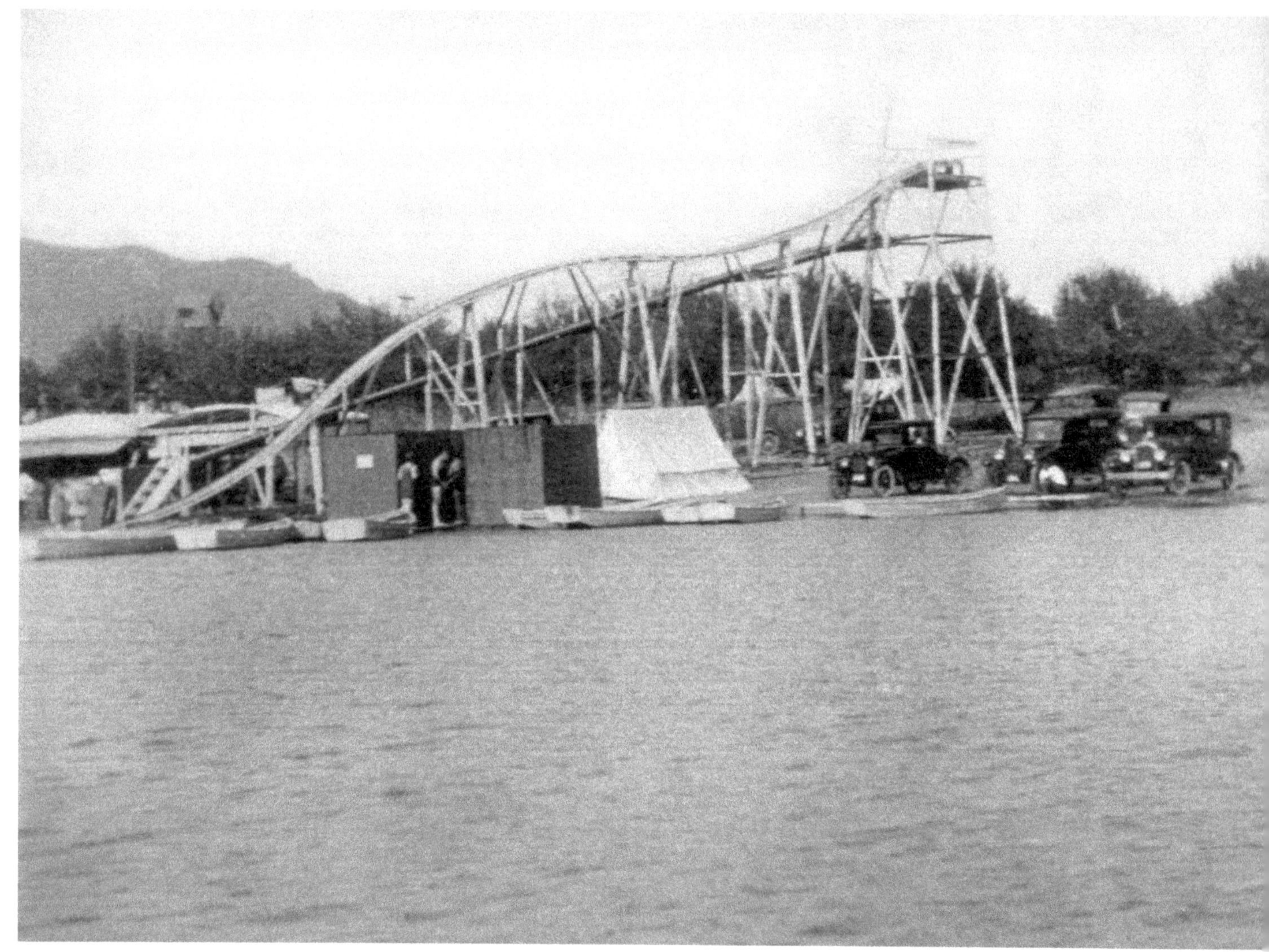

Trains were a mainstay of Sonoma County's transportation system until automobiles took their place. This was the scene in the west county when this train made its last trip from Forestville to Sebastopol, hauling passenger cars on to Petaluma in 1931.

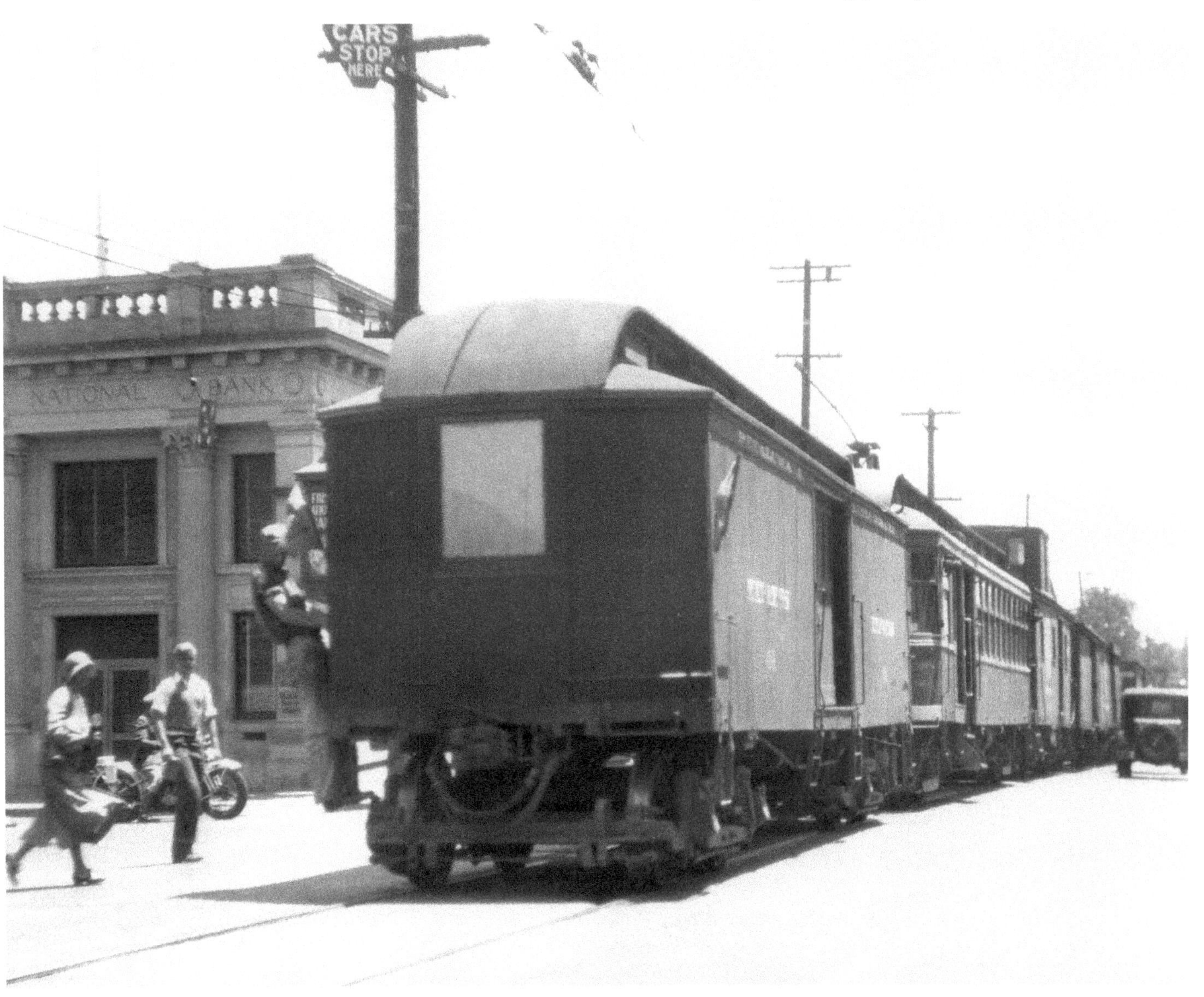

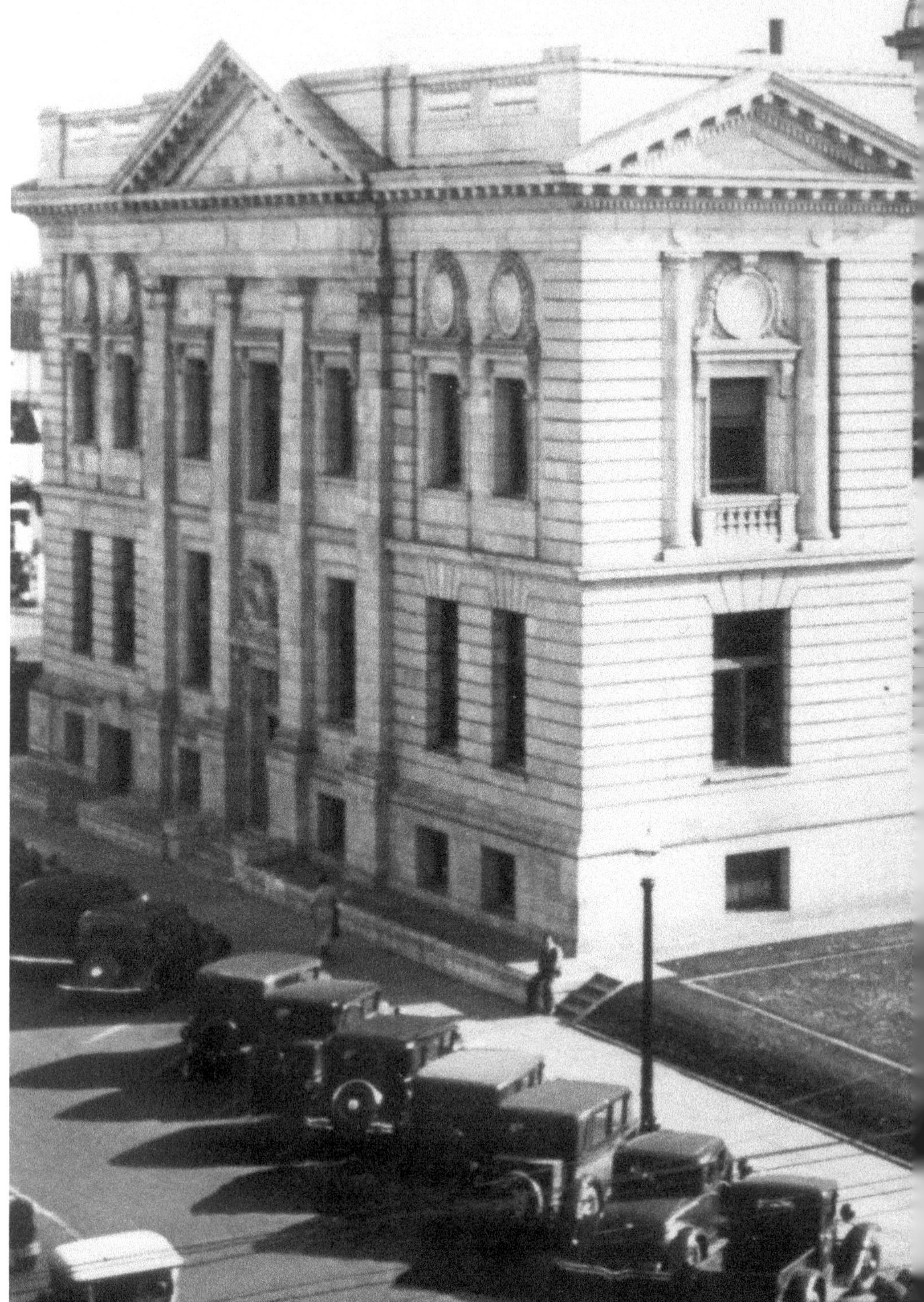

The county courthouse remained an architectural bulwark in the 1930s, although lawyers often complained that parking spaces were hard to find, and motorists complained that they were forced to detour around Courthouse Square. Further danger came from young drivers who engaged in midnight races around the building. With tears in their eyes, old-time residents watched as the wrecking ball brought the building to the ground in the 1960s.

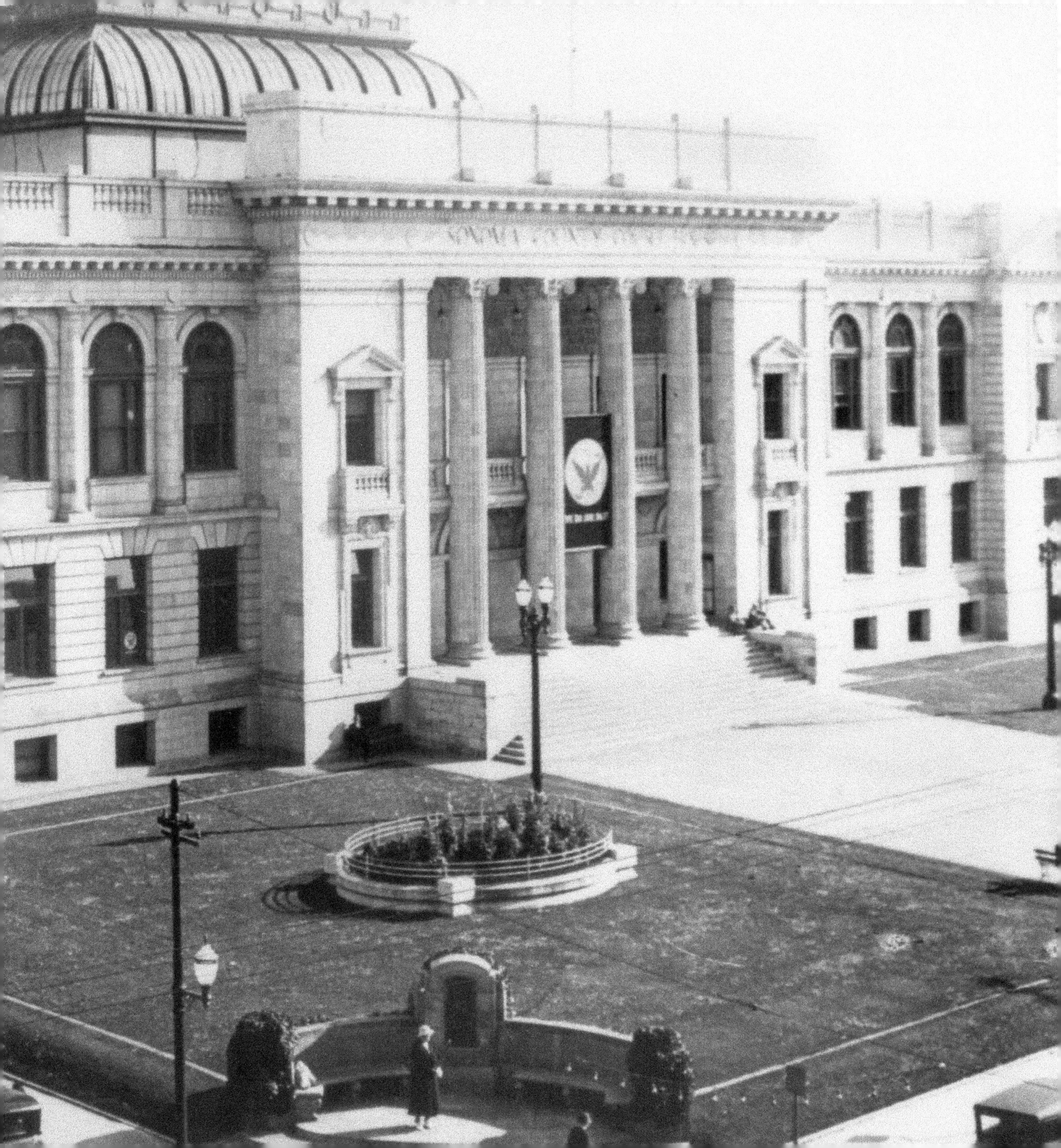

Despite the Depression, Santa Rosa of the mid-1930s had become a city of wheels. Drivers poured into the county seat to do business and enjoy diversions, including the numerous city parks. The view west on 4th Street shows the well-tended greenery in front of the county courthouse on the south side of the street and the thriving Exchange Bank building to the north.

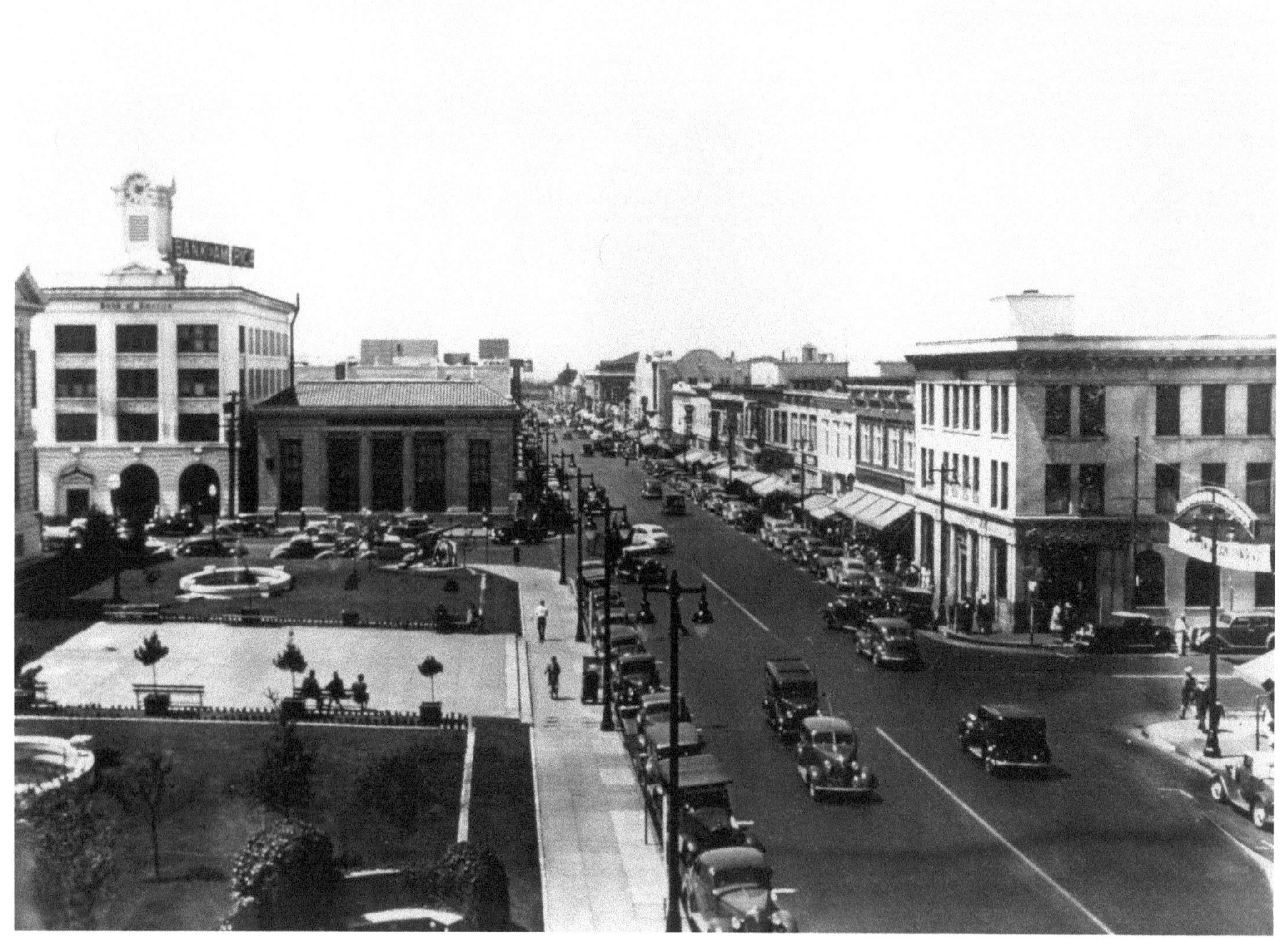

After the earthquake, the new Overton Hotel and the Occidental Hotel stood across from each other at 4th and B streets. The Overton, owned by the Bane brothers and later by philanthropist Leonard Howarth, was renamed the Santa Rosa Hotel by the time the Rosenberg family bought it in 1934. Part of the hotel was destroyed by fire on May 8, 1936.

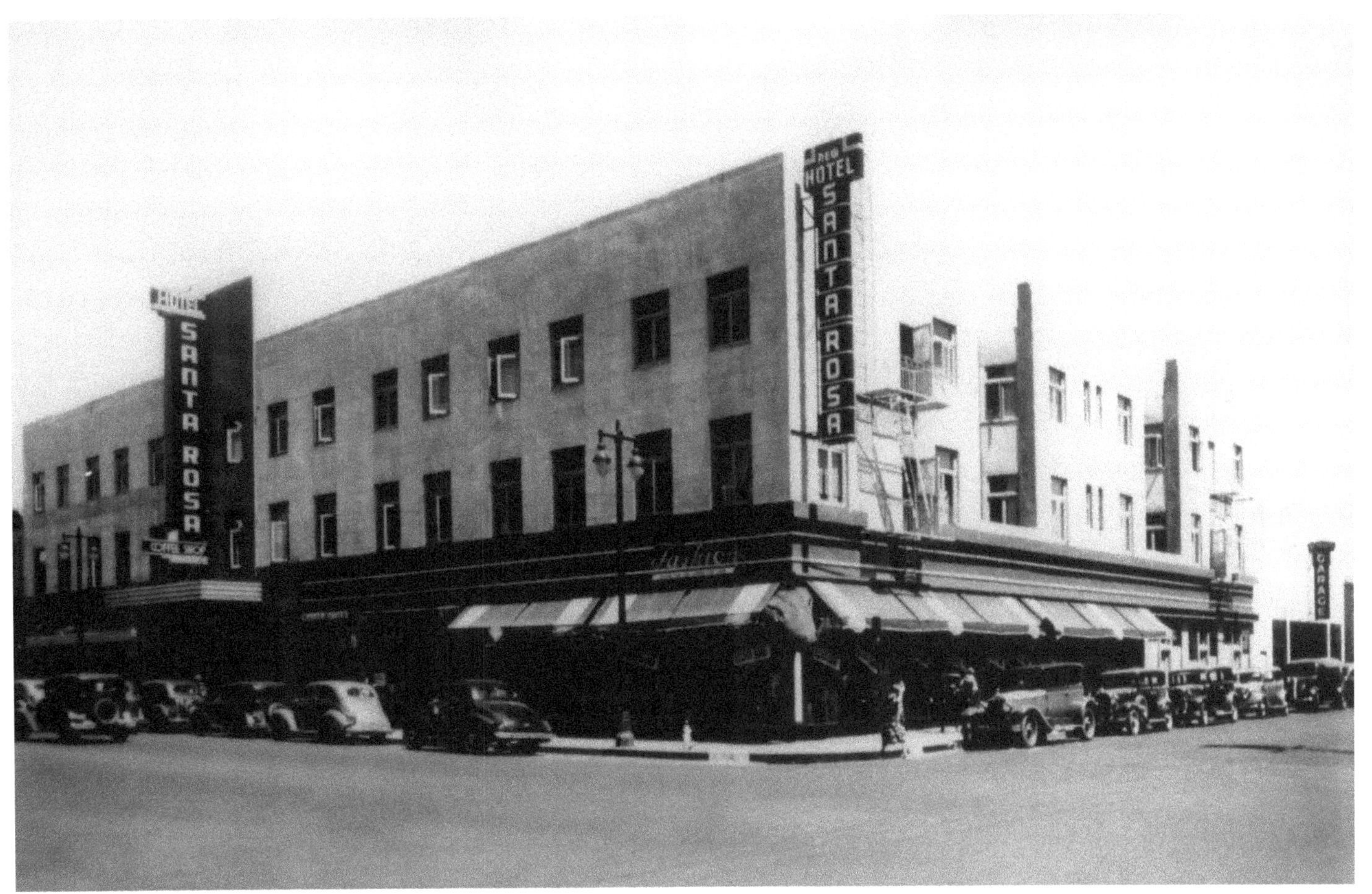

As air travel became more popular, a number of curious movers and shakers of Santa Rosa gathered in 1938 to look over a plane owned by William G. McAdoo. In the photo, not in order, were Charles Oliver Dunbar, Santa Rosa *Press Democrat* publisher Ernest L. Finley, department store owner Fred Rosenberg, Exchange Bank President Frank Doyle, W. W. Shubert, D. P. Anderson, John P. Overton, and McAdoo.

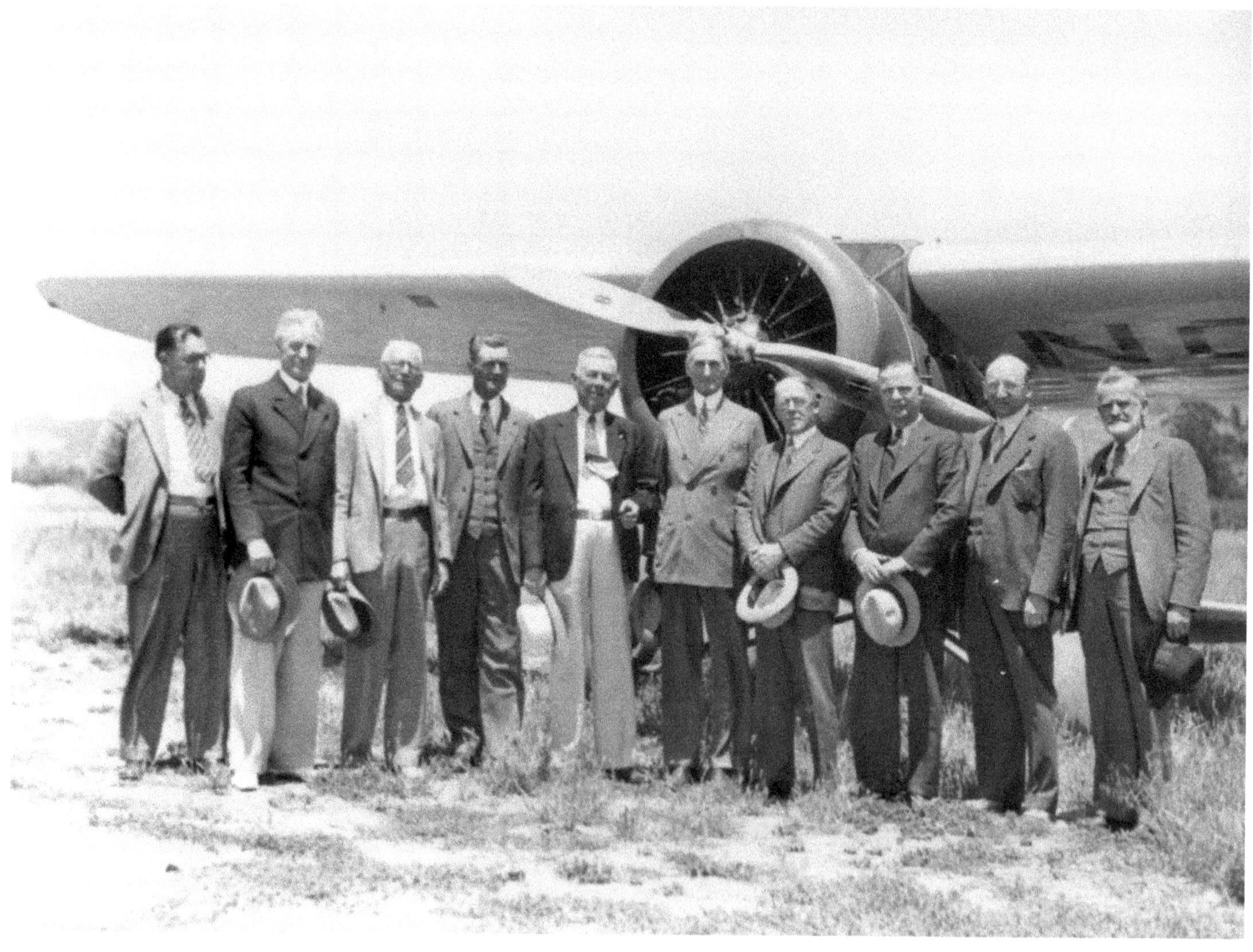

Leroy Jewett and his smartly dressed orchestra attracted large crowds of dancers at Rio Nido during the 1930s. Band members included (from left) Louie Hamilton, unknown, Ed Gundstrom, Walt Oster, Walt Hobbie, Al De Martini, Bill Hyer, Vic La Franchi, "Peewee" Leiton, Ernie Layton, Les Winslow, singer Melba Lewis, and Jewett.

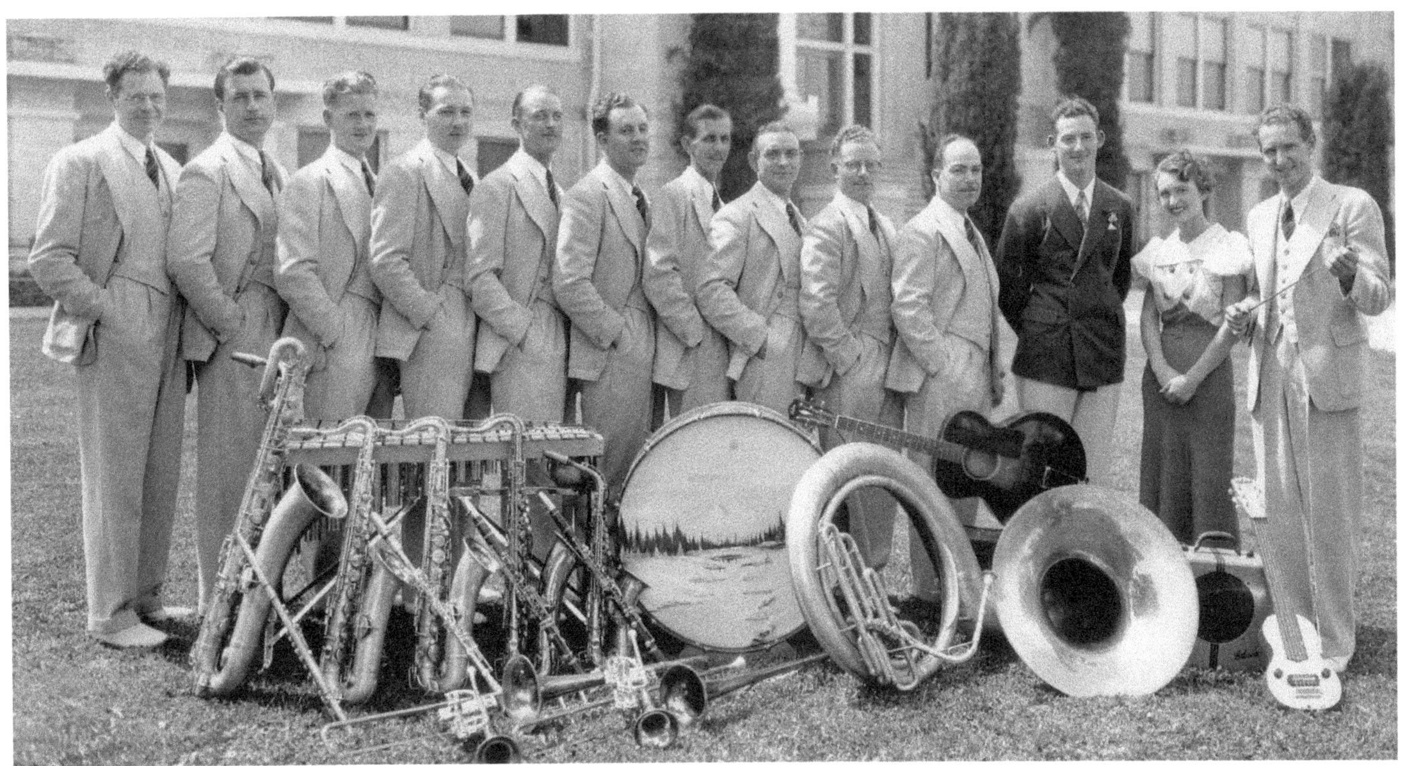

Most winters brought flood dangers along the surging Russian River. Mill Street in Guerneville went underwater in 1931, leaving residents scrambling to find higher ground. The building of the Warm Springs Dam west of Healdsburg has diminished the danger in recent years, although many residents keep rowboats and canoes handy just in case.

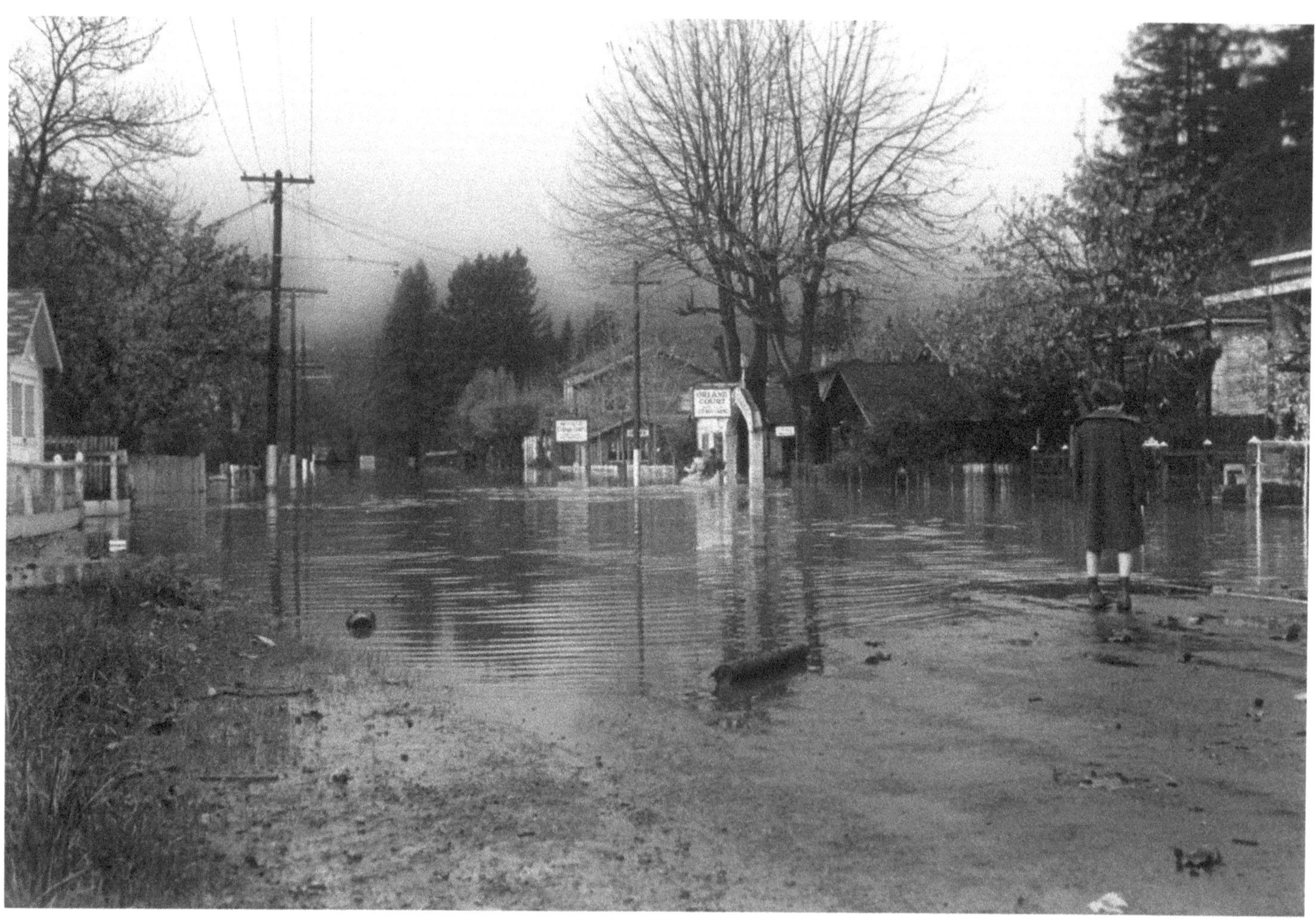

Hinkle's Union 76 Service Station in Windsor, owned by John Edward Hinkle, pumped gasoline and sold candies, ice cream, and root beer inside the store in Windsor in the mid-1930s. From left, Edward Hinkle and John Hinkle were at the pumps and George Hinkle and Sam Lawson were on bicycles.

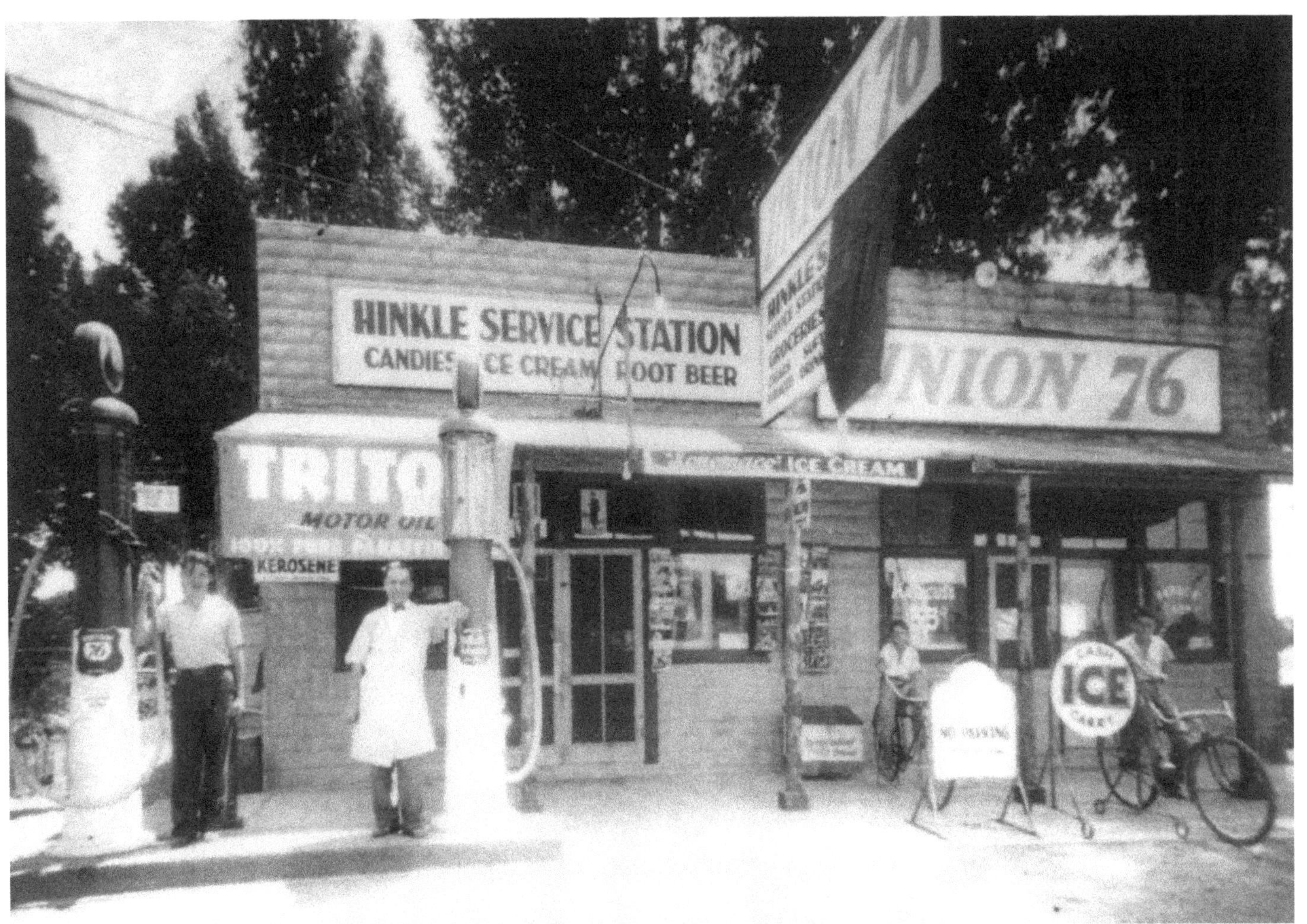

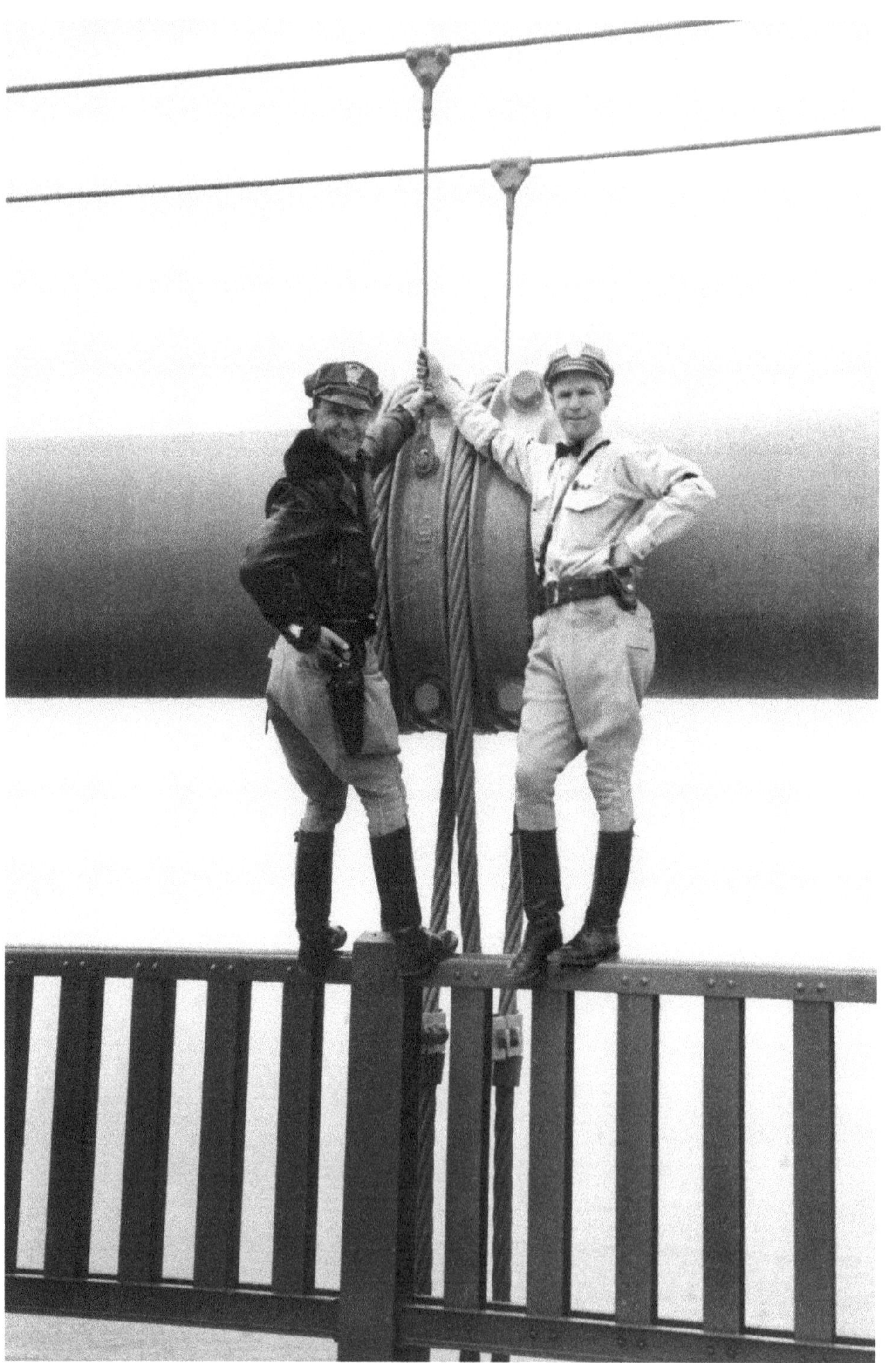

Two adventurous California Highway Patrol (CHP) officers, Irv Rohner (left) and Ira Hein, defied gravity as they teetered on the railing of the Golden Gate Bridge just before the span opened in May 1937.

This Dodge was the first privately-owned auto to cross the new Golden Gate Bridge, March 30, 1937. In front of the vehicle were (left) Santa Rosa banker Frank P. Doyle, a major advocate for building of the span, and J. H. Williams, a Santa Rosa car dealer. Doyle argued the bridge would guarantee a strong economic future for North Bay communities, including his own hometown.

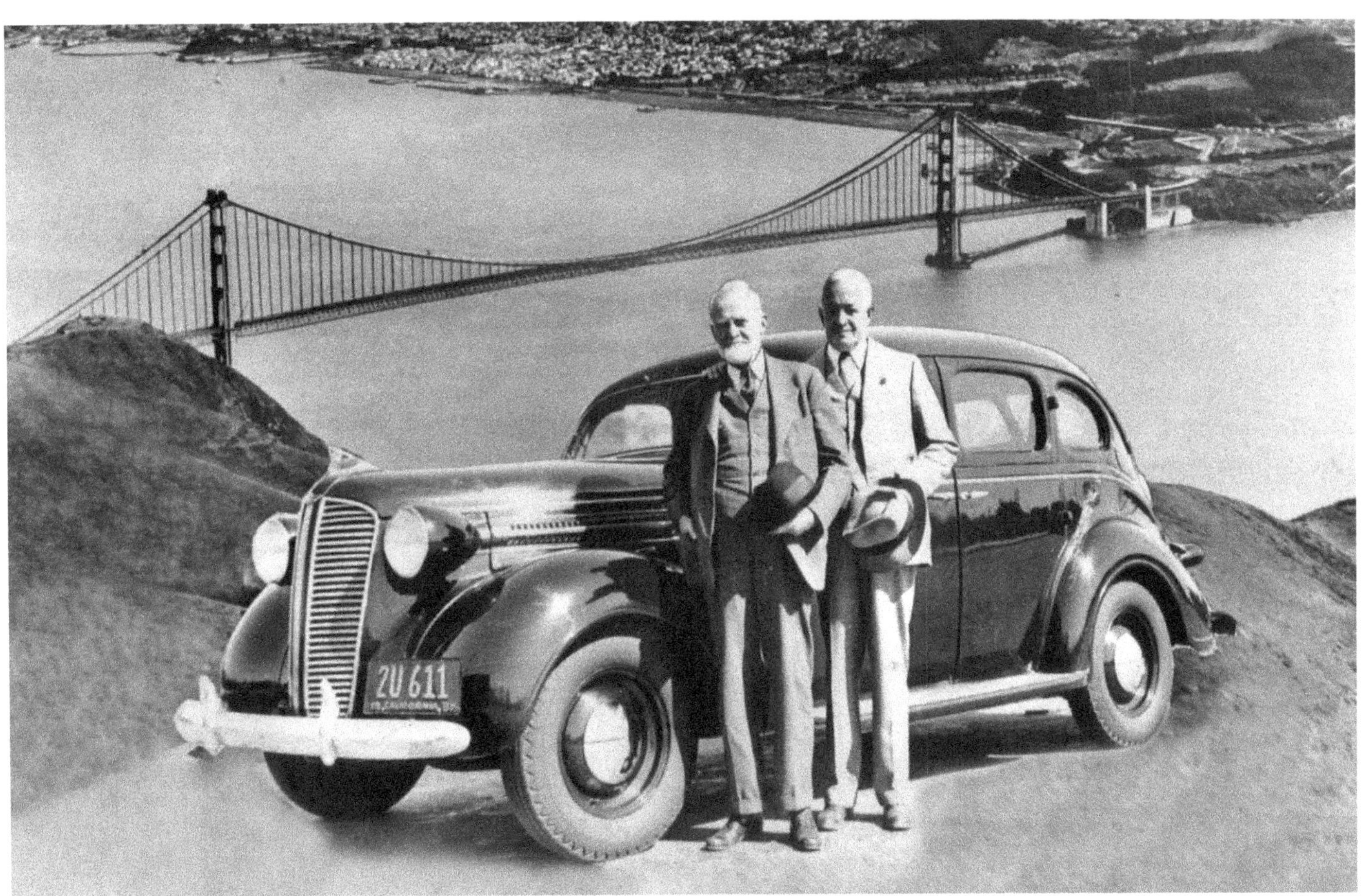

Mill Creek was one of the numerous one-room schools in Healdsburg in the 1930s. The teacher was kept busy tending to the needs of students ranging from grades one to eight. The area was mainly populated by mill workers, starting in the 1850s.

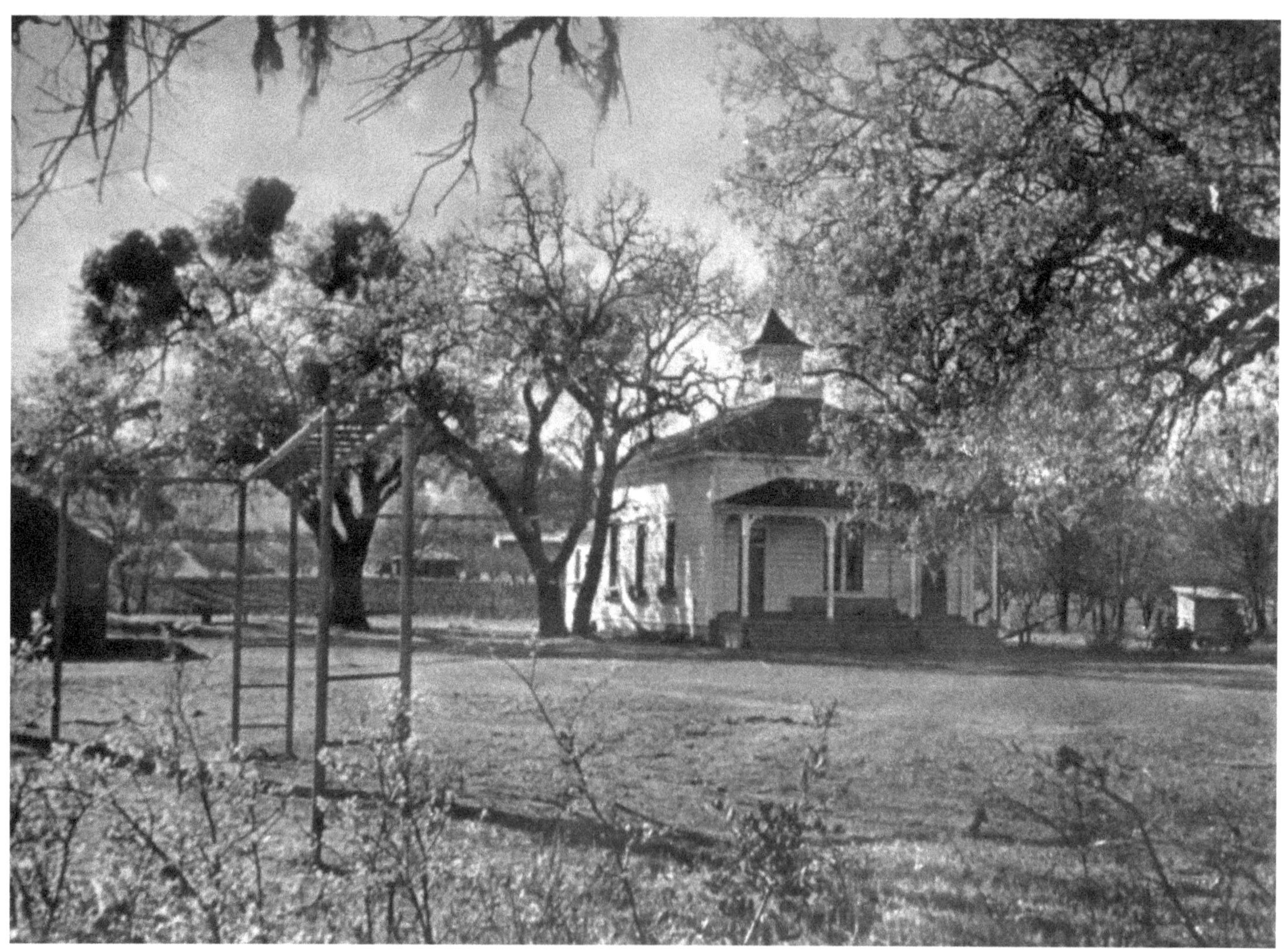

The stately Petaluma City Hall, with cars moving by in 1938, served as a center of city government at Kentucky and 4th streets. James Mott, the first paid Petaluma fireman, was hired in 1910 and, among other duties, tended to the "almost-human" firehorse named Black Bart, stabled in the Corporation Yard behind the city hall. Mott died in 1912 in a car-fire explosion. The city hall was built in 1886 and turned into a parking lot in 1955.

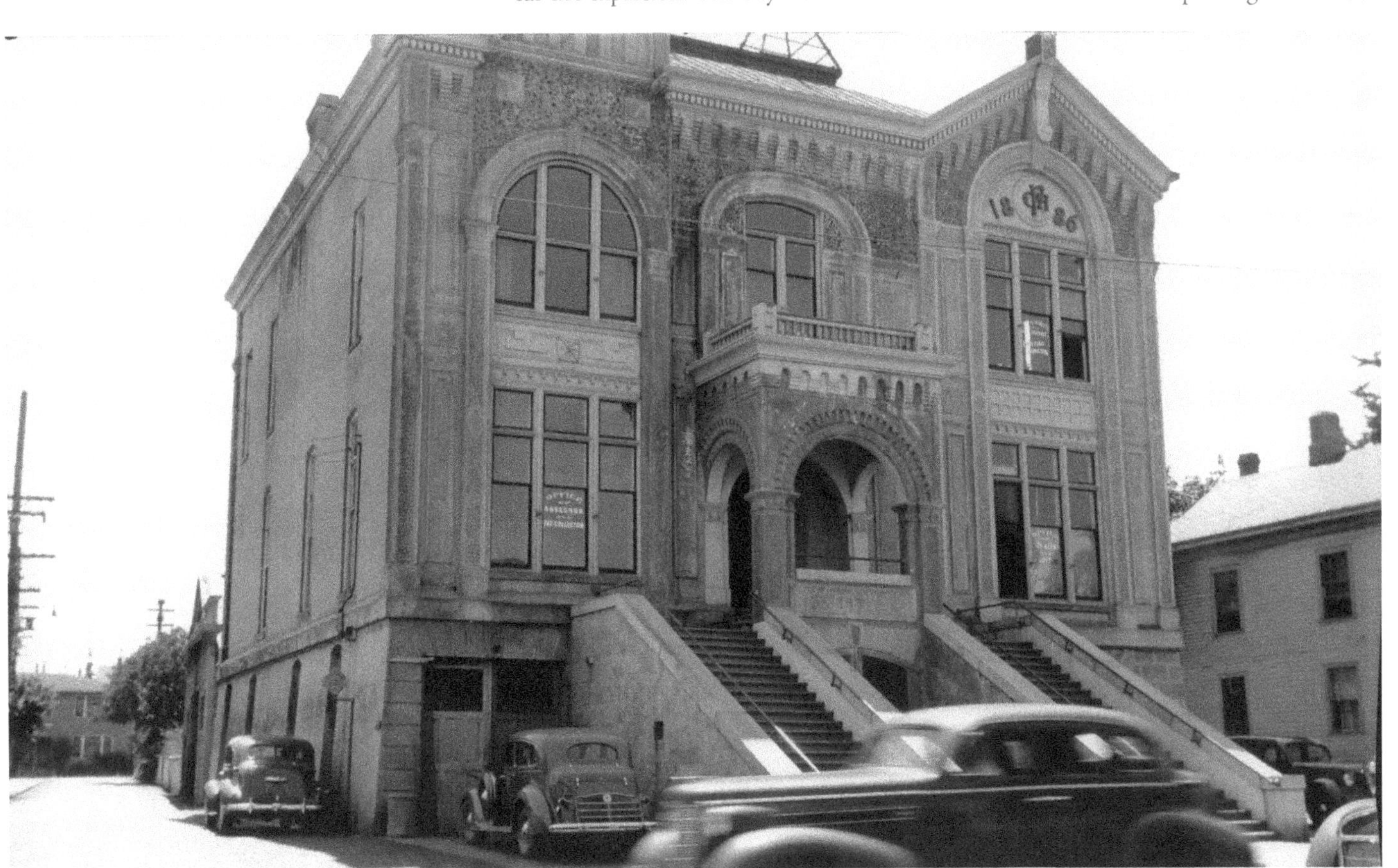

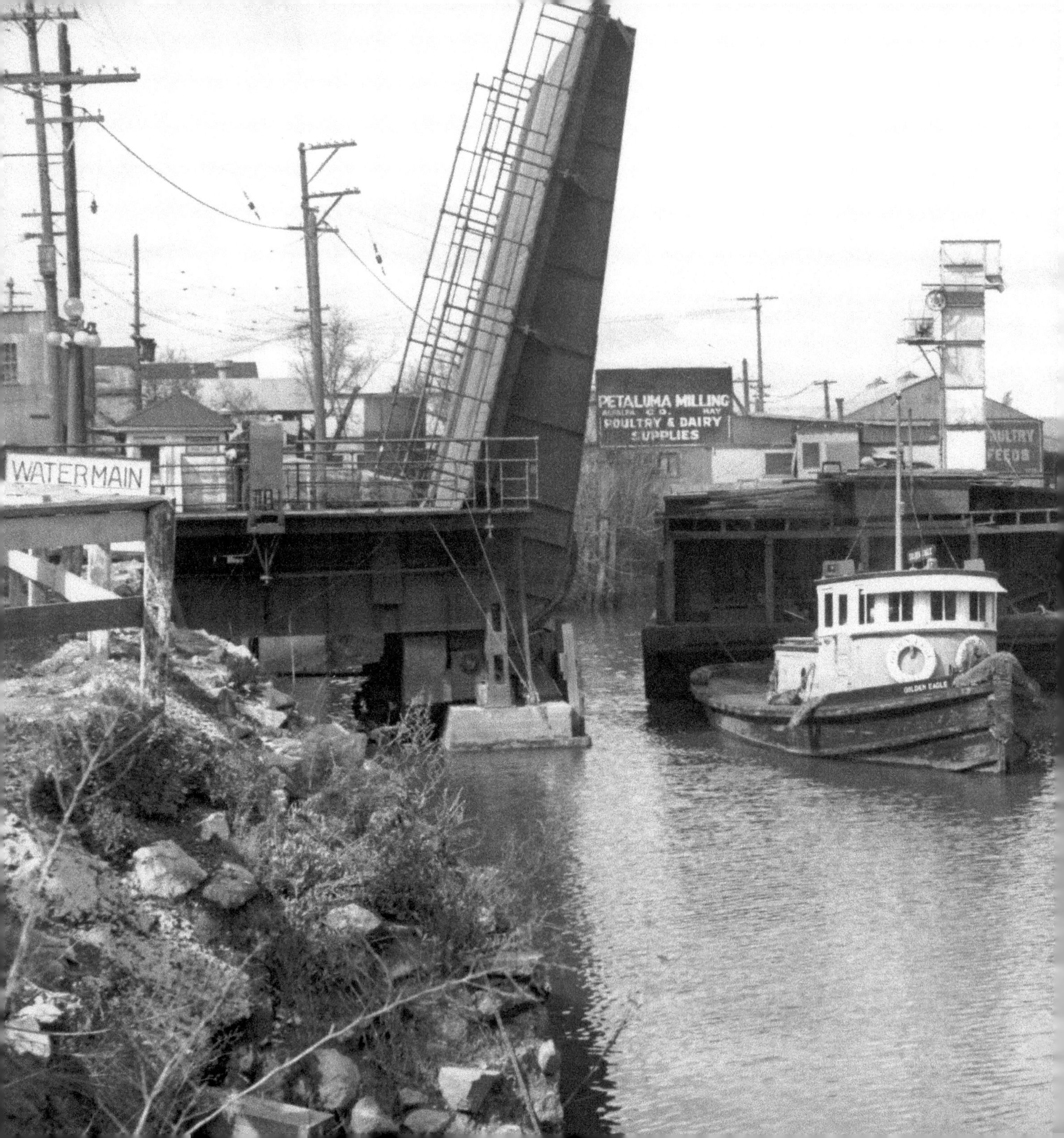
WATERMAIN
PETALUMA MILLING
CO.
HAY
POULTRY & DAIRY
SUPPLIES

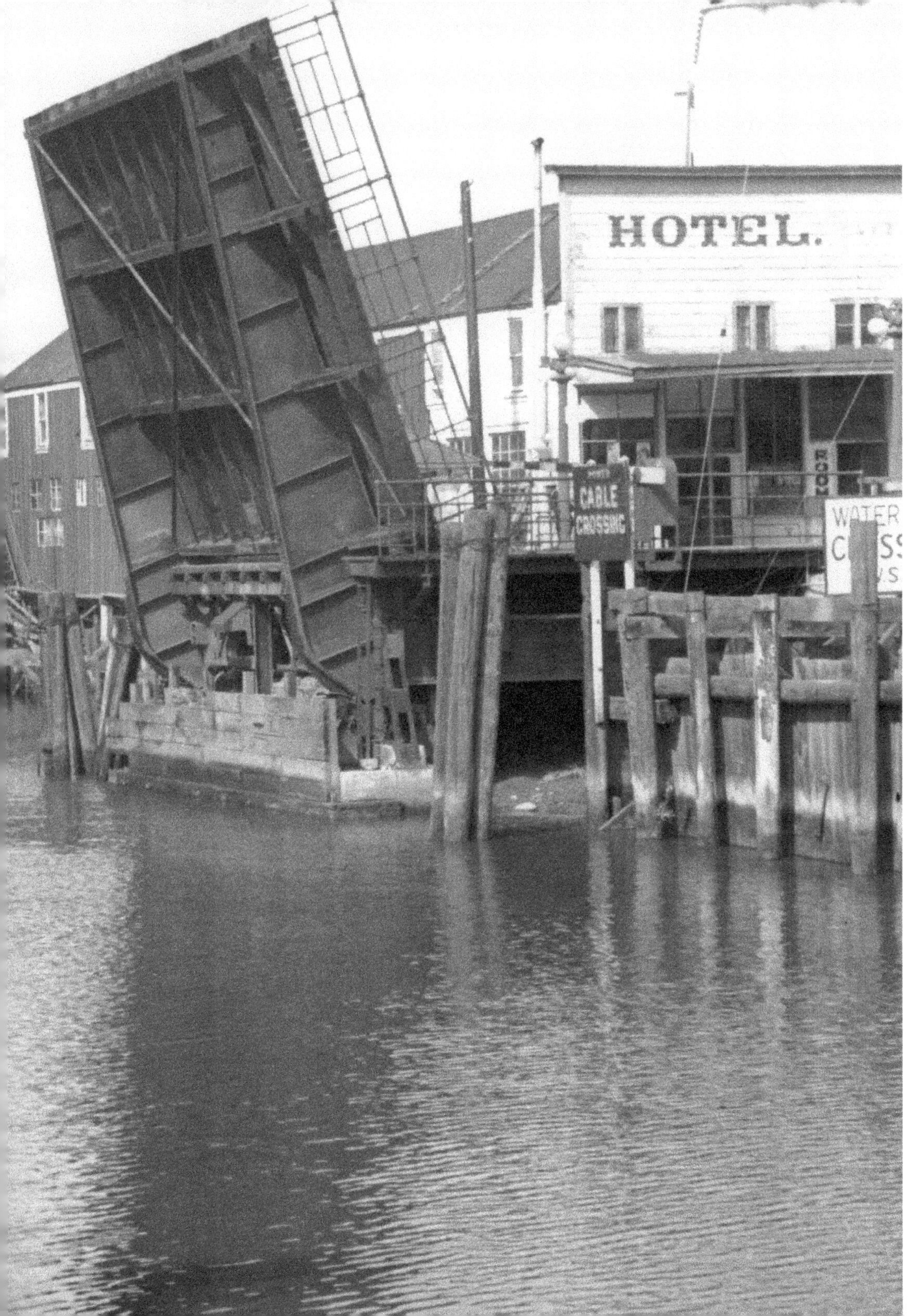


Throughout the nineteenth and well into the twentieth century, the water link between Petaluma and San Francisco was a crucial part of the local economy. Fruits, vegetables, butter, eggs and other farm products supplied the urban areas while new arrivals made their way up the Petaluma River to settle in the North Bay. The tugboat Golden Eagle was part of the process, towing a barge under the Washington Street Bridge in 1937.

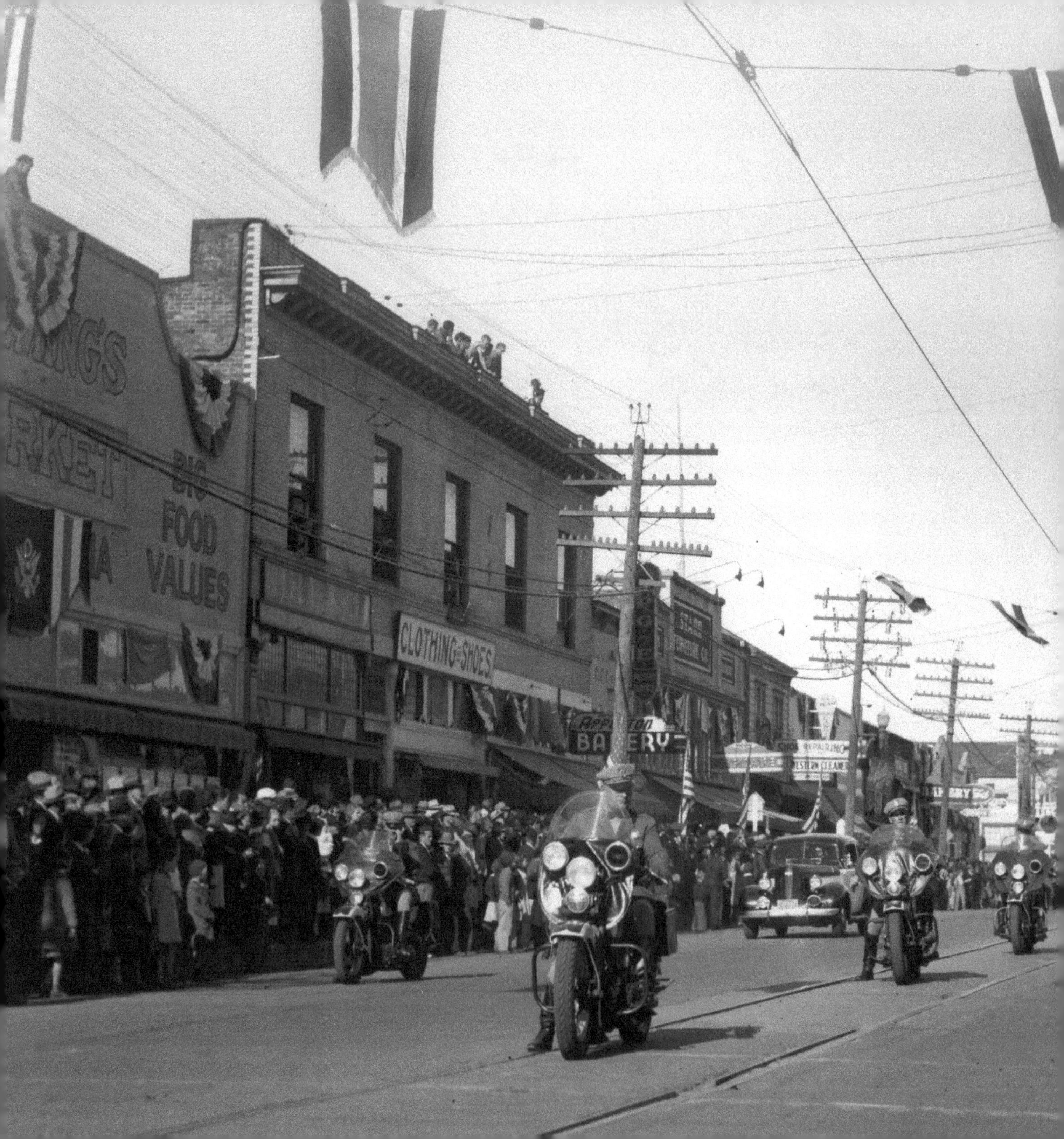
BIG FOOD VALUES
CLOTHING SHOES

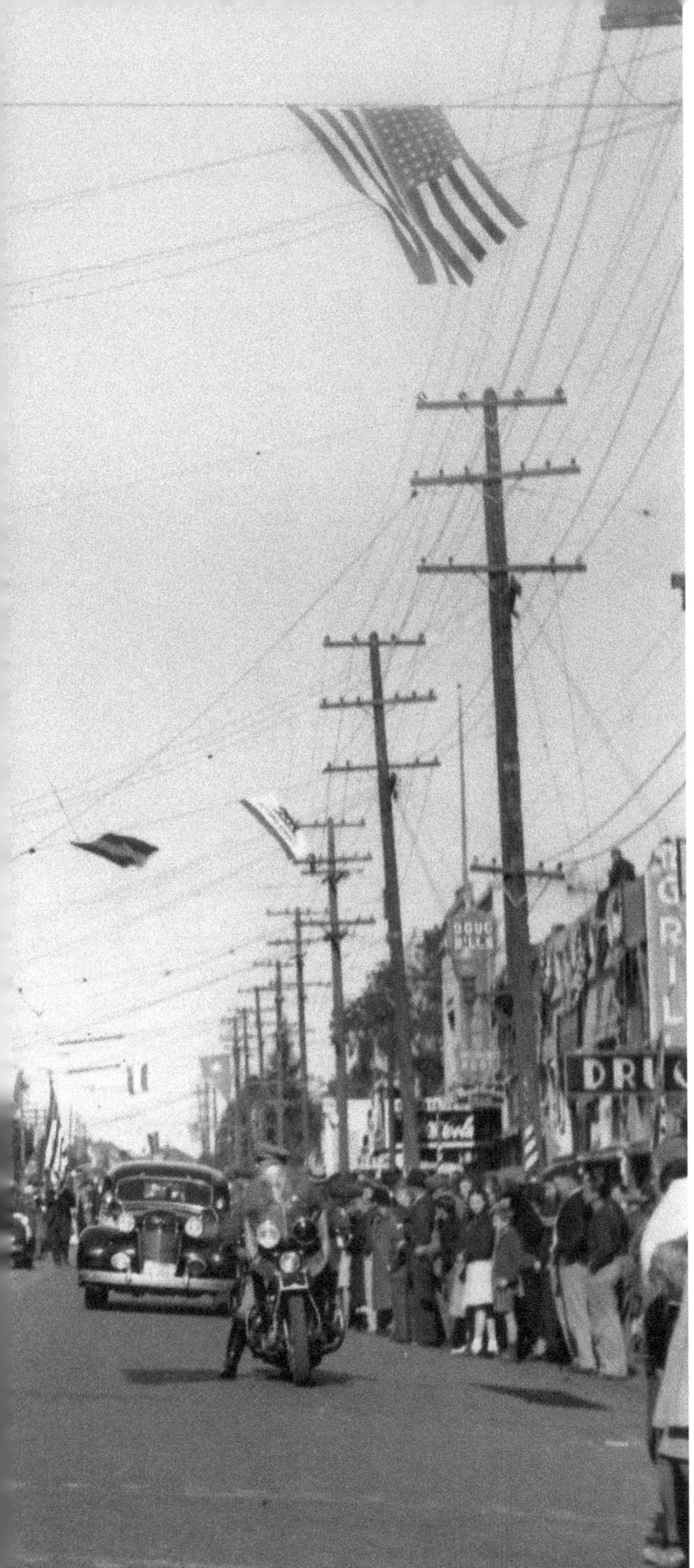

The roar of police motorcycles signaled the start of a jubilant parade when Sebastopol's finest led the way at the Gravenstein Apple Show in 1939. Sebastopol held its first Apple Fair in 1910, successfully promoting the tart Gravenstein variety. The western part of the county had 5,700 acres of apples in 1910 and 27,000 acres by 1920. Grapes became dominant, and apple orchards covered only 4,000 acres by 2000.

In 1938, a drug store and Fleming's Market and Groceteria anchored Main Street in Sebastopol. In spite of the depression, the market for fresh and dried apples helped save Sebastopol's economy during the economic downturn.

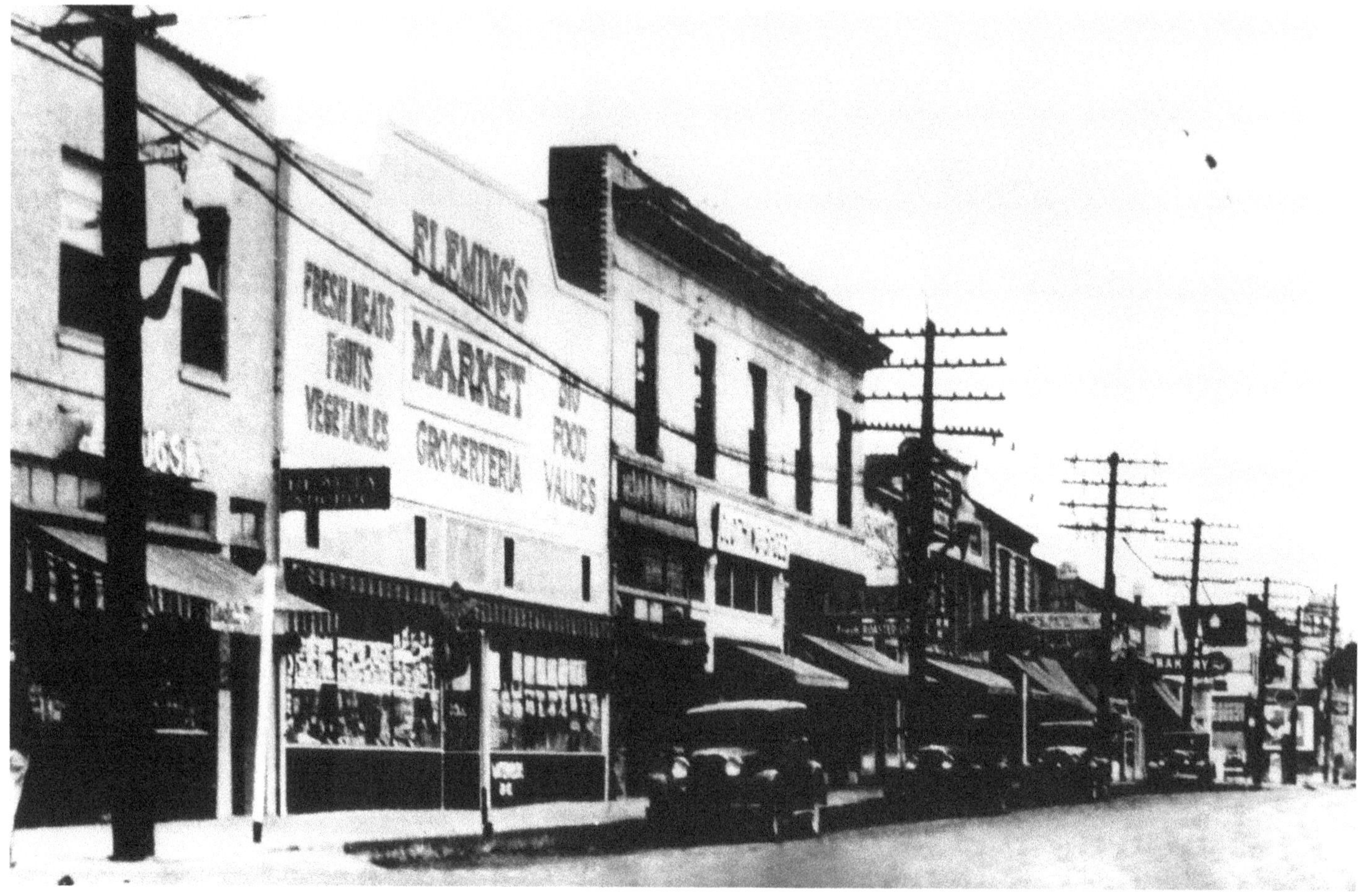

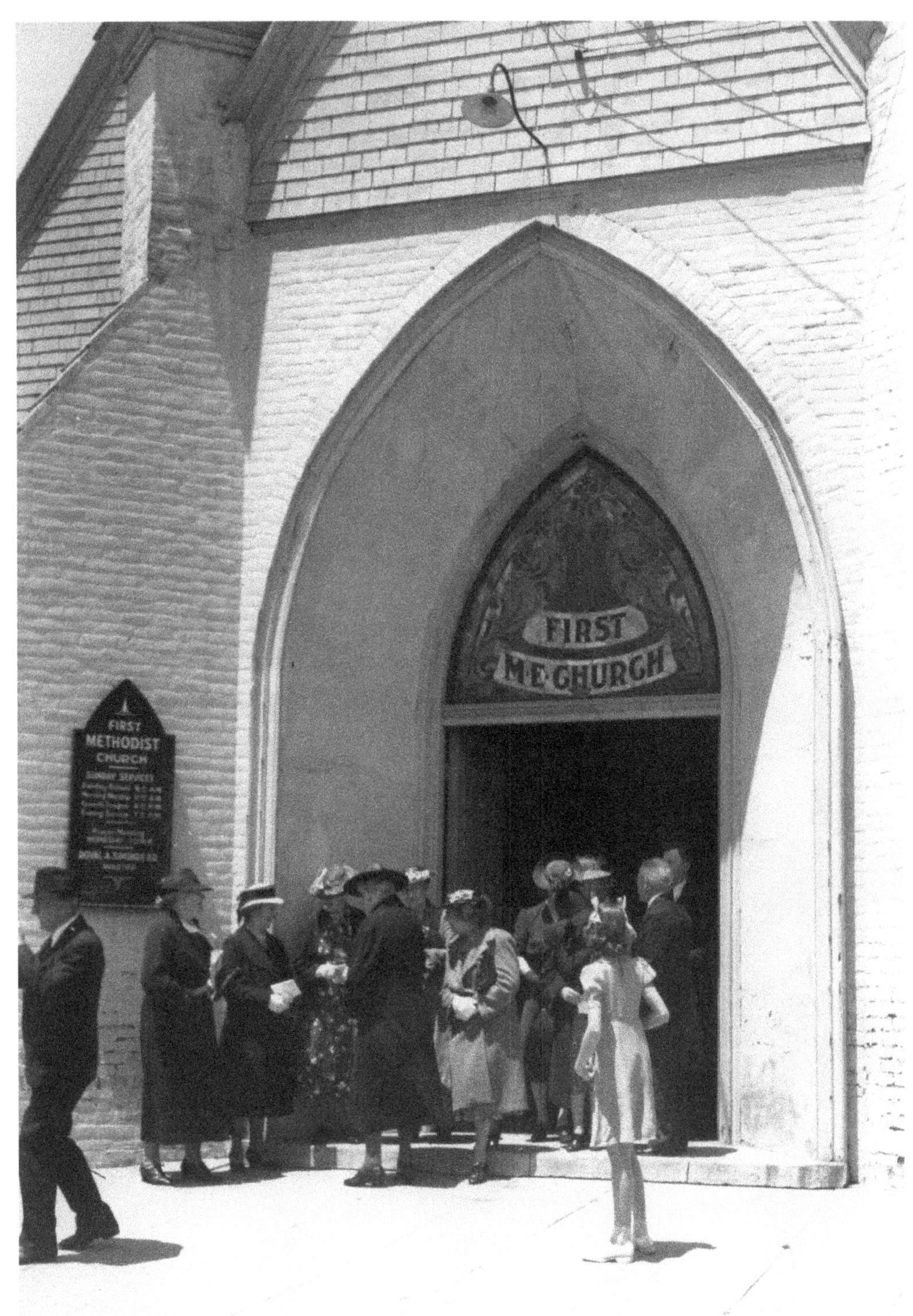


Sunday afternoon was for baseball, but Sunday morning was church time in the county. A group of worshippers were photographed leaving services at the Methodist Church at 200 Western Avenue in Petaluma in 1938.

Automobiles filled roads in the 1930s, raising a demand for more modern transportation systems, including the building of the Golden Gate Bridge. Even in sparsely populated west Sonoma County, pleas for relief from traffic snarls became part of the political discourse. A large crowd of people and cars turned out for the grand opening of the highway bridge across the Russian River on October 4, 1931.

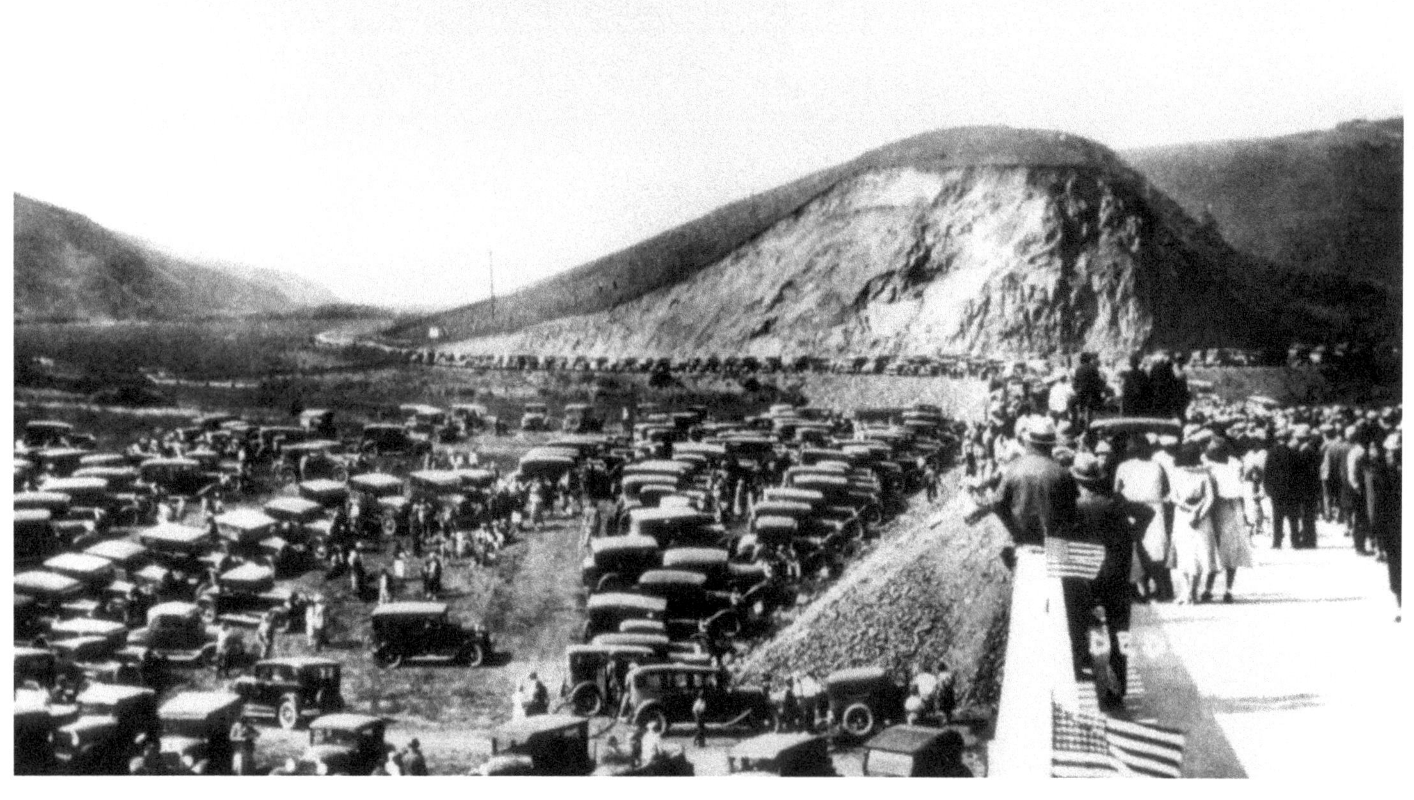

# Gains and Losses from Postwar Growth

## (1940–1979)

Sonoma County did its share to support the fight against the Axis powers in World War II. At the same time, it suffered through the program to relocate Japanese Americans in camps throughout the West. Sonoma County had a substantial number of Japanese Americans, many of whom were part of the 110,000 sent off to relocation camps during the war. In one case, Jim Miyano was sent to a relocation camp while his brother George rose to the rank of sergeant serving in the U.S. Army.

There were plenty of patriots in Sonoma County, and they quickly signed up, going to fight in places that they had previously known only as names in a geography book. At home, community leaders became game wardens and the citizenry saved lard, learned how to use ration stamps, and bought government bonds to support the war effort. The war came close to home as aircraft filled the skies on training missions from air bases in and near Santa Rosa.

The magic of movies came to the area as director Alfred Hitchcock made a star of young hometown girl Edna May Wonacott in the thriller *Shadow of a Doubt.* Don Ameche arrived in 1943 to make *Happy Land,* and Loretta Young won an Academy Award for *The Egg and I,* made in Petaluma in 1947.

Developer Hugh Codding came along after World War II to open up the area economically. He built Montgomery Village in Santa Rosa and seemed to be involved in almost every economic activity of the early post-war era. New, commuter-oriented cities like Rohnert Park cropped up, in this case replacing the old seed farm operated by Waldo Rohnert.

There were battles over the pace and direction of growth. The environment became a common part of the debate. Local residents took on powerful Pacific Gas and Electric when the utility sought to set up a nuclear power plant at Bodega Head on the Sonoma Coast. The Sea Ranch residential development became the center of a coastal access battle, and local interests locked horns for decades over whether it was a good idea to build a dam at Warm Springs on the Russian River northwest of Healdsburg.

Sonoma State became the first four-year university in the area and the boom in wine and technology triggered a spree of prosperity that changed the face of the county in the second half of the twentieth century.

In 1941, life in Santa Rosa seemed to be going on normally, but World War II was on the horizon. This scene, looking east on Fourth Street toward the White House Department Store, showed a normal shopping day. Blackouts and other disruptions became common after the war started. In one case, two policemen drove in the dark ten miles from Sebastopol to Santa Rosa to save the life of a six-month-old baby.

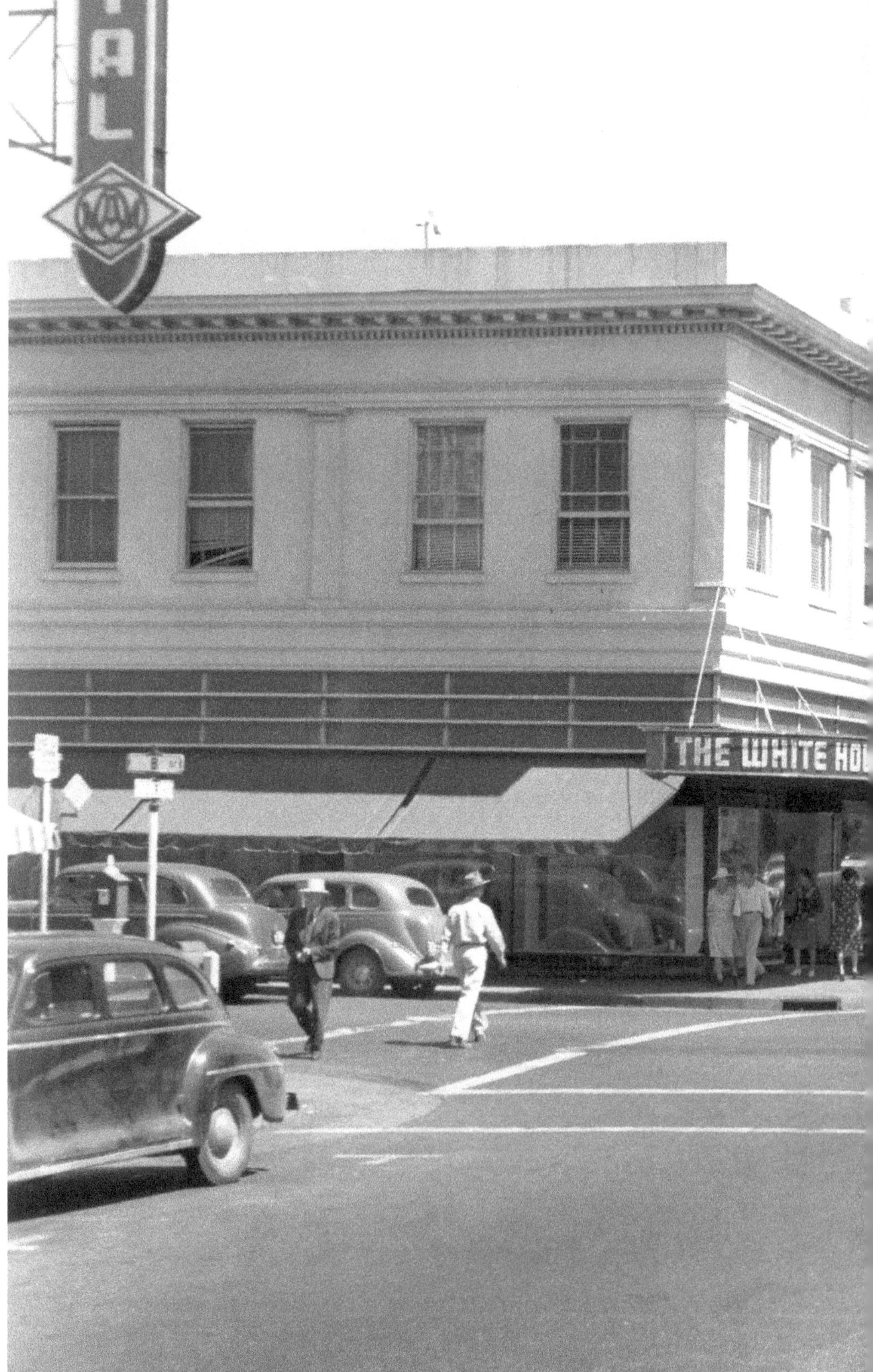

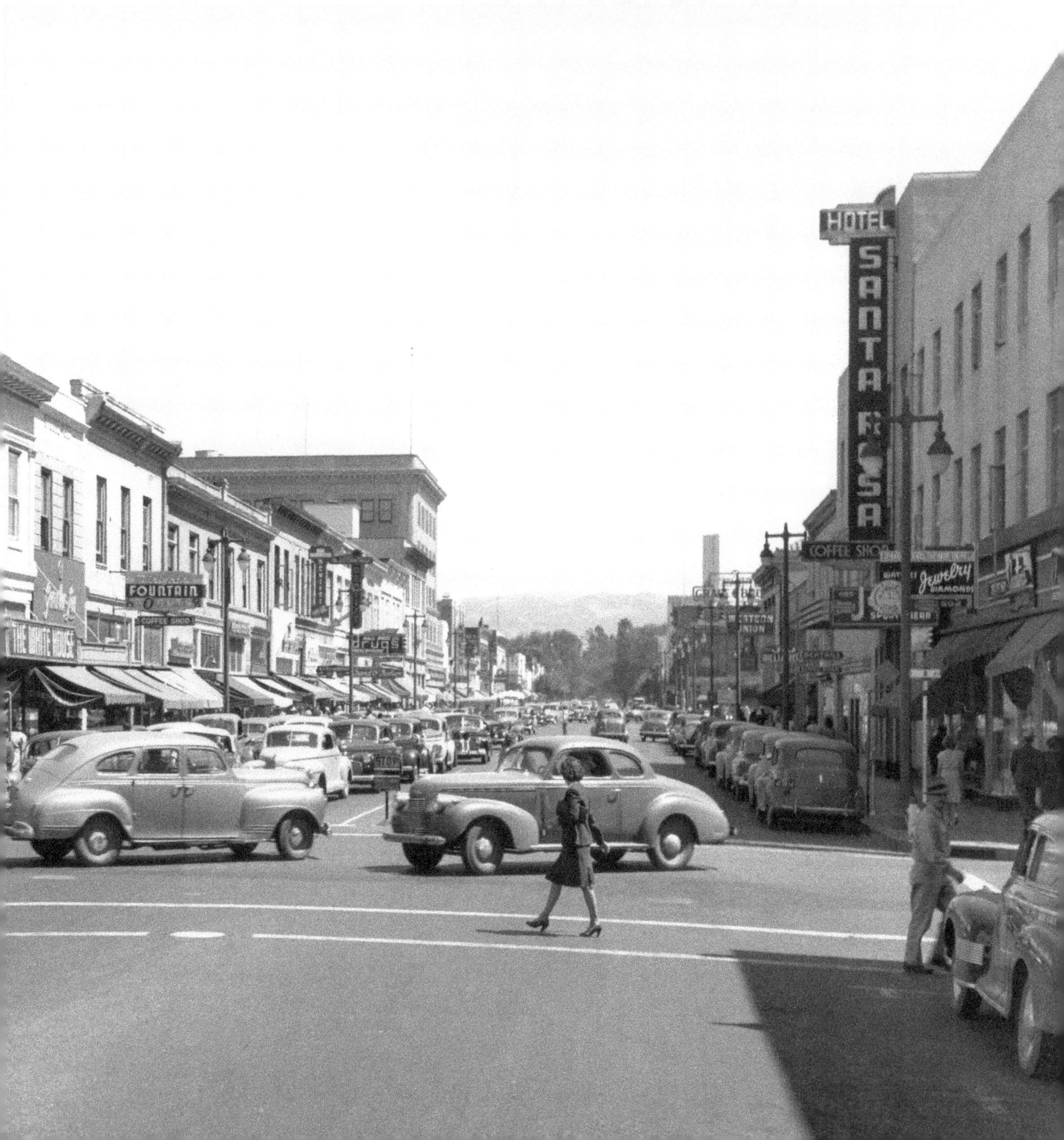
HOTEL
SANTA
COFFEE SHOP
FOUNTAIN
THE WHITE HOUSE
COFFEE SHOP
drugs
Jewelry
DIAMONDS
STOP

The one-room Sotoyome School in Windsor opened in 1872 and served the children of the community until after World War II. It became part of the Windsor School District in the 1950s.

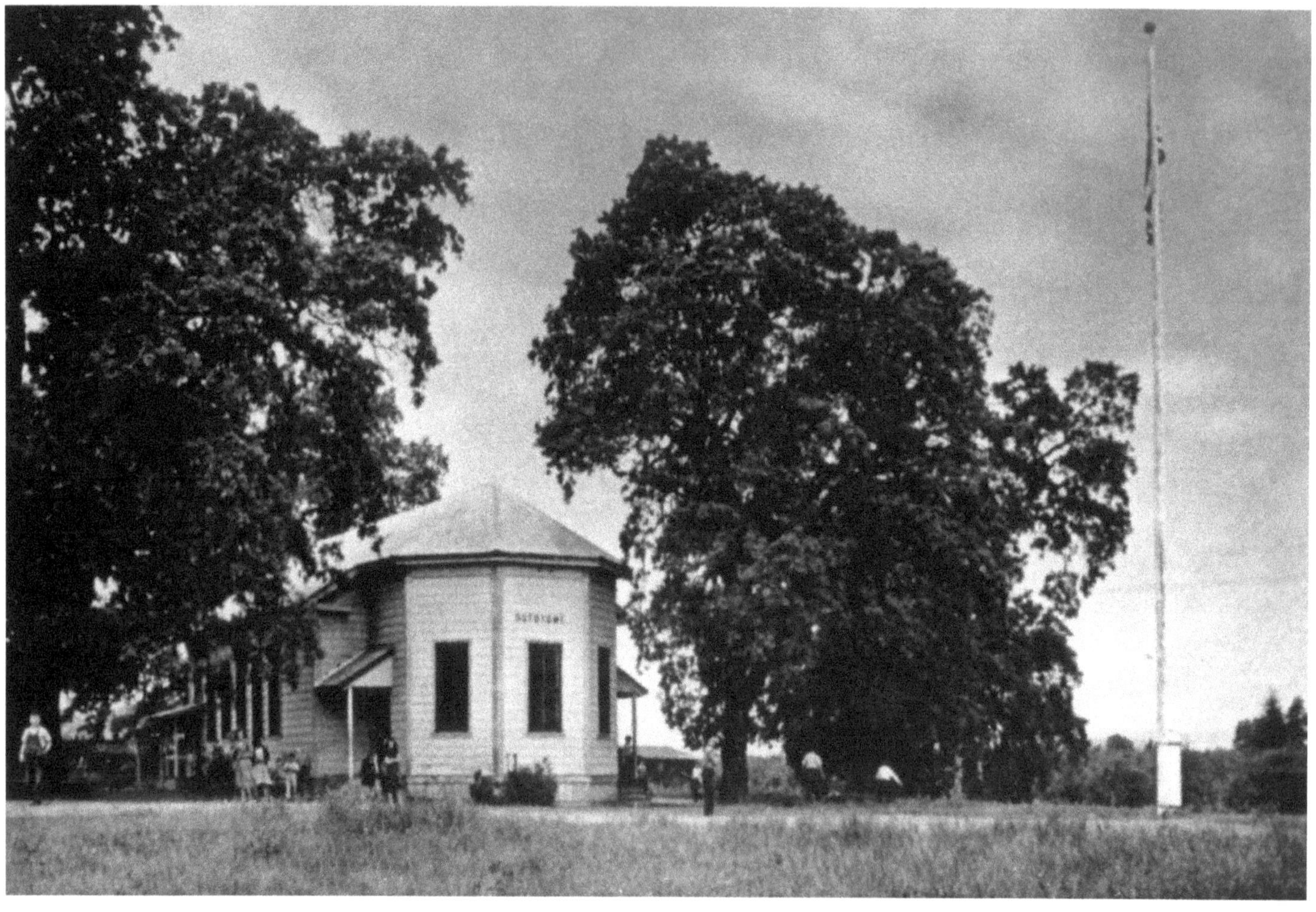

The Carithers block included the White House Department Store at the corner of 4th and B streets in Santa Rosa. It was incorporated in 1924 as W. E. Carithers and Sons, with Donald Carithers as president; William, Jr., as vice-president; and in-law Vernon Garrett as secretary-treasurer. The Carithers expanded into Napa and Vallejo in the 1930s and to Petaluma in the 1940s. The family sold its interest in the store in the mid-1960s.

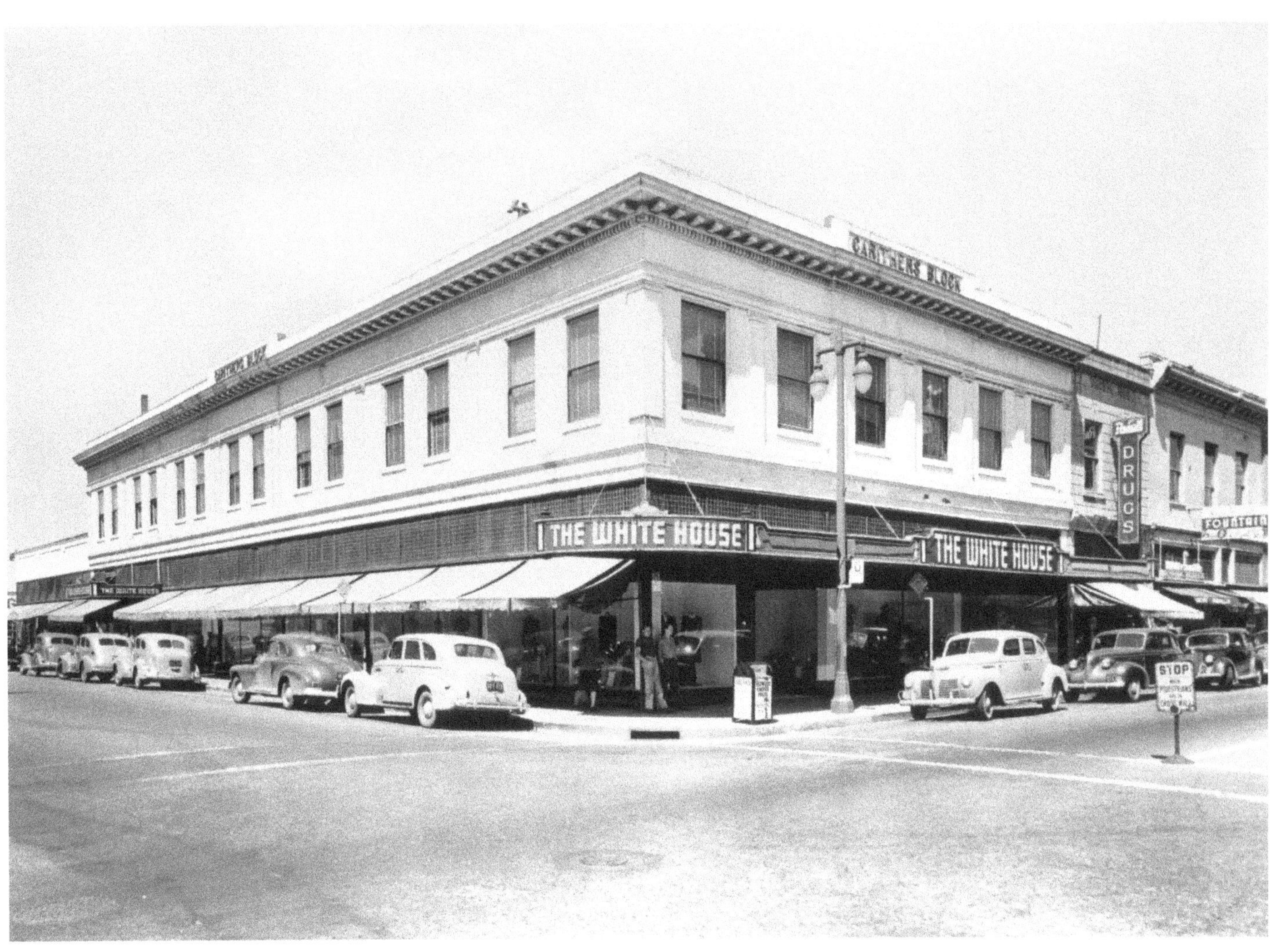

Sonoma County held its first fair in front of the Sonoma County Courthouse in 1855. In 1936, the Sonoma County Fair District was created, providing summer entertainment for people young and old through much of the twentieth century. Some went to see the animals, others entered their favorite pickle recipes in competition, but the big money was won and lost at the racetrack. Overhead view shows happy horse owners posing with a winner at the finish line.

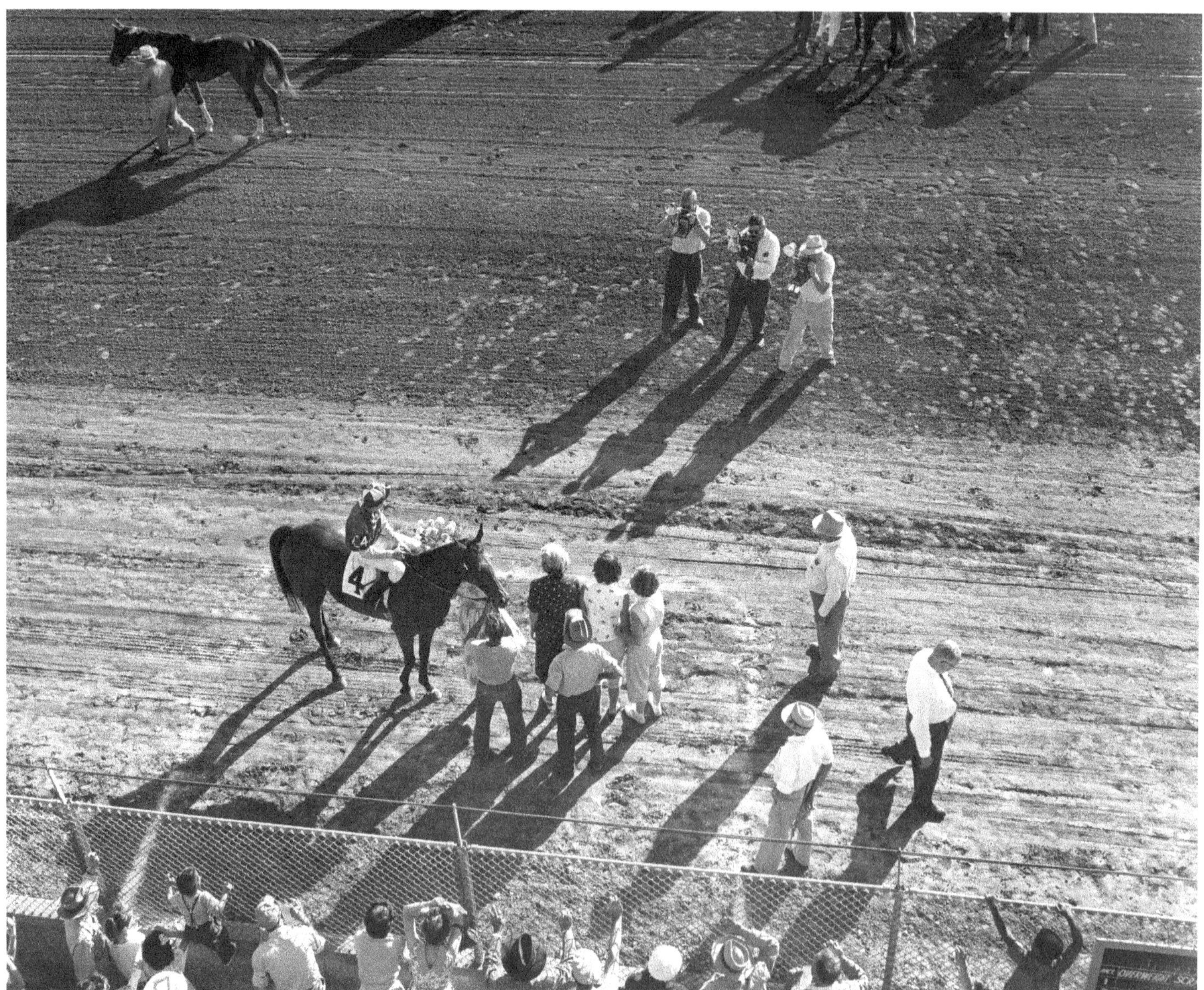

The Washoe House halfway between Petaluma and Santa Rosa, built in 1859, has served diners and travelers for many decades. Legend has it that during the Civil War a group of Petaluma soldiers went north to "punish" Santa Rosa, a "Confederate town." The "mission" ended when the Petaluma group stopped at the Washoe House to quench its collective thirst. By day's end, they had apparently lost their lust for war.

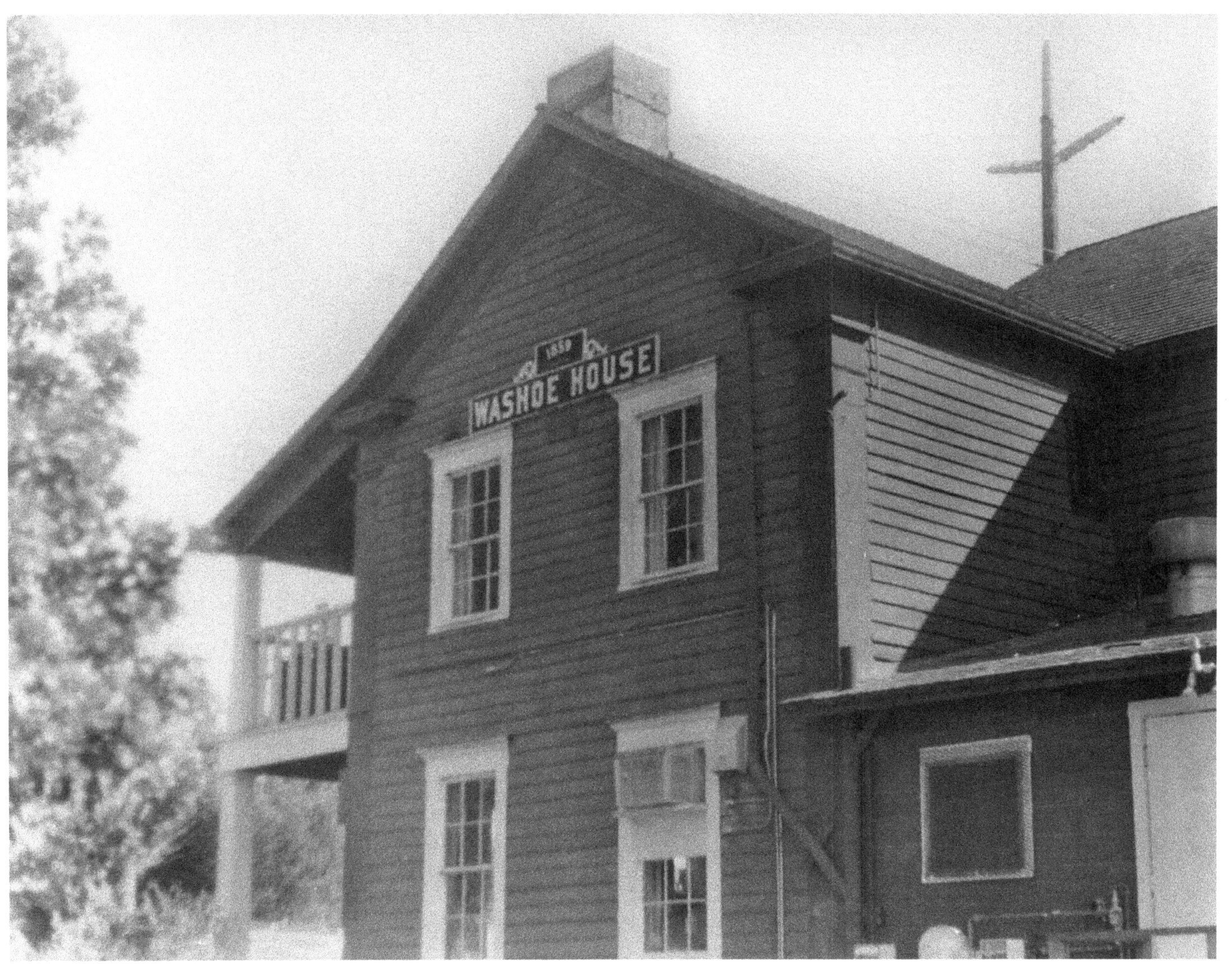

The Buena Vista Vineyards, founded by pioneer winemaker Agoston Haraszthy in 1857, holds the distinction of being the oldest stone winery in California. Buena Vista has long been recognized as the birthplace of the California wine industry. Haraszthy dug limestone tunnels into the hillside and returned to Europe in 1861 to gather the cuttings that developed the state's wine industry. This photo is a 1940s view.

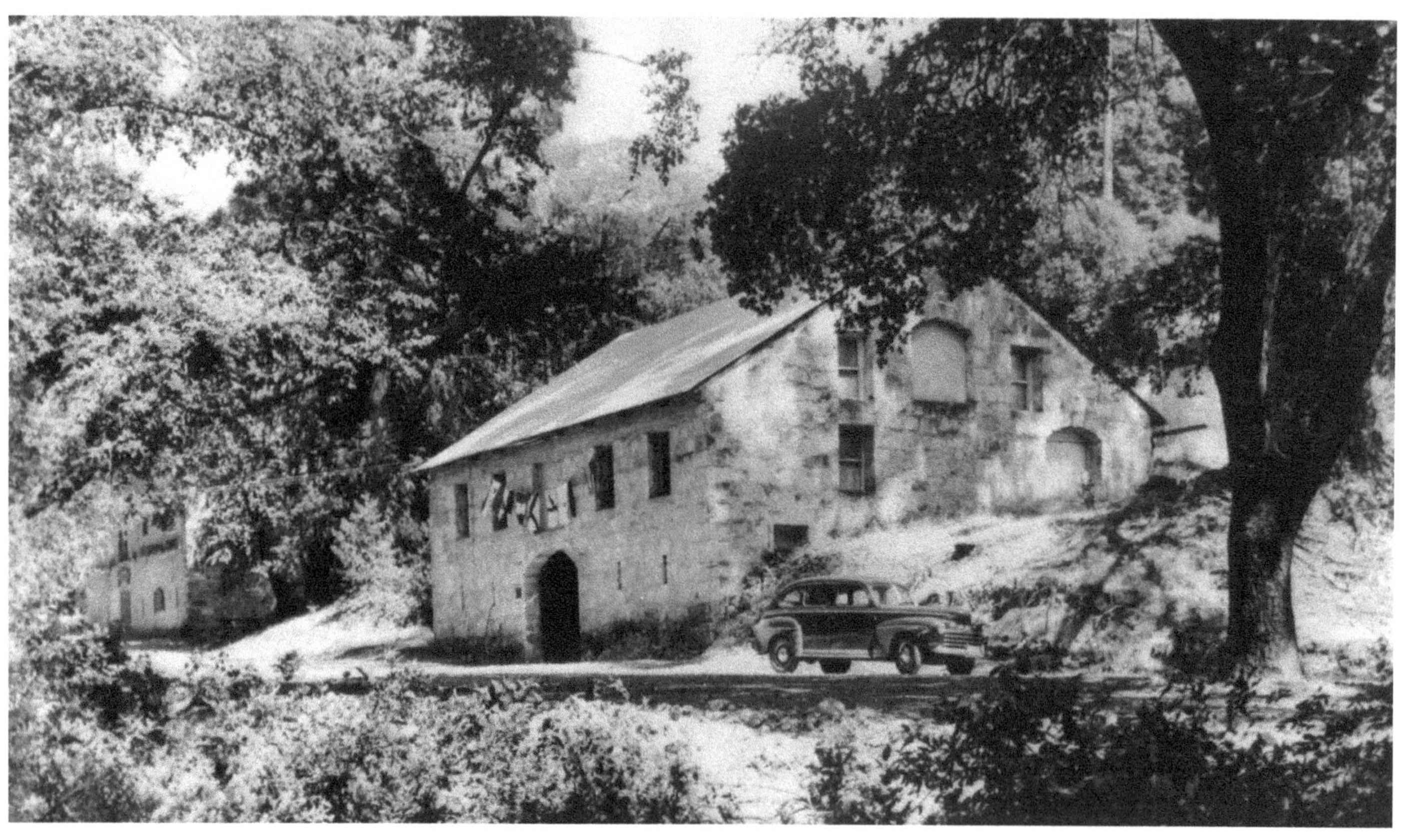

General Mariano Vallejo was an important figure in the settling of nineteenth-century Sonoma County, during both the Mexican and American periods. Vallejo and his family lived and entertained in their New England–style home for thirty-five years. To keep the rambling, two-story house warm in the winter and cool in the summer, bricks were placed inside the walls. Now part of the state park system, it is located at West Spain and 3rd streets, west a half-mile from the Sonoma Plaza. This picture was taken in 1945.

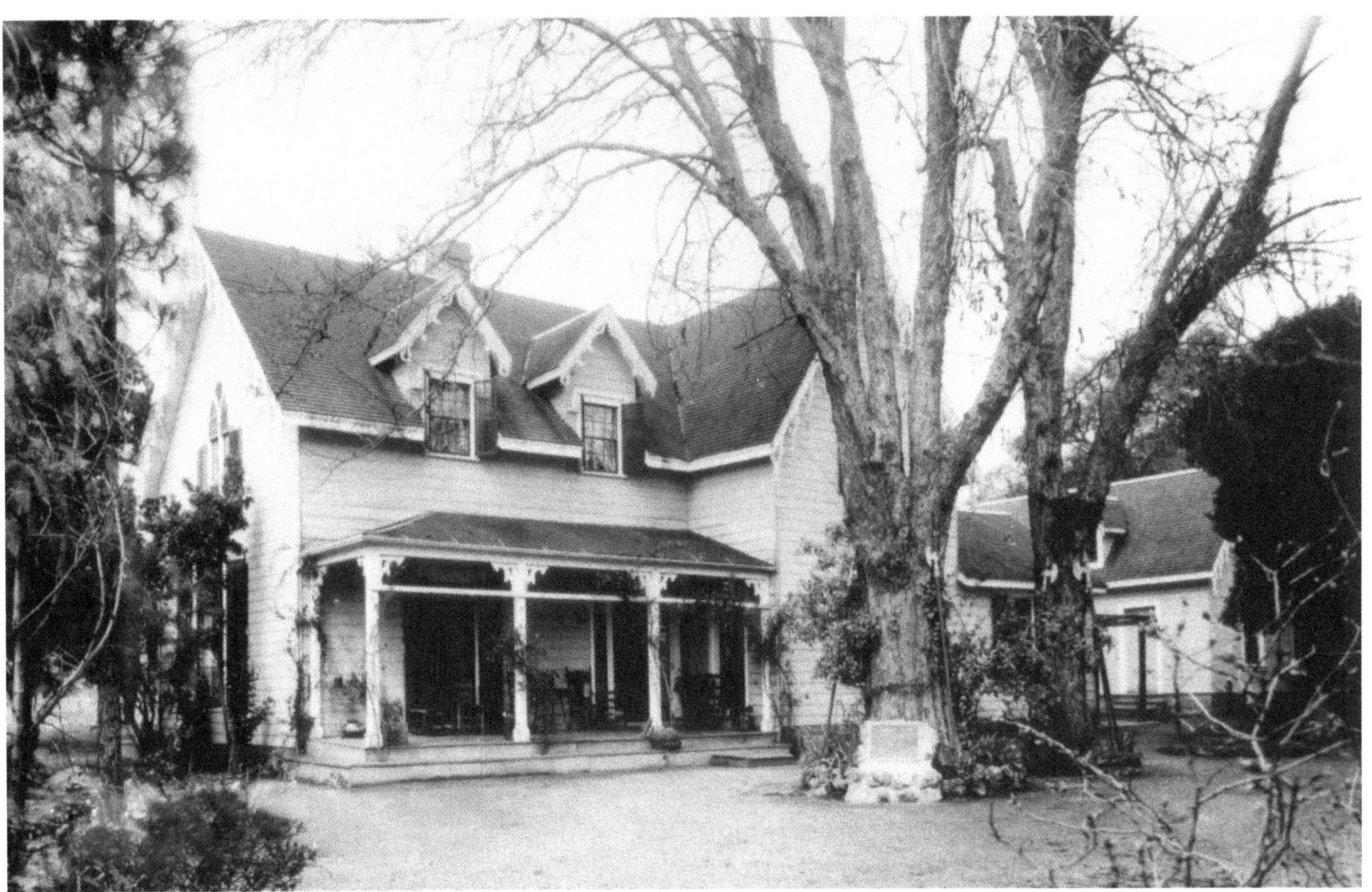

Sonoma's old Mexican garrison, built in 1836 at First and Spain streets, was an office building in the 1940s. The Sonoma Valley Chamber of Commerce and Robert A. Miller Insurance operated out of the classic building.

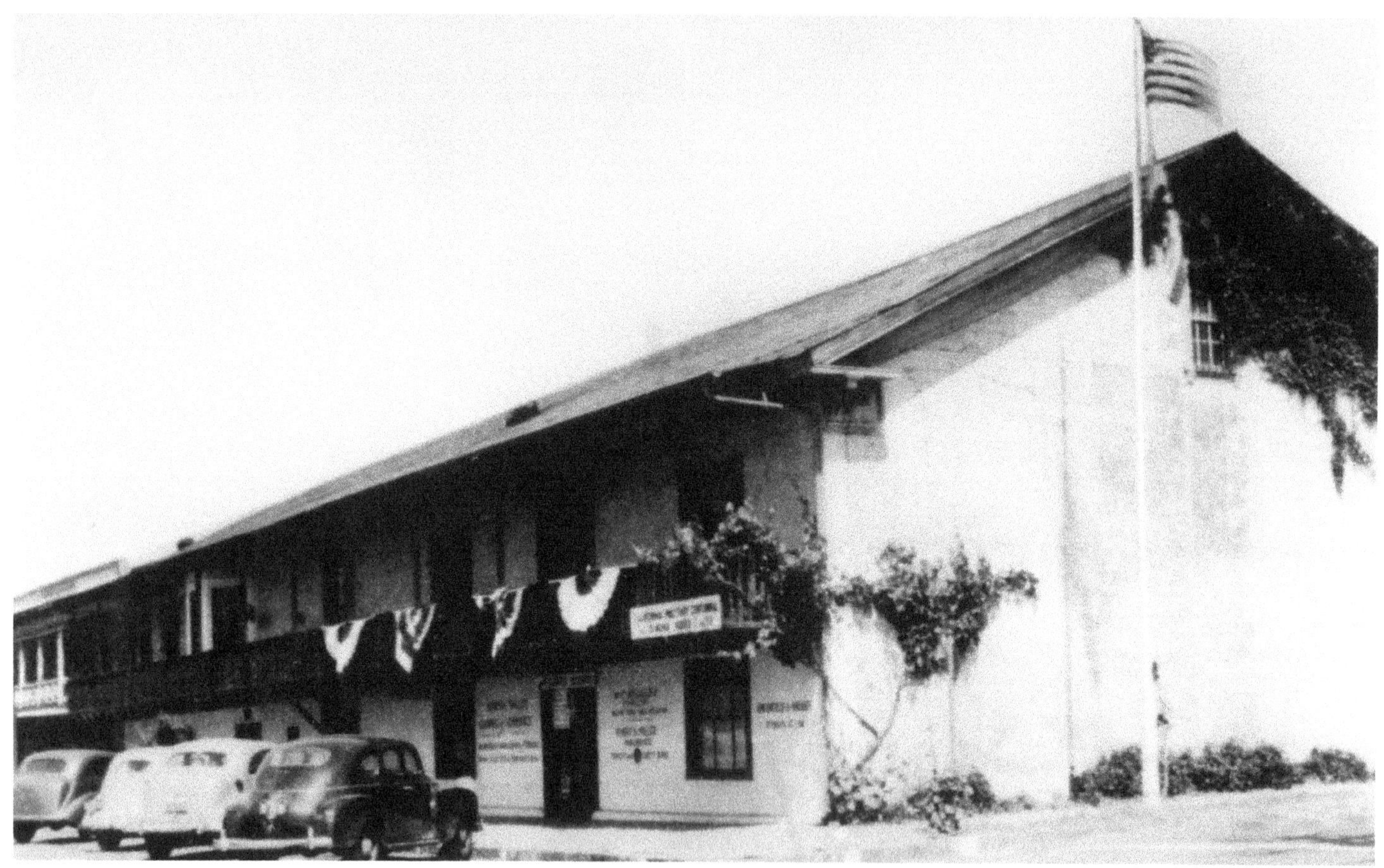

What's a coffee shop without a long string of pickup trucks, not to mention their thirsty drivers? The White Creamery in Petaluma, at left in the 400 block of 3rd Street, served up omelets, donuts, and coffee in the 1940s while people did their business at the Spence Peoples Motor Co. and Sterling Lumber Co. next door.

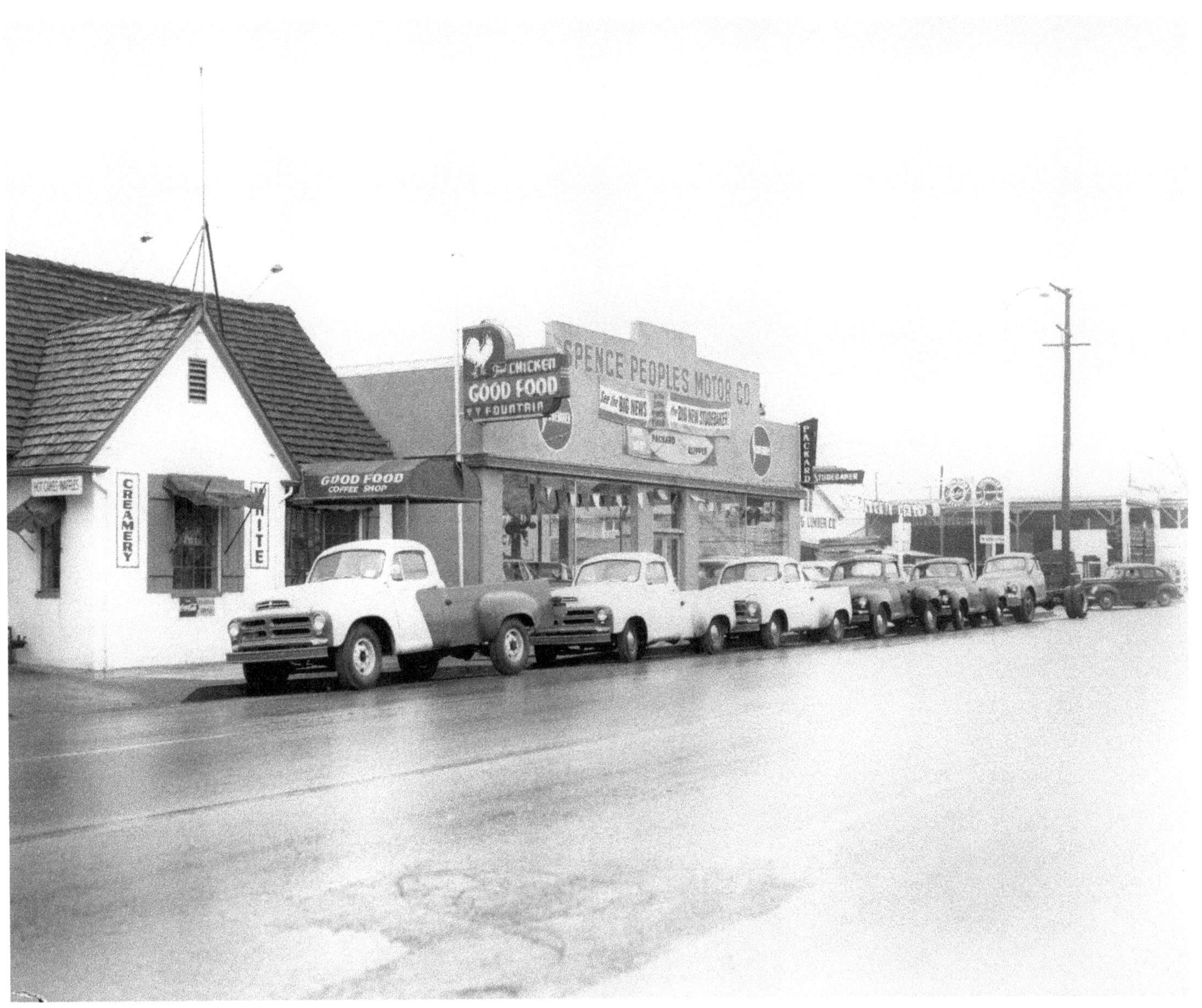

North of downtown, around Healdsburg Avenue at B and 10th streets, Santa Rosa became more residential, although the fashionable Saturday Afternoon Club met at their clubhouse at 430 10th Street. The club, founded in 1890, was considered the most influential women's group in the community, and membership was by invitation only.

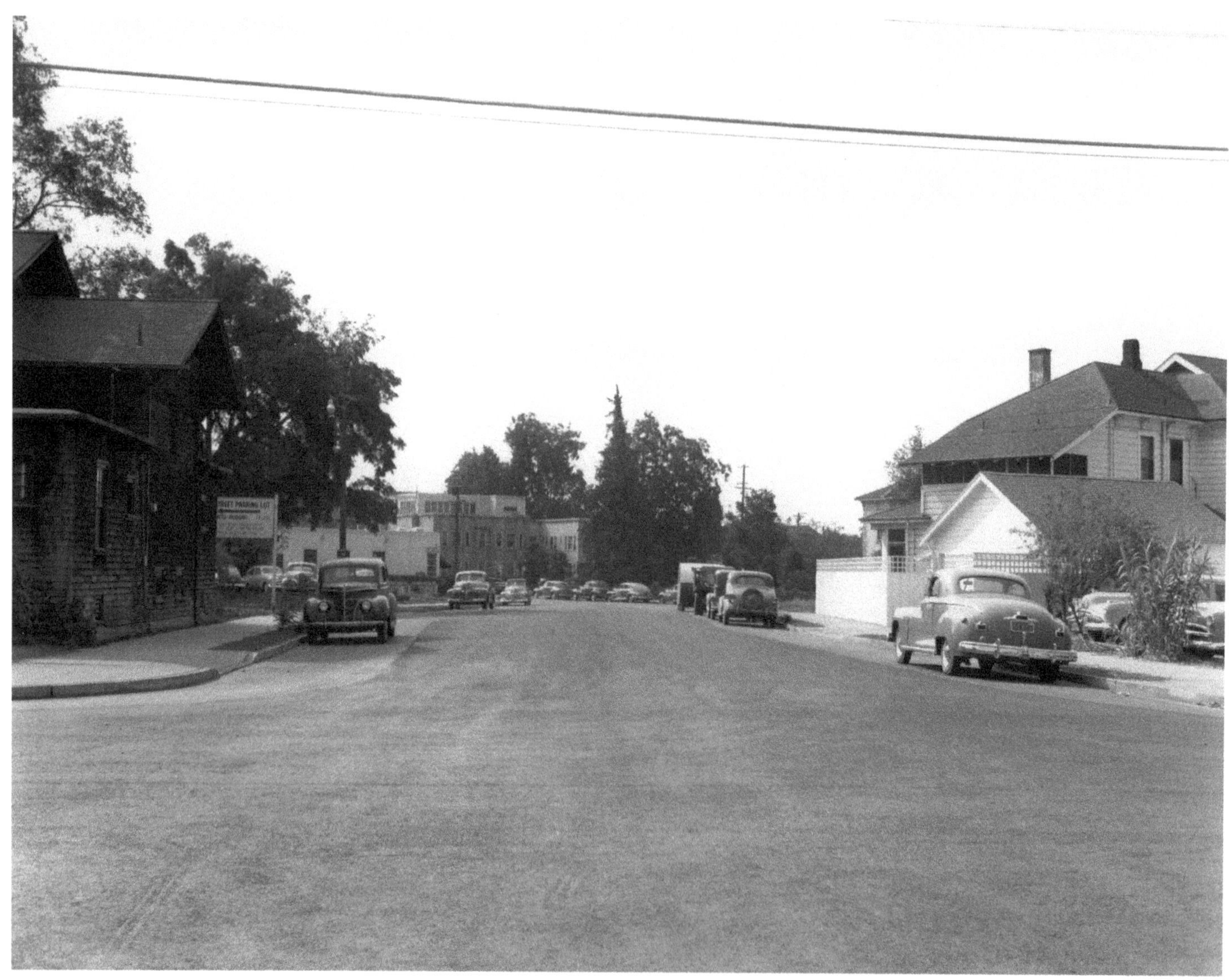

It didn't happen often, but a winter storm in 1947 left the Sonoma County Courthouse dusted in snow. Political pressures led to demolition of the venerable building in 1964, much to the chagrin of those residents who admired the historic structure.

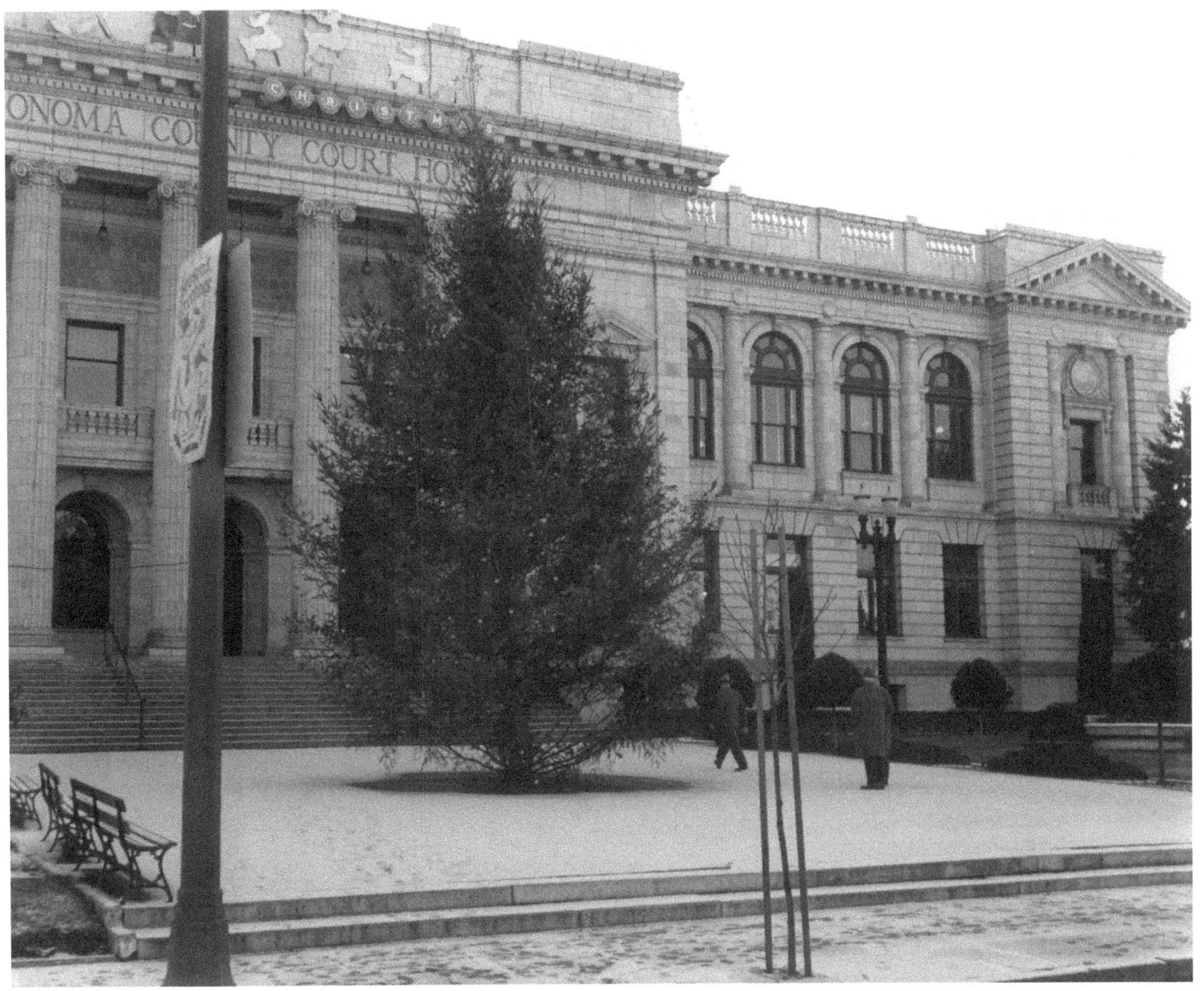

The city hall in Sonoma is a reminder of the community's historic role in the development of Sonoma County. The facility, built on the Sonoma Plaza in 1906, was built with all four sides the same, so no merchant would feel that he was facing the back door. Photo was taken in 1948.

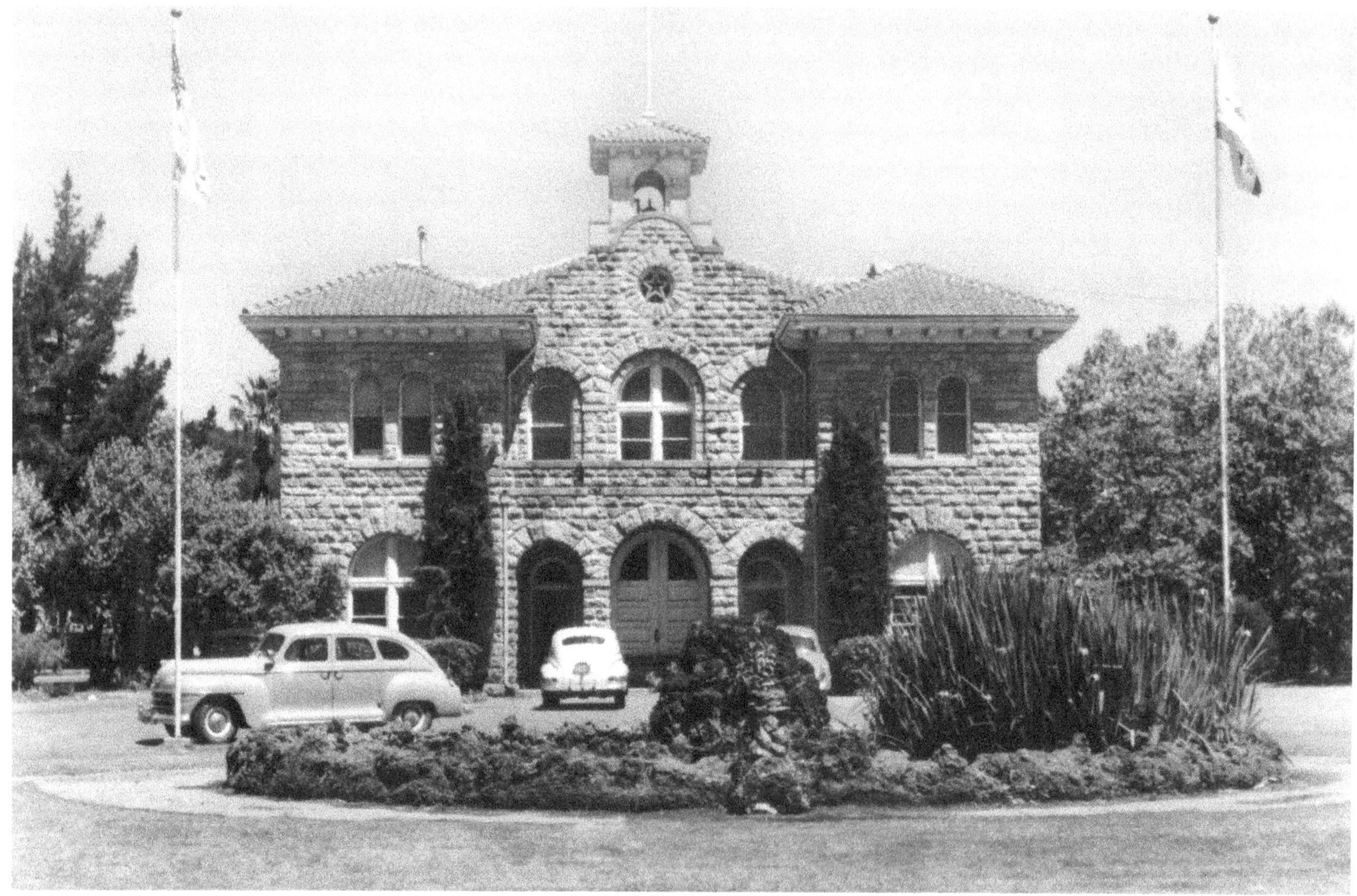

There was a great deal of controversy about where to run a postwar north-south highway through Santa Rosa, but at the insistence of local merchants, it was finally built close to the city, causing more congestion than would have occurred if it had been built farther west. Workers diligently went about the heavy-duty task of preparing the new link designated to speed access to major parts of the county.

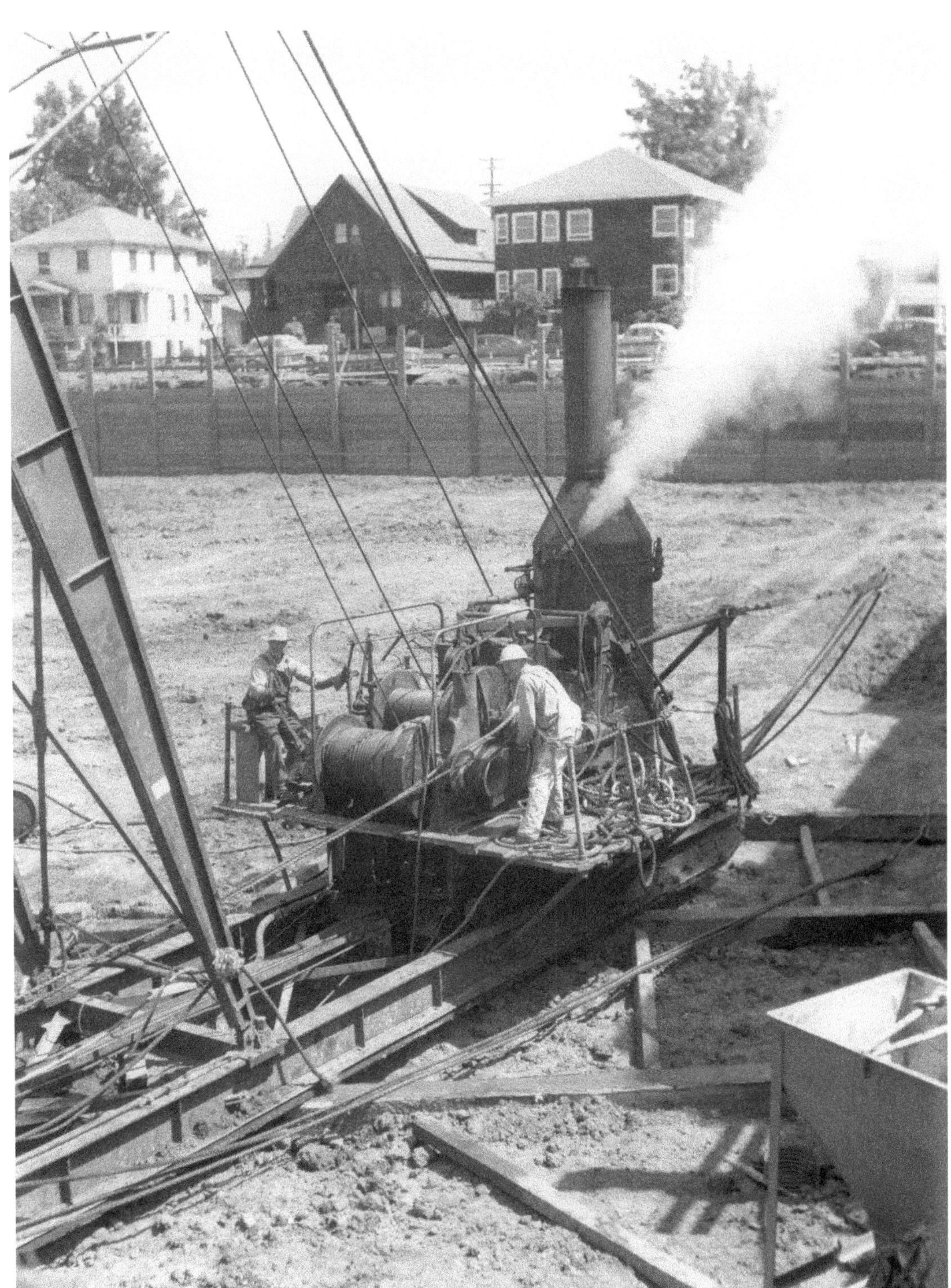

Perhaps the most unusual church in Sonoma County is the famous Church Built from One Tree, located in 1949 at Ross and B streets. Guerneville mill owner Rufus Murphy provided the redwood lumber for the Baptist facility, built in 1873. Robert Ripley featured the church in his "Believe It Or Not" column, noting that "my mother attended this church."

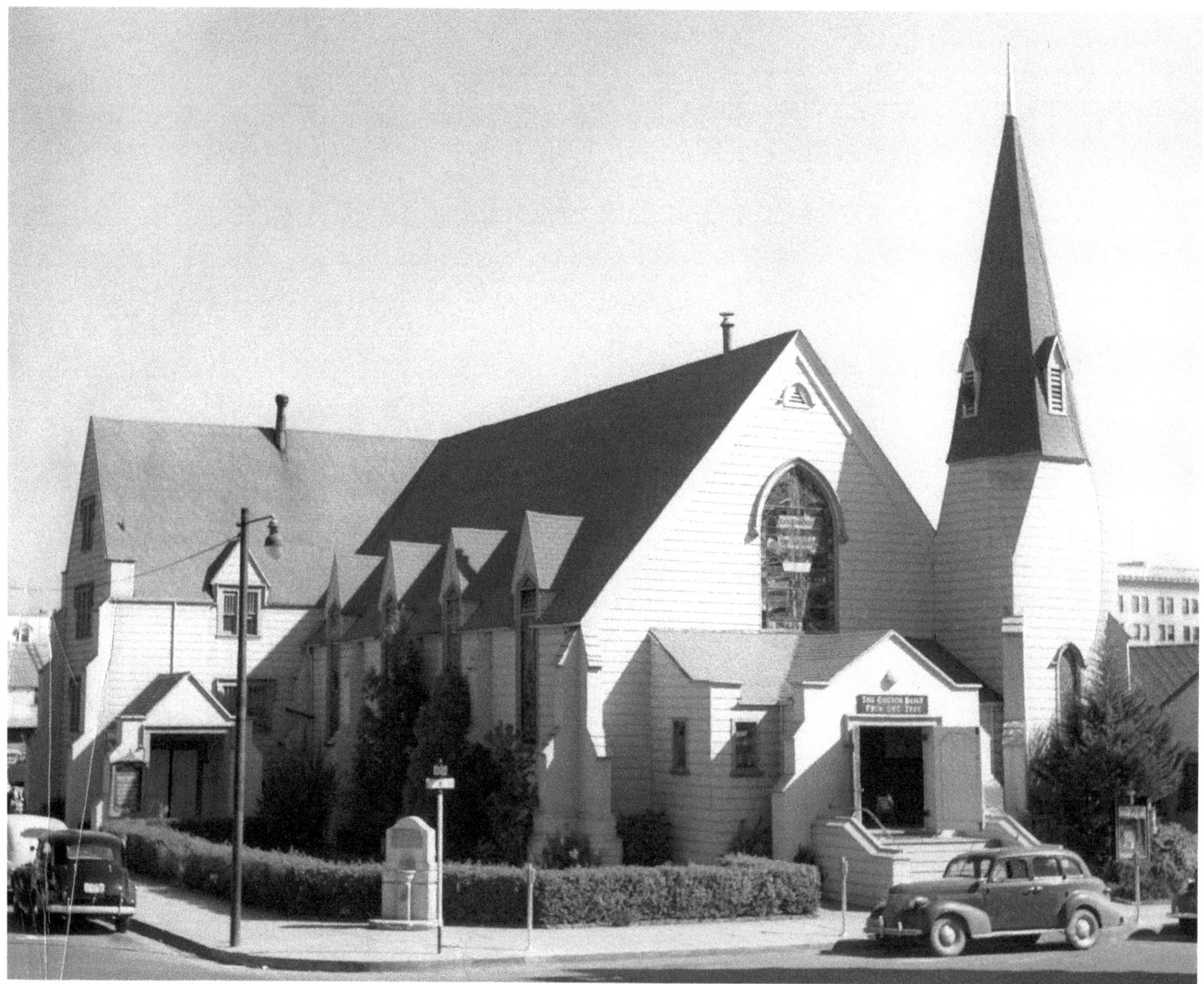

One of the more inspiring views in Santa Rosa came from the loft of the St. Luke's Lutheran Church in 1949. Richard F. Holtzen was pastor of the church at 905 Mendocino Avenue.

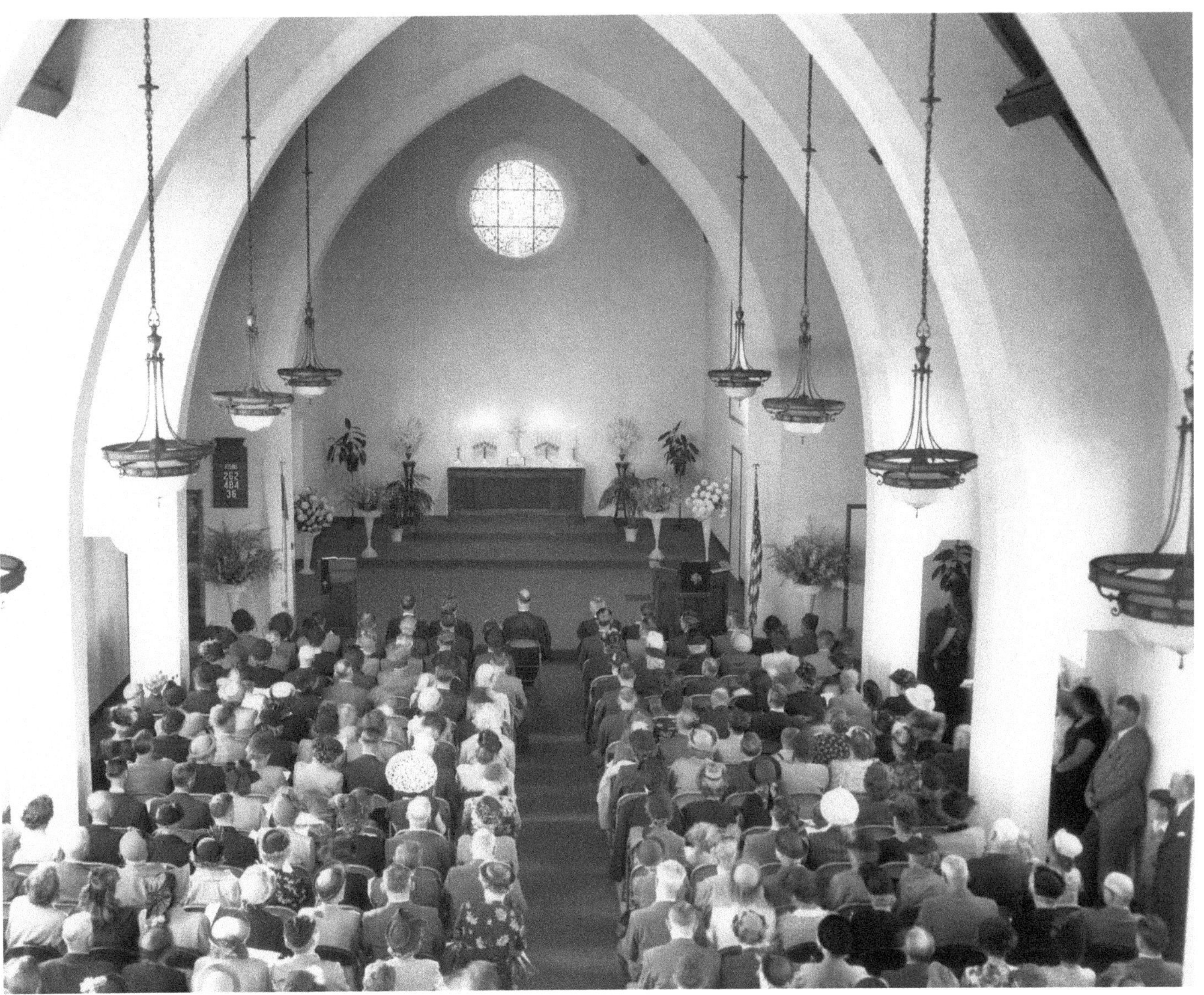

After fire destroyed the Rosenberg Department Store at 4th and B streets in 1936, father Max and son Fred bought up a big chunk of land farther east and built their "dream store" at 4th and D streets in Santa Rosa, where this photo was taken in 1950. Fred was an important benefactor to many causes until his death in 1965 at age seventy-nine. The store closed its doors in 1988, but was saved from the wrecking ball when Barnes and Noble took over the property.

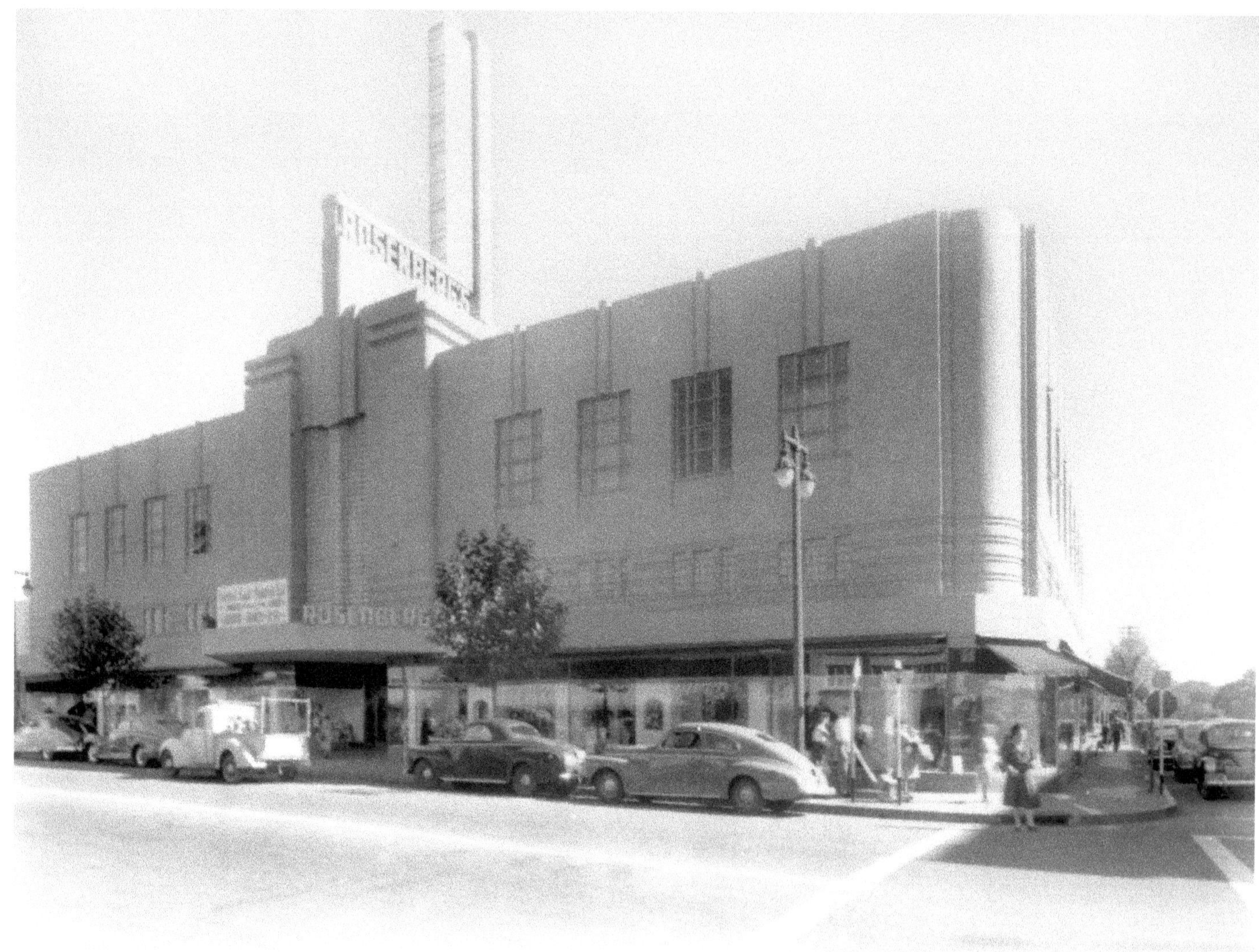

Deputy Sheriff Tom Campion successfully put his energy into developing a crack marching group through the Santa Rosa Boys Club in post–World War II Santa Rosa. The snappy marching group became one of the highlights of the annual Rose Parade in downtown Santa Rosa. The boys shown here performed for a cheering audience in 1952.

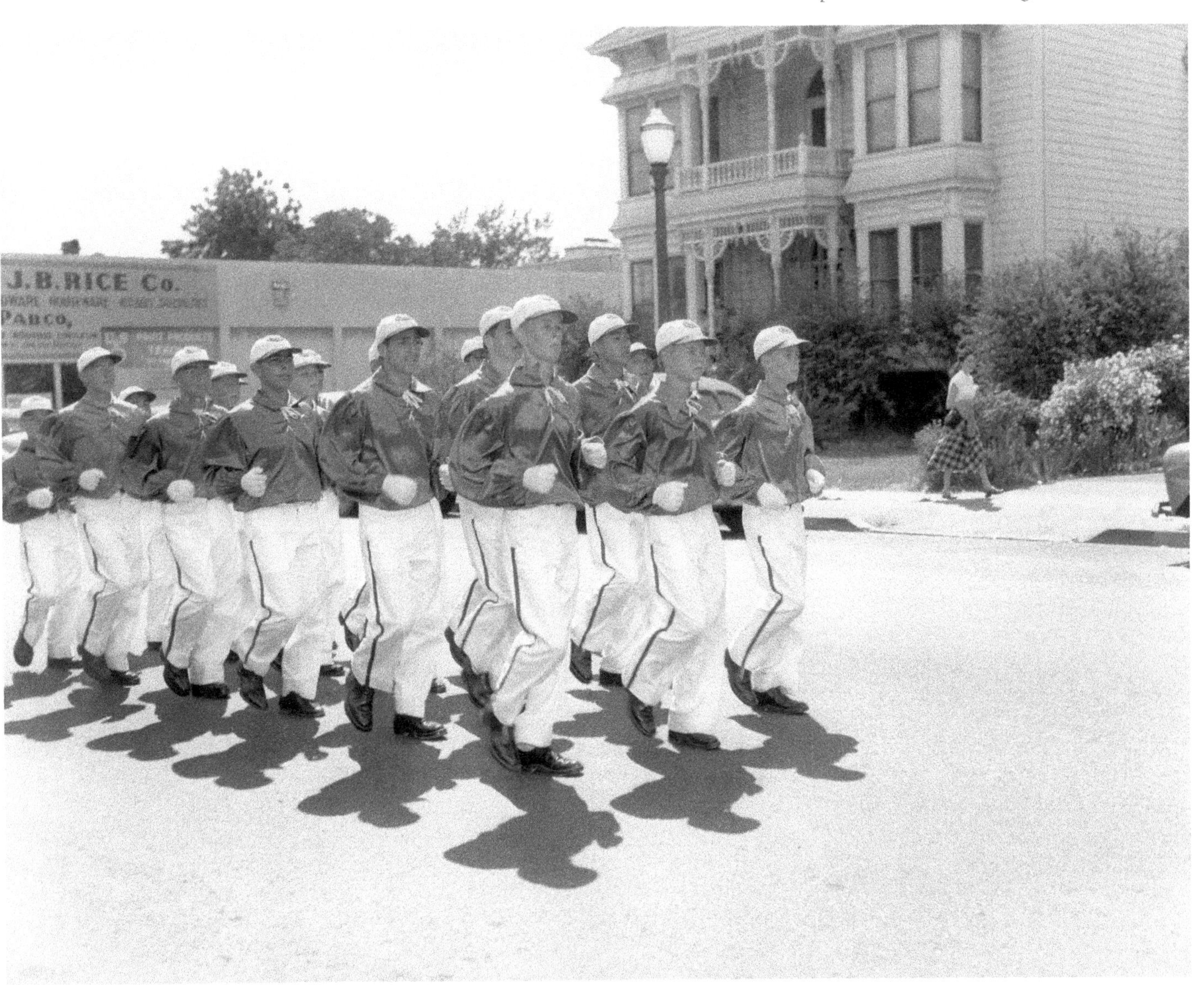

The tradition of Kanaye Nagasawa's Fountaingrove Winery carried on even after his death in 1934. In the 1950s, guests drank a toast to the success of the wine industry along with their hosts, owners Gwendolyn McBoyle Bechhold and her husband Siegfried. When Bechhold took out the vines to make room for other farm enterprises, it marked the end of more than seventy years of winemaking at Fountaingrove.

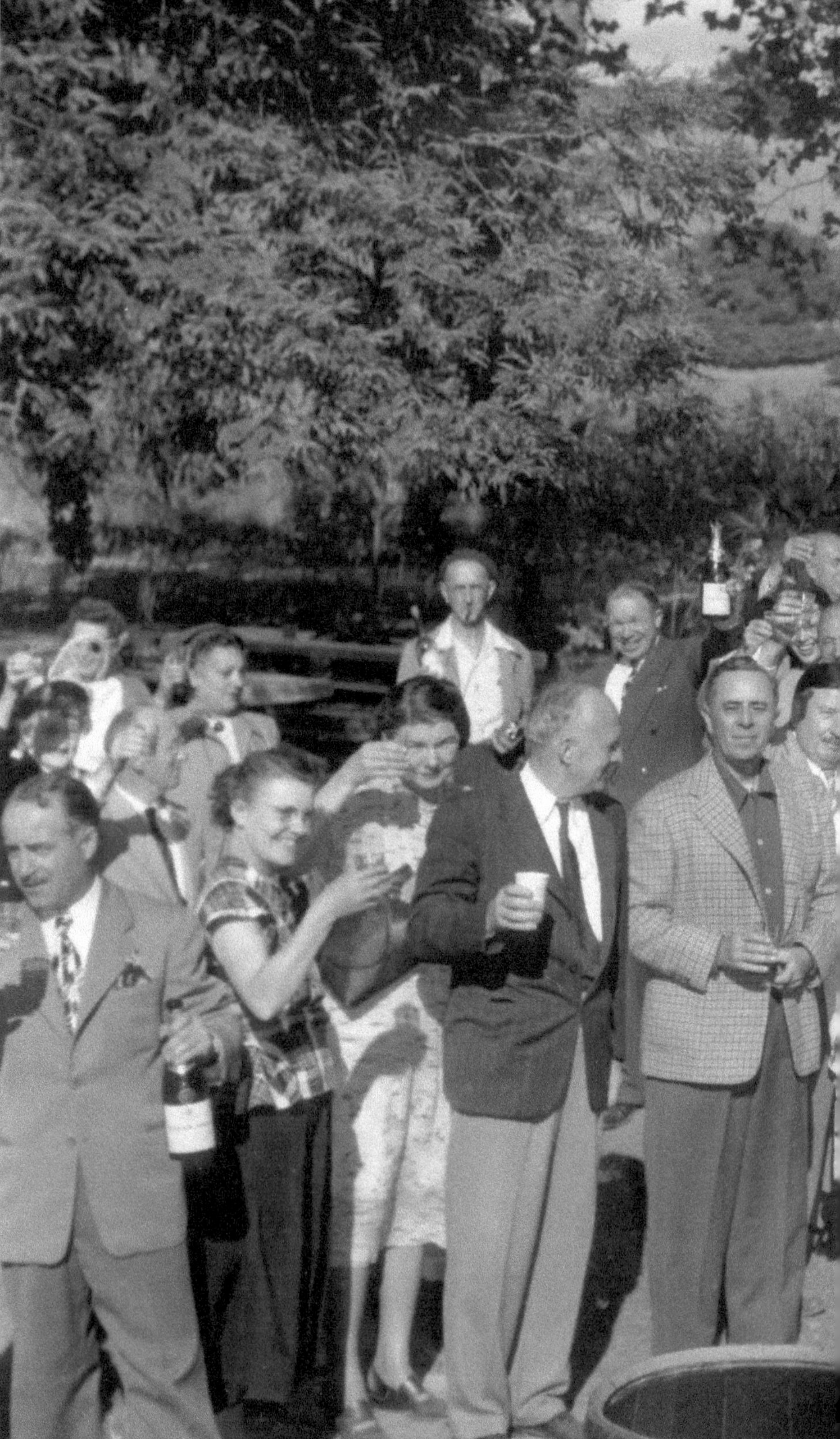

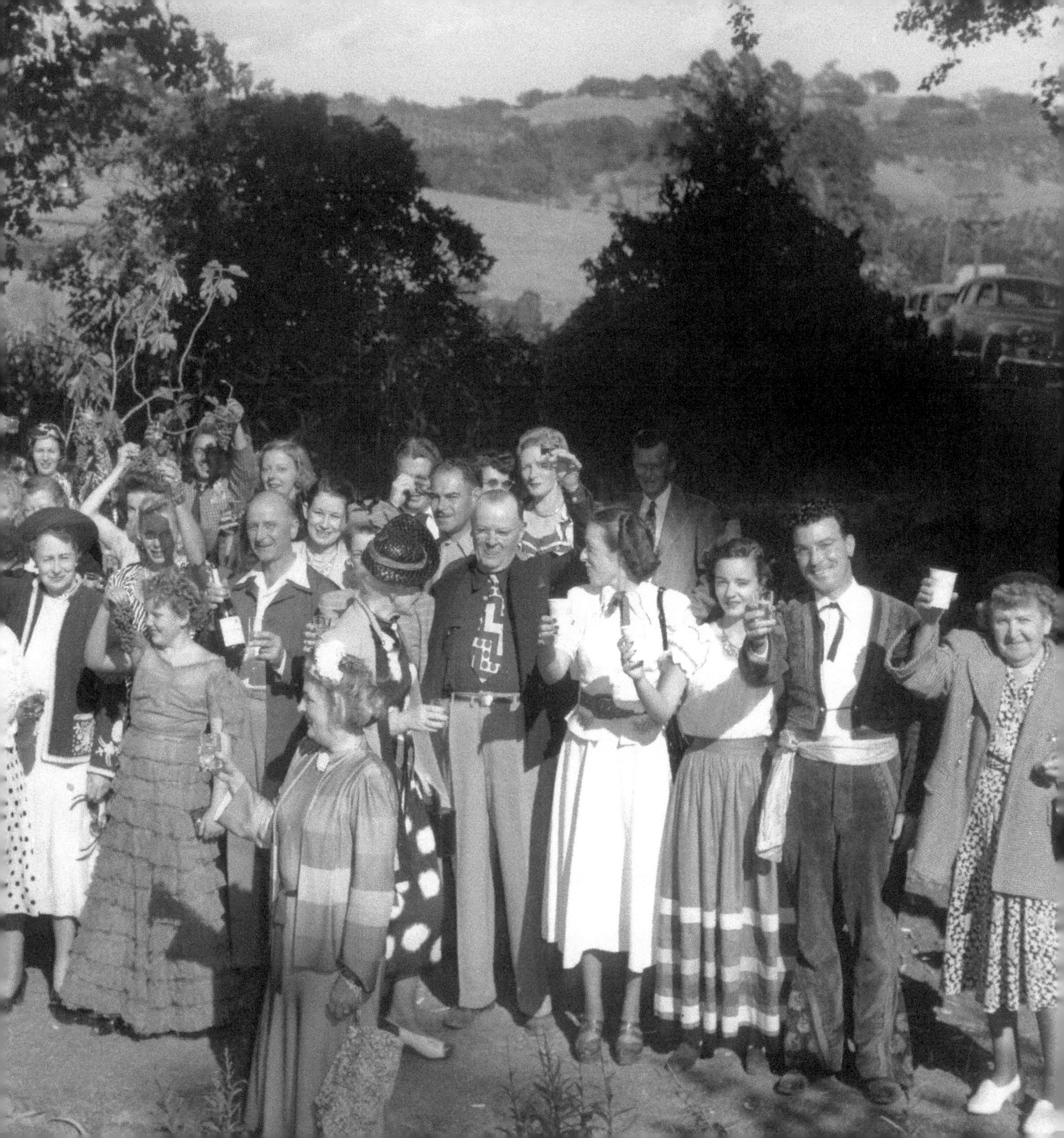

The vineyards of the Napa and Sonoma Wine Company promised a good harvest in 1952. Prohibition did damage to many operations in Sonoma County, and it took time for the area's wineries to recover. Some of the top names, including Korbel, Foppiano, Pedroncelli, Sebastiani, and Martini and Prati, joined forces after World War II to promote their product by creating the Sonoma County Winegrowers Association.

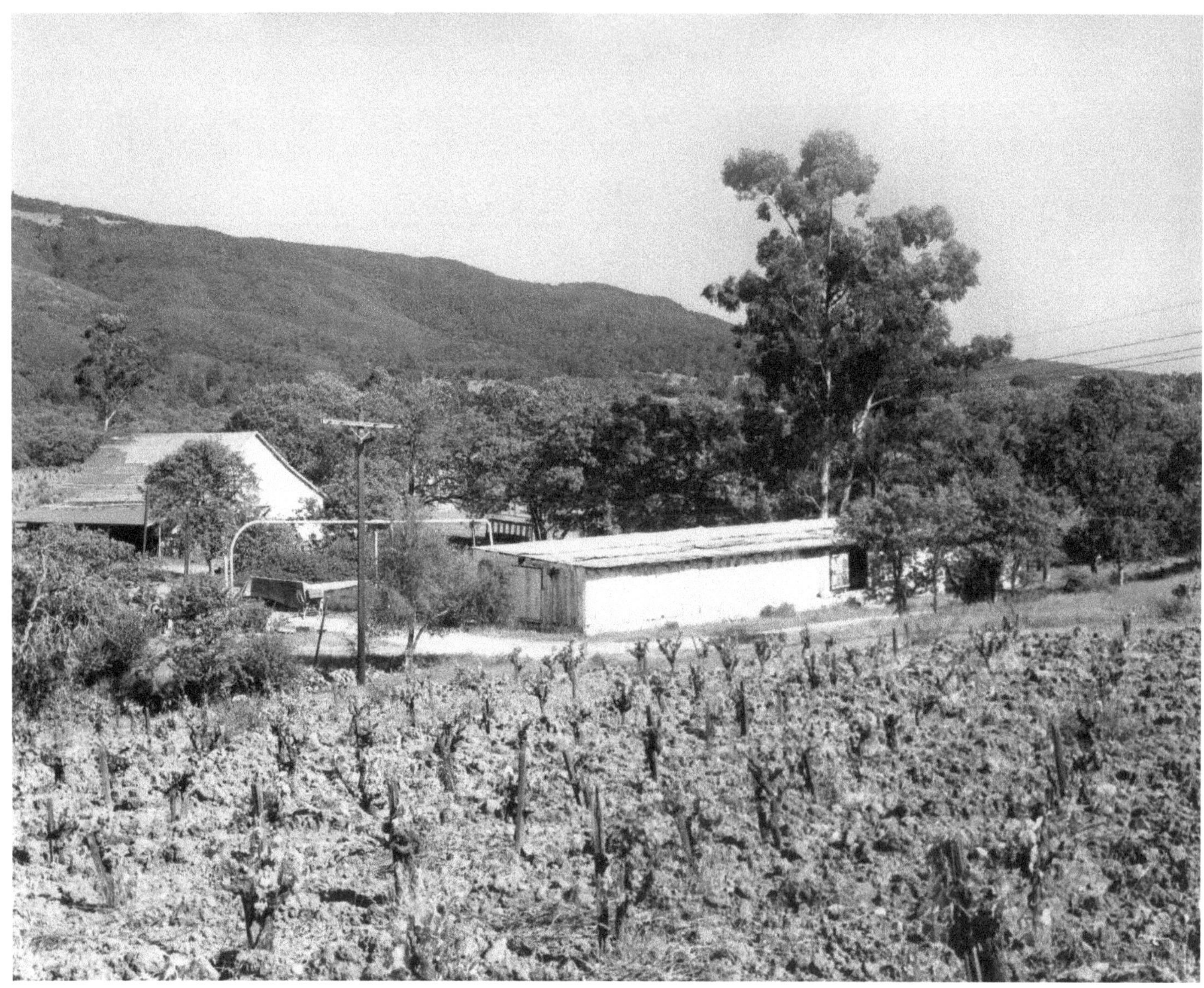

The Napa and Sonoma Wine Company's Castler Cellars showed impressive stone detail work in the 1950s.

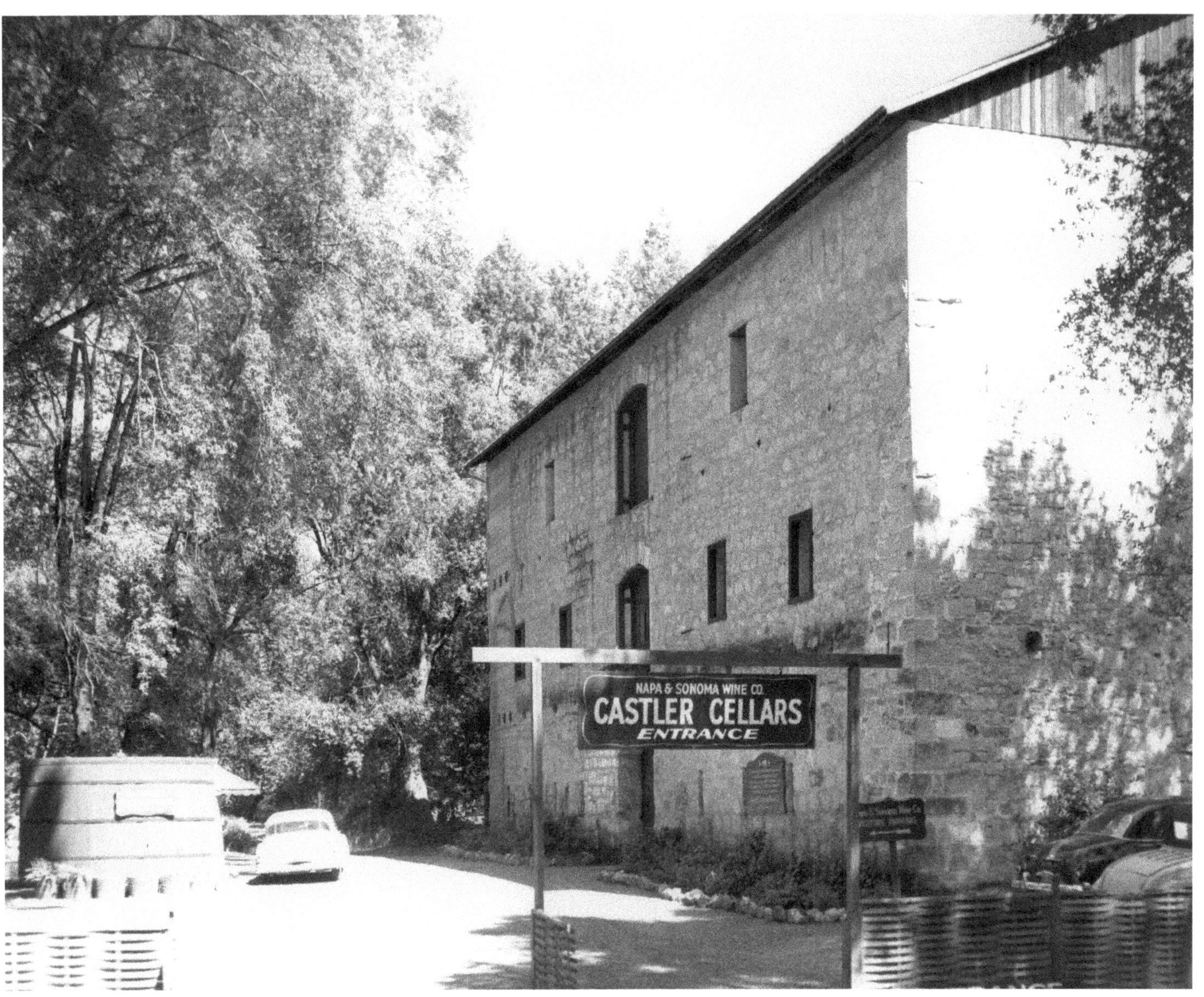

Antique vehicle owner Berkeley Nash brought out his 1902 Nash to showcase in a Santa Rosa parade in 1952. Joining him for the jaunt was doctor and historian William Shipley, author of a book on nineteenth-century Healdsburg called *Tales of Sonoma County.* In the book, Shipley, the first president of the Sonoma County Historical Society, recalled what it felt like to grow up in the small farm town north of Santa Rosa.

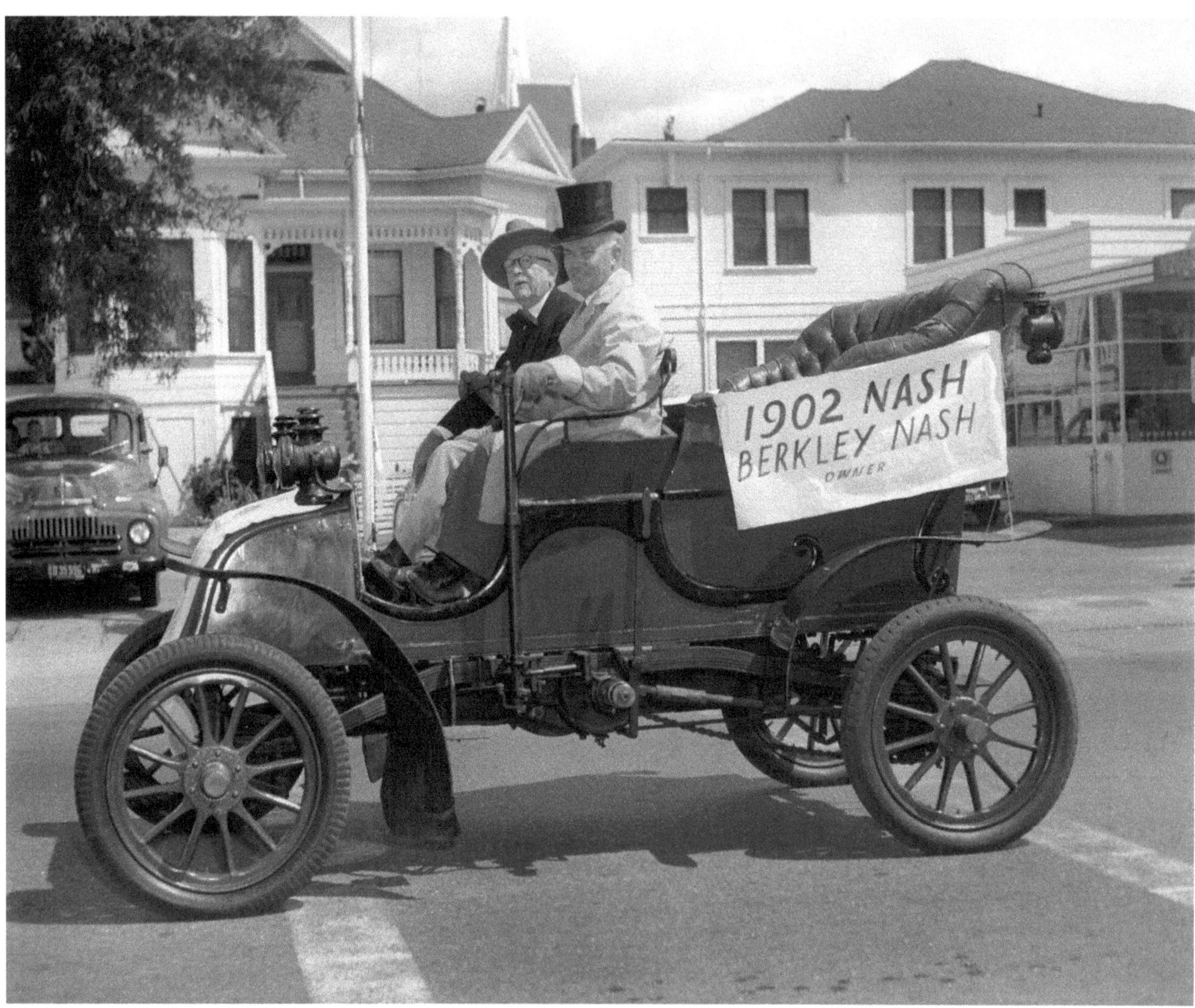

With pressures of population mounting in the late 1950s and early '60s, the Waldo Rohnert seed farm south of Santa Rosa was turned into an entirely new community called Rohnert Park. By 1958, a billboard advertised the Rohnert Park Industrial Center with facilities ideal for light industry, warehouses and service centers.

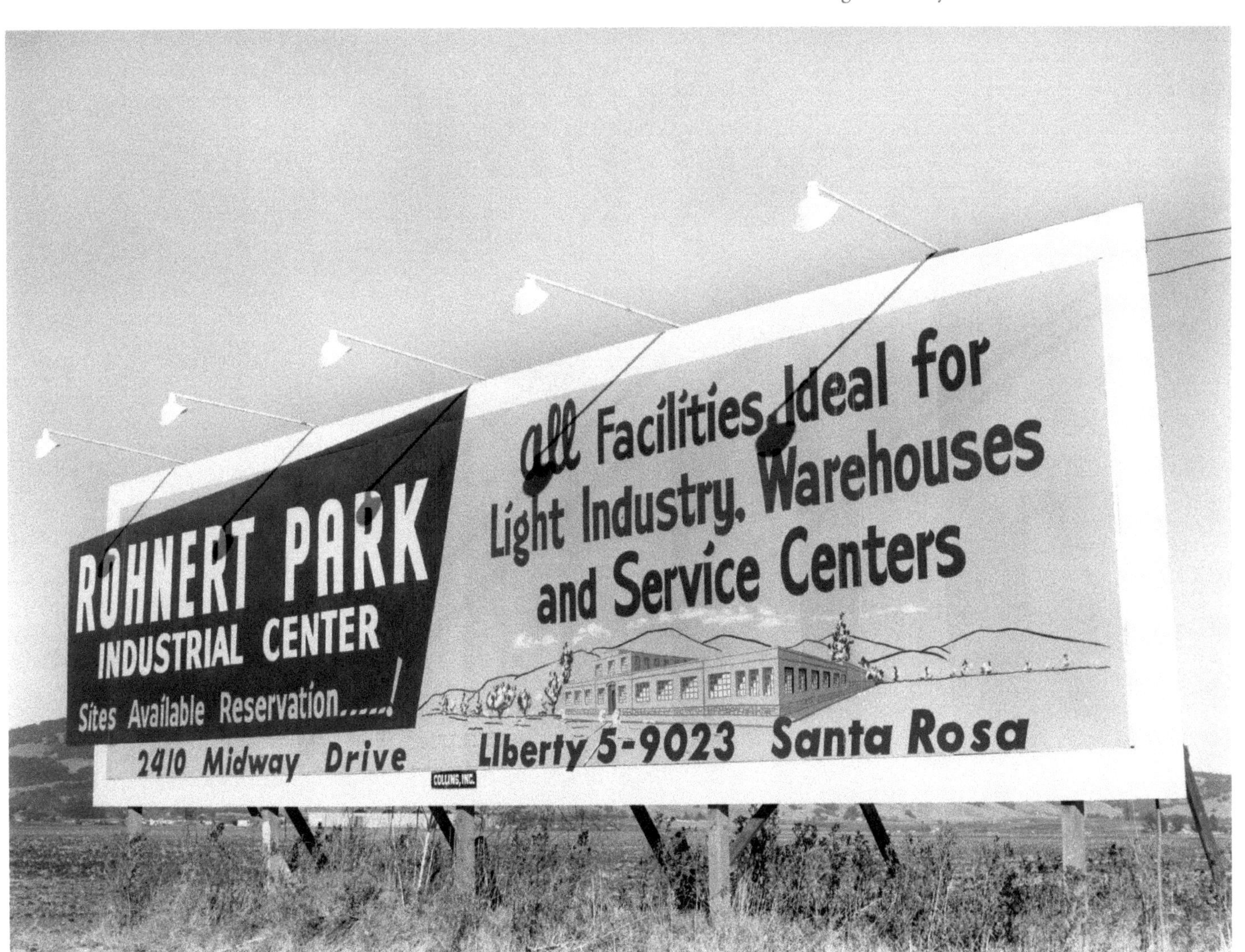

Increasing population, more traffic, more repair work—that was the formula in Petaluma in the late 1950s as painters used their striping machine on Washington Street. Val 's Richfield Station and the Sorenson Funeral Home are in the background.

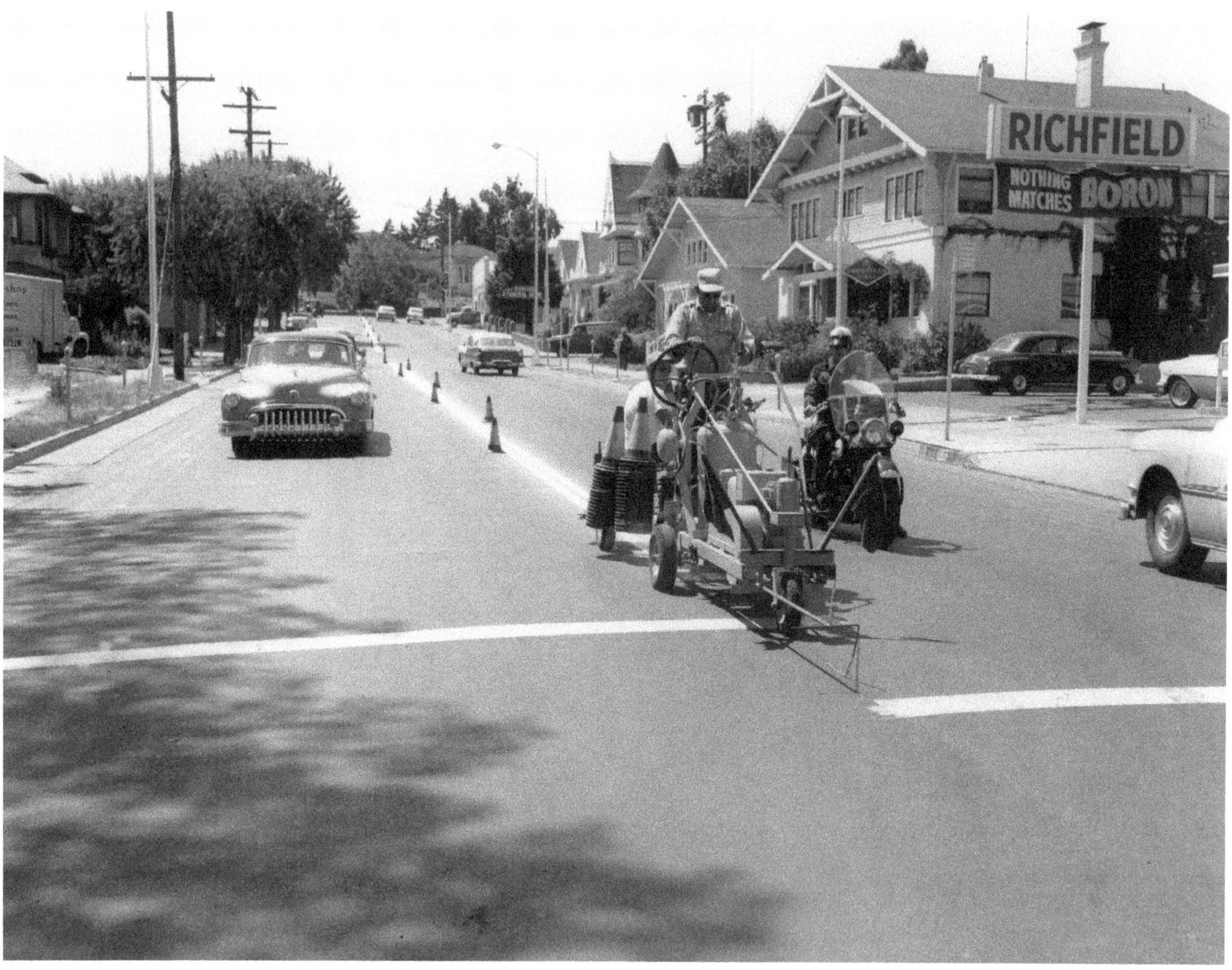

The Trinity Episcopal Church displayed a dignified presence in the 1950s at 214 East Napa Street at the corner of 2nd in Sonoma.

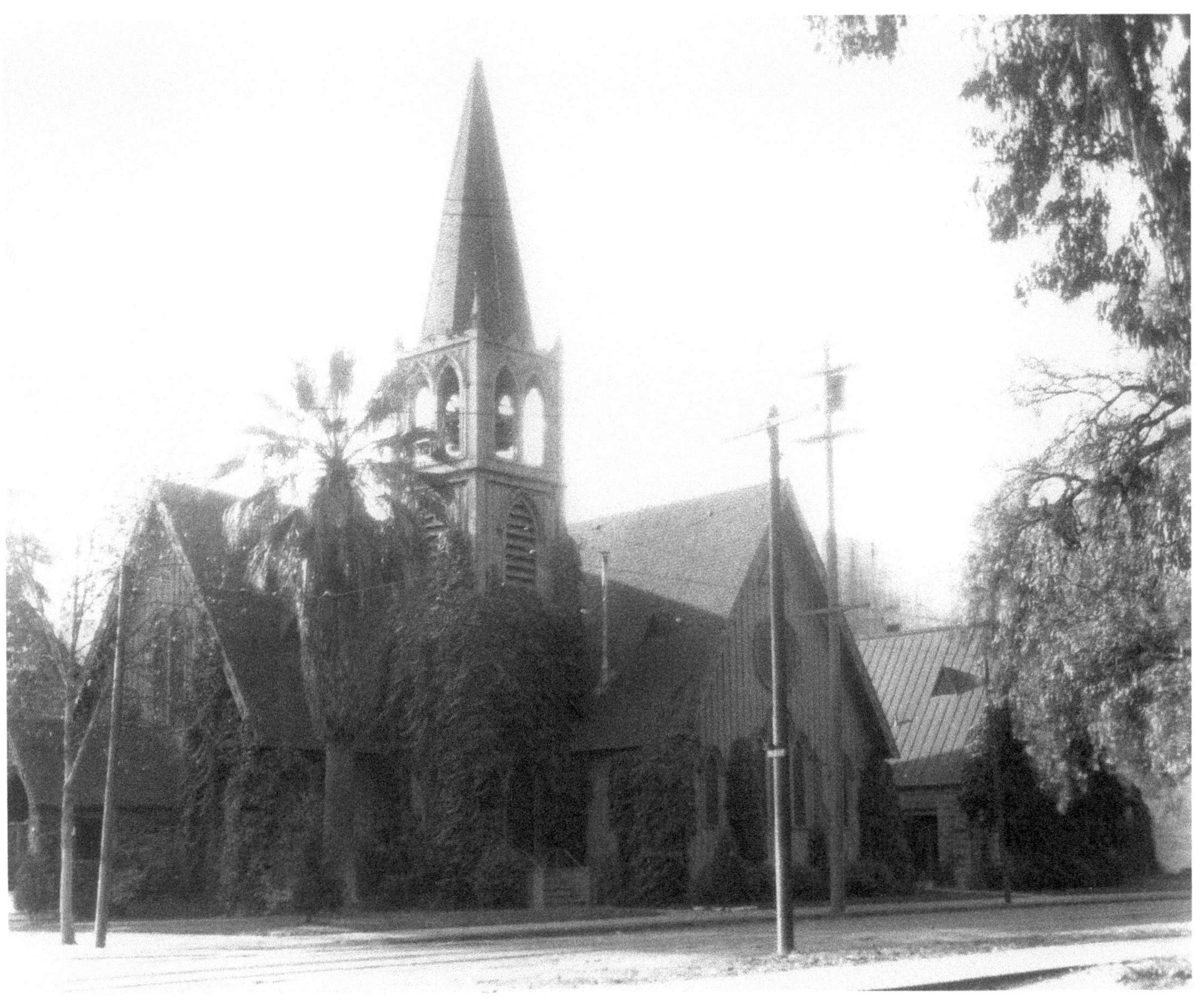

The years after World War II brought more national merchandisers to Sonoma County. Sears, Roebuck and Company offered "one-stop shopping" at 455 B Street from the early 1950s. Photo was taken in 1960.

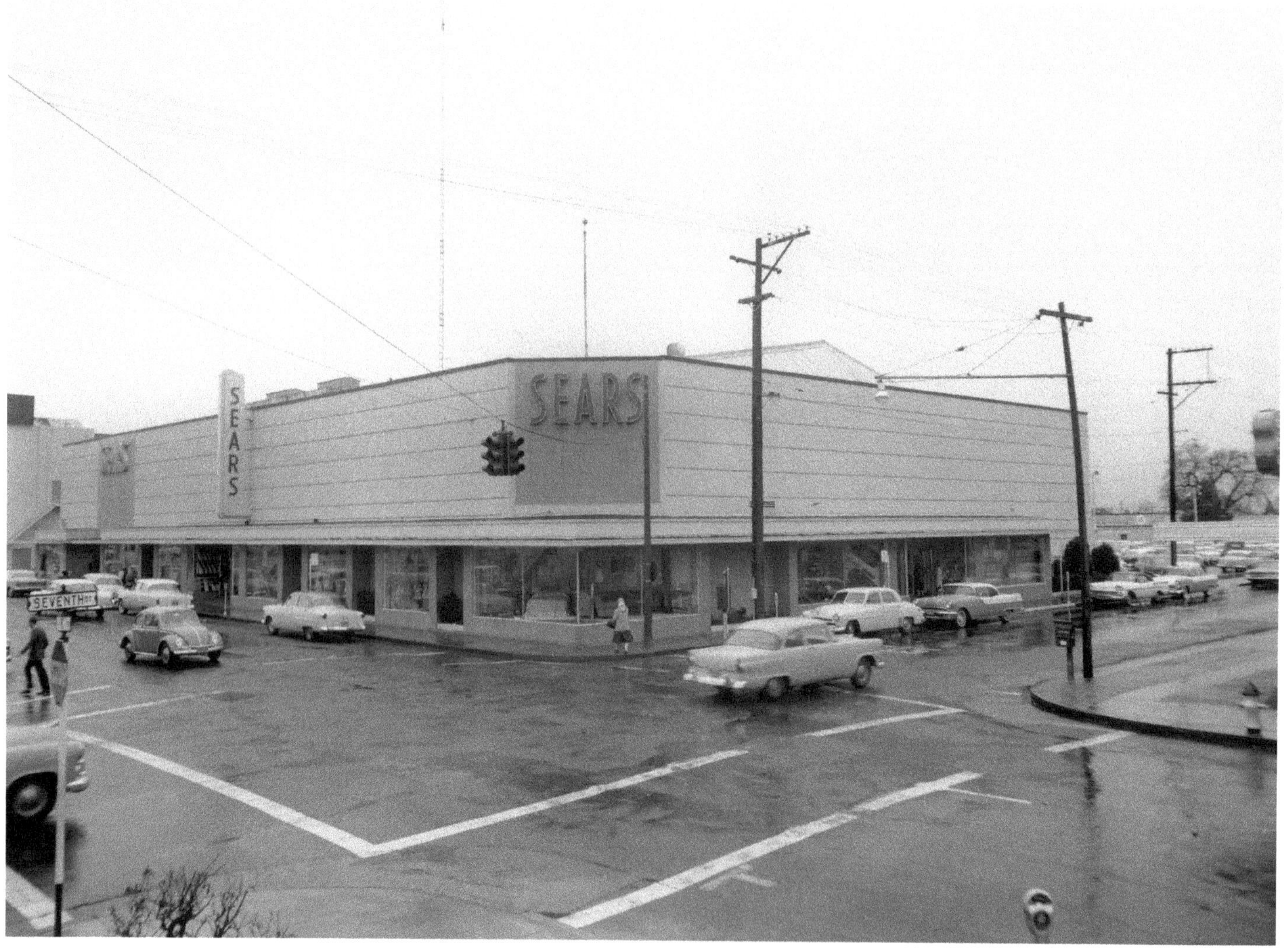

A church with modern design greeted Windsor parishioners in 1960.

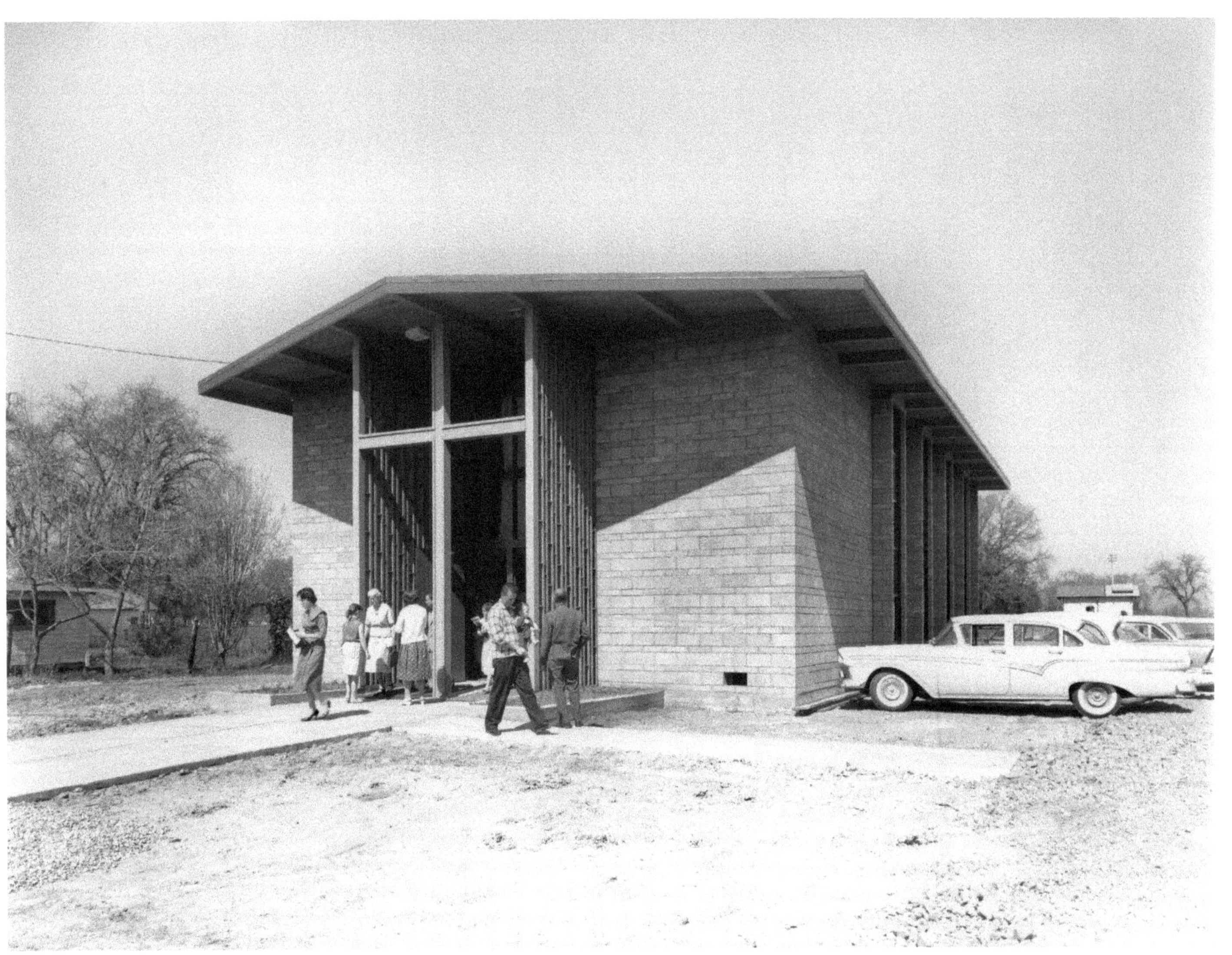

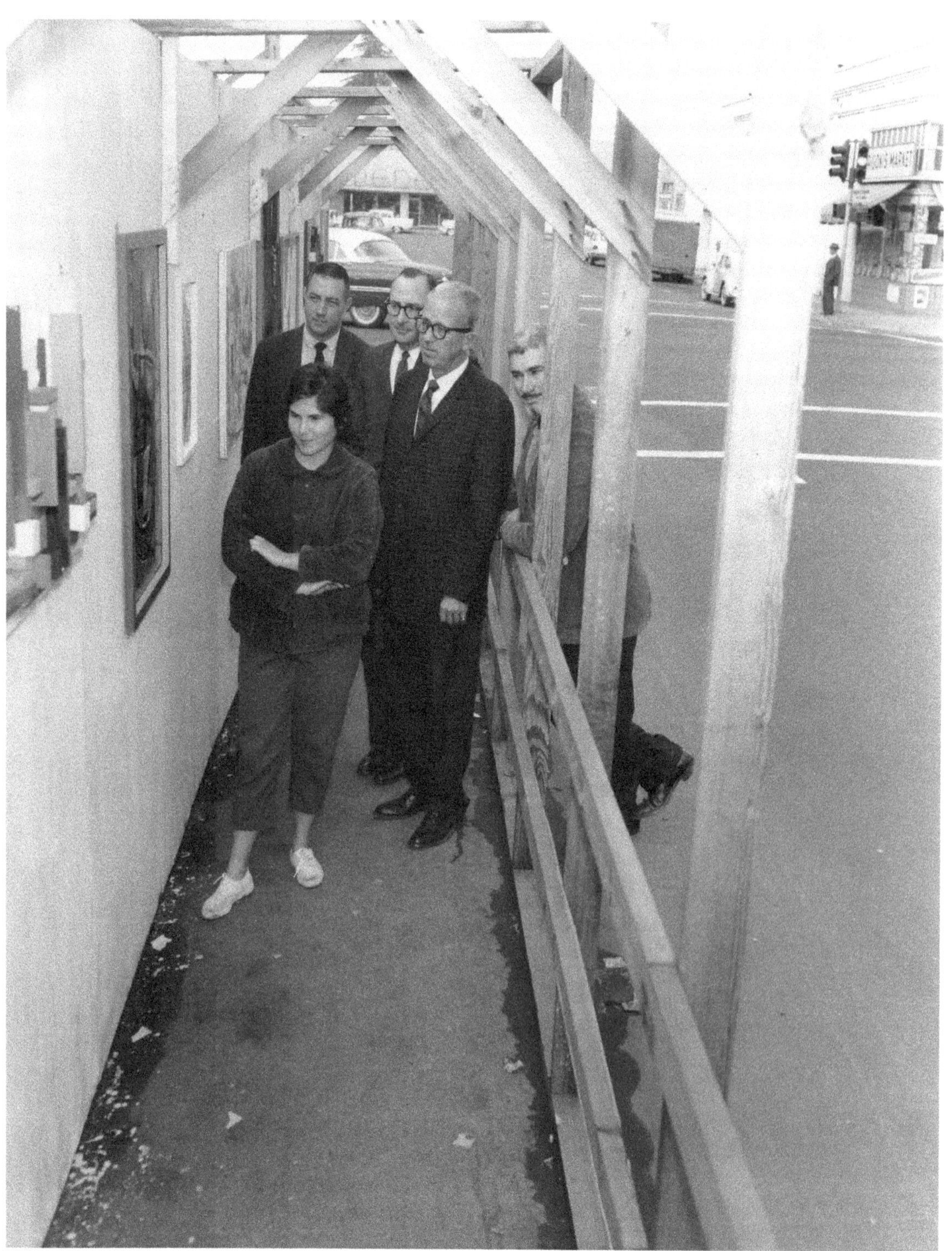

Santa Rosa Junior College, a two-year school founded in 1918 with an enrollment of nineteen students, has served a diverse population in both day- and night-school programs. As enrollment swelled, it sought to make more community contacts, as happened when the school opened an art exhibit in downtown Santa Rosa at 4th and D streets. Administrator Ran Newman, 3rd from left, and art instructor Maurice Lapp (far right), were among the people inspecting the display.

An aerial view of Rohnert Park in 1960. The "planned community" was incorporated two years later. Following a master plan, the developer divided the city into neighborhood units with 200 to 250 homes per unit. Each neighborhood was identifiable by street names that all started with the same letter of the alphabet.

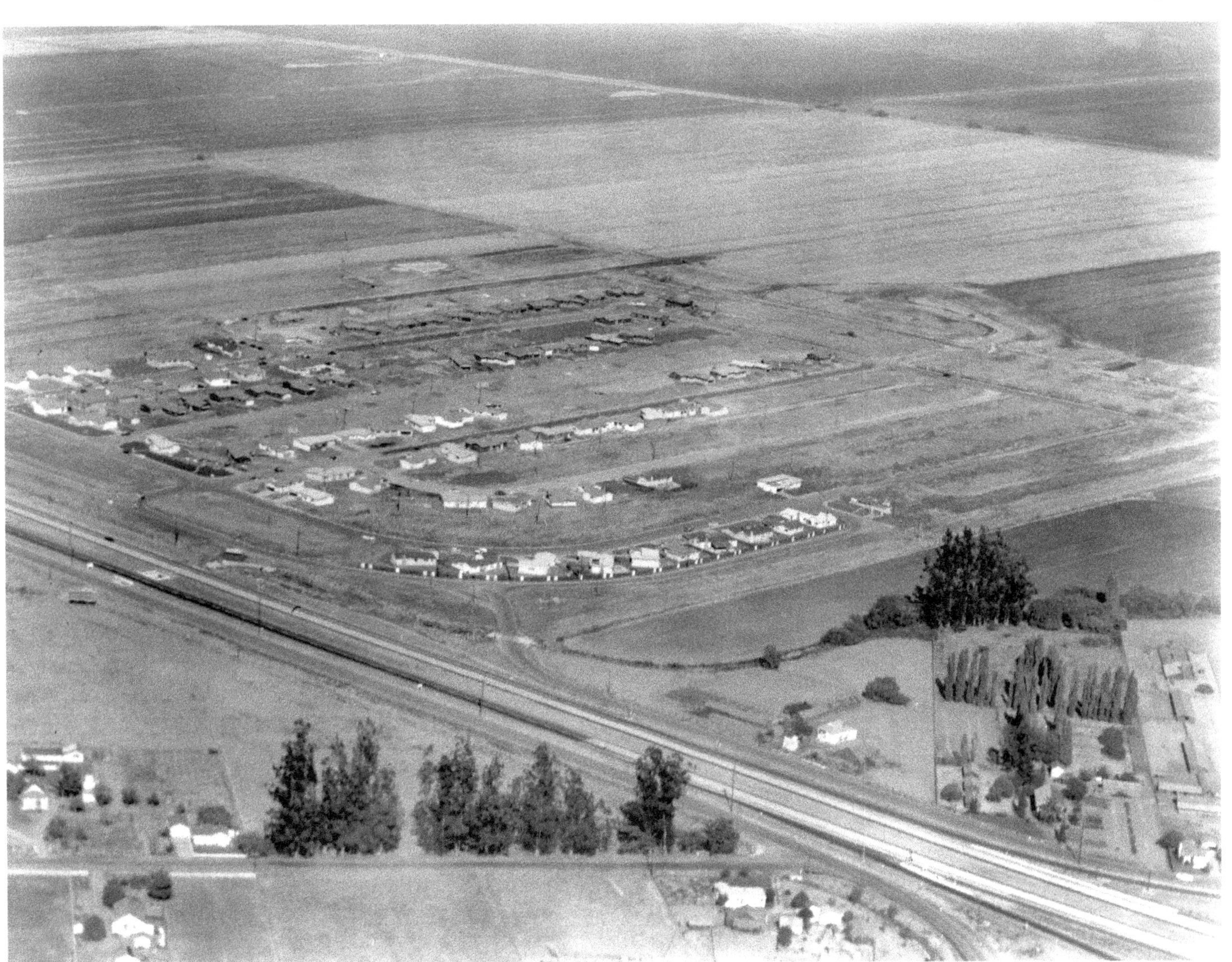

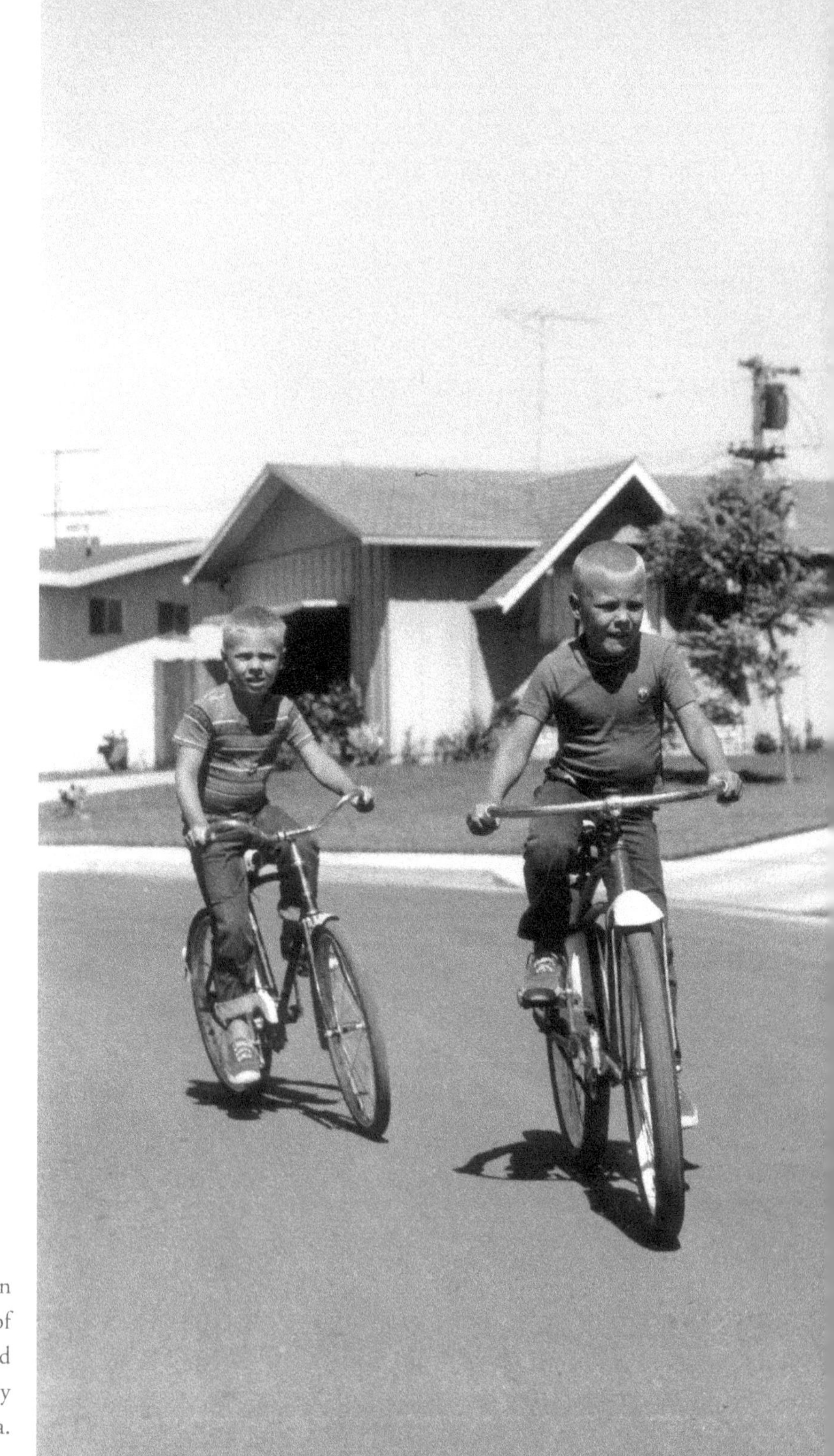

What could provide a more idyllic scene than children safely riding their bikes on the freshly paved streets of Rohnert Park in the early 1960s? The city provided a haven for many of the commuters who made daily trips to jobs in the San Francisco Bay Area.

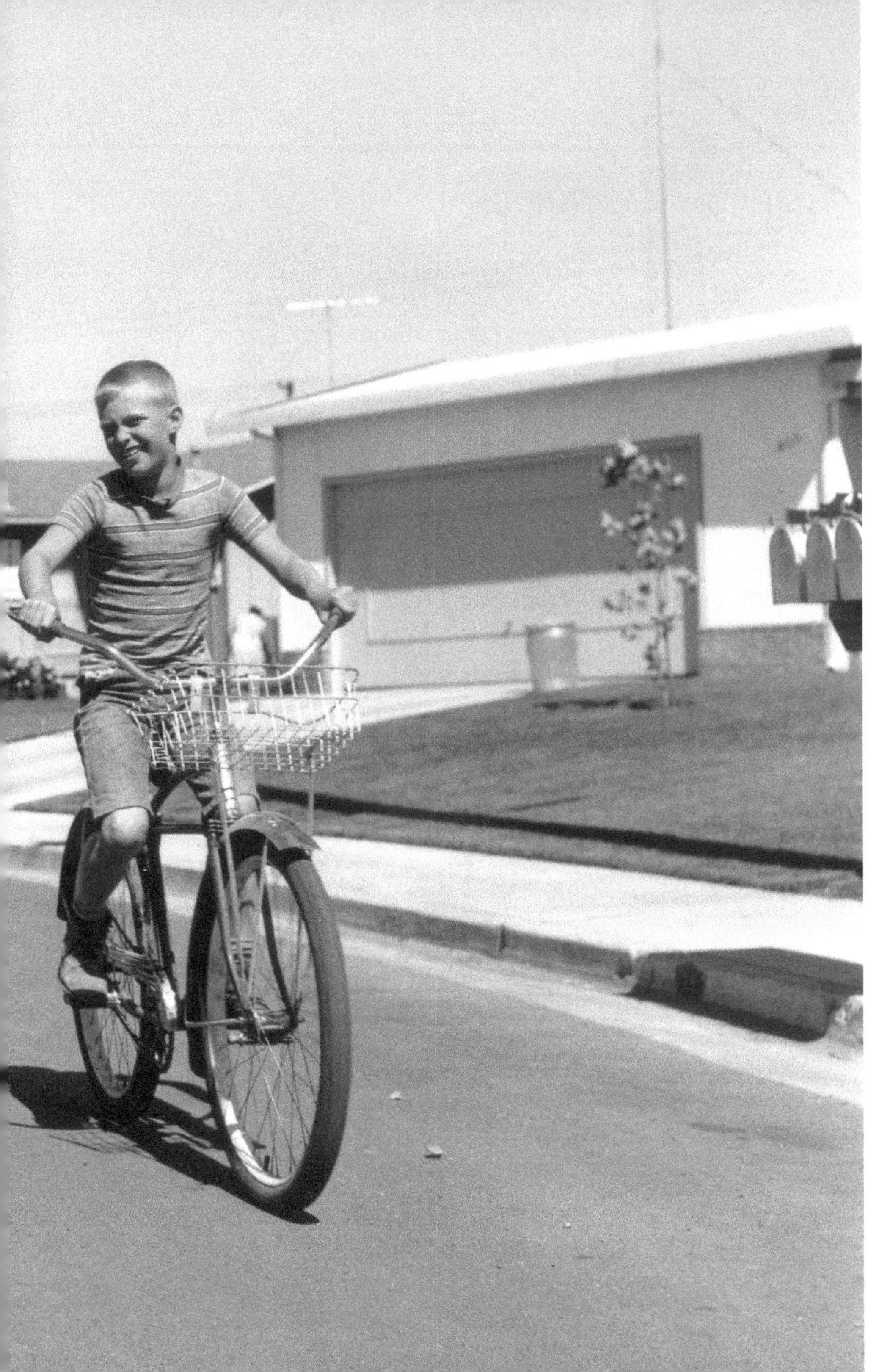

Attorney Paul Golis, with assistance from his law partner, Maurice Fredericks, was credited with creating the new city of Rohnert Park on an expanse of vacant farmland beside Highway 101 just north of Cotati. The town grew from a population of 6,000 in 1970 to 42,000 in 2000. Golis and Fredericks shared offices at 6950 Commerce Boulevard in 1961.

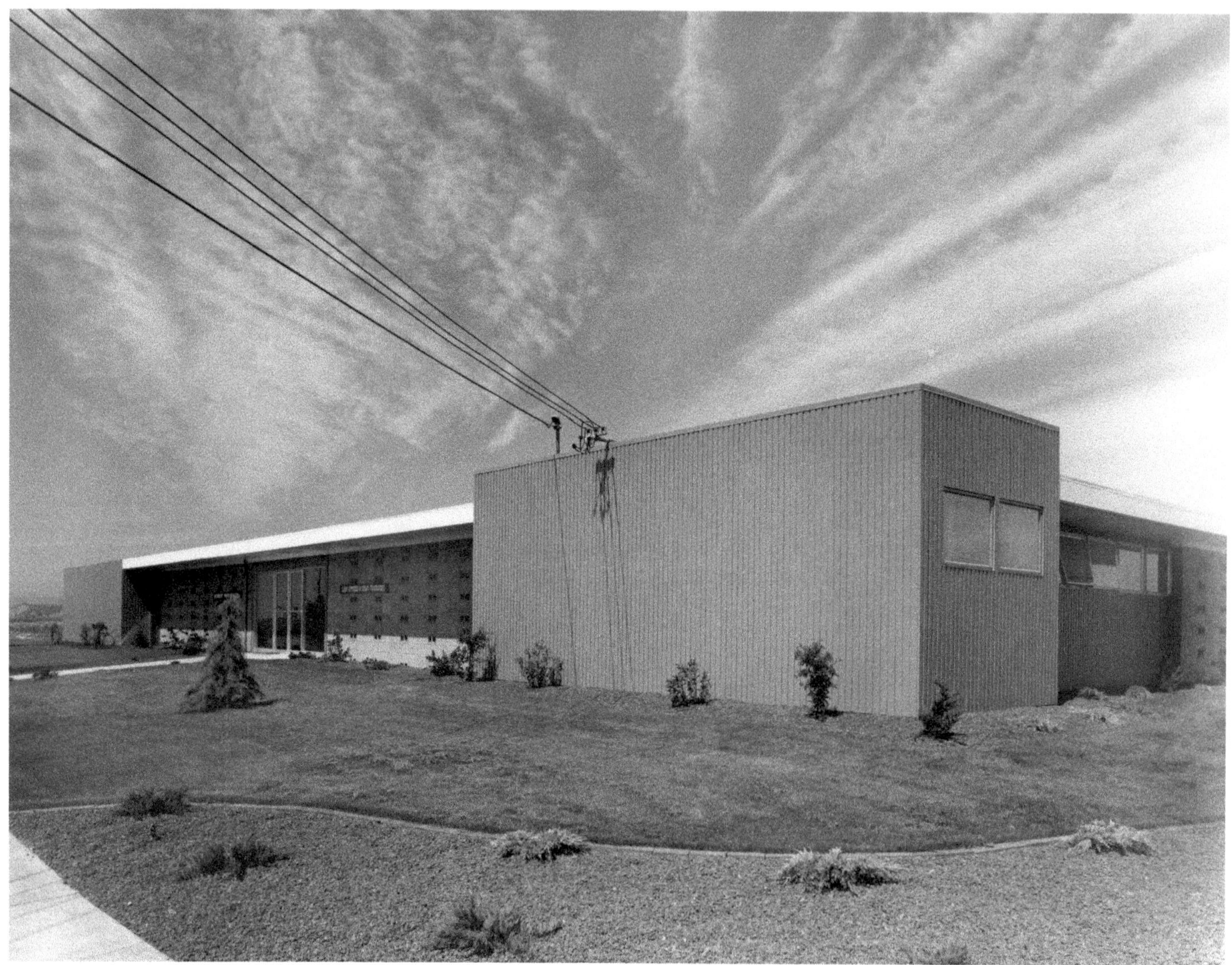

For more than 150 years, dairying has been one of the leading agricultural activities in Sonoma County. In the early 1970s, as one example, market milk brought in around $26 million a year. Many children around Petaluma were good friends with the Clover Dairy delivery men who left daily bottles of milk on their doorsteps. This fleet of Clover trucks lined up in their parking lot in Petaluma in 1963.

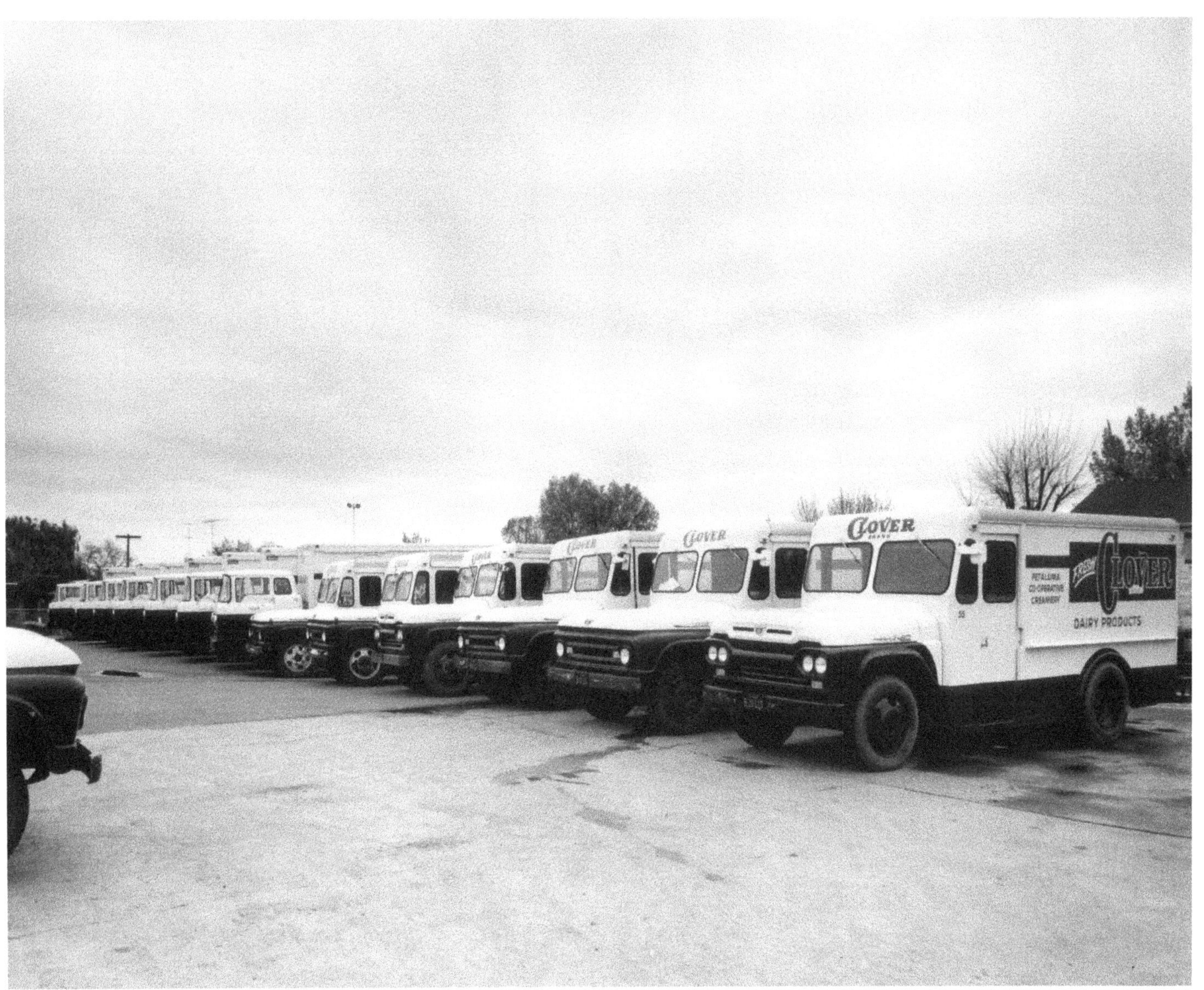

Fluor Wood Products plant came to a 155-acre site in Windsor in the 1950s. The firm also built water cooling towers and at one point had 500 employees and a $1.5 million Sonoma County payroll. Their specialties included heavy industrial installations and manufacturing of air conditioning and refrigeration units. The sales staff gathered to discuss strategy in the early 1960s.

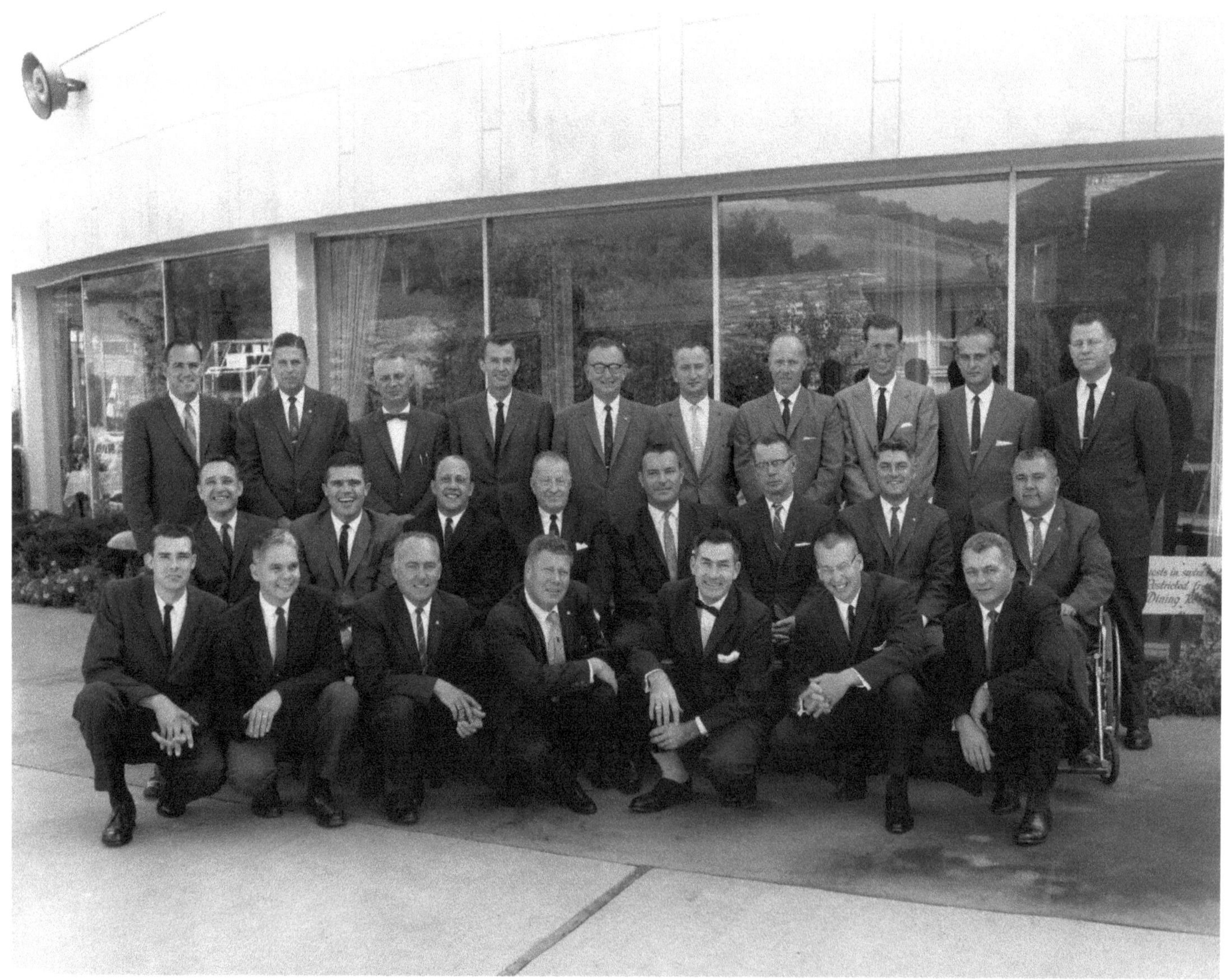

The Round Barn at Fountaingrove Winery in Santa Rosa, photographed in 1965, has withstood the test of time. The Round Barn was originally built by Kanaye Nagasawa to house sixty horses. Now located on the lower portion of the Fountaingrove hillside, it remains one of the significant historic structures north of San Francisco.

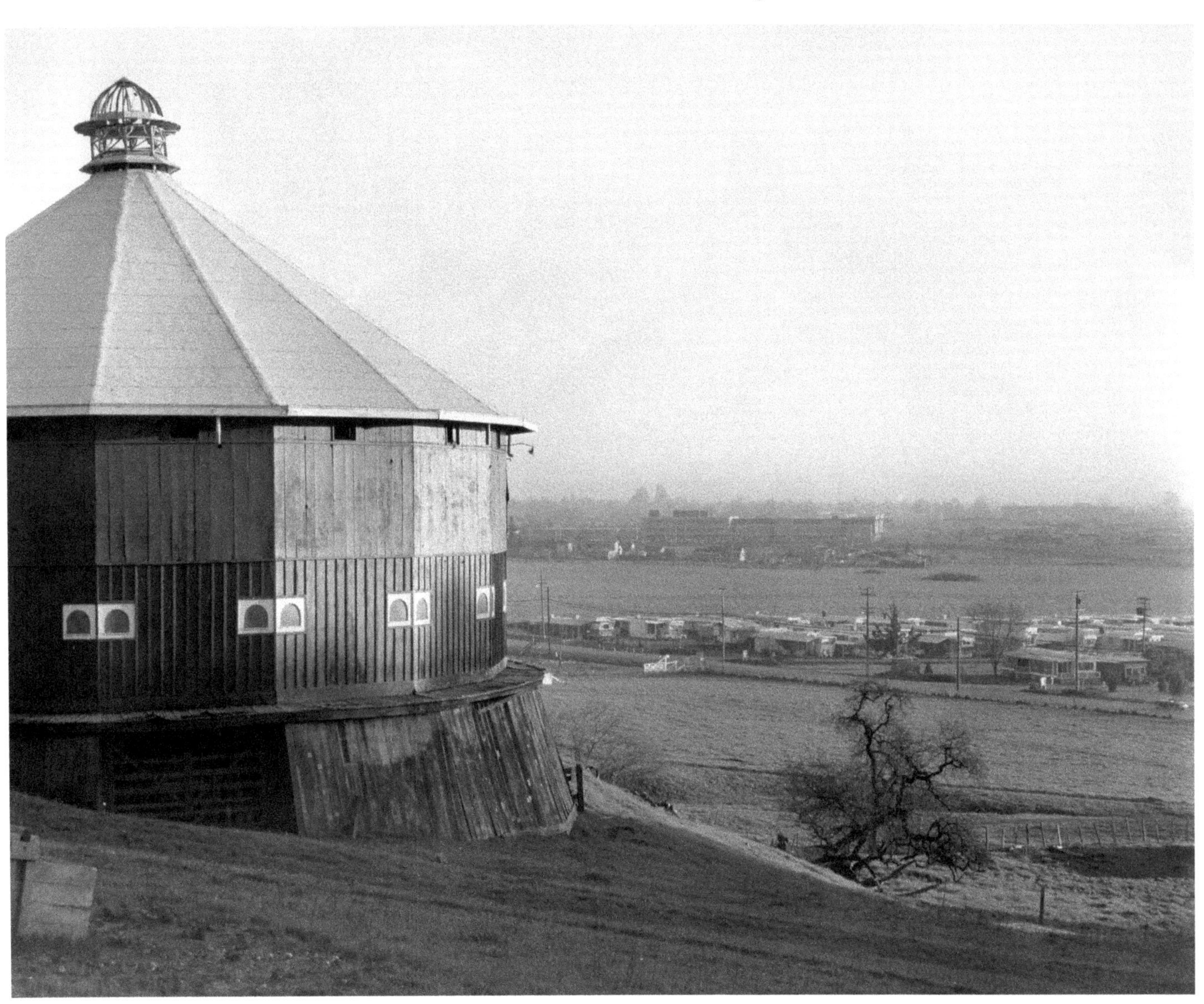

The post–World War II period presented a dilemma for a growing Sonoma County—whether to build up the downtown core or expand commercial and residential development into outlying areas. An aerial view from the north shows downtown Santa Rosa in 1965, with the Press Democrat building to the far left, a multi-story parking garage in the center, the theater block with the California and Roxy movie palaces on the far right, and the five-story-tall Rosenberg and courthouse buildings in the distance at the city center, Mendocino and 4th streets.

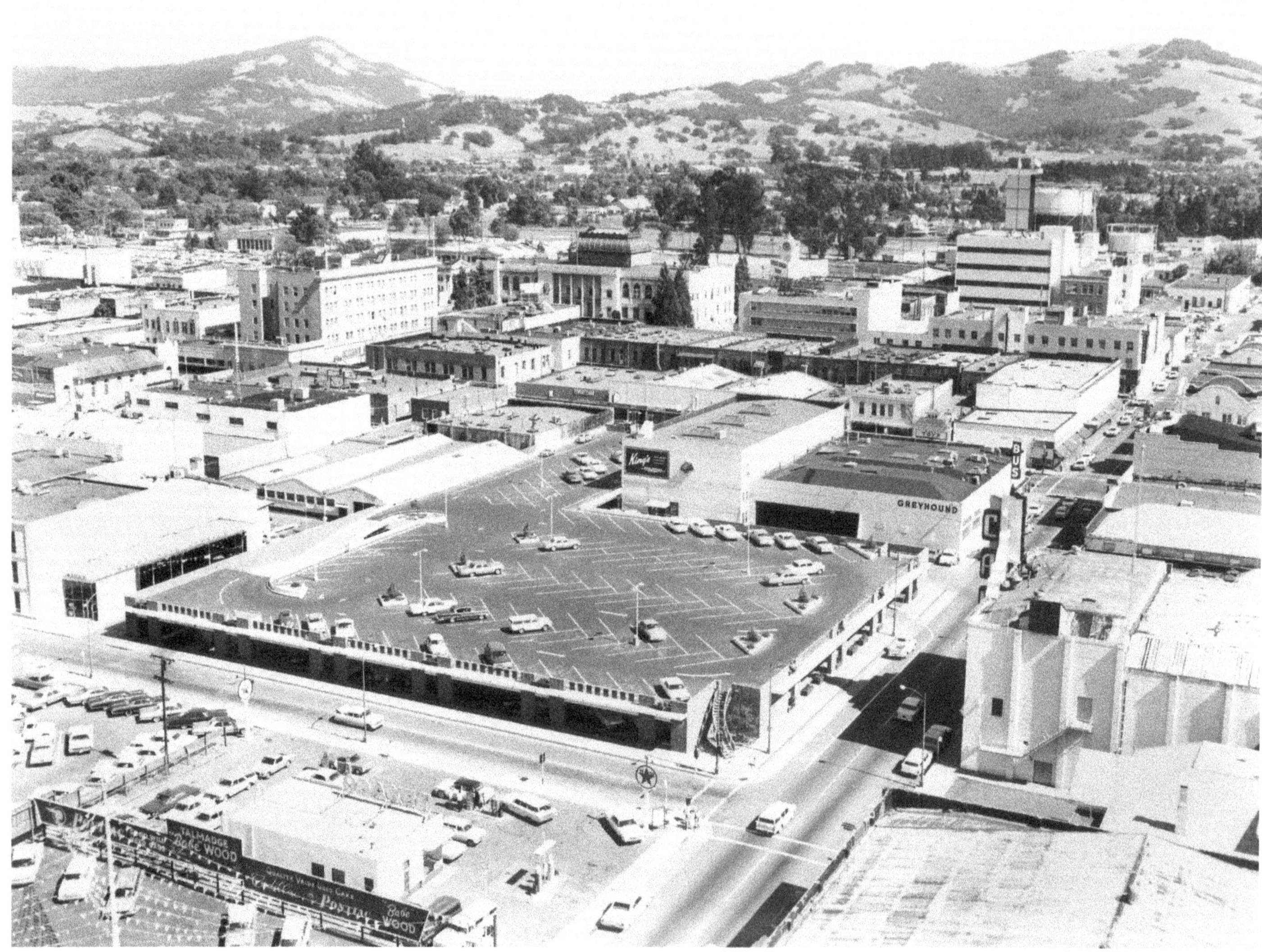

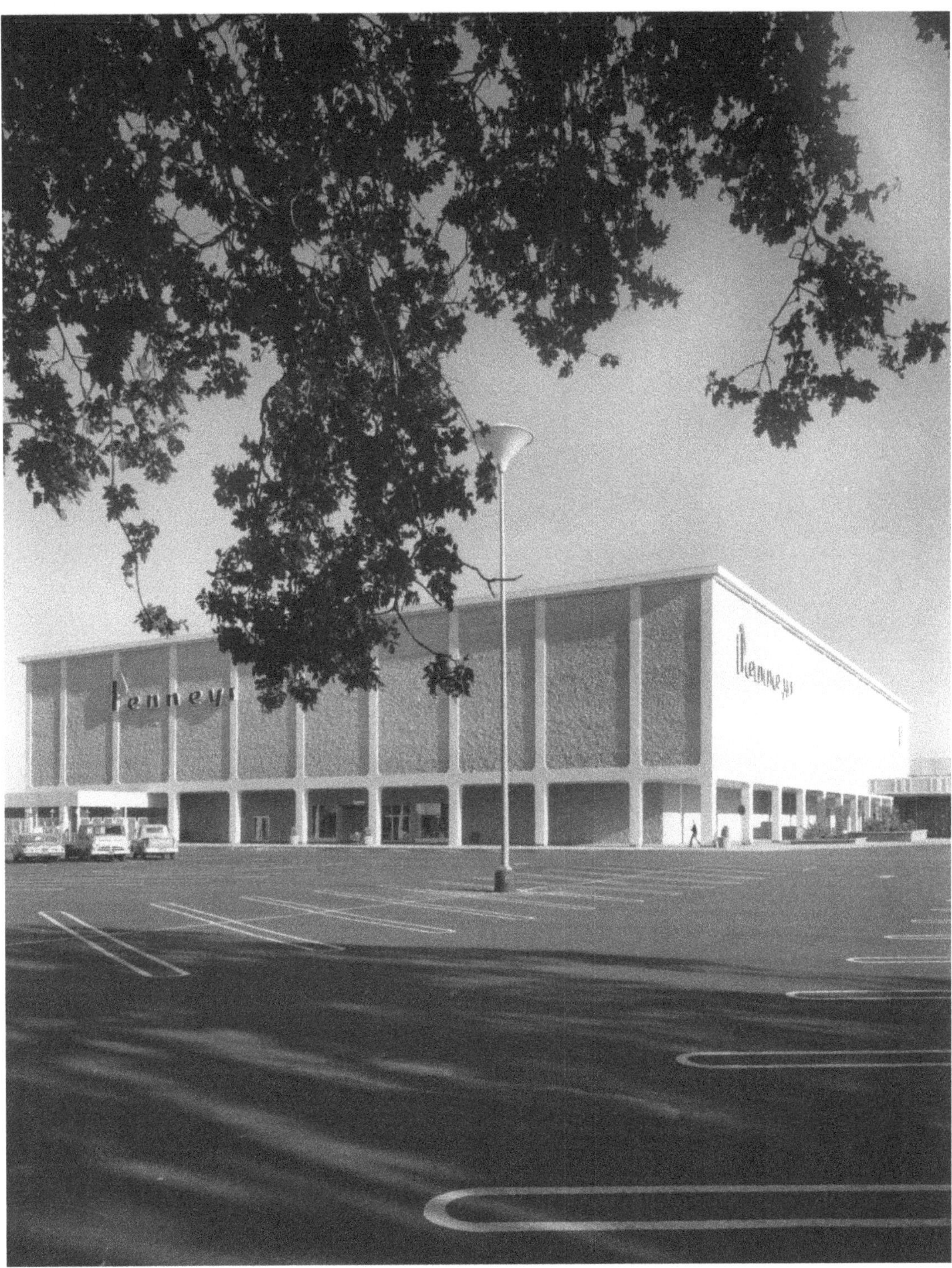


Penney's was a downtown fixture until it moved to Coddingtown in the early 1960s. The large-scale mall, one of the first of its kind, was located off Highway 101 in northwest Santa Rosa. It was part of the continuing business move away from the old downtown core. The man who made it happen was innovative developer Hugh Codding, who earlier gained attention when he built 2,600 houses in Montgomery Village after World War II.

Melvin (Dutch) Flohr, left, was a tough cop with a heart who ran the small-town Santa Rosa Police Department from 1940 to 1974. Flohr, a large man who towered over friend and foe, chased down criminals, ran some of them out of town, and spent his spare time directing traffic at busy intersections. Numerous prominent Santa Rosans recall getting a "talking to" from the chief during their rambunctious teenage years. He died in 1980.

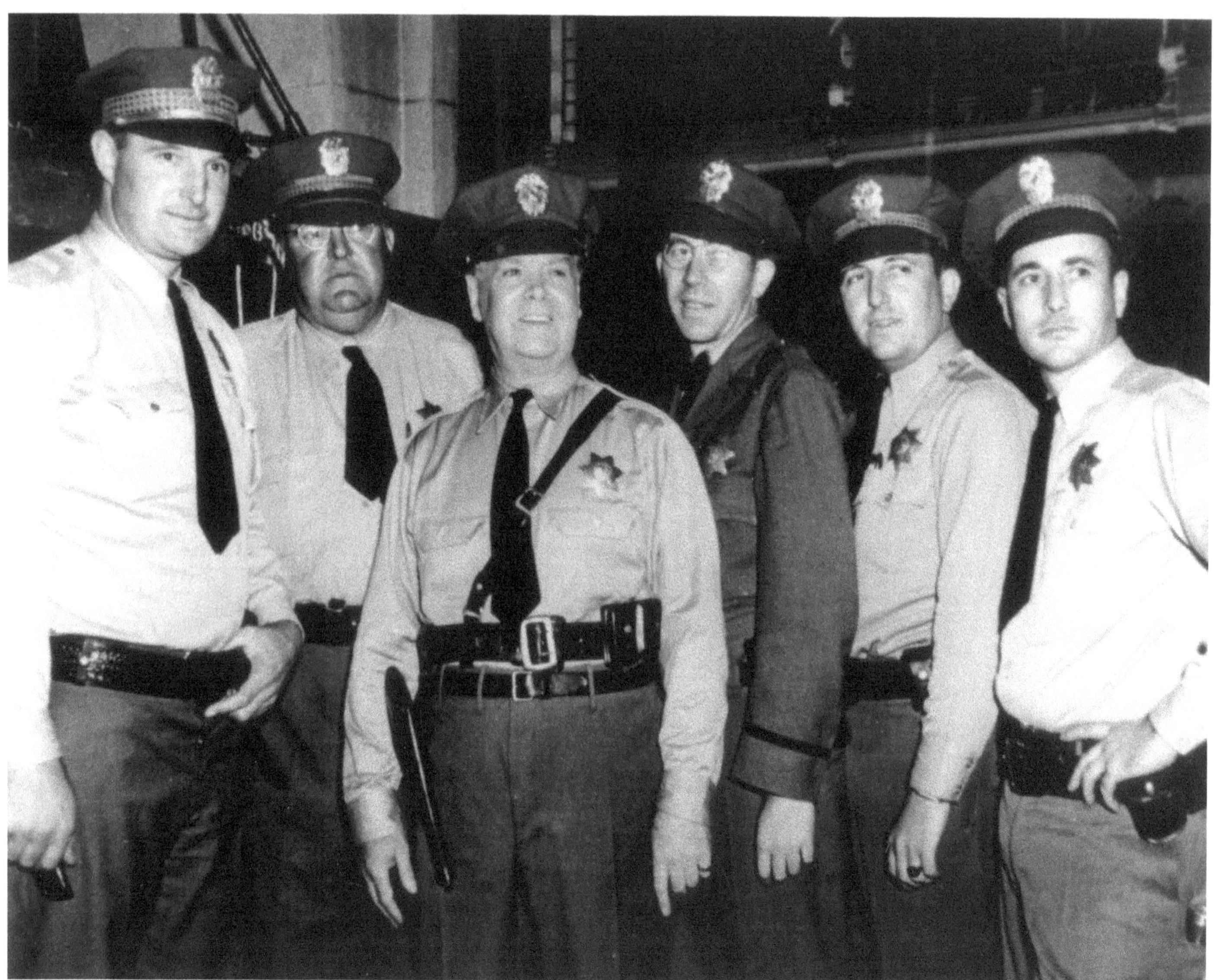

At a groundbreaking for a new downtown Bank of America in 1967, major developers of the postwar era picked up their shovels for ceremonies at the new building site. From left were financier Henry Trione, developer Hugh Codding, Bank of America executive Wayne Ancell, Urban Renewal official Trent Harrington, and D. C. Sutherland.

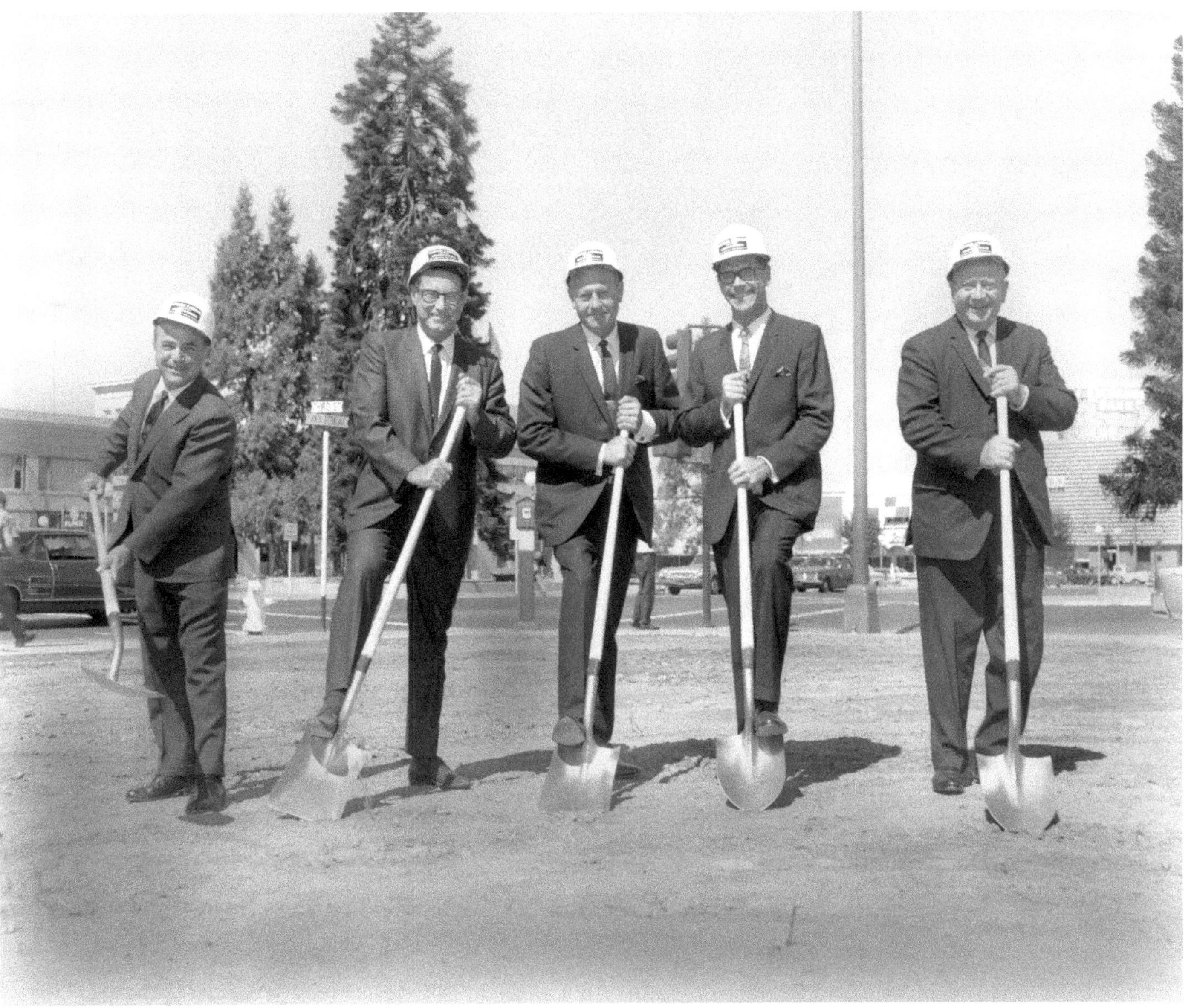

As Santa Rosa's residential subdivisions expanded east to Rincon Valley, Tusan's Department Store opened in the late 1960s. Part of the Montecito Shopping Center at 560 Montecito Center, the owners were John, Ernest, Alice, and Doris Thomas.

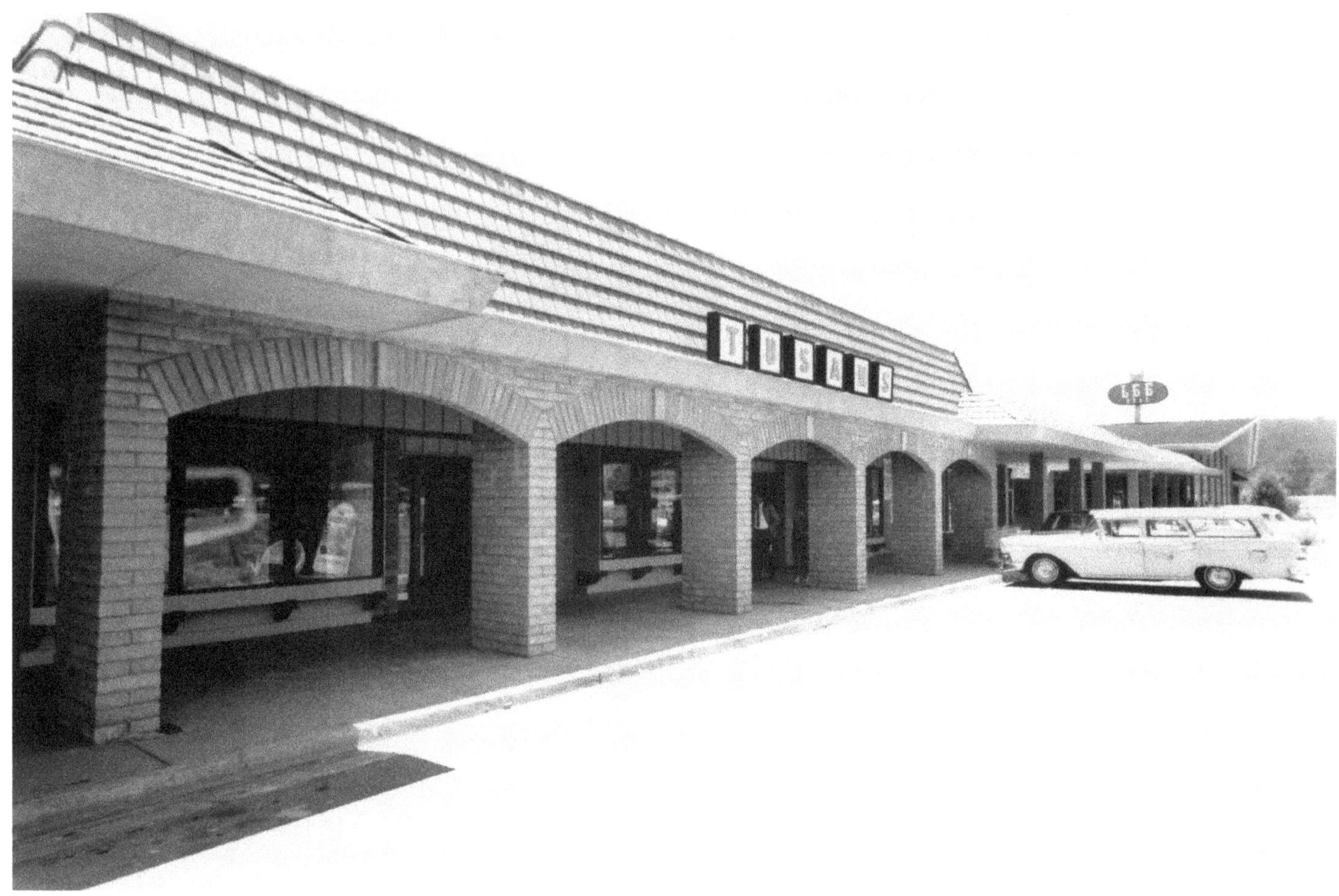

Showing that school life can be more than lectures and tests, the Santa Rosa Junior College band showed up one day in 1968 to serenade students while they enjoyed a snack on campus. The diverse campus currently serves more than 35,000 students a semester.

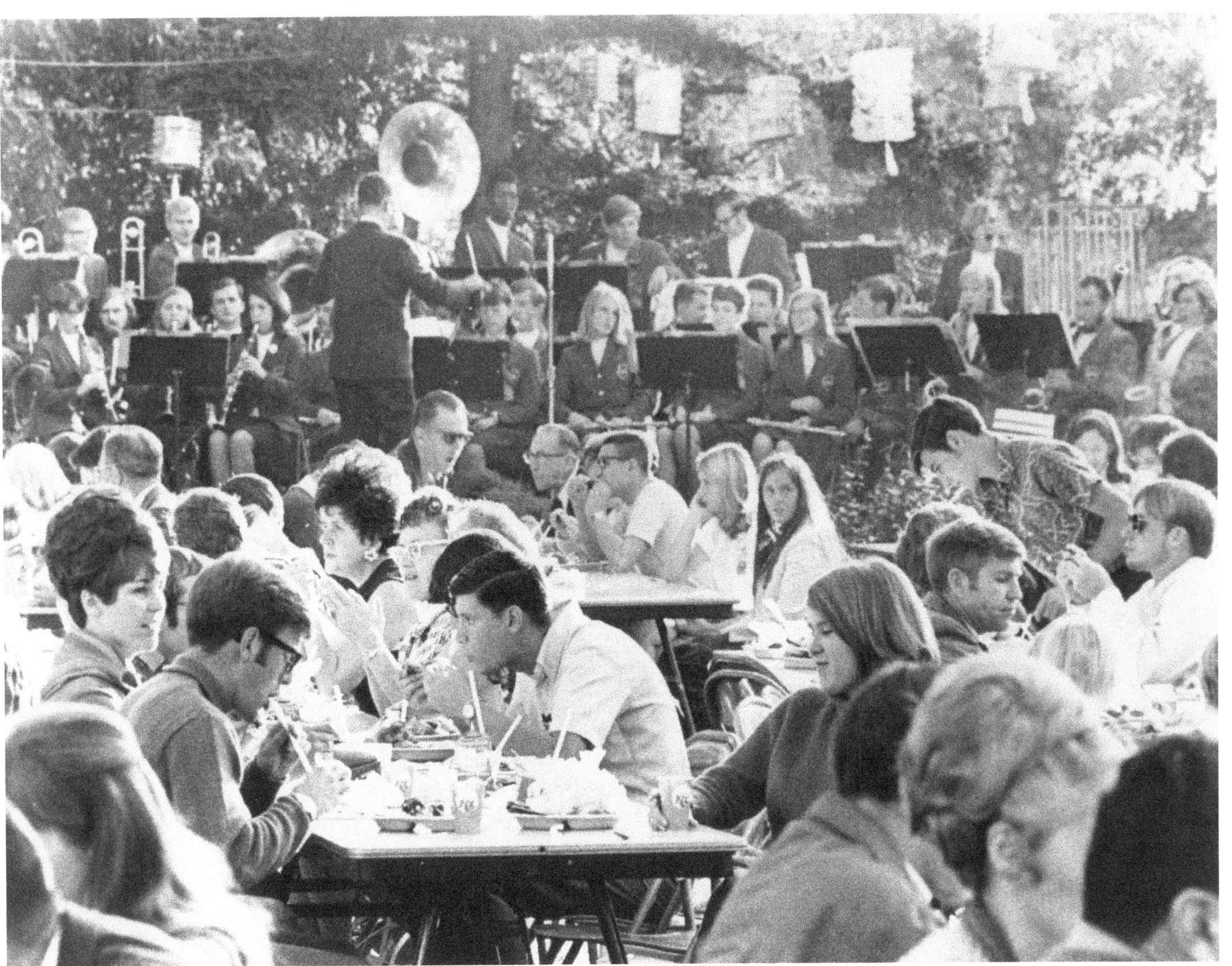

Sonoma County blended tradition and change when it replaced its historic Carnegie Library building in Santa Rosa in the 1960s. The exterior featured broken brick and the garden walls were built from stones from the 1903 Carnegie grant building. Sculptured redwood fences were another major feature. The front view of the library, before landscaping, was recorded from the northeast corner of Third and E streets.

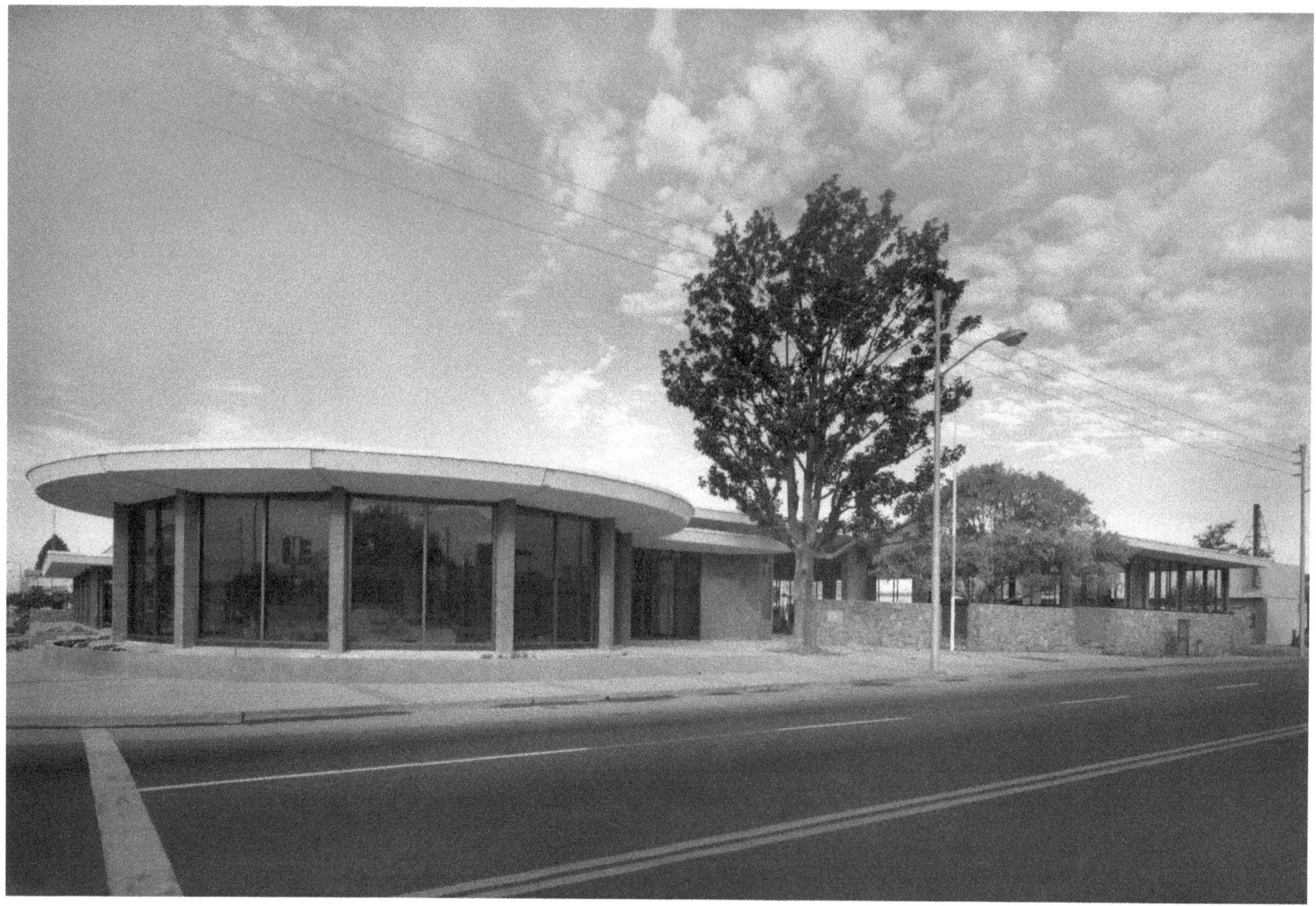

This Fluor Products employee was photographed at work on the factory floor in 1965. When a Chicago firm bought Fluor in 1969, there was still a crew of 214 employees. The plant was something of a city in itself, operating on its own electric, gas, and water system. The firm's name was changed to Ecodyne Cooling Products in 1972.

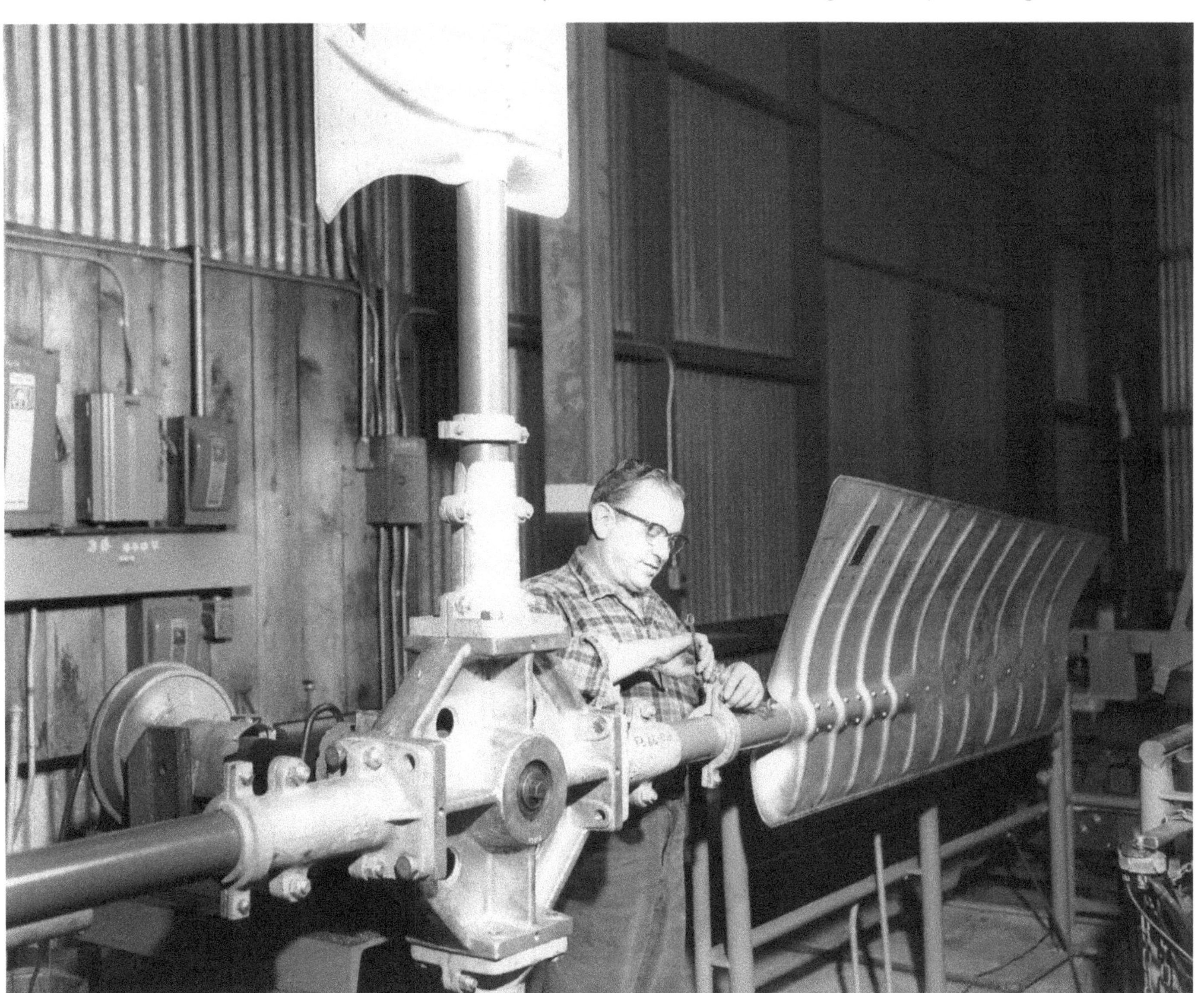

Two employees at Fluor Products use their skills to prepare a long pipe used in making cooling towers.

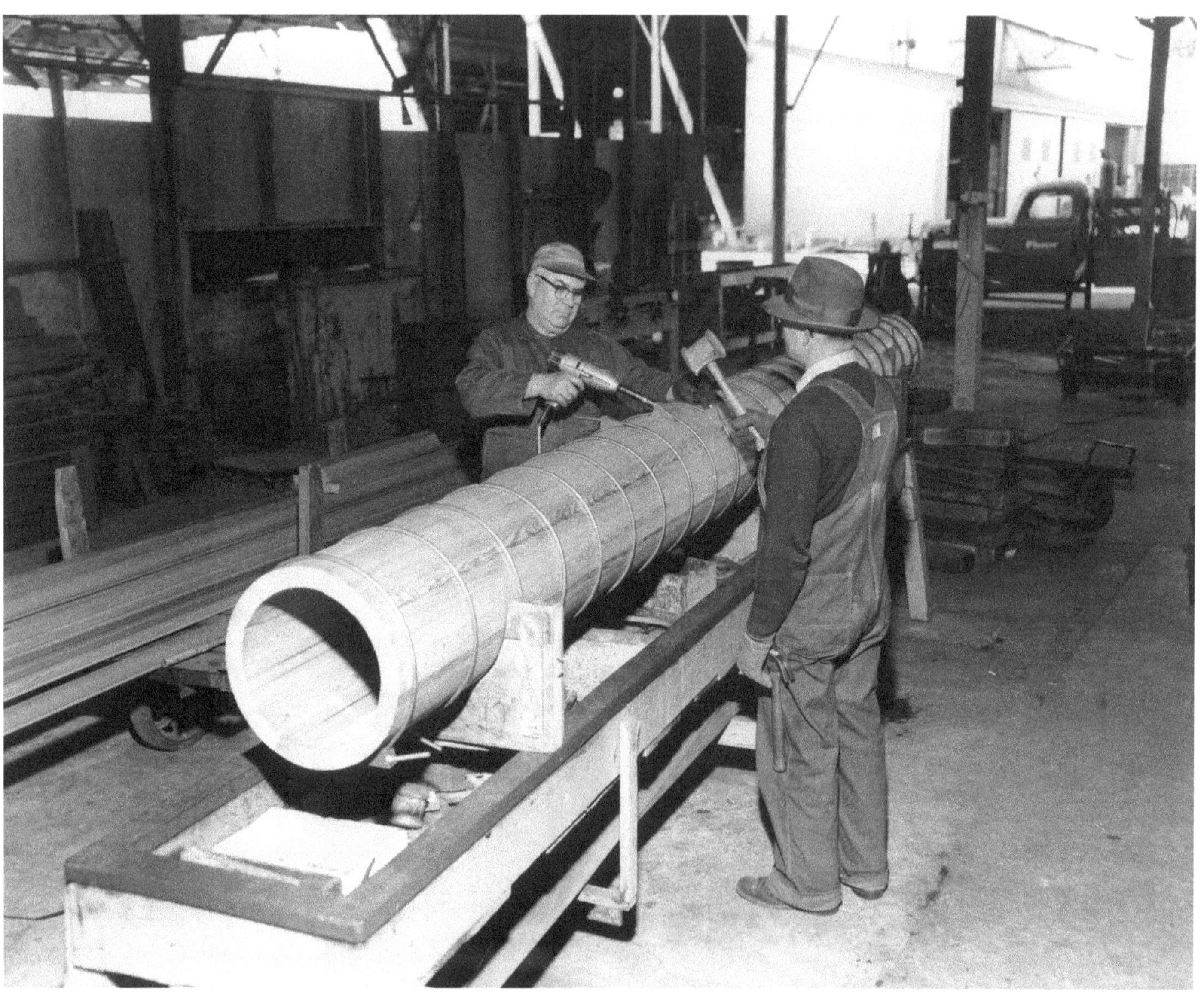

Speedspace Corporation, an offshoot of Fluor Products, manufactured laminated beams and portable buildings for schools, businesses, and industrial needs. Located in Windsor eight miles north of Santa Rosa, Speedspace was headed by merger expert Robert Kerr, former Santa Rosa mayor Charles LeMenager, and C. W. Worman, a designer of relocatable buildings. The lumber yard was an important part of the operation.

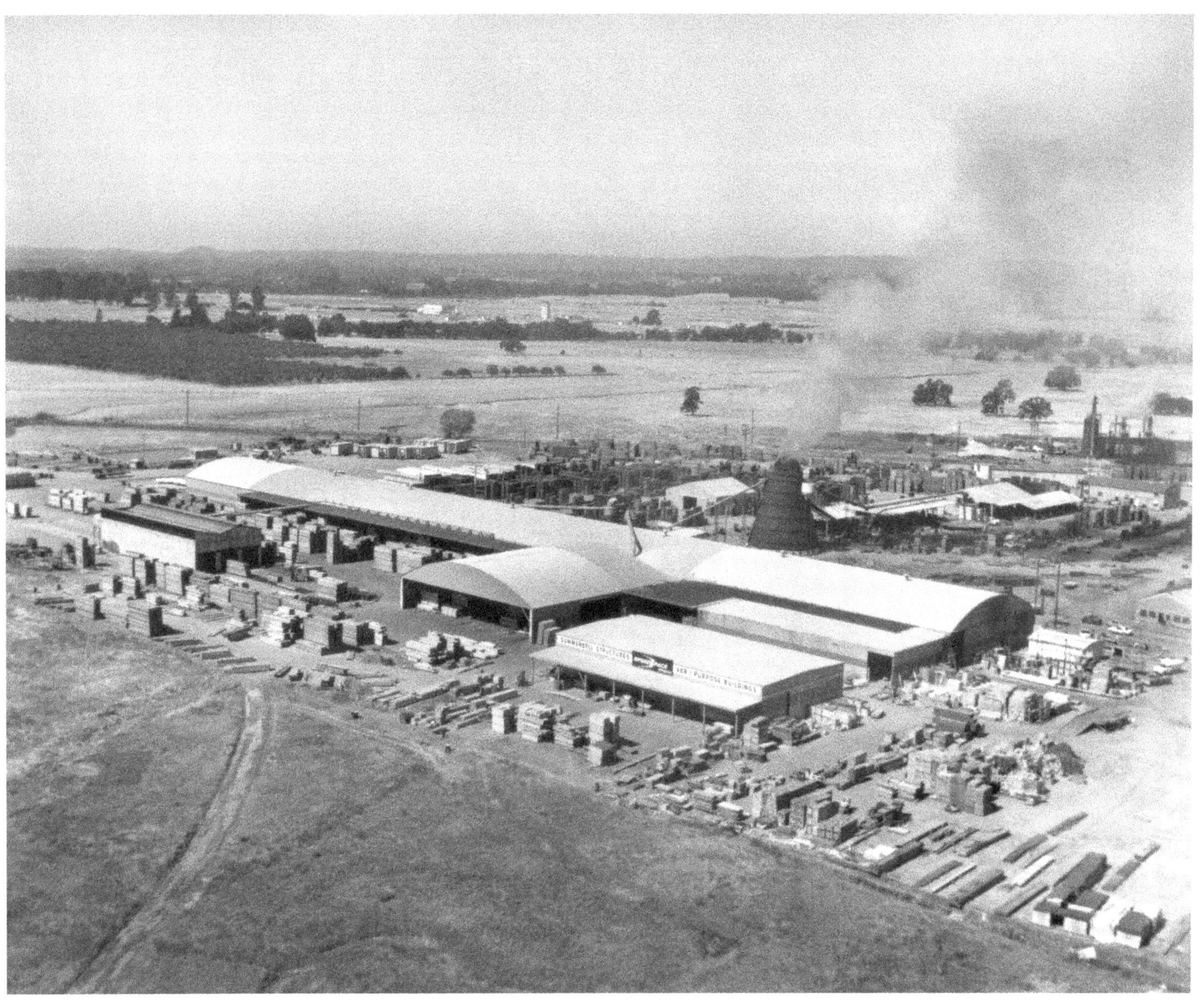

Police dispatchers Mildred Hollingsworth, Lois Tueschler, Mary Palmer, and Anne Rochester at work in Healdsburg in 1967.

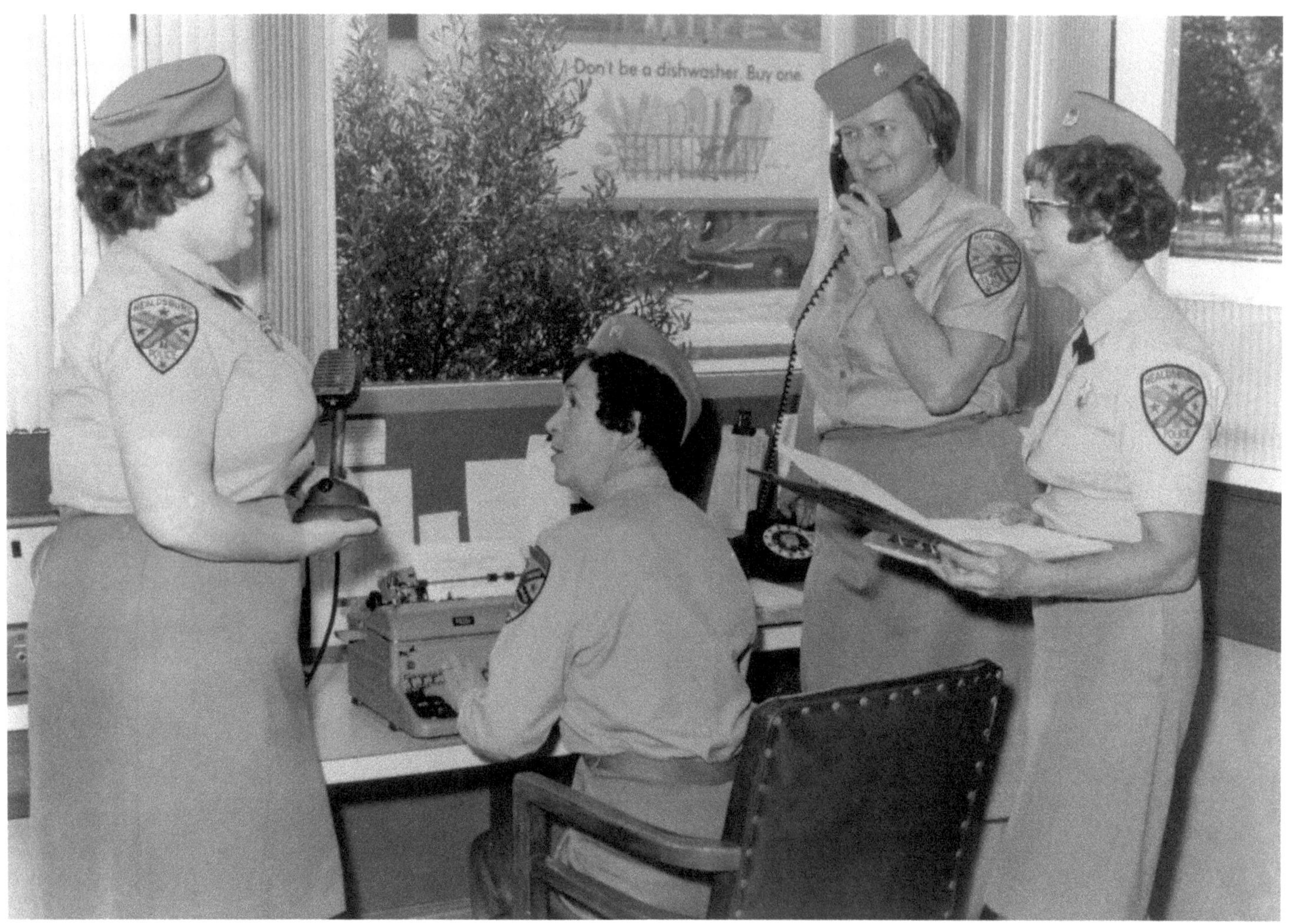

Chain stores presented a challenge to small, independent retailers in the postwar years. The Purity grocery store operated out of 455 Center Street in Healdsburg in the 1960s. The chain also offered its services in Petaluma and Sebastopol.

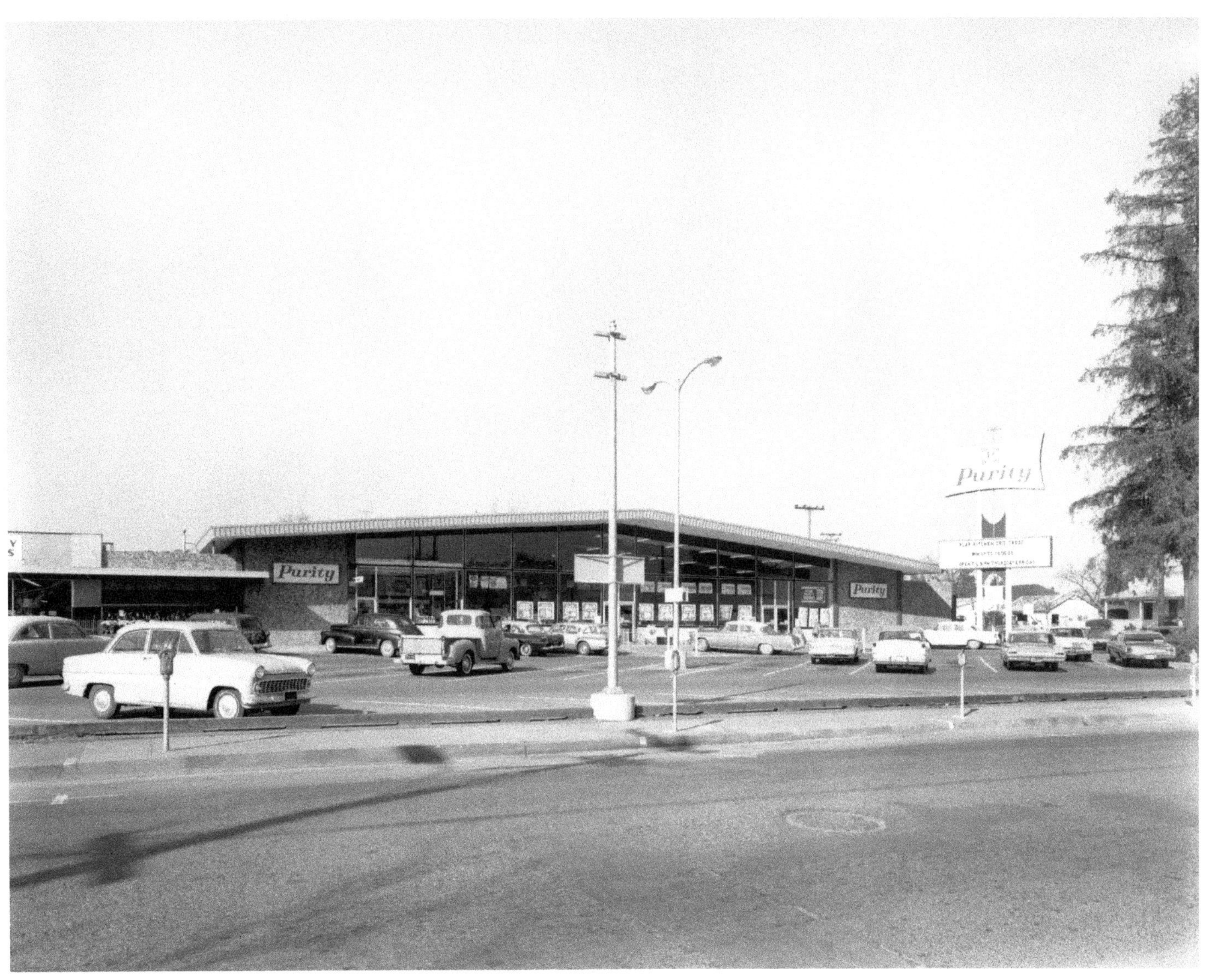

As eager crowds waited outside, Mayor Gerald Poznanovich spoke at the opening of the K-Mart Discount Department Store at 3775 Cleveland Avenue in 1970. The store provided more competition for struggling merchants downtown.

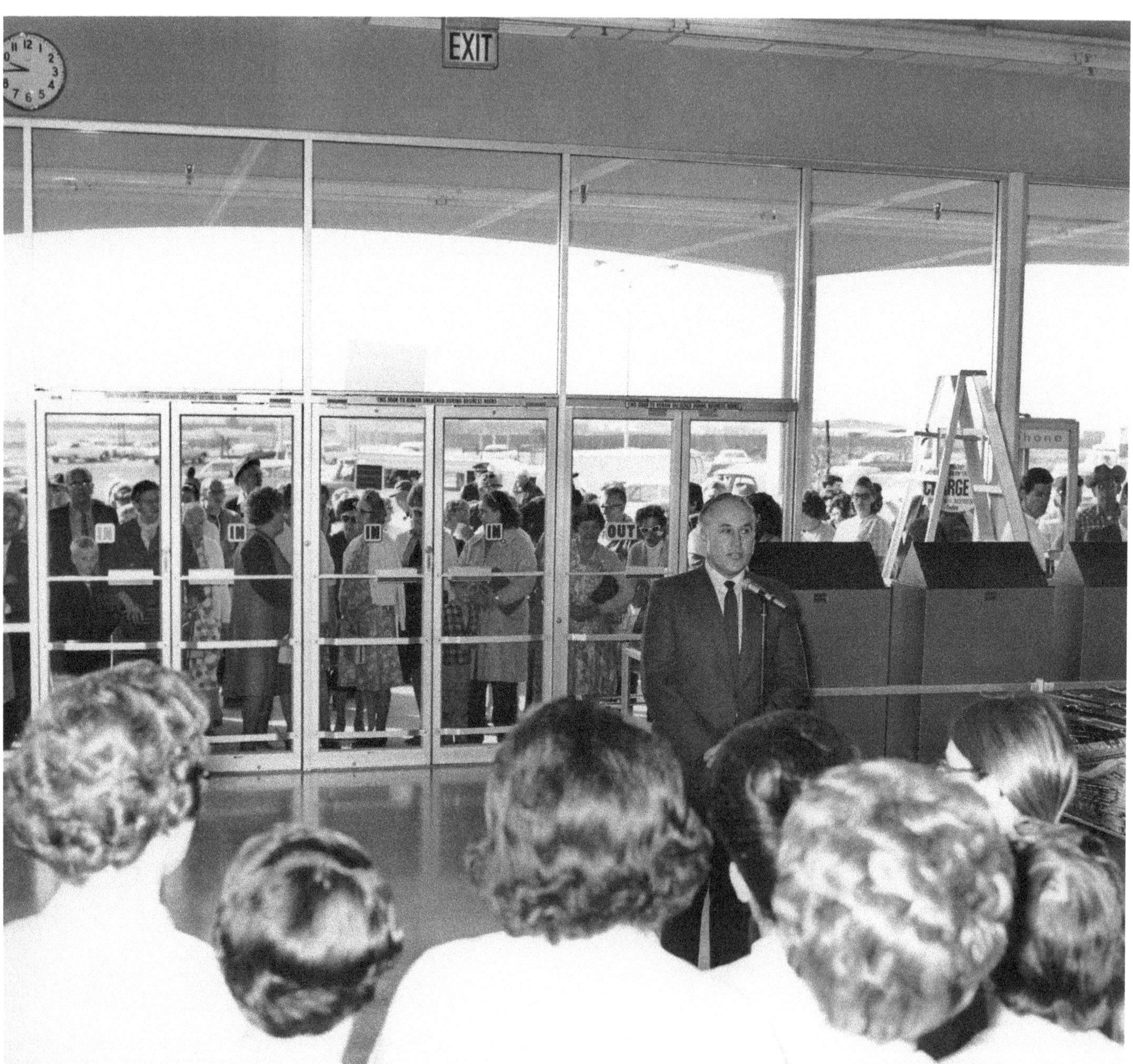

Sonoma County got an economic shot in the arm when Hewlett-Packard Corporation moved portions of its high-tech operation from Palo Alto to Santa Rosa. As the unemployment rate jumped over the ten percent mark in the early 1970s, H-P agreed to buy 200 acres at the Fountaingrove Ranch as a plant site. By 1980, it was the largest operation in the county with 2,700 employees. To discuss the impact of the rapidly-changing local economy, the Mortgage Bankers Association got together for a business meeting and tour at Windsor Winery in 1972.

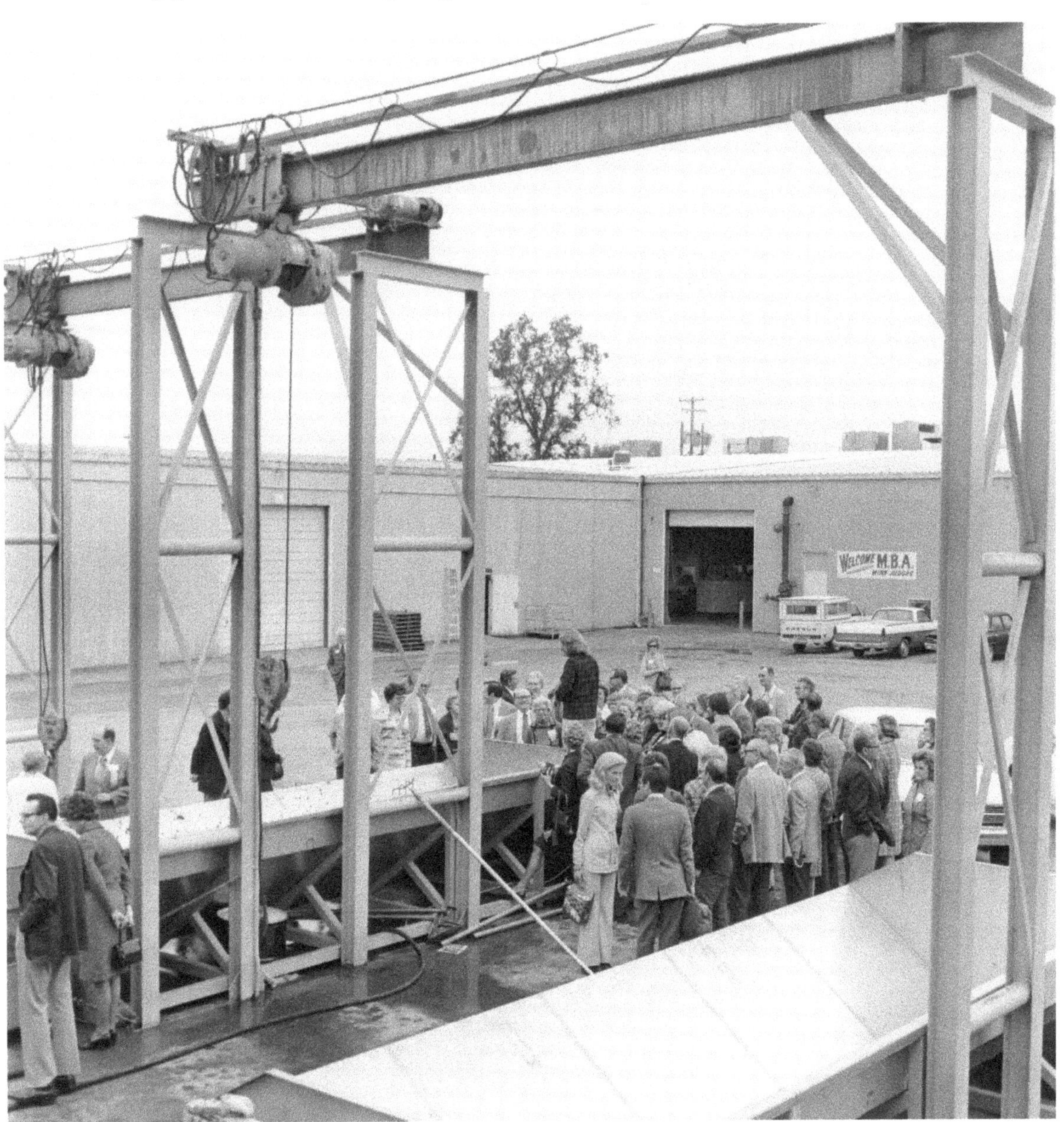

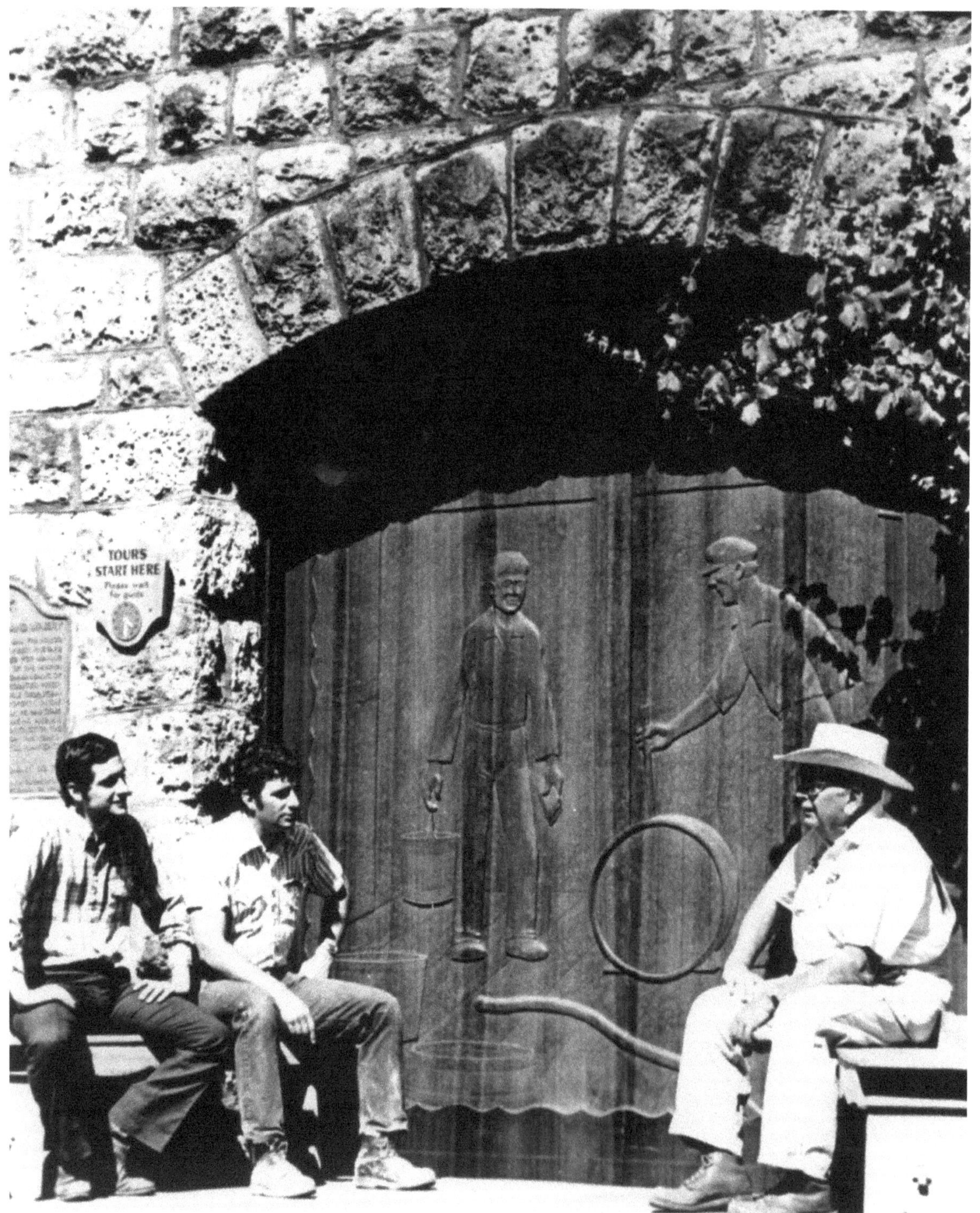


The Sebastianis, sons Don (left) and Sam and father August, gathered to discuss life in the vineyards in 1975. The Sebastiani legend goes back to 1904 when the family patriarch Samuele started growing grapes in Sonoma. His son August ran the company from 1944 to the late 1970s. Sebastiani Wineries is still family-owned and in business at its original location, just east of the Sonoma Plaza.

Sonoma State College was created in the 1961 as a small liberal arts college in an apartment complex in Rohnert Park. In 1978, the school became a university, expanding in many academic areas. Its new sign was unfurled by (left) Peter Diamandopoulos, president 1977–83, and (right) the school's first president, Ambrose Nichols (1961–70).

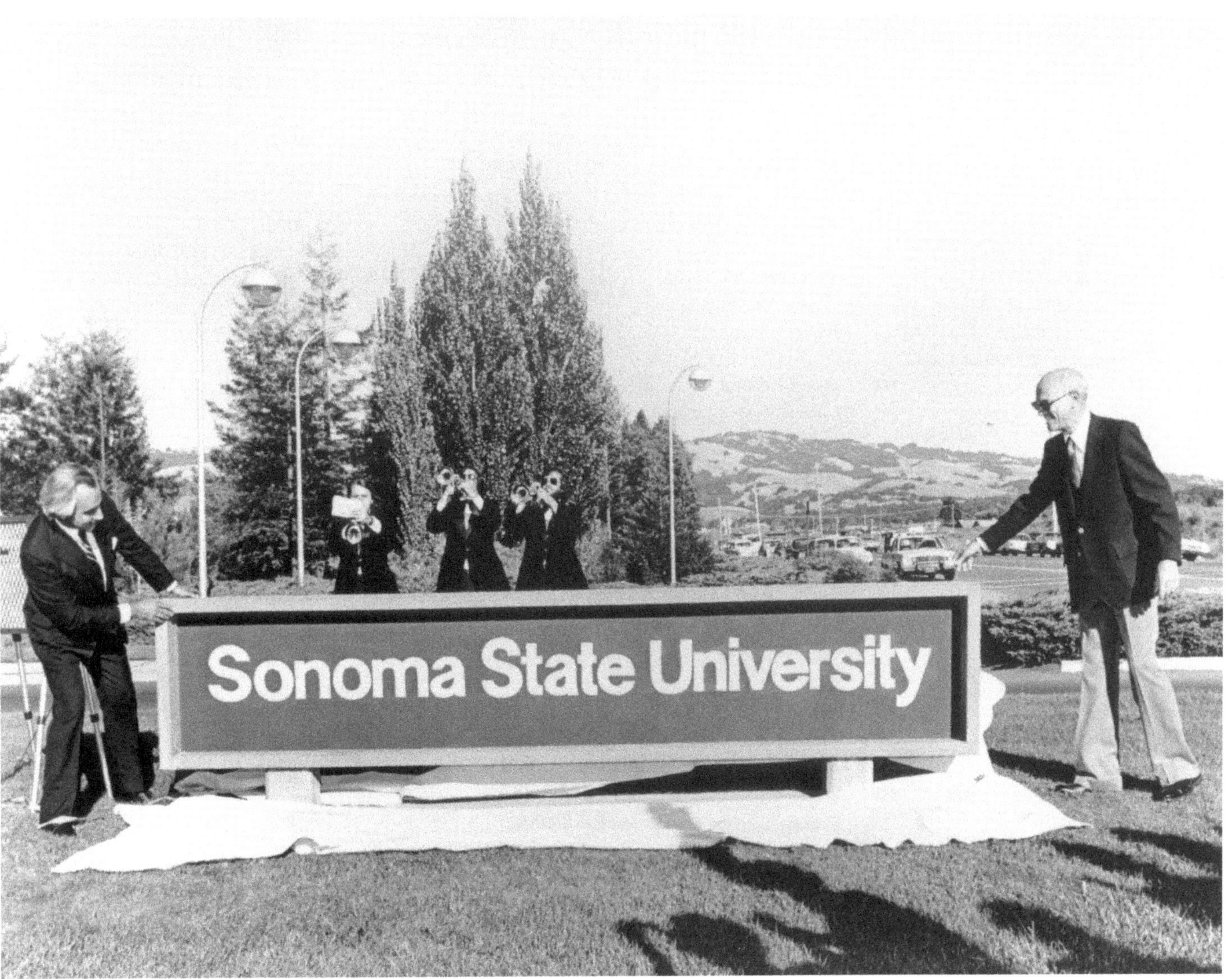

# Notes on the Photographs

These notes, listed by page number, attempt to include all aspects known of the photographs. Each of the photographs is identified by the page number, photograph's title or description, photographer and collection, archive, and call or box number when applicable. Although every attempt was made to collect all available data, in some cases complete data was unavailable due to the age and condition of some of the photographs and records.

**II** **Golden Gate Opens**
Sonoma County Library
28931

**VI** **Fighting Irish**
Harold Lapham Collection

**X** **M. Vallejo Carriage**
Sonoma County Library
20811

**2** **Old Barracks**
Sonoma County Library
11992

**3** **Gowen Building**
Sonoma County Library
8881

**4** **Sonoma Plaza**
Sonoma County Library
6243

**5** **Courthouse**
Sonoma County Library
3563

**6** **Grand Hotel**
Sonoma County Library
13027

**7** **4th Street**
Sonoma County Library
1006

**8** **Main Drag**
Sonoma County Library
572

**9** **Windsor School**
Sonoma County Library
13500

**10** **Santa Rosa Bridge**
Sonoma County Library
18697

**11** **Feed Stable**
Sonoma County Library
12601

**12** **Loggers**
Sonoma County Library
13002

**13** **Meeker Sawmill**
Harold Lapham Collection

**14** **Post Office**
Sonoma County Library
12594

**15** **Cloverdale**
Sonoma County Library
7552

**16** **Winery**
Sonoma County Library
13076

**17** **IOOF**
Sonoma County Library
12599

**18** **Windsor and Trenton**
Sonoma County Library
320349

**19** **Stables**
Sonoma County Library
2815

**20** **United States Hotel**
Sonoma County Library
7577

**21** **Hardware Store**
Sonoma County Library
6234

**22** **Loggers**
Sonoma County Library
13045

**23** **Sonoma Band**
Sonoma County Library
633

**24** **Studebaker Wagons**
Sonoma County Library
19578

**25** **Derby Block**
Sonoma County Library
8893

**26** **Icaria Scool**
Sonoma County Library
27550

**27** **Soaking Wheels**
Sonoma County Library
327593

**28** **B. F. Express Stable**
Sonoma County Library
32000

**29** **Hill Plaza Park**
Sonoma County Library
7716

**30** **Windsor Hotel**
Sonoma County Library
2401

**31** **Spring Picnic**
Sonoma County Library
29476

**32** **Petaluma Parade**
Sonoma County Library
2906

**33** **Windsor Schoolhouse**
Sonoma County Library
20415

**34** **Local Well**
Sonoma County Library
13537

**35 Sorting Mail**
Sonoma County Library
7575

**36 Local Celebration**
Sonoma County Library
13541

**37 Henry Bell's Store**
Sonoma County Library
13522

**38 Railroad Tunnel**
Sonoma County Library
13507

**39 Louis Arata**
Sonoma County Library
20418

**40 Flower Boy**
Sonoma County Library
30911

**41 Methodist Church**
Sonoma County Library
13099

**42 Road Crew**
Sonoma County Library
20412

**43 Gang Plow**
Sonoma County Library
13521

**44 Company C**
Sonoma County Library
2952

**45 Unit Marching**
Sonoma County Library
32049

**46 Saloon**
Harold Lapham Collection

**47 Wagon Market**
Sonoma County Library
2205

**48 Brewery**
Sonoma County Library
5038

**50 Hop Crop**
Sonoma County Library
1078

**51 Hops**
Harold Lapham Collection

**52 Healdsburg Wheelmen**
Sonoma County Library
2291

**53 Main Street**
Sonoma County Library
2919

**54 Prescott Mansion**
Sonoma County Library
7553

**55 Wagonloads of Grapes**
Sonoma County Library
27167

**56 Train at Howard**
Harold Lapham Collection

**57 Carnegie Library**
Sonoma County Library
3256

**58 4th Street**
Sonoma County Library
13012

**59 Hose Company**
Sonoma County Library
16284

**60 Giant Earthquake**
Sonoma County Library
6926

**61 Injured Survivor**
Sonoma County Library
6733

**62 Broken Bar**
Sonoma County Library
7699

**63 Crumbling Courthouse**
Sonoma County Library
32135

**64 5th and D Streets**
Sonoma County Library
Annex 30750

**65 Main Street**
Sonoma County Library
9086

**66 Police Station**
Sonoma County Library
6330

**67 Police Photo**
Sonoma County Library
13025

**68 White House Store**
Sonoma County Library
20291

**70 Victorian Home**
Sonoma County Library
7686

**71 Group of Students**
Sonoma County Library
20414

**72 Luther Burbank**
Sonoma County Library
1953

**73 City of Roses**
Sonoma County Library
3786

**74 Rebuilding Effort**
Sonoma County Library
3777

**75 River Road**
Sonoma County Library
3776

**76 Wine Wagon**
Sonoma County Library
27164

**77 Geyserville Winery**
Sonoma County Library
27168

**78 Schoolhouse**
Sonoma County Library
20807

**79 Railroad Tracks**
Sonoma County Library
18688

**80 Scott Hardware**
Sonoma County Library
9073

**81 Hinton Street**
Sonoma County Library
20218

**82 Unloading Barrels**
Sonoma County Library
31257

**83 Fred Wiseman**
Sonoma County Library
15589

**84 White House Store**
Sonoma County Library
1427

**85** **Charmian London**
Harold Lapham Collection

**86** **St. Rose Church**
Sonoma County Library
20384

**87** **St. Vincent's**
Sonoma County Library
7277

**88** **Washington Street**
Sonoma County Library
4772

**89** **Main Street**
Sonoma County Library
5629

**90** **"Parking Lot"**
Sonoma County Library
9074

**91** **Two Rock Band**
Sonoma County Library
15365

**92** **Apple Show**
Sonoma County Library
3018

**93** **Apple Parthenon**
Sonoma County Library
193

**94** **Grace Brothers**
Sonoma County Library
Annex 29477

**95** **Masonic Temple**
Sonoma County Library
10270

**96** **Wood-Burning Engine**
Sonoma County Library
30748

**97** **River Hay Barge**
Harold Lapham Collection

**98** **4th of July Parade**
Sonoma County Library
Annex 32336

**99** **Mendocino Avenue**
Sonoma County Library
20222

**100** **Dairy**
Harold Lapham Collection

**102** **Fire Department**
Sonoma County Library
7568

**103** **West Street**
Sonoma County Library
4874

**104** **County Courthouse**
Sonoma County Library
4004

**105** **Occidental Hotel**
Sonoma County Library
760

**106** **Shell Station**
Sonoma County Library
712

**107** **Market**
Sonoma County Library
1358

**108** **Luther Burbank**
Sonoma County Library
1952

**109** **Robert Ripley**
Sonoma County Library
583

**110** **California Theatre**
Sonoma County Library
762

**112** **Kerrigans in Car**
Harold Lapham Collection

**113** **Egg Boom**
Sonoma County Library
Annex 29485

**114** **Kerrigan Parade**
Sonoma County Library
4901

**115** **Flowered Roadster**
Sonoma County Library
7359

**116** **Parade**
Sonoma County Library
2039

**117** **Shell Station**
Sonoma County Library
1031

**118** **Hauling Work Clothes**
Sonoma County Library
Annex 32068

**119** **Rio Nido**
Sonoma County Library
3598

**120** **Train #58**
Harold Lapham Collection
Loco + 2

**121** **Gonellas**
Harold Lapham Collection

**122** **Windsor School**
Sonoma County Library
20417

**123** **Healdsburg Team**
Sonoma County Library
2464

**124** **Ernie Nevers**
Harold Lapham Collection125
Hotel Petaluma
Sonoma County Library
30748

**125** **Chicken Boom**
Sonoma County Library
30748b

**126** **Water Slide**
Sonoma County Library
2214

**127** **Train Stop**
Sonoma County Library
1627

**128** **Courthouse Square**
Sonoma County Library
2053

**130** **4th Street**
Sonoma County Library
5751

**131** **Santa Rosa Hotel**
Sonoma County Library
12581

**132** **McAdoo Plane**
Sonoma County Library
20327

**133** **Jewett Band**
Harold Lapham Collection

**134** **Russian River Flood**
Sonoma County Library
19055

**135** **Hinkle Service Station**
Sonoma County Library
20421

**136** **Patrol Atop Railing**
Sonoma County Library
Annex 28928

**137 First Car to Cross**
Sonoma County Library
28928

**138 Mill Creek School**
Sonoma County Library
20442

**139 Petaluma City Hall**
Sonoma County Library
17343

**140 Golden Eagle Tugboat**
Sonoma County Library
8781

**142 Gravenstein Apple Show**
Sonoma County Library
445

**144 Fleming's Market**
Sonoma County Library
7181

**145 Sunday Group**
Sonoma County Library
17380

**146 Tomasco Pharmacy**
Sonoma County Library
709

**148 4th Street**
Sonoma County Library
491

**150 Sotoyome School**
Sonoma County Library
20357

**151 Carithers Block**
Sonoma County Library
754

**152 Racetrack**
Sonoma County Library
227

**153 Washoe House**
Sonoma County Library
30884

**154 Buena Vista Vineyards**
Sonoma County Library
12290

**155 Vallejo Home**
Sonoma County Library
12084

**156 Garrison**
Sonoma County Library
12066

**157 White Creamery**
Sonoma County Library
9760

**158 Healdsburg Avenue**
Sonoma County Library
527

**159 County Courthouse**
Sonoma County Library
1385

**160 Sonoma Plaza**
Sonoma County Library
12085

**161 Road Preparation**
Sonoma County Library
257

**162 From One Tree Church**
Sonoma County Library
5

**163 St. Luke's**
Sonoma County Library
1310

**164 Rosenburg Store**
Sonoma County Library
13433

**165 Marching Group**
Sonoma County Library
52

**166 A Toast**
Sonoma County Library
1157

**168 Vineyards**
Sonoma County Library
232

**169 Castler Cellars**
Sonoma County Library
233

**170 Berkeley Nash**
Sonoma County Library
256

**171 Billboard**
Sonoma County Library
17428

**172 Traffic Lines**
Sonoma County Library
Annex 32007

**173 Trinity Episcopal**
Sonoma County Library
595

**174 Sears**
Sonoma County Library
16561

**175 Modern Church**
Sonoma County Library
16596

**176 Santa Rosa Junior College**
Sonoma County Library
26333

**177 Rohnert Park**
Sonoma County Library
19420

**178 Riding Bikes**
Sonoma County Library
19680

**180 Commerce Boulevard**
Sonoma County Library
19677

**181 Clover Dairy Trucks**
Sonoma County Library
Annex 28764

**182 Fluor Wood Products**
Sonoma County Library
27423

**183 Round Barn**
Sonoma County Library
5039

**184 Santa Rosa**
Sonoma County Library
23538

**185 Penney's**
Sonoma County Library
Annex 29109

**186 Police Department**
Sonoma County Library
20217

**187 Groundbreaking**
Sonoma County Library
25284

**188 Department Store**
Sonoma County Library
19558

**189 Junior College Band**
Sonoma County Library
2605

**190 Library**
Sonoma County Library
4962

**191 Fluor Employee**
Sonoma County Library
26295

**192 Welding Long Pipe**
Sonoma County Library
26296

**193 Speedspace Corporation**
Sonoma County Library
4721

**194 Police Dispatchers**
Sonoma County Library
8112

**195 Purity Grocery**
Sonoma County Library
20681

**196 Eager Crowds**
Sonoma County Library
26887

**197 Mortgage Bankers Association**
Sonoma County Library
22309

**198 The Sebastianis**
Sonoma County Library
8486

**199 Sonoma State University**
Sonoma County Library
4372

# Bibliography

The publications listed below were helpful in providing information for creating the captions in this work.

Hansen, Harvey J. and Jeanne Thurlow Miller. *Wild Oats in Eden, Sonoma County in the 19th Century.* Hooper Printing, 1962.

Heig, Adair. *History of Petaluma, A California River Town.* Scottwall Associates, 1982.

LeBaron, Gaye, Dee Blackman, Joann Mitchell, and Harvey Hansen. *Santa Rosa, a Nineteenth Century Town.* Historia Ltd., 1985.

LeBaron, Gaye and Joann Mitchell. *Santa Rosa, a Twentieth Century Town.* Historia Ltd., 1993.

Munro-Fraser, J. P. *History of Sonoma County.* Alley, Bowen and Co., 1880.

Ray, Barbara F. *Windsor,* Images of America series. Arcadia Publishing, 2004.

Thomas H. Thompson and Co. *Historical Atlas Map of Sonoma County, 1877.*

Tuomey, Honoria. *History of Sonoma County California,* Vol. I. S. J. Clarke Publishing, 1926.

Wilson, Simone. *Sonoma County, The River of Time.* Windsor Publications, 1990.

*The Historian,* a quarterly publication of the Sonoma County Historical Society.

# HISTORIC PHOTOS OF SONOMA COUNTY

The climate was good, the soil was good, and the people who came to this fertile area on the Pacific Coast of America knew they had found a special place. Native American tribes came first, Europeans and their American descendents followed. With statehood and the Gold Rush, the population swelled.

The river led to Petaluma and brought pioneers who settled in the growing cities—Sebastopol, Santa Rosa, Sonoma, Healdsburg, Cloverdale, Windsor, and many smaller hamlets. Resilient pioneers rebuilt after the 1906 earthquake and took up the challenges of Prohibition, the Depression, and war. Construction of the Golden Gate Bridge opened the way for expansion.

*Historic Photos of Sonoma County* uses striking illustrations to follow life, government, education, and events in this special place. Rare scenes captured in historic, black-and-white photographs preserve the essence of Sonoma County life from the 1850s to the 1970s.

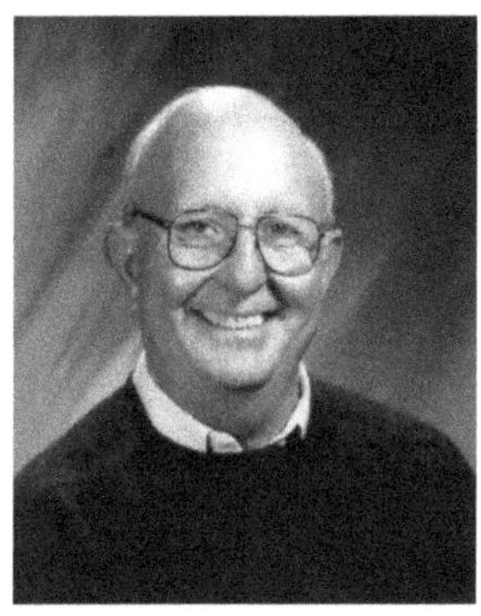

Lee Torliatt is a fifth-generation Petaluman, born on Groundhog Day, 1933. After attending San Francisco State and the University of California, Berkeley, he went on to a career in teaching and journalism.

Torliatt taught Social Science and English at Santa Rosa and Piner High Schools in Santa Rosa before retiring in 1993. He was an editor and writer at the Santa Rosa *Press-Democrat*, Petaluma *Argus-Courier*, San Francisco *Chronicle,* and *Pacific Stars and Stripes* in Tokyo.

On the board of the Sonoma County History Society, he has served as archivist and editor of the *Sonoma County Historian* quarterly magazine. He has written two major local history books, *Golden Memories of the Redwood Empire* and *Sports Memories of Sonoma County,* published by Arcadia Press. He also worked with fifth graders at Roseland School in Santa Rosa on a history of their area.

His community volunteer projects include Catholic Worker, Friends Outside, and international exchange programs. He has a daughter and two grandsons who live in Santa Rosa.

WWW.TURNERPUBLISHING.COM

www.ingramcontent.com/pod-product-compliance
Lightning Source LLC
LaVergne TN
LVHW060606110826
845154LV00003B/48
* 9 7 8 1 6 8 3 3 6 9 8 9 9 *